The Oberle Family
From Dabo to Baltimore: 1711 – 1975

Covering our French ancestors from the communes of Dabo in Moselle, Lorraine, and Engenthal-le-Bas in Bas-Rhin, Alsace, as well as their early descendants in the city of Baltimore, Maryland.

Also covered in a more limited manner are various families that have married into the Oberle line over the generations, including our Anstett, Boyle, Deumant, Dillenschneider, Dirkson, Drixel, Goldrick, Kelly, Kerber, Kiwiet, Mertz, Müller, Ruffenach, Schott, Schreiber, and Sennewick ancestors.

Rue De La Mossig going north from D224 Roadway in Engenthal-le-Bas

Frank Oberle
(Fifth Great-Grandson of Balthassar Oberlé of Dabo)
(Possibly the Sixth Great-Grandson of Johann Oberlé of Dabo)

The Oberle Family
From Dabo to Baltimore: 1711 – 1975

Copyright © 2014 by Frank Oberle
Revision III of the book originally titled "Our Oberle Ancestors."

Baltimore – Cornelius Oberle circa 1919

My father Cornelius (1917-2004) of Baltimore, Maryland is the 4th great-grandson of the first Balthassar Oberle (1711-1788) of Dabo, Lorraine, France

ISBN-13: 978-06-1595-529-2
ISBN-10: 06-1595-529-0

Preface

This brief history, as well as those I've prepared for several other branches of our family, is intended to give my own children and grandchildren, as well as their descendants, some sense of where they came from and a little perspective on the differences between the lives of earlier generations and our own.

Compared to most of the other families in our lineage, some lines of which arrived before the American Revolution, and others before the Civil War, our first Oberle ancestor arrived in the United States at a relatively late date, although still early enough to arrive before the Statue of Liberty and the introduction of Coca Cola.

This book will discuss eight generations of our Oberle-side ancestors – five generations, outlined in a chart on page 51, who were born and lived in what is now France – and another three generations, diagrammed on page 144, who were born in the United States.

Other books I've written related to my family's history include:

Our Gonce Ancestors
ISBN: 9-780615-923147

Abraham Rudolph Gonce – Missouri Pioneer
ISBN: 9-780615-912448

Our Hulshoff and Kerchner Ancestors[1]
ISBN: 9-781616-002626

The following page identifies our Oberle ancestors whose signatures are shown on the rear cover of the book.

---

[1] The Hulshoff book includes reproductions of manuscripts by Fr. Frank Kunkel (1870 - 1951) about the Kern and Kerchner ancestors on my Mother's side of the family.

Some Signatures of Our Ancestors (from the rear cover)

Balthassar Oberlé (II)
about 1745 – 1786 <u>id1675</u>

... Balthassar's son (François) Joseph Oberlé
Mar 1773 – Apr 1834 <u>id1154</u>

Joseph Müller
1772 – May 1836? <u>id1161</u>

... Joseph Müller's daughter, Catherine Müller
Jul 1799 – Unknown <u>id1157</u>

... Catherine M's daughter, Catherine Ruffenach
Jul 1821 – Nov 1864 <u>id1147</u>

... Catherine R's husband, Seraphin Oberlé (I)
May 1811 – Jan 1890 <u>id708</u>

... Seraphin's grandson, Joseph Oberle
Dec 1887 – Aug 1954 <u>id81</u>

... Joseph's wife, Katherine G. Goldrick
Mar 1884 – Apr 1975 <u>id80</u>

... Joseph & Katherine's son, Cornelius F. Oberle
Sep 1917 – Oct 2004 <u>id196</u>

The signatures of our early Oberlé ancestors François Joseph and Seraphin appear to end with the letter "n," but this is actually an "e." See the section titled "Reading 18th and 19th Century French and German Handwriting" on page 150 of Appendix I: Languages of Our Ancestors

Where signatures of earlier ancestors may seem to appear on some of the records shown in the book, note that they have what appears to be small "o" or "x" characters adjacent to the name; this indicates that these ancestors "signed" the documents with their "mark." Also observe that the females were generally able to sign their full names (and could often read and write) a generation or two before the males could. This is typical of the time, and reflected the need for males to "earn their keep" at an early age, while at least minimal education was deemed an asset for anyone planning to raise children.

Also note that, in the times and places described in the history of our family in Dabo and Engenthal-le-Bas, women did not take the surnames of their husbands once they married. Thus when, for example, François Joseph Oberlé's wife Marie-Anne Schreiber died in 1823, the record of her death lists her as Schreiber, although refers in the record to her husband by name. See page 34.

Table of Contents

Rue De La Mossig going north from D224 Roadway in Engenthal-le-Bas..i
Baltimore – Cornelius Oberle circa 1919...ii

Preface..iii

Some Signatures of Our Ancestors (from the rear cover)..iv
 Balthassar Oberlé (II)..*iv*
 ... Balthassar's son (François) Joseph Oberlé...*iv*
 Joseph Müller..*iv*
 ... Joseph Müller's daughter, Catherine Müller...*iv*
 ... Catherine M's daughter, Catherine Ruffenach..*iv*
 ... Catherine R's husband, Seraphin Oberlé (I)..*iv*
 ... Seraphin's grandson, Joseph Oberle..*iv*
 ... Joseph's wife, Katherine G. Goldrick..*iv*
 ... Joseph & Katherine's son, Cornelius F. Oberle..*iv*

Our Oberlé Ancestors..1

An 1888 German Map of the New World – Baltimore City..1

INTRODUCTION   3
The name Oberlé...3
Lothringian History...3
 Seal of King Lothar II..3
 Emperor Henry III..4
The Oberlé's "Ancestral Homeland".. 4
 Map of Our Family's Universe in the 17th through 19th Centuries...5
The Commune of Dabo..5

OUR LOTHRINGIAN ANCESTRY   6
Johann Oberle, son of Johann Oberle and Anna-Maria Anstett..6
 Church of the old Marmoutier Abbey..6
 Mauri Monastery – 1726 Birth record of Joannis Oberle...7
 (Suspected) Children of the elder Johann Oberle & Anna-Maria Anstett............................8
The Mertz family and Anne-Marie Mertz..9
Balthassar (I) Oberlé and Anne-Marie Mertz...9
 Paroisse de Dabo – 1788 Death Record of Balthassar [I] Oberlé..10
 Children & Grandchildren of Balthassar (I) Oberlé & Anne-Marie Mertz........................11
Johann (Jean) Schott & Anne-Marie Sennewick..12
 Children & Grandchildren of Jean Schott & Anne-Marie Sennewick...............................12
Church and State – the Reversal of Power...13
 Louis XV..14
 Paroisse de Dabo – 1766 Marriage Record of Balthassar [II] Oberlé & Anne Marie Schott......15
Balthassar (II) Oberlé and Anne-Marie Schott...16
 Children & Grandchildren of Balthassar (II) Oberlé & Anne-Marie Schott.....................16
 Paroisse de Dabo – 1772 Birth Record of Antoine Oberlé..17
 Paroisse de Dabo – 1774 Birth Record of Maria Catharina Oberlé......................................18
The Müller Family and Marie Ann Müller...19

Children of Antoine Muller and Marie Anne Jung..*19*
Paroisse de Dabo – 1776 Death Record of Anne Marie Schott..................................20
Paroisse de Dabo – 1777 Marriage Record of Balthassar [II] Oberlé & Marie-Anne Muller.....21
Balthassar (II) Oberlé and Marie Anne Müller..22
Children & Grandchildren of Balthassar (II) Oberlé & Marie Anne Müller.......................*22*
Migration to Engenthal-le-Bas..23
Paroisse de Dabo – 1786 Death Record of Balthassar [II] Oberlé............................24
Marie Anne Schreiber..25
née à Bürckengal ? née à Bür Keugal ?..25

OUR ALSATIAN-FRENCH ANCESTRY   25
Commune of Engenthal-le-Bas...25
Entering Engenthal-le-Bas at the modern D224 & D218 road junction....................25
Modern day welcome Sign to Wangenbourg and Engenthal on the D224 highway............26
A View of Engenthal-le-Bas; photograph taken in March 2004................................26
Engenthal-le-Bas – Cut timbers curing on the roadside..27
Commune of Obersteigen..27
Obersteigen – Chapelle de l'Assomption de la Verge..27
The First Generation to Live in Engenthal-le-Bas..28
Several Views of the Wangenbourg Castle Ruins just outside Engenthal................29
Engenthal-le-Haut – 2004 View from the Route de Panorama.................................30
Engenthal-le-Bas – View of La Mossig on the north side of Route de Windsbourg (D224).......30
François Joseph Oberlé and Marie Anne Schreiber...31
Signature of (François) Joseph Oberlé..31
Engenthal – The Mairie (Town Hall) in 2004..32
Commune d'Engenthal – 1811 Birth Record of Seraphin (I) Oberlé........................32
Commune d'Engenthal – 1793 Birth Record of Hubert Oberlé, son of François Joseph.............33
Commune d'Engenthal – 1823 Death Record of Marie Anne Schreiber..................34
Commune d'Engenthal – 1834 Death Record of François Joseph Oberlé................35
Children & Grandchildren of François Joseph Oberlé & Marie Anne Schreiber...................*36*
Cemeteries in and around Engenthal..38
André Ruffenach & Catherine Drixel..38
Joseph Müller & Catherine Deumant...39
Signature of Joseph Müller..39
Muller-Deumant-Drixel-Ruffenach Chart..39
Commune d'Engenthal – 1798 Birth Record of Catherine Müller............................40
The French Revolutionary Calendar...41
Commune d'Engenthal – 1832 Death Record of Catherine Deumant......................42
Commune d'Engenthal – 1818 Marriage Record of Antoine Ruffenach & Catherine Müller....43
Antoine Ruffenach & Catherine Müller..44
Signature of Catherine Müller..44
Children of Antoine Ruffenach and Catherine Müller..*44*
Commune d'Engenthal – 1842 Death Record of Antoine Ruffenach........................45
Seraphin (I) Oberlé and Elizabeth Stiltz..46
Children & Grandchildren of Seraphin (I) Oberlé & Elisabeth Stiltz....................................*46*
Seraphin (I) Oberlé and Catherine Ruffenach...47
Signatures of Seraphin Oberlé and his wife Catherine Ruffenach............................47
Children & Grandchildren of Seraphin (I) Oberlé & Catherine Ruffenach..........................*47*

Signature of Armand Oberlé 47
    Commune d'Engenthal – 1850 Marriage record of Seraphin Oberlé & Catherine Ruffenach....48
    Commune d'Engenthal – 1890 Death Record of my 2nd great-grandfather Seraphin Oberle....50
Diagram of our Lothringian and French Oberlé Ancestors...51
Seraphin [II] Oberlé – Our Last Ancestor in France...52
    Commune d'Engenthal – 1855 Birth record of Seraphin Oberlé (II)...52
    Commune d'Engenthal – 1864 Death record of Catherine Ruffenach Oberlé................................53
The Franco-Prussian War...54
    Napoleon III surrenders his Sword and Colors to Friedrich Wilhelm...56
    Seraphin [II] Oberlé circa 1874 in Wassellone, Alsace...57
World War II – Seraphin's grandsons return to Alsace..58

SNEAKING INTO AMERICA (THE LONG WAY)   59

The Seaport of Emden...59
    Modern Map showing the Town of Emden in Ostfriesland, across from the Netherlands..........59
The Kiwiet Family..60
Gerhard Kiwiet & Josephine Dirkson..60
Seraphin [II] Oberle & Sarah Johanna Kiwiet..61
    Emden – St. Michael Katholische Kirche...62
The Migration to Baltimore..62
Seraphin III comes to America...63
    Port of New York – 1882 Segment of passenger manifest page for the ship Salier......................64
    Baltimore – 1900 U.S. Census page segments showing family of "Lewis" Oberle....................65
Seraphin returns to Engenthal...66
    The S. S. Cassel..66
    Port of Baltimore – 1905 Alien Passenger Arrival Manifest for the S.S. Cassel..........................67
    Baltimore – 1910 U.S. Census showing family of Seraphin Oberle (II).....................................68
    Baltimore – 1910 U.S. Census segments showing family of Seraphin Oberle (III).....................69
    Baltimore – 1910 U.S. Census: closeup of sheet for Frank Oberle's family (see page 73).........70
    Baltimore – 1920 U.S. Census showing family of Seraphin [II] Oberle.....................................71
    Baltimore – 1920 U.S. Census showing family of Seraphin [III] Oberle....................................72
    Baltimore – 1920 U.S. Census showing the family of Frank Oberle...73
    Baltimore – 1930 U.S. Census showing family of Seraphin (II) Oberle......................................74
    Baltimore – 1930 U.S. Census showing family of Seraphin (III) Oberle.....................................75
Seraphin's Employment in Baltimore...76
    Baltimore – 1920 Photo of Workers at the Stieff Piano Company Factory..................................76
    Baltimore – Seraphin and Sarah in their later years..77
    Baltimore – Seraphin II circa 1925...78
    Baltimore – Oberle headstone at Holy Redeemer Cemetery...79
    Baltimore – Oberle Infants' Stone in Lot 30 of Holy Redeemer Cemetery.................................79
Children & Grandchildren of Seraphin (II) Oberle & Sarah Johanna Kiwiet........................80
    Seraphin and Barbara Oberle..80
    Mary E. (Sr. Alvina) Oberle...80
    Eddie and Marie Oberle..80
    Francis Joseph (Frank) Oberle..81
    The future Fr. Jerry Oberle, Frank Oberle, and Fr. Joe Oberle..81
    Tom Jelks in early 2011..81
    Frank Oberle with Fr. Joe Oberle circa 1938...82
    Bill and Nina Oberle and family in 1954...82

One of my daughters in Esopus NY with Fr. Jerry Oberle in 2005 82
Baltimore – Oberle Family Portrait, circa 1900 83
Four of the Oberle brothers and two sisters: 84
Ireland in the Nineteenth Century (The Goldrick & Boyle Families) 85
    Home Counties of Martin Goldrick and Catherine Boyle 85
    U.S. Congress – 1848 "Passenger Bill of Rights" passed on May 17th 86
The Goldricks of County Sligo, Ireland 87
    Baby Book of Cornelius Oberle 88
The Boyles of County Donegal, Ireland 89
    Catherine Boyle, circa 1862 89
    Baltimore – 1900 U.S. Census segments showing Catherine (Boyle) Goldrick's Family 90
    Baltimore – 1870 U.S. Census segment showing the Holland Family 90
Martin Goldrick and Catherine Boyle 91
    Catherine Boyle Goldrick, circa 1915 91
    Baltimore – 1910 U.S. Census showing the family of Catherine Boyle Goldrick 92
    Close-ups of portions of my 2nd great-grandparents' tombstone at Old St. Mary's Cemetery ... 93
    Children & Grandchildren of Martin Goldrick & Catherine Boyle ***94***
    1949 – Mildred Dunn 94
    Map of areas where the Oberles and Goldricks lived from 1900 to 1926 95
Catherine Goldrick becomes Katie with a "K" 96
    Catherine Goldrick's Baptismal Certificate from St. Ann's 96
    Katie Goldrick and Joe Oberle circa 1911 or 1912 98
Joseph Oberle & Katherine Goldrick 98
    1901-1902 Loyola College (H.S.) Booklet, page 67 99
    1902-1903 Loyola College (H.S.) Booklet, page 68 99
    1902-1903 Loyola College (H.S.) Booklet, page 69 99
    1902-1903 Loyola College (H.S.) Booklet, page 71 99
    Atlantic City – Postcard of Katie and Joe 100
    Another early postcard of Joe and Katie 100
    Joseph Oberle's World War I Draft Registration Card of 5 June 1917 101
    Seraphin and Frank Oberle's World War I Draft Registration Cards of 12 September 1918 102
    Babe Ruth Strikes Out ***103***
    1998 to 2009 – The Vanishing Babe Ruth Baseball 103
    Office of Cashier/Vice-President in the Citizen's National Bank Building 104
    Baltimore – 1919 Photo of Katie and her Kids 104
    Baltimore – circa 1920: Cornie, Sis, & Joe Oberle 105
    Baltimore – circa 1920: Cornie, Joe, & Sis 105
    Baltimore – circa 1920: Cornie, Joe, & Sis 105
    Baltimore – circa 1920: Katie, Cornie, Sis, & Joe 105
    Baltimore – circa 1920: Sis, Cornie, Joe, & Joe Jr. 105
    Baltimore – circa 1923: Cornie & Sis 105
    Baltimore – 1920 U.S. Census showing family of Joseph Oberle 106
    Baltimore – 1926: the new home at 213 Midhurst Rd. on move-in day 107
    Baltimore – mid-1930s: The Oberle Family 108
    Granddad Oberle driving his 1931 Dodge with "Sis" and "Cornie." 108
    Baltimore – 1930 U.S. Census showing family of Joseph Oberle 109
    Baltimore – 1940 U.S. Census showing family of Joseph Oberle 110
Joe & Katie's Family during World War II 110
    Tom Jelks Book Cover 111

Joe, Katie, Joe, Jr. and Sis in back yard at Midhurst Road..112
Joe, Jr., Sis and Francis in back yard at Midhurst Road..112
The Post-World War II Years...113
    Baltimore – 1954 Obituaries of Joseph Oberle...114
    Katie and Joe in their garden in the early 1950s..115
    Katie Goldrick Oberle shortly before her death..116
    My inheritance – and still working!..116
    Baltimore – 1975 Death Certificate of Katherine G. Oberle...117
    Baltimore – 1975 Obituaries of Katherine G. Oberle..118
    Baltimore – Graves of Joseph and Katherine Goldrick Oberle at New Cathedral Cemetery....119
    Children and Grandchildren of Joseph Oberle & Katie Goldrick..119
Rosalie Gonce and our Gonce Ancestors...120
    Rosalie Gonce as a child in 1926...120
Cornelius Oberle and Rosalie Gonce...120
    Receipt for original birth report of Cornelius Oberle..120
    Duplicate Baptismal Certificate obtained for Catholic approval of his wedding in 1941.........121
    Cornie in about 1927 (age 10)...121
    Cornelius Oberle – October 2, 1936 application to Johns Hopkins University.......................122
    Ro and Cornie after a 1938 CSMC Social Event..123
    Baltimore American – Sunday, May 25, 1941..125
    Baltimore – 1941 Wedding Party of Ro and Cornie at Blessed Sacrament Church................126
    Savannah, Georgia – Mrs. Skeffington's "The Georgian Tourist Home"................................127
Cornelius and Rosalie – World War II...127
    Savannah, Georgia – January, 1942: Ro and Cornie Oberle..128
    Dad's Pacific Theater Assignments in WW-II...129
    Papua, New Guinea – Modern-day shoreline..130
    20 March 1942 and 24 July 1942 Promotion Records for Cornelius Oberle............................131
    Map showing my parents' home at 721 Radnor Avenue...132
    Our 3-bedroom Baltimore row house at 3918 Rexmere Road...132
    Ft. Meade, MD – 1945 Report of Separation for Cornelius Oberle..133
    Ft. Meade, MD – 1945 Separation Qualification Record for Cornelius Oberle......................134
    Cornelius Oberle – Post-World War II application to Johns Hopkins University...................135
Settling into Civilian Life..136
    Baltimore – 1948: Sally Pope & the author...136
    Baltimore – 1949: Tommy and his big brother..136
    Baltimore – 1950: Tommy and his big brother..136
    Atlantic City – 1951: Rosalie and her children..136
    Baltimore – 1951 photographs of me and my siblings Tommy and Mary on Rexmere Road...137
    Baltimore – 1953: The author and his grandmother Katie..137
    New York State – 1953: Cornelius and his children..137
    Philadelphia – 1956: The author and his sister Mary...137
    Baltimore – 1955: After Dad's graduation from Johns Hopkins...137
    Tucson – 1975: Ro and Cornie at Colossal Cave...139
    Legend City – 1982: Cornie and Ro on water slide...139
    Illinois – 1990 visit to new granddaughter...139
    Illinois – 1999 last visit together to Buffalo Grove..139
    Bel Air – 2004: Cornie and one of his great-grandsons...140
    Lincolnshire – 2010: Rosalie with her new great-grandson...140
To Be Continued:..140

Bel Air – 2004 Death Certificate of Cornelius F. Oberle..141
Obituaries and photos of Cornelius and Rosalie Oberle's headstone.................................142
Lincolnshire, Illinois – 2013 Death Certificate of Rosalie Gonce Oberle...........................143
Three Generations of Oberles from Seraphin (II) to Cornelius and his Siblings............144
"Nancy" & "Joe"..144
"Bud" & "Sis"..144
"Ro" & "Cornie"..144
Gladys & Francis...144

Appendix I :: Languages of Our Oberle Ancestors................................145
Signature of (François) Joseph Oberlé...145

THE LANGUAGES OF OUR ANCESTORS   147
Elsässisch.. 147
Lothringer Platt.. 147
Medieval (Church) Latin... 147
French... 149
German... 150
Reading 18th and 19th Century French and German Handwriting....................... 150

Appendix II :: Getting There..155
Scene by the D224 Roadside in Romanswiller between Wasselonne and Engenthal.................155

DRIVING FROM STRASBOURG TO ENGENTHAL   157

FAMILY REMNANTS IN ALSACE?   162
Kilstett, Alsace – Oberle Hotel & Restaurant in 2004..162

Appendix III :: Connecting Balthassar to François Joseph.................163
Signature of Balthassar [III] Oberlé...163

IS BALTHASSAR OBERLÉ REALLY OUR ANCESTOR?   165
Naming Conventions.. 165
Ages and Gaps... 166
Convergence in Engenthal.. 166
Demonstrated Family Connections.. 167
Engenthal – 1800 Death Record of Magdalena Oberle...168
Engenthal – 1800 Death Record of Michall Oberle..169
Engenthal – 1812 Marriage record of Balthasar III Oberle and Elisabeth Dieda.................170

Appendix IV :: The 1864 Boyle Photo Album.......................................173
Outside Views of the 1864 Boyle Photo Album...173
Diagram of our only identified Boyle, Goldrick and Kelly Ancestors........................174

THE 1864 BOYLE PHOTO ALBUM   175
Source of the Album... 175
Physical Description of the Album... 176
Title and Dedication Pages.. 177
Existing Indexes to the Photographs... 178

Surnames Mentioned in the Indexes..179
Locations where the Photographs were taken...179
Implications of The Dedication Poem...180
Descriptions of the Album's Photos..181
    Page 1 Photo – ("Mabel")...181
    Page 2 Photo – Catherine Boyle...182
    Page 3 Photo – (Mr. Sands)..183
    Page 4 Photo – ("Grandmother")...184
    Page 5 Photo – (Unknown Male)...185
    Page 7 Photo – (Unknown Female)...186
    Page 10 Photo – (Unknown Male)...187
    Page 11 Photo – (Unknown Male)...188
    Page 15 Photo – ("C. Dowd")..189
    Page 16 Photo – ("L. Holland"?)..190
    Page 18 Photo – ("Margaret")...191
    Page 19 Photo – (Unknown Male)...192
    Page 21 Photo – Archbishop Bayley..193
    Page 22 Photo – (Unknown Females)..194
    Page 24 Photo – (Unknown Female)..195
    Page 25 Photo – (Martin Goldrick?)..196
    Page 28 Photo – (Unknown Male)...197
    Page 29 Photo – (Unknown Male)...198
    Page 30 Photo – (Unknown Female)..199
References for Dating Photographs...200

Appendix V :: Joseph Oberle Currency Examples..........................201
    Montage of Series 1929 National Bank Notes signed by Joseph Oberle......................201

SAMPLE CURRENCY SIGNED BY JOSEPH OBERLE   203
    $100 Series 1902 Large Bill..204
    $ 20 Series 1902 Large Bill..205
    $10 Series 1902 Large Bill...206
    $ 5 Series 1902 Large Bill..207
    $100 Series 1929 Small Bill...208
    $ 50 Series 1929 Small Bill..209
    $ 20 Series 1929 Small Bill..210
    $ 10 Series 1929 Small Bill..211
    $ 5 Series 1929 Small Bill..212
    Currency Bequests in Katherine Oberle's Will...213
    The Serial Number 1 Five Dollar Note..213
    $ 5 Series 1902 Large Bill – Serial Number 1 - Front..214
    $ 5 Series 1902 Large Bill – Serial Number 1 – Back..215
    Baltimore – Citizens National Bank Building..216

Appendix VI :: Wills of Joseph and Katherine Oberle....................217
    An Early Baltimore Map..217

THE WILLS OF JOSEPH AND KATHERINE OBERLE   219
    Katie Goldrick Oberle circa 1948..220

Joseph Oberle's Will of 8 March 1948 – Page 1 221
Joseph Oberle's Will of 8 March 1948 – Page 2 (Signature Page) 222
Joseph Oberle's Inventory Cover Sheet of 28 September 1954 – Page 1 223
Joseph Oberle's Inventory of 28 September 1954 – Page 1 224
Joseph Oberle's Inventory Certification Sheet of 28 September 1954 – Page 1 225
Joseph Oberle's Inventory Accounting Work Sheet – Page 1 226
Joseph Oberle's Inventory Accounting Work Sheet – Page 2 227
Audit Statement for Settlement of Joseph Oberle's Estate – 28 September 1954 228
Notary Statement for Settlement of Joseph Oberle's Estate 229
Katherine Goldrick Oberle's Original Will of 26 January 1956 – Page 1 230
Katherine Goldrick Oberle's Original Will of 26 January 1956 – Page 2 231
Katherine Goldrick Oberle's Original Will of 26 January 1956 – Page 3 232
Katherine Goldrick Oberle's Original Will of 26 January 1956 – Page 4 233
Katherine Goldrick Oberle's Original Will of 26 January 1956 – Page 5 234
Katherine Goldrick Oberle's Original Will of 26 January 1956 – Page 6 (Signature Page) 235
Katherine Goldrick Oberle's First Codicil of 3 February 1959 – Page 1 236
Katherine Goldrick Oberle's First Codicil of 3 February 1959 – Page 2 237
Katherine Goldrick Oberle's Second Codicil of 19 April 1963 – Page 1 238
Katherine Goldrick Oberle's Second Codicil of 19 April 1963 – Page 2 239
Inside Page from Deed to Lot 575-W in New Cathedral Cemetery in Baltimore, MD 240
Outside Cover from Deed to Lot 575-W in New Cathedral Cemetery in Baltimore, MD 241

Appendix VII :: Descendants of Balthassar Oberlé of Dabo 243

Paroisse de Dabo – 1743 and 1766 Parish Register Covers 243

DESCENDANTS OF BALTHASSAR OBERLE   245

Engenthal – 1811 Birth Register Cover 252
Engenthal – 1834 Death Register Cover 252
Engenthal – 1855 Birth Register Cover 252

Appendix VIII :: Ancestors of Joseph Oberle of Baltimore 253

Baltimore – 1913: Joe and Katie Oberle, with Joe's siblings Tommy and Theresa in the rear .. 254

ANCESTORS OF JOSEPH OBERLE   255

Baltimore – 1913: Anna, Tommy, Katie and Theresa Oberle 256

Appendix IX :: Other Children of Joseph and Katherine Oberle 257

JOSEPH FRANCIS OBERLE   259

Baltimore – 1920: Joe Oberle, Jr. 259
Baltimore – 1942: Joseph Oberle 260
The Borig Family 260
Children of Richard F. and Mary Borig *260*
The Greeley Family 261
Baltimore – 1860 U.S. Census showing family of Patrick Greeley 261
Henry Richard Borig and Mary J. Greeley 262
Baltimore – 1917: World War I Draft Card of Henry Richard Borig 262
Baltimore – 1920: U.S. Census showing family of Joseph Greeley 263
Baltimore – 1942: World War II Draft Card of Henry Richard Borig 263
Children of Henry Borig and Mary Greeley *263*

Joseph Oberle and Catherine Borig..264
   Baltimore – 2019 Hillenwood Road...264
   Austria – 1978: Joe and Nancy...265
   Headstones of Joseph and Catherine (Nancy) Oberle...265

KATHERINE GERTRUDE OBERLE (MILLER)   266
   Katherine Oberle circa 1919..266
   Katherine Oberle circa 1934..266
   1944 – Letter from Katherine Oberle to her brother Cornelius...........................267
  The Matchmaker Shirley Jacobi's Family and Margaret Mary Jacobi..................268
   Baltimore – 1872 Passenger Manifest Page for the S.S. Ohio..............................268
   1900 Census showing family of "Joseph" (actually Jacob) Jacobi......................269
   Children of Jacob and Barbara Jacobi...*270*
  The Miller Family..270
   Children of Joseph A. and Mary L. Miller..*270*
  Francis Miller and Margaret Mary Jacobi...271
   Philadelphia – 1940 U.S. Census showing family of Francis Joseph Miller.......271
   Children of Frank J. Miller and Margaret Mary Jacobi.....................................*272*
  Katherine Oberle and Norbert Miller...272
   "Bud" Miller and his fiancee Katherine Oberle...272
   Norbert and Katherine after their Wedding..273
   Katherine and Norbert...273
   Bel Air: Katherine visits family..273

FRANCIS XAVIER OBERLE   274
   Baltimore – Francis Oberle circa 1940..274
  World War II...275
  Normandy to St. Lo – Some Context...275
   France – 19 August 1944 V-Mail from Francis to his brother Cornelius............276
  The Battle of the Bulge – A Respite...277
  Post-War Years..278
  The Maroney Family and Gladys "Bookie" Maroney...278
   Virginia – 1940 Census showing family of James E. Maroney............................279
   1942 – "Old Man's" Draft Card of James E. Maroney..280
  Francis Oberle and Gladys Maroney..280
  The Mayberry Years...281
   Francis, Gladys, and their infant son..281
  The Stafford Years..283
  Deaths and After...284
   Two-sided headstone of Francis and Gladys Oberle..285
  The Oberle School – Gladys is Remembered..285
   The Gladys H. Oberle School..285
   Baltimore – Joseph Oberle, Sr. and his youngest son, Francis at Midhurst Road...................286

Appendix X :: Suggestions for Further Research..........................287

SUGGESTIONS FOR FURTHER RESEARCH   289
   Oberle Research..289
   Schreiber Research..289

Kiwiet Research...289
Boyle Research...290
Goldrick Research..292
Goldrick-Boyle Research..293

Appendix XI :: Index of Surnames...295
SURNAME INDEX   297
Appendix XII :: Family Group Sheets..301
EXTENDING THE LINE…   301

OUR OBERLÉ ANCESTORS

From Dabo to Baltimore

*An 1888 German Map of the New World – Baltimore City
Seven Years after our first Oberle ancestor arrived there ...*

Introduction

The name Oberlé

Some reasonably reliable sources suggest that the name Oberle is related to the name Albrecht[2], but the most common etymology I've encountered is that the name is formed from the Middle High German "ober" (upper one) and the diminutive suffix "ele." This, in effect, refers to someone who lived at the higher/upper end of a town – suggesting that the name Oberle didn't appear until after the nomadic period of the Allemanic tribes. At first blush, this might imply that the name originated in what is now Germany, but the entire area in which the early Oberles (not only those known to be related to our family) lived in the late seventeenth and early eighteenth centuries was Germanic, so the Middle High German etymology likely isn't significant.

We first encounter our own Oberlé forebears in the early eighteenth century in the French town now known as Dabo, although at that time it was called Dagsburg, the name it had under German control.

Lothringian History

To fully appreciate our ancestors' lives, it will be helpful to first review some history of the areas in Alsace and Lorraine where they lived.

In the year 843, twenty-nine years after the death of Charlemagne, the Treaty of Verdun divided his empire among his three grandsons Charles the Bald, Louis, and Lothar. In 855, when Lothar died, his son Lothar II inherited his father's portion which then became known as Lotharingia[3]. Lotharingia – what we now call Lorraine – is located in the northeastern part of modern France.

In 959, Lotharingia itself was divided in two, and the southern portion was given the name Mosellane, later known as Moselle. Over its subsequent history, the geographical and political makeup of Lotharingia, eventually known as Lothringen, changed often, although Moselle, the home of our earliest identified Oberlé ancestors, was always part of the territory.

Seal of King Lothar II

---

[2] Ancestry.com, for instance, says that "Oberle" is "from an Allemanic pet form of the personal name Albrecht."
[3] Lotharingia is short for "Lotharii Regnum," which means the kingdom of Lothar.

Emperor Henry III

In 1048, the Holy Roman Emperor Henry III, known as "Henry the Black," willed Lothringen to Gerard IV, the Duke of Elsass (Alsace). The Duke and his descendants ruled the combined region for almost four hundred years.

During the Thirty Years War, which began in 1618, the area was beset not only by almost continuous fighting, but was decimated by recurring famine and several outbreaks of the plague. In the two year period from 1635 to 1637, the Duchy of Lothringen lost about half its population to the disease.

France conquered Lothringen for a short time in 1663 and again in 1670, renaming it Lorraine. The Nijmegen peace agreement of 1678 then established Alsace as part of France as well. With the Treaty of Ryswick in 1697, however, the French King Louis XIV formally turned the province of Lothringen over to Duke Leopold[4], although Louis still retained Alsace.

By the early eighteenth century, Duke Leopold had managed to negotiate international recognition for the Duchy's neutrality. For the next fifty years or so, the area remained relatively peaceful while sporadic war raged all around it, resulting in the immigration of many refugees from Switzerland, Burgundy, Savoy, Franch-Comté and Germany. Not having located any relevant records earlier than 1726, it is difficult to determine whether our Oberlé ancestors were already living in Lothringen by this time (which I suspect), or emigrated from Germany or Switzerland[5] during this period.

The Oberlé's "Ancestral Homeland"

During the entire eighteenth and nineteenth centuries, and quite possibly before that, our Oberle-side ancestors lived in a ten square mile area near the border of what is now Lorraine and Alsace. These Provinces[6] are located in what is now the northeastern part of France (also see the maps in the Appendix beginning on page 157). The Departments of Moselle in Lorraine and Bas-Rhin in northern Alsace share a common border along the eastern edge of the Vosges mountain range.

---

[4] His full name was Duke Leopold Joseph, and he ruled from the castle known as Château de Lunéville.

[5] Although the name Oberle is quite common in Germany and Switzerland in later years, I haven't encountered it in records of Burgundy, Savoy or Franch-Comté until much later, leading me to guess that our forebears probably didn't originate in those areas. Migratory patterns (directions) also make Swiss origins seem unlikely.

[6] In simplified terms, the French geopolitical subdivisions are Province (more or less equivalent to a State in the U.S.), Department (similar to a County), Arrondissement (an administrative district within a Department), Canton, and Commune (Town). Note that Lorraine, then known as Lothringen, was part of Germany until 1766.

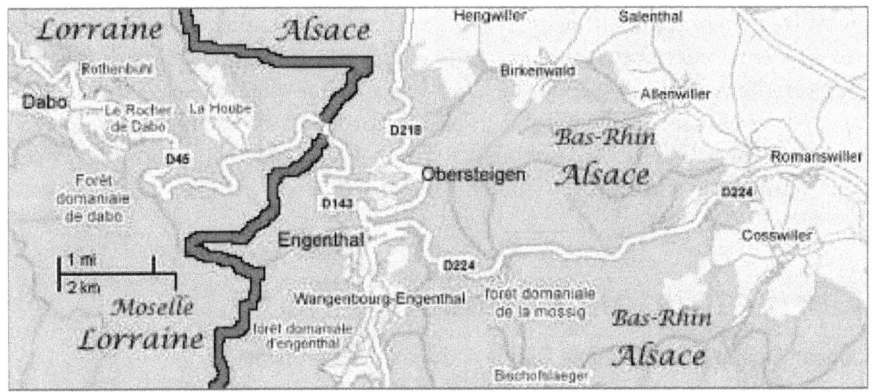

Map of Our Family's Universe in the 17th through 19th Centuries
The mountainous route from Dabo (in Lorraine, left) through Engenthal to Romanswiller, both in Alsace

The Commune of Dabo

The small town of Dabo, Lorraine, seen on the far upper left of the map above, is located in the present-day Department of Moselle and Arrondissement of Sarrebourg, and is where I've located the records of the earliest known of our Oberlé ancestors. The town itself is located almost at the peak of the Vosges Mountains, a little west of the modern day ski resort at Le Rocher de Dabo (literally, "The Rock of Dabo"). The picture above right was taken from Le Rocher de Dabo with the small town of Dabo itself in the distance.

The language spoken in Lothringen at this time was a German dialect known as *Lothringer Platt* (called *Lorraine Franconian* or *Platt Lorrain* in French)[7]; as the only extant records from this period appear to be church records in Latin, however, the *Platt* language isn't relevant to this discussion.

Until 1766, the town, as part of the Germanic duchy of Lothringen, was known as Dagsburg. Other than Rothenbuhl to the north, towns such as Obersteigen and Engenthal-le-Bas, although only a few miles away, were effectively in a different country. There was some level of trade and travel between Dagsburg and these "foreign" communes, but it was made inconve-

---

[7] A full discussion of the languages spoken by or relevant to our ancestors is provided in an appendix beginning on page 147. This includes basic terms required to read the records reproduced in this book.

nient by many factors other than political borders and the accompanying bureaucracy. As mentioned earlier, areas outside Lothringen were still plagued by periodic warfare; the town of Dagsburg, being quite close to the border, needed to remain somewhat isolationist in order to avoid this fighting. One of the earliest Oberles we encounter with a Dagsburg connection, however, may actually have been born while his mother was traveling in Alsace.

Our Lothringian Ancestry

Johann Oberle, son of Johann Oberle and Anna-Maria Anstett

The earliest evidence of an Oberle I've so far located who is likely related to our family is a Johann Oberle, whose birth the previous day was reported at the Mauri Monastery on 28 January 1726[8]. Johann himself is certainly not our direct ancestor, but I suspect that his older brother Balthassar id1704 [9] is. As I interpret the record, Johann's birth was reported by the delivering midwife (Barbara Higard) at the Mauri Monastery in Alsace after she and the baby's mother Anna-Maria Anstett[10] of Dagsburg spent the night at the hostel there.

Church of the old Marmoutier Abbey
Rebuilt in the 1760s – other Mauri Monastery buildings later served other functions; one is the current Town Hall.

The infant's father, also named Johann, apparently did not accompany the women to report the birth. It would be interesting to know why he wasn't present, or why Anna-Maria was in Alsace, but it seems unlikely that any information will surface to explain those circumstances.

The Anstett family is also mentioned on page 12 where it is reported that Rosalie Schott, the younger sister of my 4th great-grandmother Anne-Marie Schott, married Joseph Anstett in Dagsburg.

Because the relationship among Johann, Anna Maria, and the remainder of our ancestral line given in this book is still unproven, this generation of the Oberle line is not included in the Descendant Chart given on page 245.

---

[8] The report of Johann's birth is in Latin, so his name appears as Joannis Oberle. Languages used in vital records of Alsace and other areas mentioned are discussed later in this book on page 147. The Mauri Monastery, about five miles northeast of Engenthal, was later known as the Marmoutier Abbey, the site of which is on the Route Romaine d'Alsace in present day Marmoutier.

[9] The ID numbers are from my genealogy database and are provided for cross-referencing other books and documents related to our ancestors.

[10] The report mentions that Anna-Maria's mother Catherine, a daughter of Michael Simon, was living at the time, but that her father was deceased, giving us the names of two more generations.

OUR OBERLE ANCESTORS

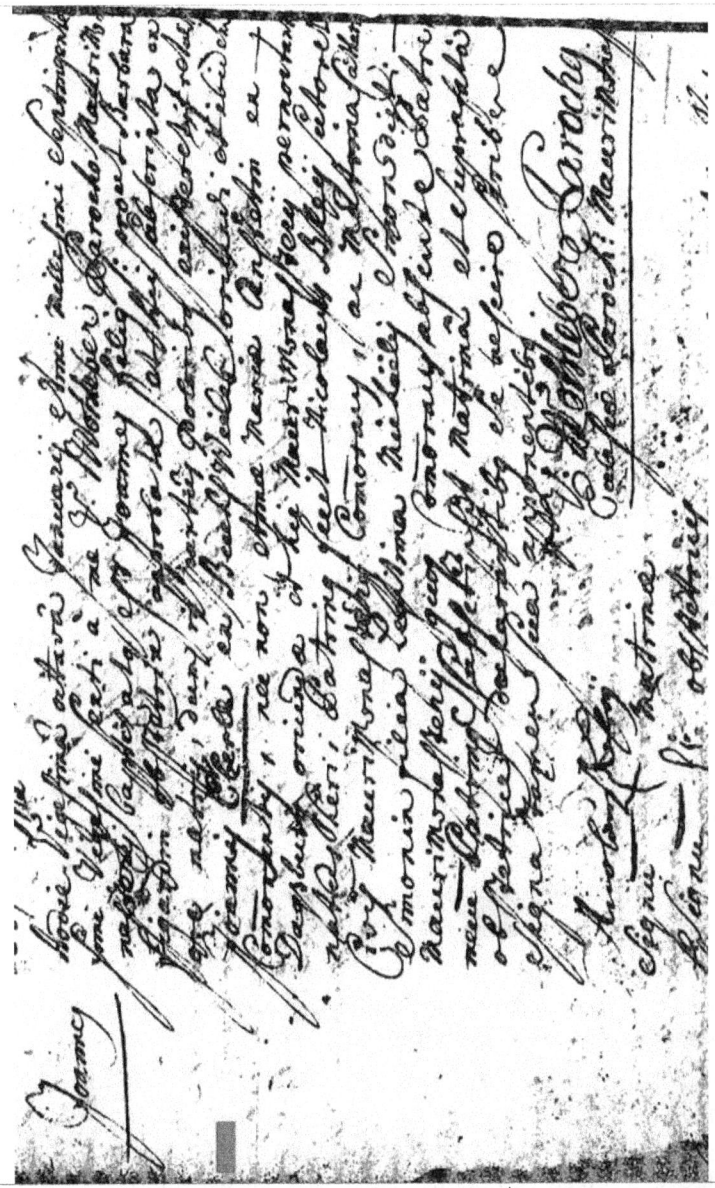

Mauri Monastery – 1726 Birth record of Joannis Oberle

Joannis Oberle, born on 27 January 1726, was possibly a brother of our oldest known ancestor

Birth report found in the Wangenbourg Church Records, evidently transferred from the Mauri Monastery when it was closed during the French Revolution.

It is unusual in that it is the only record from Alsace that I have found with the surname Oberlé prior to the return of Lorraine to France in 1766. Line 7 shows the name of the child's mother "Anna Marie Anstett from Dagsburg". Dagsburg, later Dabo, although not that far from Wangenbourg, was part of the Germanic Duchy of Lothringen, and is where our other ancestors were located at this time.

The first two lines give the reporting date: "twenty-eighth of January, Year one thousand seven hundred twenty-seven"; line nine begins "natus heri" ("born yesterday"), hence the birth date of the 27th.

Other discernible names are "Barbara Higard" (midwife - lines 3 & 4), and the godparents "Nicolaus Bley" (line 9) and "Catherine Simon, daughter of Michael" (lines 10-11). It appears to me that line 3 says that the child is the "son of Joannis," hence the conclusion that Joannis Oberle is the father.

Translated Data

■ 7 ■

(Suspected) Children of the elder Johann Oberle & Anna-Maria Anstett

Johann and Anna Marie, in addition to being the younger Johann's parents, are very likely the parents of several other children, although I have been unable to locate any of their birth records to support this. Circumstantial, but admittedly weak, evidence[11] suggests that Johann and Anna Maria may also be the parents of Balthassar Oberlé, who is almost certainly my 5th great-grandfather.

- Antonius (Anthony) Oberlé id4305, born in 1724, married Catherine Langbour id4306 at some point before September 1747. Anthony may actually be the child of Jacques Oberlé id4310, a sibling of Johann's, and Eve id4311 Schwoerer.

- **Balthassar [I] Oberlé** id1704, (born between 1709 and 1718, probably in 1711, died 27 April 1788). Balthassar is very likely our family's direct ancestor and will be discussed in more detail beginning on page 9 below. To avoid any confusion with his son Balthassar as well as those named Balthassar in several succeeding generations of his descendants, I will refer to him as "Balthassar [I]." Balthassar may be Johann's sibling rather than his son, but not enough records exist to clarify this.

- Ludovicus (Ludwig) Oberlé id4298, married Anna Maria Rammier or Rammin and had at least one child, Johann Wilhelm id4300 who was born and died in August 1749. Anna Maria's surname is possibly Ramm, and she is possibly a sibling of the Catherine Rammin who married Jacob Oberle below, since the Latin form *Rammin* would often be used to indicate "child of Ramm." Ludwig may also be a nephew of Johann rather than his son, but he is definitely the brother of Anthony above.

- Catherine Oberlé id4290, (born about 1722, died 5 May 1790). Catherine was married to Joseph Brodnig id4291, but I am unaware of any children.

- Johann (Joannis) Oberlé id5215, (born 27 January 1726). Johann is discussed above, and his birth record is illustrated on page 7. I've encountered no further information about Johann.

- Jacobus (Jacob) Oberlé id4292, (born about 1730). Jacob was married to Catherine Hamm id4293. Catherine's surname is possibly Ramm, and she is possibly a sibling of the Anne-Marie Rammin who married Ludwig Oberle above. Jacob and Catherine had at least one daughter:
  Catherine Oberlé id4224, (born about 1750); married Antonius Rollin id4295 on 21 January 1770 in Dabo.

If further evidence can establish that Johann and Anne-Marie are indeed Balthassar's parents, they would be my 6th great-grandparents. Because of the

---

[11] These children were all born in the same time frame, and I have been unable to identify any other possible parents. If they are not all Johann and Anna Maria's children, they are certainly Johann's nieces or nephews.

uncertainty regarding our relationship to Johann, he is not included in the ancestor chart on page 51, and is discussed solely for general interest.

The Mertz family and Anne-Marie Mertz

Anne-Marie Mertz id4221, was born in Nancy, Muerth et Moselle, Lorraine, France. One published genealogy[12] gives Anne-Marie's surname as Matz, rather than Mertz, but I believe that to be incorrect, since Mertz was a fairly common surname in both the Nancy and Dagsburg areas in this period. I've located no information on her parents.

Balthassar (I) Oberlé and Anne-Marie Mertz

It is certain that this Balthassar [I] Oberlé id1704 is the father of Balthassar [II] Oberlé id1675; it is likewise certain that François Joseph[13] Oberlé id1154, is our direct ancestor. Although fairly compelling, however, the evidence that François Joseph is Balthassar [I]'s grandson (i.e. the son of Balthassar [II]) is still circumstantial. Unless some evidence surfaces to disprove this assumption, though, I consider it very likely that Balthassar id1704 and Anne-Marie Mertz id4221 are my 5th great-grandparents. The reasons for this conclusion will be discussed in more detail in an appendix beginning on page 165.

Balthassar was likely born in about 1711, since his 1788 death record, shown on page 10, gives his age as seventy-eight.

As can be seen from the birth dates of their confirmed children, it seems likely that Balthassar and Anne-Marie were married in 1746 or 1747. Since Balthassar would have been over thirty years old by the time of that marriage, it is possible that Anne-Marie may not have been his first wife, although I have uncovered no evidence of a previous marriage or other Oberle births.

Balthassar and Anne-Marie lived their entire married lives in Dabo. Because extant church records seldom mention anyone's profession, we will likely never know what Balthassar did for a living or anything else about them. Most residents of the Dabo area were illiterate farmers or laborers, however, and we know from his son Balthassar's id1675 death record (see page 24) that Balthassar [I] was unable to sign his name; it is therefore likely that he was a typical rural peasant.

My 5th great-grandmother Anne-Marie Mertz died in 1787[14].

Her husband Balthassar died in Dabo on 27 April 1788; as can be seen from his death record (see page 10), he outlived his son Balthassar, my 4th great-grandfather, by almost two years.

---

[12] by Isabella Warth of France.
[13] My third great-grandfather François Joseph Oberlé is introduced on page 16.
[14] This year is reported by Annick Keiner of France, although he gives no source; I haven't found any record to verify this, and haven't been able to contact Mr. Keiner, but the record of her husband's death in 1788 indicates that Anne-Marie had predeceased him so I have no reason to question Mr. Keiner's information.

1711-1975 History

Death 27 APR 1788
of
Balthassar Oberlé (id1704)
age 78

Reported by:
Joannis Oberlé (id4309)
Son of decedent
and
Petrus Oberlé (id4222)
Son of decedent

Observations:
This Balthassar [I], likely my 5th great-grandfather, outlived his son Balthassar [II], my 4th great-grandfather, by slightly over two years.

Balthassar's son Johann, who reported his father's death, made a mark next to his name (Sig + joannis Oberle), indicating that he himself was unable to sign his name, and was therefore likely illiterate. Pierre (signing his name in the Latin form "Petrus") seems to have been able to write his name.

Balthassar's wife Anne Marie Mertz (id4221) (a129) is not mentioned in the death record; she had died the previous year.

Paroisse de Dabo – 1788 Death Record of *Balthassar [I] Oberlé*

Balthassar [I] Oberlé[id1704] *is the husband of Anne Marie Mertz*[id4221]

Translated Data

Children & Grandchildren of Balthassar (I) Oberlé & Anne-Marie Mertz

In order to retain a focus on our direct line, this section will provide only a brief commentary on Balthassar (I) and Anne-Marie's children and grandchildren.

- **Balthassar (II) Oberlé** id1675, (born about 1745, died in 1786). Balthassar is almost certainly our family's direct ancestor; he and his family will be discussed in more detail beginning on page 16 below. To avoid confusion with his father and son, I refer to him as "Balthassar II."

- Pierre Oberlé id4222, (probably born in about 1748), married Marie-Thérése (Theresa) Schmidt id4223 in 1787. Pierre and Theresa had at least four daughters, all born in Dabo.
  Maria-Therese Oberlé id4298, (born 28 July 1788)
  Anna Maria Oberlé id4308, (born 2 November 1789)
  Marie-Catherine Oberlé id4307, (born 27 March 1790, died before 1797)
  Marie-Catherine Oberlé id4231, (born 1797, died 1842); married Jacques Spengler id4230 in 1817.

- Antonius Oberlé id4304, (born before 1751). He is mentioned as the godfather on the birth record of his niece Anne-Marie Oberlé id4267 (see page 16) on 7 April 1767, but I have no other information about him.

- Magdalena Oberlé id4238, (died 18 December 1800). I have no firm evidence that Magdalena is a member of this family, but the circumstances suggest that is likely. Her death was reported in Engenthal (see page 168), where others of the family are known to have moved in the late eighteenth century.

- Anne-Marie Oberlé id4228, married Martin Linkenheld id4227 in 1778, and had at least two daughters:
  Maria Elisabeth Linkenheld id4248, (born 5 July 1780)
  Martina Linkenheld id4249, (died 20 November 1781)
  Female Infant Linkenheld id4266, (born and died 26 June 1789)
  Maria Anna Linkenheld id4265, (born 10 February 1790)
  Anne-Marie Oberlé appears to have lived her entire life in Dabo.

- Catherine Oberlé id1703, (born about 1759, died 22 October 1829 at age 70). Catherine was married to Jean Weinmann id1702 (who died before Catherine). I suspect that Catherine may earlier have been married to Henri Sali id4255, and had at least one son with him.
  Antoine Sali id1252, (born about 1784, died 20 April 1814). Antoine will be mentioned when discussing Maria Caecilia Oberle id1229 on page 22. Catherine also died in Engenthal.

- Michel Oberlé id4225, (born 1765, died 24 November 1800). Michel married Odile Schott id4226 (born 1771) in 1799, but had no children I am aware of. Michel also died in Engenthal (see page 169).

- Joseph Oberlé id4229. In about 1758, Joseph married Catherine[15] Drixel id4296 and they had a daughter Francisca, born on 15 October 1759. Catherine seems to have died, possibly in childbirth and, when he was about 48, Joseph married the much younger Françoise Gemmerle id4247 (born 13 August 1750) in Steinbourg (Bas-Rhin region of Alsace) on 6 February 1798. I am unaware of any children. Françoise was the daughter of Jean Gemmerle id4220 and Madeleine Vierling id4246.

- Joannis Oberlé id4309. Johann married Catherine Michel id4258 on 25 November 1783 in Dabo, and had three children:

    Catherine Walburga Oberlé id4260, (born 12 October 1784, died bef 1786)
    Catherine Walburga Oberlé id4261, (born 25 March 1786)
    Johann Martin Oberlé id4263, (born 13 December 1789)
    Maria Catherine Oberlé id4543, (born 6 April 1792)

Johann (Jean) Schott & Anne-Marie Sennewick

I have uncovered very little information about my 5th great-grandparents. Jean Schott id4250, who seems to have had four brothers, had already died before his daughter Anne-Marie's marriage to Balthassar Oberlé on 27 May 1766. According to one source[16], Anne-Marie Sennewick id4251 had passed away much earlier, in 1748, but I have a record from early February of 1765 which seems to show Jean and Anne-Marie sponsoring the marriage of their son Joseph id4274; unfortunately the beginning of the record is missing and I can't be certain. Anne-Marie had at least one sister, Barbara.

Children & Grandchildren of Jean Schott & Anne-Marie Sennewick

- Joseph Schott id4274. Joseph is known only from the death record of his sister Anne-Marie's husband Balthassar Oberlé id1675 on 4 March 1786, where he is one of those reporting the death. The partial record alluded to above is a marriage to Elisabeth Laurent, likely his wife.

- **Anne-Marie Schott** id4228, (born about 1738, died 18 June 1776). Anne-Marie is almost certainly our family's direct ancestor; she and her family will be discussed in more detail beginning on page 16 below.

- Rosalie Schott id4275, married Joseph Anstett id4276 and had two children that I know of:

    Antonius Anstett id4277

---

[15] This is not the same person as my fourth great-grandmother (id1228) who was married to Andre Ruffenach and was the paternal grandmother of Catherine Ruffenach, the first Seraphin's mother.

[16] Genealogy of Nicole Delor and Dominique Martin of France.

Unnamed infant daughter id4278, who died on 27 May 1766.

- Maria Barbara Schott id4279, married Anthony Dillenschneider id4280 and had at least one child:

  Maria Barbara Dillenschneider id4281.

- Johannes Schott id4282, married Marie Christoph id4286 and had at least one son:

  Peter Schott id4287, (died 27 April 1766)

- Antonius Schott id4283, married Anna Maria Ramm id4284 on 29 April 1766 and had at least one child:

  Anna Maria Schott id4285 (born 14 July 1770)

  Antonius later married Marie Anne Schreiber id4259 on 12 October 1773, but I haven't located any children from that marriage. I am also unaware of what relationship there is between this Marie Anne Schreiber and my younger 3rd great-grandmother of the same name id1155 (see page 25).

Church and State – the Reversal of Power

The next generation of our ancestors was born at the end of what was known in France as the *Ancien Régime*, and were going to be living through one of the more tumultuous periods of French, if not human, history. It is helpful, therefore, to review how the contemporary state of politics and the sources of political power came to be.

In early western history, it is evident that there was little if any distinction between civil and religious authority; for the most part, they were one and the same. Although the early Jewish patriarchs had no particular knowledge of trichinosis, for example, they realized that those who ate pork often suffered painful deaths. They therefore banned the consumption of pork – this was not considered at the time[17] to be a religious stricture per se – simply the type of guidance expected from an enlightened leadership.

Over the centuries however, as civilization became more complex, political and religious authorities became more distinct – each evolving to fill its own particular role. There was still, however, at least in the Christian world, an understanding that civil authority derived its power from the consent of the religious. Later power struggles within the Catholic Church, and between the church and various civil authorities, led ultimately to a reversal of this balance in the areas occupied by the Holy Roman Empire.

On December 20, 1046, Henry the Black (1017–1056), whom we met back on page 4, convened the Council of Sutri in order to prepare for his coronation. In order to satisfy popular beliefs and prevent any later challenges to his

---

[17] ... although, like many other early pragmatic strictures, this eventually became entrenched as a tenet of the religion itself.

authority, Henry needed to subscribe to the pretense that in order to become the Holy Roman Emperor and fully exercise the power of that office, he needed to be crowned as emperor by God's representative on earth – the Pope. First, however, he needed to establish who exactly of the three existing claimants to the papacy was legitimate.[18] In a deliciously pragmatic move, Henry deposed all three and declared the papacy temporarily vacant. After Adalbert of Bremen refused the papacy, Henry selected Bishop Suidger, his own earlier appointee to the See of Bamberg, who became Pope Clement II. Clement then proceeded to crown Henry as the Holy Roman Emperor. The new balance of power was now clear – if not to the public at large, at least to the political and religious players themselves.

By the time the next generation of our ancestors was growing up, even the public had become aware of the distinct separation of church and state although, as peasants, most were now simply serving two masters – masters who sometimes unfortunately had conflicting agendas.

The French King Louis XV, in a speech given before the Parliament of Paris in 1766[19], further reinforced the idea that the power of the Kings wasn't reliant on any outside approval from the church – or any other government legislatures or courts. He said:

Louis XV

"To attempt to establish such pernicious innovations as principles is to affront the magistrature, to betray its interests and to ignore the true, fundamental laws of the state, as if it were permissible to disregard the fact that in my person alone lies that sovereign power whose very nature is the spirit of counsel, justice and reason. From me alone the courts receive their existence and authority. The fullness of this authority, which they exercise in my name only, remains permanently vested in me, and its use can never be turned against me. Legislative power is mine alone, without subordination or division. It is by my sole authority that the officers of my courts effect, not the creation of the law, but its registration, promulgation and execution, and that they have the right of remonstrance, as is the duty of good and faithful counselors. Public order in its entirety emanates from me. I am its supreme guardian. My people are one with me, and the rights and interests of the nation – which some dare to make into a body separate from the monarch – are of necessity united with my own and rest entirely within my hands."

---

[18] A discussion of this period of papal history is far beyond the scope of this book, but the three claimants were Pope Benedict IX, Pope Sylvester III, and Pope Gregory VI, who each represented a differing faction of Roman nobility. Gregory VI's claim to the papacy, interestingly enough, was that he had purchased it in good faith from Benedict IX two years earlier.

[19] Recall that this was the year in which the French assumed control of Lothringen/Lorraine, our Oberlé ancestors' hometown.

Marriage 27 MAY 1766
of
Balthassar Oberlé (id1675) (a64)
son of Balthassar Oberle (id1704)
and Anna Maria Mertz (id4221)
and
Anne Marie Schott (id4224)
daughter of Jean Schott (id4250), deceased, and Anne Marie Sennewick (id4251)

Witnesses:
Balthassar Oberlé (id1704)
Father of the groom Balthassar Oberlé,
Anthony Schott This could be one of two people:
(id4271) Uncle of the bride, or
(id4283) Brother of the bride
and
Georgiu Lambour The uncle of Anna Marie Ramm (id4284), sister-in-law of the bride.
Note: The bride's brother had just married Anna Marie Ramm on 29 April of 1766.

Translated Data

Hodie vigesimo septimo mensis May anni millesimi septingentesimi
sexagesimi sexti tribus proclamationibus in hac Ecclesia publice factis
nullo detecto impedimento a me infra scripto parocho in Dagsburg pro-
vie recepto mutuo consensu sacro matrimonii vinculo in facie Ecclesiae
conjuncti fuerunt Balthasar Oberle filius Balthasaris Oberle
civis hujatis et Annae Mariae Martz conjugum hic comorantium et
Maria Schott filia defunctorum Joannis Schott quondam civis hujatis
et Annae Mariae Sennewick conjugum, ambo comorantes in hac
parochia. adfuerunt testes Balthasar Oberle, Antonius Schott
Fridericus Apreterius cives hic comorantes et Georgius Lambour
civis et Schafferhoff hujus parochiae qui mecum subscripserunt
excepto sponso qui notam fecit declarans se nescire scribere.

Paroisse de Dabo – 1766 Marriage Record of Balthassar [II] Oberlé & Anne Marie Schottt

Balthassar [id1675] and Anne Marie [id4242] were married on 27 March 1766

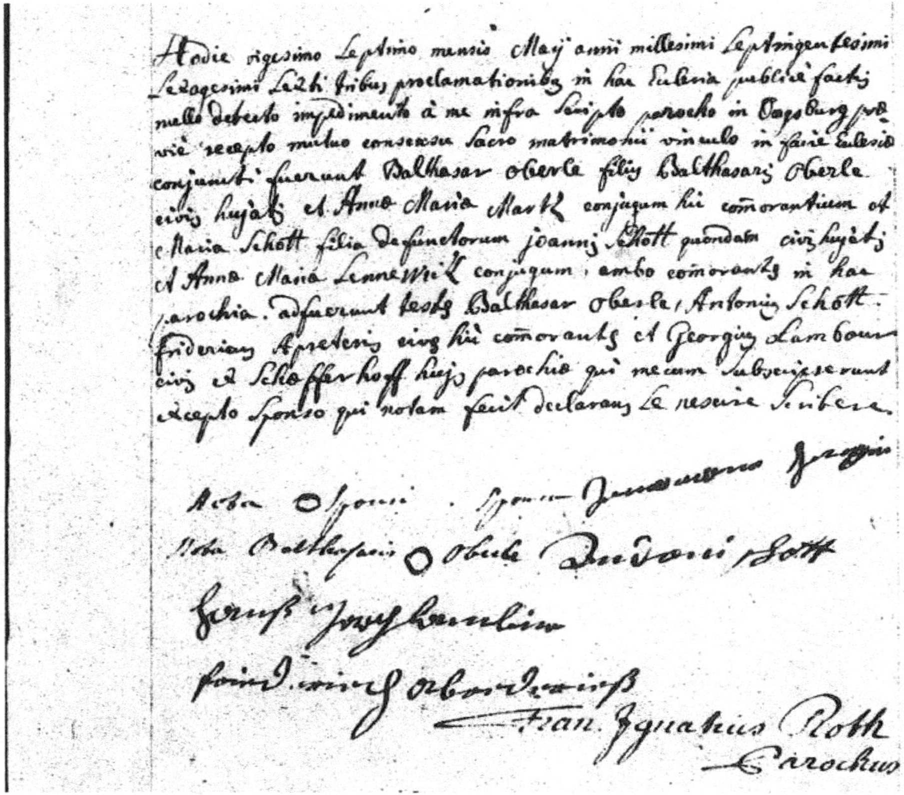

Balthassar (II) Oberlé and Anne-Marie Schott

My 4th great-grandfather Balthassar Oberle id1675 was married in Dabo, Lorraine, France on 27 May 1766 to his first wife, Anne-Marie Schott id4224, daughter of Jean Schott id4250 and Anne-Marie Sennewick id4251, my 5th great-grandparents. Anne-Marie died in 1777 after having at least six children with Balthassar, although the estimated dates of the childrens' births would suggest that there may have been earlier children.

Children & Grandchildren of Balthassar (II) Oberlé & Anne-Marie Schott

- Anna Maria Oberlé id4267, (born 7 April 1767, died before 1778). Anna-Maria's death year isn't known, but Balthassar had another child of the same name in 1778 (see below) with his second wife, suggesting that this Anna Maria may have died as a child.

- Maria Barbara Oberlé id4233, (born on 23 October 1769). Barbara married François Joseph Schmitt on 22 April 1800 in Dabo, but had no children I am aware of.

- Antoine Oberlé id4236, (born on 2 March 1772, died in July 1807). Antoine married Marie Anne Dillenschneider id4237 on 21 November 1805 in Dabo, and had at least one child:

  François Joseph Oberlé id4241, (born 29 January 1806, died 29 July 1834). This François lived his entire life in Dabo as far as I can tell.

  The record of Antoine Oberlé's birth is shown on the facing page. Since the birth record for our ancestor François Joseph Oberlé id1154 cannot be located, this record of his next older sibling Antoine will help to narrow down his date of birth.

- **François Joseph (Joseph) Oberlé** id1154, (born about March 1773, died 24 April 1834 at age 62). My 3rd great-grandfather Joseph, as he was usually known, is our family's direct ancestor, and will be discussed in more detail beginning on page 31. Although almost all references to him are under the name Joseph, we know his full name to be François Joseph from his son Hubert's id1180 death record of 27 January 1848.

  I have so far been unable to locate François Joseph Oberlé's birth record, but estimate his month and year of birth as follows:

  Joseph's death record of 1834 (see page 35) gives his age as 62. This implies that he was born between 25 April 1772 and 24 April 1773[20]. Placing his pregnancy between Antoine's birth (2 March 1772) and Marie Catherine's conception (19 May 1773) with a sufficient buffer would imply a birth some time in February or March of 1773.

---

[20] This may appear to be a math error, but the ages used in this part of Europe are generally analogous to ordinal numbers, whereas in the United States we give our ages as cardinal numbers. In France, for instance a child is "2" if it is in its second year, whereas in the our country, a child born on the same date would be "1," since it has only completed one year of life.

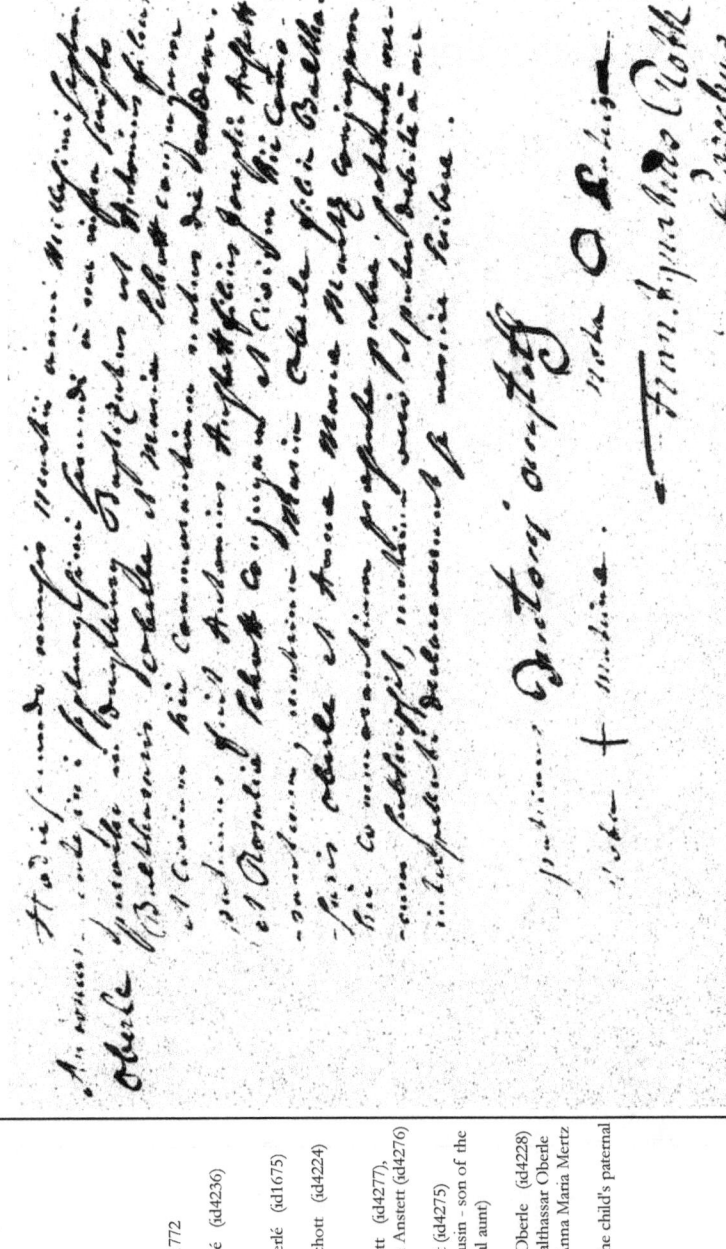

Paroisse de Dabo – 1772 Birth Record of Antoine Oberlé

Antoine Oberlé id4236 *is the next older sibling of our ancestor François Joseph Oberlé* id1154

Translated Data

Birth 2 MAR 1772
of
Antoine Oberlé (id4236)

Parents:
Balthassar Oberlé (id1675)
and
Anne-Marie Schott (id4224)

Witnessed by:
Antoine Anstett (id4277), son of Joseph Anstett (id4276)
and
Rosalie Schott (id4275)
Godfather (cousin - son of the child's maternal aunt)
and
(Anna) Maria Oberle (id4228) daughter of Balthassar Oberle (id1704) and Anna Maria Mertz (id4221)
Godmother (the child's paternal aunt)

1711-1975 History

Parvisse de Dabo – 1774 Birth Record of Maria Catharina Oberlé

Maria Catharina (id1696) is the next younger sibling of our ancestor François Joseph Oberlé (id1154)

Translated Data

Birth 19 FEB 1774
of
Maria Catherina Oberlé (id1696)

Parents:
Balthassar Oberlé (id1675)
and
Anne-Marie Schott (id4224)

Witnessed by:
Jacob Ruffenach (id4228)
son of the deceased Jacob Ruffenach and Claudia [illegible]
and
Anna Maria Oberlé (id4228) daughter of Balthassar Oberlé (id1704) and Anna Maria Mertz (id4221)
Godmother (the child's paternal aunt)

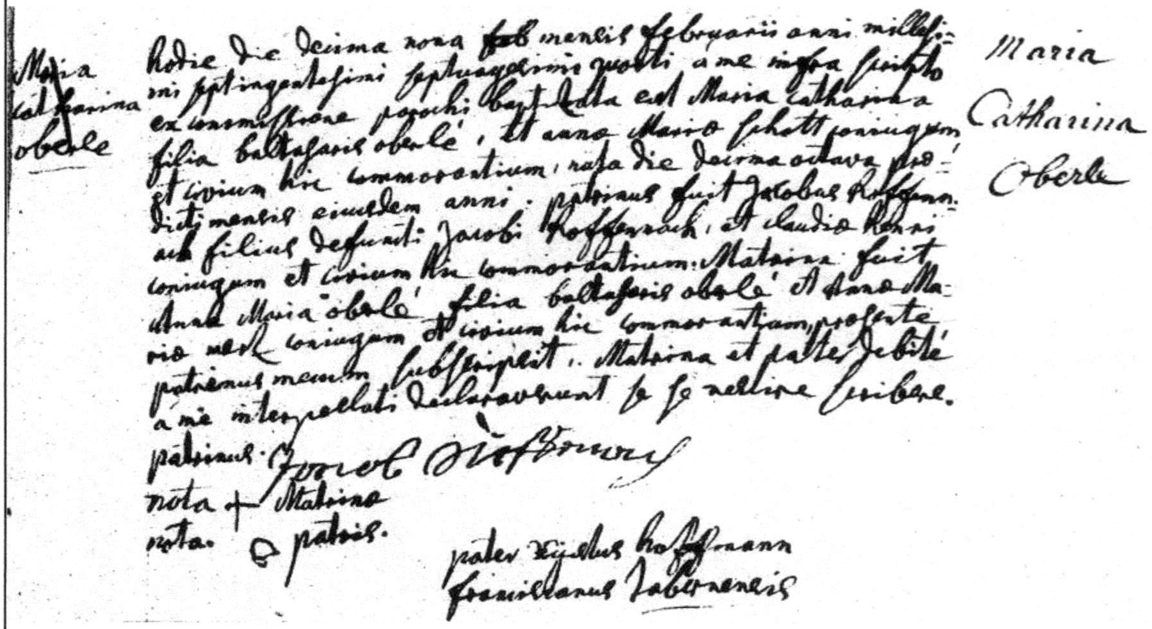

■ 18 ■

Children & Grandchildren of Balthassar (II) Oberlé & Anne-Marie Schott (continued)

- ◆ Marie Catherine Oberlé id1696, (born 19 February 1774 in Dabo, died 21 March 1822 in Engenthal-le-Bas at age 48); married to Dominique Burger id1697, with whom she had three children.

    (Evidence that the Catherine married to Dominique Burger is the same as the Catherine who is Balthassar and Anne-Marie's daughter is only circumstantial, but seems reasonable given all the available information.)

    Sofia Burger id2279 (born 1807, died 17 March 1809)

    Hubert Burger id1629, (born about 1810)

    Sophie Burger id2229, (born 28 June 1817)

    The record of Catherine's birth is shown on the facing page. Since the birth record for François Joseph Oberlé id1154 cannot be located, this record of his next youngest sibling will help to narrow down his date of birth.

- ◆ Maria Elisabethe Oberlé id4256, (born 11 March 1776). I have located no further information about Elisabethe.

My 4th great-grandmother Anne-Marie Schott died in Dabo on 18 June 1776. The report of her death as recorded in the Parish records there is shown on the following page.

The Müller Family and Marie Ann Müller

Marie Anne Müller id1676 was the daughter of Antoine Müller id4242 and Marie Anne Jung id4243.

Because my 4th great-grandfather's second wife Marie Ann is not one of our ancestors, I've made no attempt to trace her line any further back than her parents, or to identify the descendants of her siblings.

Children of Antoine Muller and Marie Anne Jung

- ◆ Marie Anne Müller id1676 became Balthassar (II) Oberlé's second wife; see page 22.

- ◆ Andre Müller id4244, married Marie Anne Burger in Dabo on 9 November 1779.

- ◆ Joseph Müller id4245, married Marie Anne Kilhofer in Dabo on 25 April 1780.

It seems reasonable to suspect that my 4th great grandfather Joseph Müller id1161 (see page 39) is related to this family, but I haven't yet made any attempt to pursue this line.

Death 18 JUN 1776
of
Maria Anna Schott (id4224)
age about 38 (triginta circiter et octo - thirty and about eight)

Reported by:
Balthassar Oberlé (id1675)
Husband of decedent
and
Jacob Schott (id4289)
(I believe this is Maria Anna's cousin)
and
Antony Schott (id4283)
(I believe this is Maria Anna's brother)

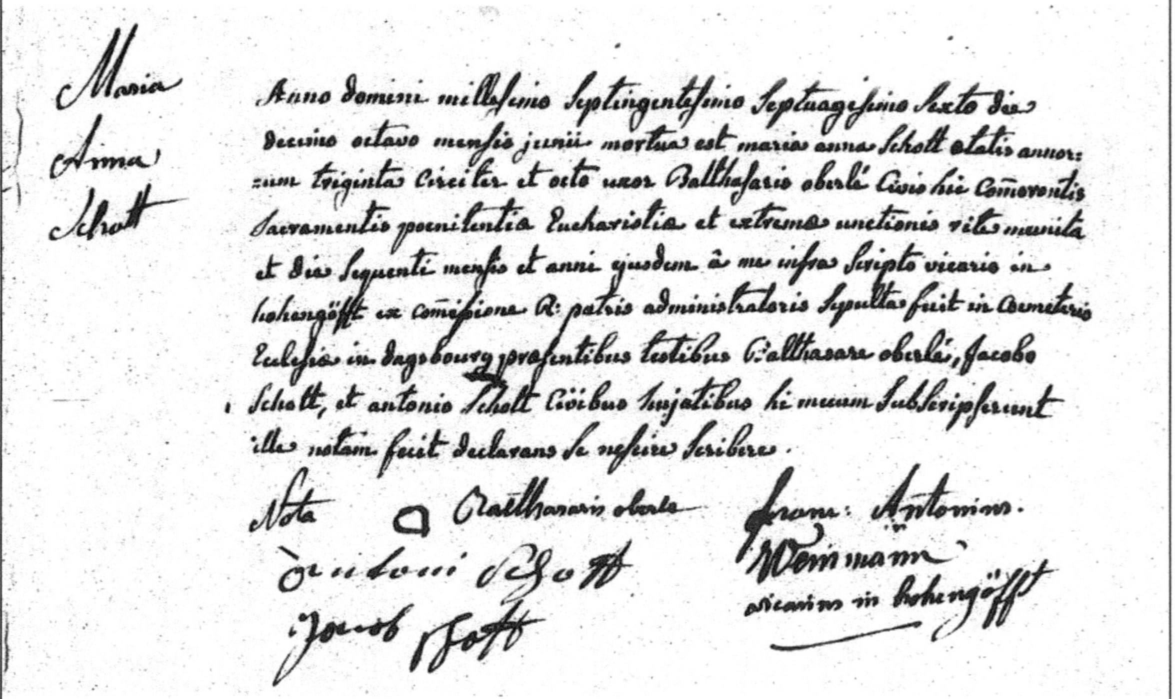

Observations:

The large "mark" to the left of Balthassar's signature, which I originally believed to indicate he could not sign his name, seems to be have been placed to indicate that the signatures of Antoni and Jacob Schott were made for them by the pastor Franciscus Georgius, and that Balthassar (II) could, in fact, sign his name.

This is not certain, however.

Translated Data

Maria Anna Schott

Anno domini millesimo septingentesimo septuagesimo sexto die decimo octavo mensis junii mortua est maria anna Schott aetatis annorum triginta circiter et octo uxor Balthasaris oberlé civis hic comorantis sacramentis poenitentiae Eucharistiae et extremae unctionis rite munita et die sequenti mensis et anni ejusdem à me infra scripto vicario in hohengöfft ex comissione R: patris administratoris sepulta fuit in coemeterio Ecclesiae in dagsbourg praesentibus testibus Balthasare oberlé, Jacobo Schott, et antonio Schott civibus hujatibus hi mecum subscripserunt ille notam fecit declarans se nescire scribere.

Nota ◻ Balthasaris oberle

Antoni Schott

Jacob Schott

fran: Antonius Weinmann vicarius in hohengöfft

Paroisse de Dabo – 1776 Death Record of Anne Marie Schott

My 4th great-grandmother Anne Marie Schott (id4224) was the first wife of Balthassar [II] Oberle (id1675)

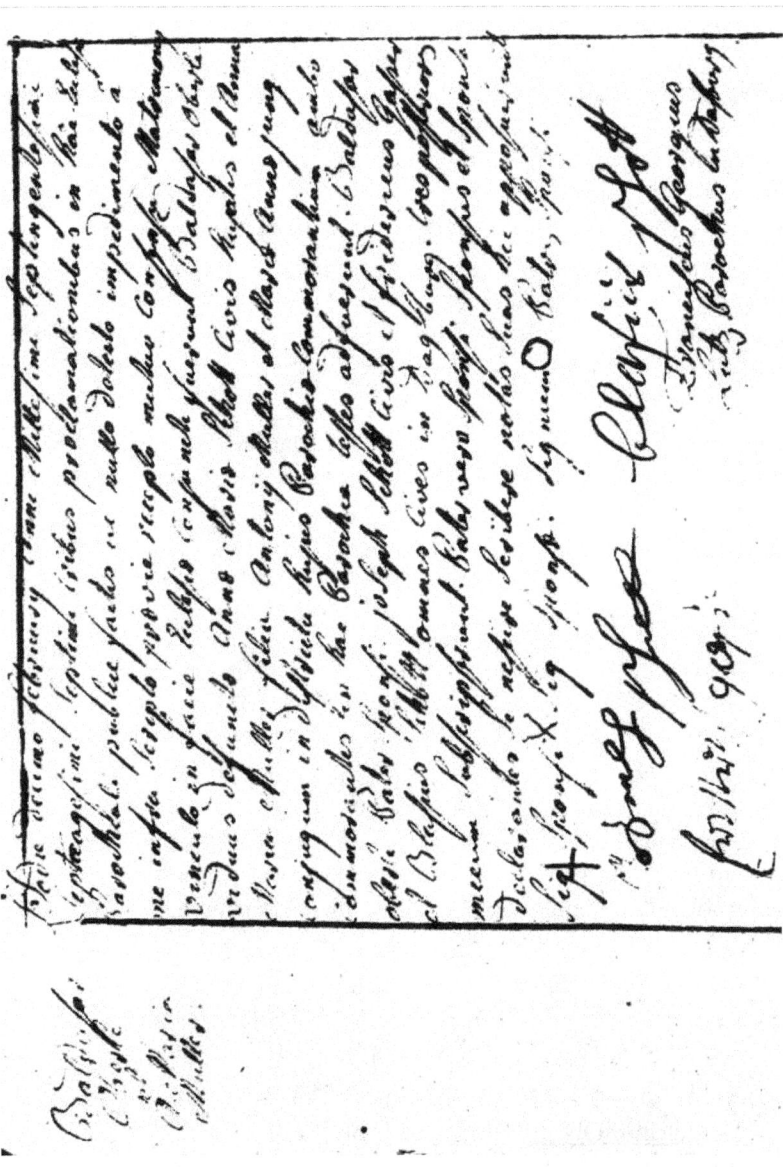

Paroisse de Dabo – 1777 Marriage Record of Balthassar [II] Oberlé & Marie-Anne Muller

Marie-Anne Muller (id1676) was the second wife of my 4th great-grandfather Balthassar [II] Oberle (id1675)

Marriage 10 February 1777
of
Balthassar Oberlé (id1675)
widow of Anne Marie Schott
(id4224)
and
Anna Maria Muller
daughter of Anthony Muller
(id4242) and Marie Anne Jung
(id4243)
Fredericus Gasper
unidentified
Sponsors:
Joseph Schott (id4311)
Brother of Balthassar Oberlé's
deceased wife Anne Marie Schott,

and
Blasius Schott (id4273)
Cousin of Balthassar Oberlé's
deceased wife Anne Marie Schott.

Translated Data

Balthassar (II) Oberlé and Marie Anne Müller

After his first wife Anne-Marie Schott's death, Balthassar married Marie Anne Müller <u>id1676</u> on 10 February 1777; the record of this marriage is shown on the previous page. There is evidence that Balthassar and Marie Anne were already living in Wangenbourg, a little south of Engenthal-le-Bas, by the late eighteenth century.

Children & Grandchildren of Balthassar (II) Oberlé & Marie Anne Müller

This section will provide only a brief commentary on Balthassar and Marie Anne's children and grandchildren, since none of them fall into our direct line. Since children from both of Balthassar [II] Oberlé's marriages migrated to Engenthal-le-Bas in the same time frame, however, this data helps to establish a family connection.

- Marie Anne (Anna) Oberlé <u>id4235</u>, (born 16 March 1778). Anna married Stéphane Bentz (born 1771) in 1799. I am unaware of any children, but haven't specifically researched this.

- Maria Caecilia (Cecile) Oberle <u>id1229</u>, (born 22 November 1779, died 1848). Cecile married Antoine Sali <u>id1252</u> (born about 1784, died 20 April 1814), and they had at least two children:

    Marie Anne Sali <u>id2249</u> (born July 1811).

    Françoise Sali <u>id1253</u> (born 30 January 1814, died 1883).

    Cecile's husband Antoine Sali is the son of Catherine Oberle and her second husband Henri Sali. Not enough detail is available to determine this for certain, but I believe that this Catherine Oberle is my genealogy id #1703, the daughter of Balthassar [I] Oberlé <u>id1704</u> and Anne-Marie Mertz <u>id4221</u>, which would make Cecile and her husband Antoine first cousins. Cecile and Antoine both migrated to and died in Engenthal-le-Bas.

- Balthassar (III) Oberlé <u>id1691</u>, (born about 1781, died 10 May 1829 at age 48); married Marie Elisabethe (Elisabethe) Dieda <u>id1689</u>, daughter of Joseph Dieda <u>id1694</u> and Madelaine Saly <u>id1695</u>. Balthassar and Elisabethe both died in Engenthal-le-Bas. The couple had at least eight children:

    Gaspard Oberlé <u>id1677</u>, (born 1 February 1813, died 11 April 1814.)

    François Melchior Oberlé <u>id1678</u>, (born April 1815.)

    Marie Elisabethe (Elisabethe) Oberlé <u>id1682</u>, (born 21 May 1818); had at least one child, Casimir Oberlé <u>id1687</u> before marriage; later married Jean Auer <u>id2262</u> and had seven other children.

    Françoise Oberlé <u>id1679</u>, (born 12 June 1820, died on 23 September 1845.) Françoise had at least one child, Auguste Oberlé <u>id1688</u>, with an unknown father, and I never located any record of a subsequent marriage.

    Balthassar (IV) Oberlé <u>id1680</u>, (born 17 May 1822); married Marie Anne Gersinger <u>id1690</u> and had at least nine children.

Joseph Oberlé ⁱᵈ¹⁶⁸¹, (born 11 December 1824.)

Caspare Oberlé ⁱᵈ¹⁶⁹², (born 20 June 1827.)

Catherine Oberlé ⁱᵈ¹⁶⁹³, (born 30 August 1829); married Antoine Schwaller ⁱᵈ²²¹⁹ and had at least eight children:

- Maria Geneviève Oberle ⁱᵈ⁴²⁴⁰, (born 23 March 1785, died 1814). Geneviève married Hubert Schwaller ⁱᵈ⁴²³⁹ (born 1777) in 1807, and they had at least one child:

    Marie Therese Schwaller ⁱᵈ⁴²⁵² (born 1812)

    Based on the date of their marriage, it seems likely that Maria Geneviève and her husband may have had other children.

Balthassar (II) Oberlé died on 4 March 1786; the report of his death is shown on the next page.

Balthassar's second wife Marie Anne's date of death is unknown[21], but she was known to be living on 16 April 1812 when her son Balthassar (III) ⁱᵈ¹⁶⁹¹ was married in Engenthal.

Migration to Engenthal-le-Bas

In the latter part of the eighteenth century, after Lorraine became part of France, several members of the family migrated to Engenthal-le-Bas, now known simply as Engenthal.

Of the six children my 4ᵗʰ great-grandparents Balthassar Oberlé and Anne-Marie Schott had, at least two, including our ancestor François Joseph Oberlé ⁱᵈ¹¹⁵⁴ and his sister Marie Catherine Oberlé ⁱᵈ¹⁶²⁶, made this migration. I found no record of Joseph's marriage, which probably took place in about 1792, in either Dabo or Engenthal-le-Bas, but all of his children, grandchildren, and great-grandchildren were born and lived in Engenthal.

This suggests the possibility that Joseph may have been married in his wife's home town, but although I have a name for that town, I have never located it and believe I may be misreading it. See "Marie Anne Schreiber" on page 25 for more information.

Balthassar (III) Oberlé ⁱᵈ¹⁶⁹¹, Joseph's half-brother, also migrated to Engenthal, as did Joseph's aunts, Magdalena ⁱᵈ⁴²³⁸ and Catherine ⁱᵈ¹⁷⁰³, and his uncle, Michel ⁱᵈ⁴²²⁵.

---

[21] I haven't been able to locate any record of her death in Dabo or Engenthal.

1711-1975 History

Death 4 MAR 1786
of
Balthassar Oberlé (id1675)
age 42

Reported by:
Balthassar Oberlé (id1704)
Father of decedent
and
Josephus Schott (id4274)
Brother of decedent's first wife
Marie Anna Schott (id4224)

Observations:

Since no birth record for this Balthassar has been found, his year of birth must be estimated. Since his age is forty-two, he must have been born in about 1745. Note that his father outlived him.

Translated Data

Paroisse de Dabo – 1786 Death Record of Balthassar [II] Oberlé

Balthassar [II] Oberlé (id1675) was the husband of Anne-Marie Schott (id4224) and Marie-Anne Muller (id1676)

Marie Anne Schreiber

At some time around 1765, in a town whose name appears to be Bürckengal (see the segment from her death record to the right), my 3rd great-grandmother Marie Anne Schreiber [id1155] was born[22] to as yet unidentified parents.

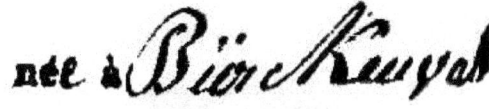

née à Bürckengal ? née à Bür Keugal ?

Earlier, on page 12, mention was made that Antoine Schott [id4283] had also married someone named Marie Anne Schreiber. Schreiber was a reasonably common name in Dabo, and since my 3rd great-grandmother managed to meet and marry François Joseph Oberlé either there or in Engenthal, it seems safe to assume that Bürckengal must have been fairly close by.

Our Alsatian-French Ancestry

Commune of Engenthal-le-Bas

Engenthal, as it is now known, is located in Alsace at the confluence of the roads shown in the map on page 5. The town is in the Department of Bas-Rhin (literally, "Lower Rhine") – counter-intuitively, it is north of Haut-Rhin ("upper Rhine") because the Rhine River dividing France and Germany flows from south to north.

Entering Engenthal-le-Bas at the modern D224 & D218 road junction

For those who get the opportunity to visit this area, specific instructions for driving from Strasbourg to Engenthal and the other communities discussed in this book are provided in an appendix beginning on page 157.

---

[22] Marie Anne Schreiber's death record of 1 May 1823 (see page 34), lists her as being 58 years old at the time of her death, and as coming from (née à) Bürckengal, a town I have not yet been able to identify or locate (the entry could very well say "Bür Kengal," or something similar, but no variant I tried led anywhere). As mentioned earlier, the French custom then, as it is now, is to consider a child's age to be one year at birth ("age one" therefore, is interpreted as indicating that a child is in its "first year," rather than as having lived for at least one year, as it does in the U.S.) – hence the estimated birth year.

Modern day welcome Sign to Wangenbourg and Engenthal on the D224 highway.

Engenthal-le-Bas (lower Engenthal – in this case it is north of, as well as at a lower altitude than, upper Engenthal) is nestled in the foothills of the Vosges Mountains west of Strasbourg[23]. The town spreads over the side of a gently sloping hill and, like all the areas adjacent to the Vosges, is surrounded by forests of oak interspersed with a variety of conifers, chief among which is the Wangenbourg Pine for which the area is noted. Because of these natural resources, the area was (and remains) a major regional source of the wood used in home construction, furniture making, etc. Thus, forestry work provided a significant source of employment in the area, providing occupations such as tree cutting, milling, and transportation.

A View of Engenthal-le-Bas; photograph taken in March 2004

---

[23] Since Engenthal is too small to be shown on any but the most detailed maps, step-by-step directions for locating it and driving there from Strasbourg (the nearest major city) are given on page 157.

There were a number of *bucheron* (lumberjacks) among the Oberlé males, including two of our direct line ancestors[24]. But because of sensible approaches to forest management (or perhaps originally due simply to poor technology), the forests are still abundant, and these industries are still active in and around the Engenthal area. This can be seen from the many sawmills and staging areas for cut timber all around the area (see the photo above right, taken in March 2004).

Engenthal-le-Bas – Cut timbers curing on the roadside

Another common occupation in this general area of Alsace was grape growing and wine production, although Engenthal was not supported as much by this activity in the eighteenth and nineteenth centuries as it was by forestry.

Commune of Obersteigen

The town of Obersteigen is located just north of Engenthal-le-Bas. So far as I am aware, none of our Oberle ancestors actually lived there, but this is where the local Catholic parish church was located.

The area near the border of Alsace and Lorraine where our ancestors lived in the eighteenth and nineteenth centuries, par-

Obersteigen – Chapelle de l'Assomption de la Verge

This is where my 3rd great grandparents François Joseph Oberlé and Marie Anne Schreiber were likely married in 1791.

---

[24] This would be Seraphin (I) [id708] and his son Seraphin (II) [id25] who eventually came to the United States. Several of the younger Seraphin's brothers and uncles also were *bucheron*.

ticularly near Dabo and Engenthal, was heavily Roman Catholic then[25], as was most of Alsace, and remains so today.

Dabo had its own Catholic parish (Paroisse de Dabo), from which several records are reproduced in this document. The area surrounding Engenthal, though, was served by the Chapelle de l'Assomption de la Verge in Obersteigen, first constructed in the thirteenth century, and which is still in use today.[26] The lower picture on the previous page shows my daughter in front of the entrance to the Chapel's cemetery, where the last male Oberlé to live in Engenthal was buried in 1995[27].

The First Generation to Live in Engenthal-le-Bas

To place my 3rd great-grandfather François Joseph Oberlé's generation in historic perspective, his birth occurred just over two years after the birth of Beethoven, a little over three years before the American Declaration of Independence, and almost simultaneously with the outbreak of revolutionary change across much of western civilization, particularly in France and in the American Colonies. By the time this generation had reached its twenties, the long established balance between church and state would be cracked if not broken – music and the arts would be dramatically changed – and politics and the relationships between rulers and ruled would begin their steady transformation to present day forms of government.

Three of our ancestor Balthassar [I] id1704 Oberlé's children are known to have been born in Dabo and died in Engenthal, and four of his son Balthassar [II] id1675 Oberlé's children, including François Joseph id1154, relocated to Engenthal as well. All of Joseph's children and grandchildren, as well as those of his half-brother Balthassar, were born there.

The reason for the Oberlés' migration isn't known, and may likely never be, since the history of such small localities is very difficult to unravel. Consider, however, that the nearby border had recently disappeared with the annexation of Lorraine by France in 1766 – just a few years earlier.

---

[25] In 1807, the population of Engenthal-le-Bas was 99% Roman Catholic, and that of Engenthal-le-Haut (Wangenbourg) was 95% Roman Catholic. The remainder was Calvinist. Although there was a significant Jewish population in other parts of Alsace (including the family of the great 19th century composer-pianist Charles-Valentin Alkan), it doesn't appear that the Jewish were ever a presence in the towns of the Vosges foothills. Religious distribution information is from http://www.rootsweb.ancestry.com/~fraalsac/alsaceaz/alsacewz.htm.

[26] It wasn't until 1870 that a church was built in what is now Wangenbourg-Engenthal itself; my great-grandfather Seraphin (II) would likely have seen the church, but there are no family burials or relevant headstone inscriptions among the graves at the church that we were able to see.

[27] This was Arthur Oberlé id 91116, son of Charles Oberlé id 91114 and Marie Linkenheld id91115; these I believe are descendants of Balthassar (IV). The young woman staffing the Wangenbourg-Engenthal tourist center during one of the days we visited told us that her grandmother was an Oberlé, but we were unable to meet the grandmother or obtain any further information.

The town and castle in adjacent Wangenbourg, originally built by the mostly absentee Lords of Wangen[28] in 1295, was the home of the feudal-era overlords of the area. After the French gained control of Alsace in 1678, the abandoned castle became the new headquarters for the local French military administrator and garrison, which had previously had to make do with substandard quarters in neighboring Lorraine. The photos to the left and below show the remains of this castle.

Several Views of the Wangenbourg Castle Ruins just outside Engenthal (All of the photos on this page were taken in early 2004)

When the French military garrison was finally removed from the area a few years later, the soldiers left the castle, but not before damaging the Keep and the Battlements. With the local symbol of feudal, and later military, oppression now effectively a ruin, conditions in the entire area may have seemed to be improving from the long years of war and feudal oppression. The world might have appeared somewhat more open to opportunities in the nearby valley that was now freely accessible.

On the right, one of my daughters is standing on an access bridge over the now empty moat surrounding the Wangenbourg Castle.

---

[28] Hence "Wangen-Bourg", or the Burg (city) of the Wangens.

1711-1975 HISTORY

Engenthal-le-Haut – 2004 View from the Route de Panorama

*Left:
Engenthal-le-Bas – View of La Mossig on the north side of Route de Windsbourg (D224)*

La Mossig, fairly narrow at this point, eventually continues east through Romaswiller, Wasselonne and Marlenheim, then south to Kirchheim, Odratzheim, Scharrachbergheim-Irmstett, Soultz-les-Bains and Avolsheim. La Mossig supplies irrigation and some drinking water for many of these towns – all visible in the maps beginning on in the Appendix beginning on page 157. The river's appearance here is somewhat deceiving, since it overflows its banks periodically.

François Joseph Oberlé and Marie Anne Schreiber

In about 1791, François Joseph Oberlé [id1154] and Marie Anne Schreiber [id1155] were married, likely in a religious ceremony at the Chapelle de l'Assomption de la Verge in Obersteigen[29] or perhaps in Bürckengal.

Signature of (François) Joseph Oberlé

The population of Engenthal was 510 at the time. Joseph was neither a farmer nor a logger, and seems to have made his living as a *Journalier* or day-laborer[30]. Nonetheless, he seems to have been our first provably literate male Oberle ancestor, although his father Balthassar may also have been.

These were "interesting times" in which to begin a family in France[31], even in the relatively remote area of Alsace: King Louis XVI was beginning to see indications that not everyone agreed with his divine right to rule. In October 1787, when François Joseph was about twenty years old, the Duc d'Orleans objected that one of King Louis's proclamations regarding tax changes was illegal. Louis replied "It is legal because I wish it." He prevailed then, but this was one of his final political victories. France had by then entered the depressing era of rampant poverty depicted in Victor Hugo's *Les Misérables*, and 1787 was the year the seeds of the French Revolution took hold. The storms and floods of that year ruined the harvests across the country; the drought of the following year, and the severe hailstorm of 13 July 1788, ruined the economy. Nobles and landowners, not wishing to feel the pinch, responded arrogantly by raising the payments and taxes expected from the common farmers and laborers. The following winter (of 1789/90) was also particularly severe, adding to the misery and frustration of the general population.[32] To be sure, Engenthal (and Alsace as a whole) was only indirectly affected by many of these conditions, mostly suffering from the secondary results of the national economic crisis. Nonetheless, the French Revolution of 1789 was inevitable, and was supported widely across all of France, including Alsace, and particularly by the increasingly marginalized Catholic Church and clergy.

But in 1790, when the framers of the new constitution refused to provide any special status for the Catholic religion in France, support from the church, the clergy, and the majority of rural Catholics for the revolution began to wane. Due to continuing attempts by all the parties to rebalance power and position, revolution and crisis remained the norm until Napoleon Bonaparte effectively took power in November of 1799.

---

[29] See a picture on page 27. There is no civil marriage recorded in the Engenthal records that I could find, and the parish records from the church for this period were lost many years ago.

[30] François Joseph's profession was given by his sons Seraphin and Joseph when they reported their father's death at age 62 on 24 April 1834. See the report of his death on page 35.

[31] There are many excellent books on this period. I recommend *Revolutionary France 1770-1880*, by François Furet, ISBN 0-631-17029-4, for a very readable discussion.

[32] This has been linked to a persistent El Niño that occurred in the years 1789 to 1793.

Engenthal – The Mairie (Town Hall) in 2004

Joseph Oberlé and Marie Anne Schreiber began their family in Engenthal, and had six children between 6 February 1793 and 27 May 1808. Their seventh and last child, Seraphin [id708], my 2nd great grandfather, was born on 20 May 1811. For clarity, I will be referring to him as Seraphin I in order to distinguish him from his son and grandson – also named Seraphin. His birth record is shown below:

Translated Data
*Commune d'Engenthal –
1811 Birth Record of
Seraphin (I) Oberlé*

Birth 20 May 1811 of Seraphin [I] Oberlé (id708)
Parents:
   Father: Joseph Oberlé, age 40, Laborer (id1154)
   Mother: Marie Anne Schreiber (id1155)

Witnesses:
1. Florent Soeder,   Laborer, age 36
2. Jean Pfund,   Laborer, age 37

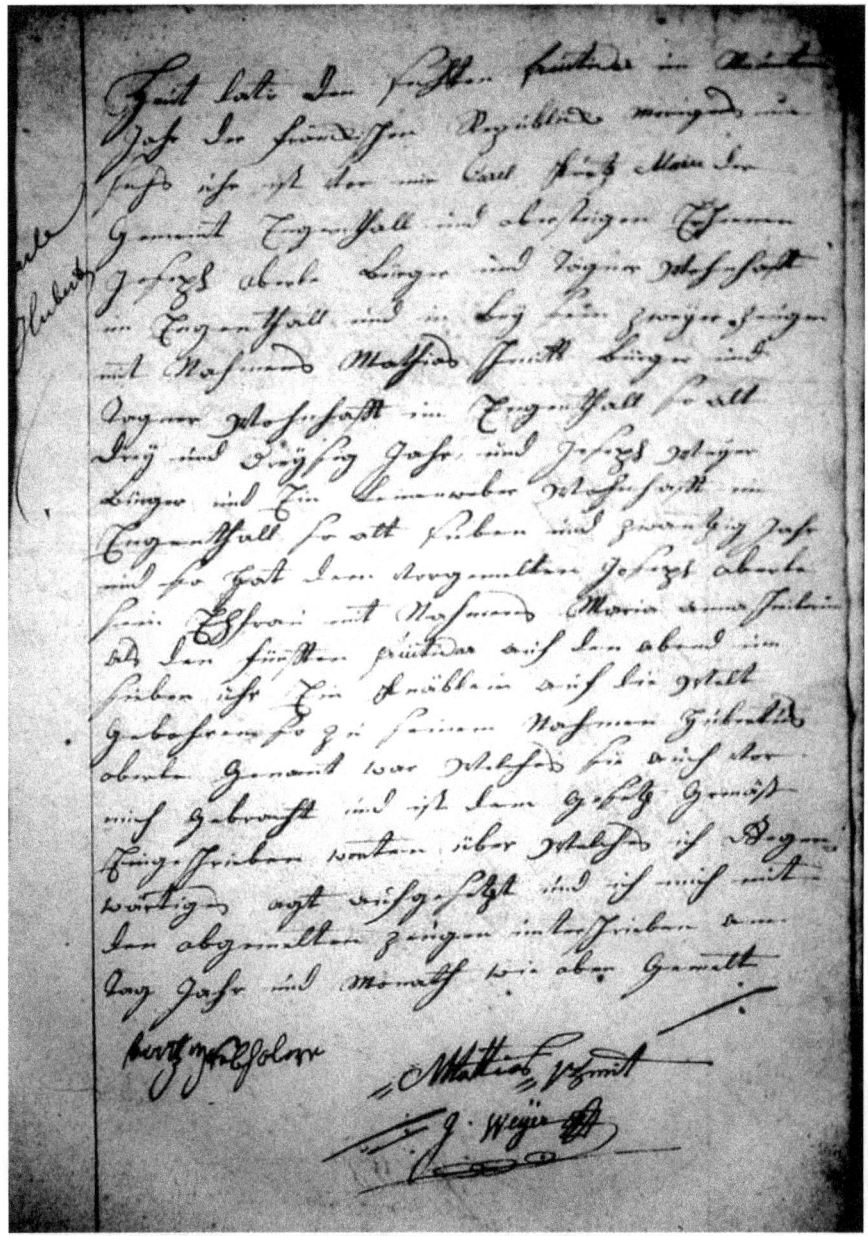

Commune d'Engenthal – 1793 Birth Record of Hubert Oberlé, son of François Joseph

My 3rd great grandfather François Joseph Oberlé's full name is known from his son Hubert's birth record, above – see the end of the fourth line and beginning of the fifth. This type of handwritten record was replaced by printed forms like those on the previous page when Napoleon came to power.

1711-1975 History

My 3rd great-grandmother Marie Anne Schreiber died in Engenthal on 1 May 1823 at age 58. The record of her death is shown below:

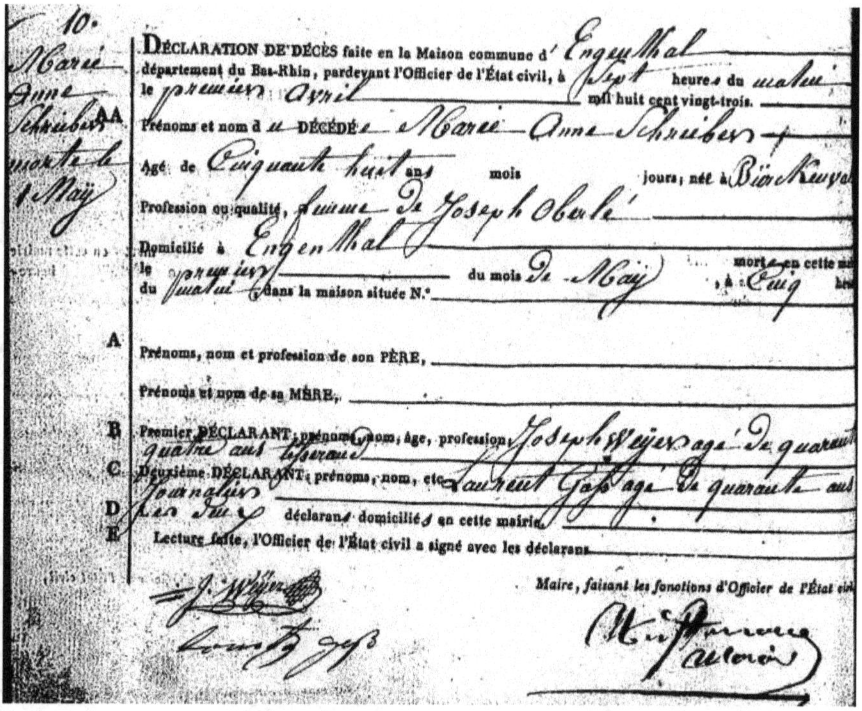

Translated Data

*Commune d'Engenthal –
1823 Death Record of Marie
Anne Schreiber*

Death 1 MAY 1823
of
Marie Anne Schreiber
age 58
(id1155)
wife of
Joseph Oberlé
(id1155)

Reported by:
1. Joseph Weyer
age 44
Weaver
2. Laurent Gass
age 40
Laborer

Note the conflict between the dates shown on this form. The title says "morte le 1 May," while the first part of form says "sept heures du matin le premiere Avril mil huit cent vingt-trois." Since the second part of the form says "le premiere du mois May," I have assumed "Avril" to be an erroneous entry and recorded a date of 1 MAY 1823. This conclusion is supported by the sequence of the records as well.

OUR OBERLE ANCESTORS

My 3rd great-grandfather François Joseph (Joseph) Oberlé died in Engenthal on 24 April 1834 at age 62, almost eleven years after his wife's death. As can be seen in the report of his death below, my 2nd great grandfather Seraphin [I] was one of the two family members that reported the death.

Translated Data

Commune d'Engenthal – 1834 Death Record of François Joseph Oberlé

Death 24 APR 1834
of
Joseph Oberlé
  age 62
  Laborer
  (id1154)
  Widower of
  Marie Anne Schreiber
  (id1155)

Reported by:
Seraphin Oberlé
  age 23
  Laborer
  Son of decedent
  (id708)
and
Joseph Oberlé
  age 39
  Profession: Seieur (??)
  Son of decedent
  (id1230)

This is an early example of Seraphin's signature; in many later examples, he signed with only his last name.

Children & Grandchildren of François Joseph Oberlé & Marie Anne Schreiber

- Hubert Oberlé id1180, (born 6 Feb 1793[33], died 27 Jan 1848); his birth record, shown on page 33, is the only place where his father's full name is given. Hubert married Catherine Ruschmeyer id1181 (born about 1803/1805), daughter of F. Ruschmeyer id1232 and Anne Marie Bahr id1233, and had at least six children:

    Barthalome Oberlé id1182 (born 23 August 1831).

    Marie Anne Oberlé id1451 (born 1 June 1833, died 30 June 1865)

    Catherine Oberlé id1183 (born 14 August 1835).

    Hubert Oberlé id1184 (born 7 December 1837).

    Louise Oberlé id1185 (born 2 August 1840).

    Louis Oberlé id1186 (born 13 July 1843).

    Save for the second child Marie Anne, I have located no death records for Catherine or her children, suggesting that the family may have left the area after Hubert's death, but I have not pursued this possibility.

- François Joseph (Joseph) Oberlé id1230, (born abt 1795, died 6 Oct 1854) was married first to Marie Anne Ruffenach id1255 (born about 1793, died 30 June 1836), daughter of Antoine Ruffenach id1259 and Catherine Schneider id1260, but they had no children that I could discover. Joseph's second marriage was to Anastasie Müller id1256 (born about 1798), daughter of François Anton Müller id1261 and Anastasie Dachraus id1262, and they had at least three children:

    Aloyse Oberlé id1257 (born 15 January 1838, died 10 October 1840)

    Catherine Oberlé id1258 (born 4 March 1841)

    Marguerite Oberlé id1452 (died 24 March 1842)

- Catherine Oberlé id1160, (born 9 Jun 1798), married Louis Rolling id1254 (born between 1793 and 1798, died 10 September 1864). They had at least three children.

    Seraphin Rolling id2260, (born 17 Apr 1831)

    Louis Rolling id1556, (born 5 Oct 1833, died 23 Aug 1855). Louis died of cholera at age 21 during his military service in the Army of the Orient.

    Catherine Rolling id2261, (born 22 October 1840)

    The gap between the second and third children suggests that there may have been other children born, but I could find no record of any.

---

[33] I have "translated" many dates from this period for convenience. The very odd French Revolutionary Calendar was begun on what would have been 22 September 1792, but became 1 Vendemiaire l'an I (Year 1) of the Revolution. This calendar had twelve months of exactly thirty days each, followed by a makeup month to correct for that mismatch with nature. Napoleon later re-established the Gregorian calendar, which took effect on 30 Fructidor an XIV (Year 14), and which became 17 September 1806.

- François Antoine Oberlé id1231, (born about 1799/1800, died 14 May 1846) first married Françoíse Berlier id1319, with whom he had one child:

  Marie Anne Oberlé id1320, (born 7 April 1829)

  Antoine's first wife Françoíse Berlier died in childbirth on 19 August 1830, after which he married Marie Anne Deumand id1239, and they had at least nine children:

  François Oberlé id1240, (born 4 March 1832, died 11 October 1837, age 5)

  Joseph Oberlé id1241, (born 11 March 1833, died 8 September 1868)

  Sophie Oberlé id1242, (born 28 December 1834), had twins Elisabeth and Vendalin Oberlé with an unknown father ("pere inconnu" reported on birth record). Neither twin lived more than ten days. Sophie later married François Joseph Spengler and had at least one child with him.

  Seraphin Oberlé id1243, (born 16 January 1837)

  Elisabethe Oberlé id1244, (born 3 December 1838), married Jean Linkenheld and had six children.

  François Oberlé id1245, (born 27 December 1840)

  Aloyse Oberlé id1246, (born September 1842)

  Catherine Oberlé id1247, (born 10 November 1844)

  Florent Oberlé id2278, (born 8 June 1846)

- Armand Oberlé id1187, (born about 1805/1806, died 13 Nov 1870), married Marie Anne Spengler id1188 (born 2 December 1800), daughter of Jean-Pierre Spengler and Elisabeth Deumant. They had at least seven children:

  Jean-Baptiste Oberlé id1189, (born 17 August 1828), married Catherine Mettling and had four children: Basile, Joseph, Emilie, and Elisabeth.

  Armand Oberlé id1190, (born 28 August 1830, died 6 March 1838, age 7)

  Marie Anne Oberlé id1191, (born 12 December 1832), married Ferdinand Spengler and had eight children.

  Joseph Oberlé id1192, (born 19 September 1834)

  Therese Oberlé id1193, (born 27 MAY 1836, died 18 MAY 1871), married Joseph Linkenheld and had five children.

  Adelaïde (Adele) Oberlé id1194, (born 18 September 1839), married Joseph Clodong and had five children.

  Armand Oberlé id1195, (born 24 February 1842, died 27 January 1863)

- Elisabethe Oberlé id1167, (born 27 May 1808), apparently never married, but had one child with an unknown father:

  Veronique Oberlé id1211, (born 8 February 1836, died 13 April 1836)

- **Seraphin (I) Oberlé** id708, (born 20 May 1811, died 7 January 1890). Seraphin is our family's direct ancestor, and will be discussed beginning on page 46. As mentioned above, I will be referring to this Seraphin as Seraphin I to avoid confusion with my great-grandfather and his son.

Cemeteries in and around Engenthal

In addition to the Catholic cemetery in Obersteigen, there are several cemeteries in the Engenthal area that have been in use for several hundred years – all of which appear very well maintained. The one shown on the left is just outside of Engenthal on the road to the old castle. Unfortunately, as is quite common in this part of Europe, cemeteries are unable to expand and graves are recycled for the interment of newer "occupants" as space is needed. For that reason, we encountered no grave that was more than one hundred years old.

Since all of our direct ancestors in Engenthal-le-Bas died more than one hundred years ago, there are no photographs of their headstones presented in this book.

André Ruffenach & Catherine Drixel

I have not located birth records for either of my 4th great-grandparents André Ruffenach ID1227 or Catherine Drixel ID1228 in Engenthal or Dabo but, based on the presence of both family names in church records of Dabo, suspect that they also may have come from that town.

In about 1788, André and Catherine had a son Antoine id1156 in Engenthal, who was my 3rd great-grandfather and is discussed on page 44. André and Catherine had earlier had at least one other child, a daughter Cecile id1159. Cecile married Antoine Stiltz id1158 after the death of his first wife and had a daughter, Elisabeth id1146, with him who became the first wife of my great-great-grandfather Seraphin [I] Oberlé id708, although she is not our ancestor.

Because the relationship among our Drixel and Ruffenach ancestors is much better illustrated graphically, I have provided a diagram on page 39 that will help in picturing the structure of these families, as well as the unrelated, but still connected, Stiltz family. Seraphin's wives Elisabeth Stiltz and Catherine Ruffenach are marked with large asterisks on the right side of the diagram.

Joseph Müller & Catherine Deumant

We only know about my 4th great grandfather Joseph Müller id1161 and his wife Catherine Deumant id1210 because of their appearance in the vital records of their children[34], although we do have a civil record of Catherine Deumant's death (shown on page 42).

Signature of Joseph Müller
Joseph is my 4th great-grandfather

Because of the low population (<600) in Engenthal at the turn of the 19th century, I suspect there may be some relationship between my 5th great grandmother Marie Anne Müller id1676 (Balthassar [II]'s second wife) and this Joseph Müller id1161; so far, however, I've been unable to confirm that.

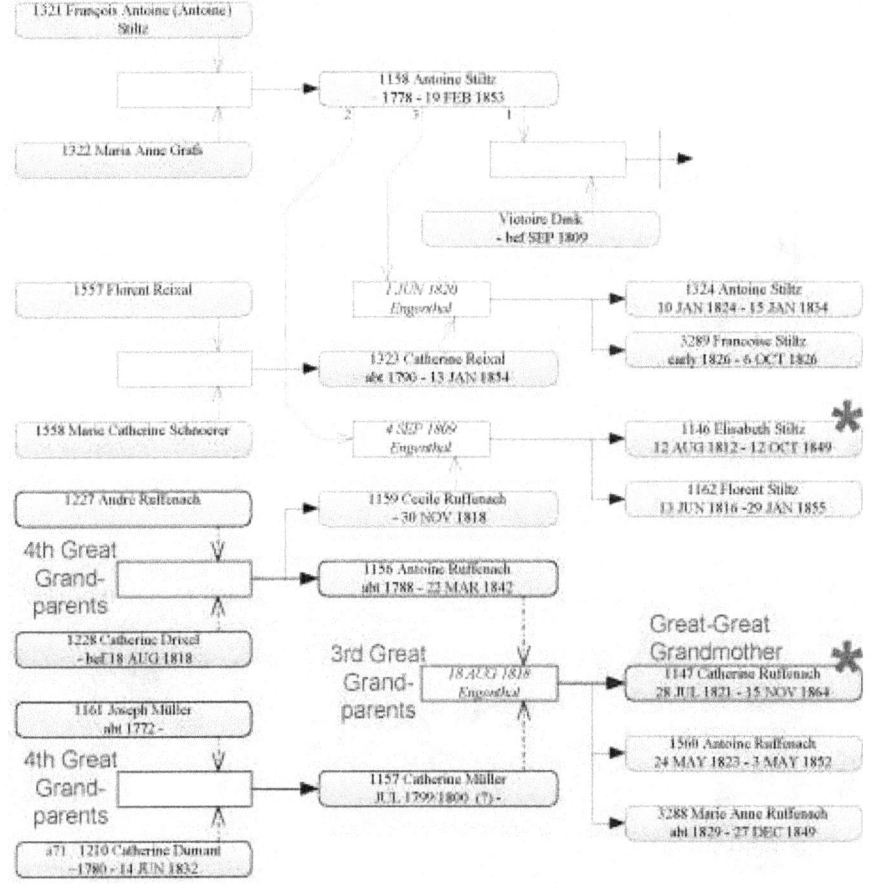

Muller-Deumant-Drixel-Ruffenach Chart

---

[34] For example, see the record of their daughter Catherine's marriage shown on page 43.

The chart above illustrates our confirmed Müller and Deumant[35] ancestors, as well as our Ruffenach and Drixel forebears that are discussed below.

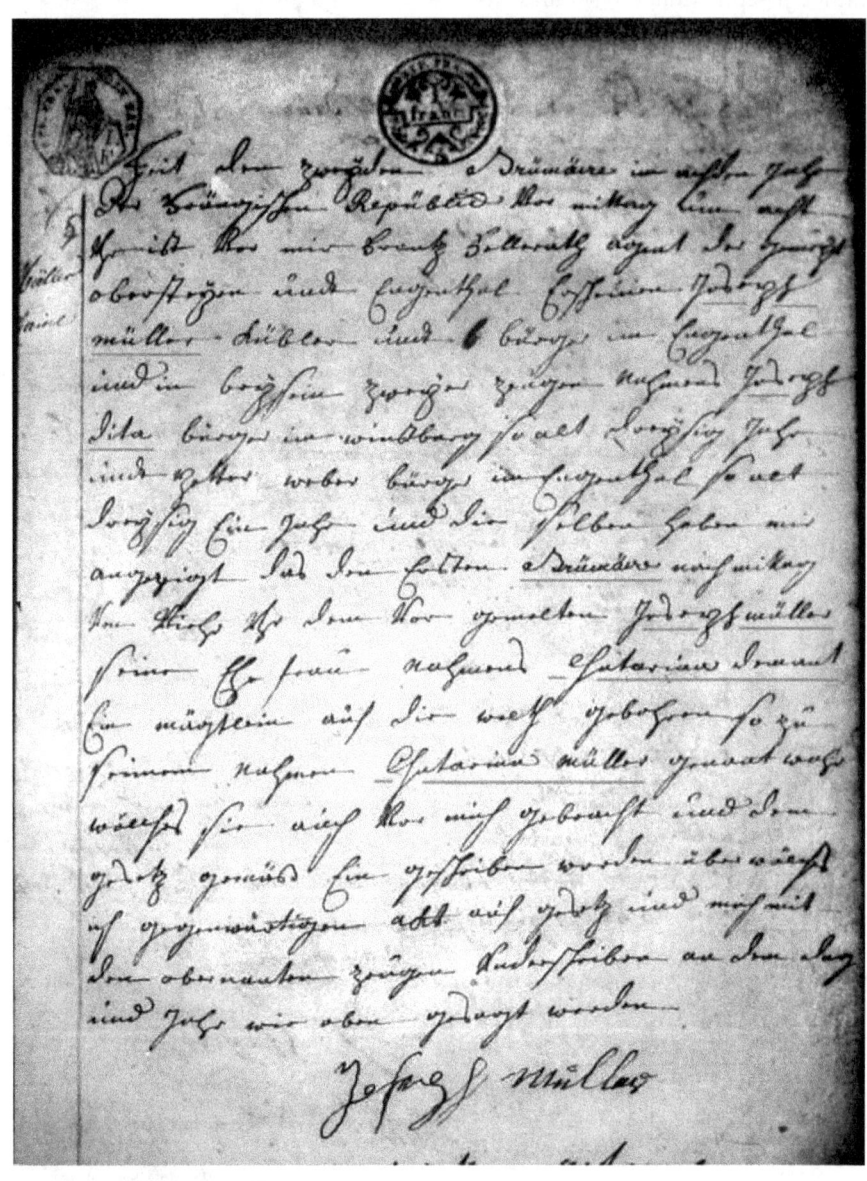

Commune d'Engenthal – 1798 Birth Record of Catherine Müller
Catherine Müller id.I.57 *was the wife of Antoine Ruffenach* id.I.56*; they are my 3rd great-grandparents.*

---

[35] The spelling of this surname varies quite a bit in extant vital records; it is also spelled "Deumand," "Dumant," "Demand," and "Demant."

A translation of the key data from Catherine Müller's Engenthal birth record is shown below on the left. Like the earlier birth record of Hubert Oberlé shown on page 33, this pre-Napoleonic French record can be difficult to decipher, not only because of the handwriting and free format, but the use of the annoying French Revolutionary Calendar.[36]

Birth ?? Brumaire an 7*
of
Müller, Catherine
(id1157)
Parents:
  Father
    Joseph Müller
      age ??

    (id1161)
and
  Mother
    Catherine Dumant
      age ??

    (id1210)

Witnesses:
1. **
    age

2.
    age

* Brumaire (underlined in the 10th line) is the second month of the French revolutionary calendar and, for the year 7, was equivalent to the dates 22 OCT 1798 and 20 NOV 1798 inclusive. If there is a specific date mentioned, I can't make it out. I am only guessing the year 7 from the context of other records and the sequence of months in other records.

** Joseph Dita (sic, whom I assume to be Joseph Dieda in the absence of other Ditas in Engenthal records) is mentioned, but I can't determine the context.

Obersteigen and Engenthal are mentioned on the fourth line.

Catherine Müller's name can be seen on line 14. Her father Joseph's is on line 11 and her mother Catherine Deumant's is on line 12.

The French Revolutionary Calendar

This rather odd Calendar took effect when 22 September 1792 became 1 Vendemiaire an I (year 1; the years were usually stated pretentiously as Roman Numerals.) The year was divided into 12 months with exactly 30 days each:

      Vendemiaire
      Brumaire
      Frimaire
      Nivose
      Pluviose
      Ventose
      Germinal
      Floreal
      Prairial
      Messidor
      Thermidor
      Fructidor

Since this totaled only 360 days, five or six "Jour Complementairs" were added as extra days to the end of each Year to synchronize the calendar to the sun. Events occurring during these periods were marked with "J-Comp" as the month.

Napoleon Bonaparte decreed an end to this silliness after he came to power, and the French Republic Calendar ended on 10 Nivose l'an XIV (31 December 1805), followed by January 1st of the Gregorian year 1806. Nonetheless, since there is no simple method of converting these dates, determining dates in records from this period can be tedious.

---

[36] This is also commonly called the French Republic Calendar.

My 4th great grandmother Catherine Deumant died on 14 June 1832 in Engenthal; the record of this is shown below:

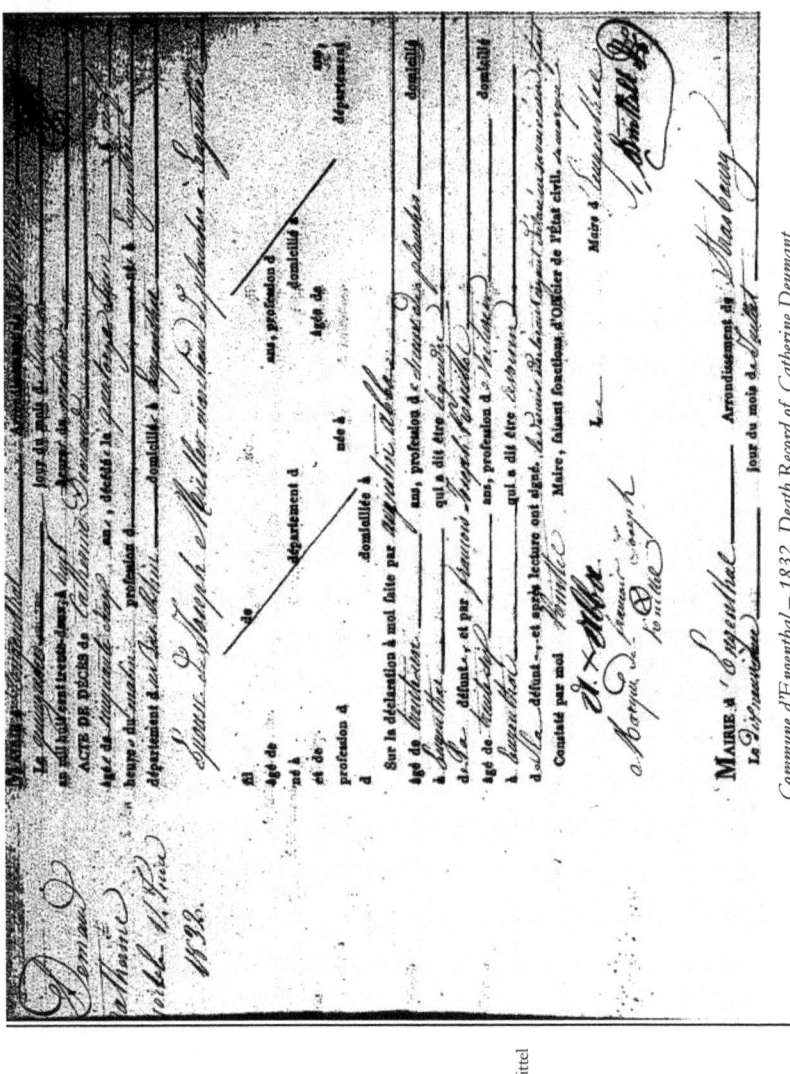

Commune d'Engenthal – 1832 Death Record of Catherine Deumant

Catherine Deumant (id1210) was the wife of Joseph Müller (id1161) and mother of Catherine Müller (id1157)

Death 14 JUN 1832 of
Catherine Deumant
age 52
(id1210)
spouse of
Joseph Müller
(id1161)

Reported by:
1. Augustin Abba
age 31
dieux des plauches ??
legeudre ?? of deced.
2. Francois Joseph Knittel
age 36
vaitur ??
lesarin ??

Translated Data

Commune d'Engenthal – 1818 Marriage Record of Antoine Ruffenach & Catherine Müller
See translation of key elements in the sidebar on the next page.

Antoine Ruffenach & Catherine Müller

My 3rd great-grandfather Antoine Ruffenach's older sister Cecile id1159, who married Antoine Stiltz id1158 after the death of his first wife, had a daughter Elisabeth id1146 – marked in the earlier chart (see page 39) with the upper asterisk – who became the first wife of my great-great-grandfather Seraphin Oberlé id708, although she is not our ancestor.

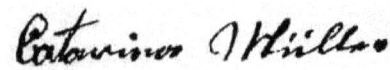

Signature of Catherine Müller

Translation of key elements from Record on Previous Page

Marriage 18 APR 1818
between
Antoine Ruffenach
age not given
Laborer
(id1156)
Parents:
Andre Ruffenach
(id1227)
and
Catherine Drixel
(id1228)
and
Catherine Müller
age not given
(id1156)
Parents:
Joseph Müller
(id1161)
and
Catherine Dumant
(id1210)

Witnesses:
1. Ferdinand Lustenberger,
age 43
profession ??
2. Antoine Weber
age 40
Laborer
3. Joseph Witta
age 22
profession ??
4. Florent Ruffenach
age 40
Weaver

(Section C) Marriage Banns announced beginning Sunday 9 AUG 1817 then daily.

Note that, at the bottom, Antoine made his mark ("marque de Antoine X Ruffenach"), and Catherine signed her own name.

Antoine himself married Catherine Müller id1157 on 18 April 1818; the record of their marriage is shown on the previous page, with a translation of the key facts from that record immediately to the left. Catherine's signature above is taken from this record. The small "x" that can be seen between our ancestor's first and last names confirms that, unlike his wife, Antoine was not able to write his own name.[37]

Children of Antoine Ruffenach and Catherine Müller

♦ Catherine Ruffenach id1147, (28 July 1821 – 15 November 1864).[38] My great-great grandmother Catherine was about nine years younger than her first cousin Elisabeth Stiltz, who was her husband's first wife.

♦ Antoine Ruffenach id1560, (24 May 1823 – 3 May 1852).

♦ Marie Anne Ruffenach id3288, (about 1829, died 27 December 1849)

Antoine Ruffenach died on March 22 1842; the record of his death is shown on the next page.

I have found no record of Catherine Müller's death, but she likely died after 1871 when her grandson (and my great grandfather) Seraphin left Alsace in the service, however unwilling, of the Kaiser.

---

[37] In this period, such a circumstance was not unusual, as the males were usually expected to earn their keep as early as they were able.

[38] Was Catherine Ruffenach a "very heavy" woman? Her son Seraphin is reported to have described his mother that way. In his genealogical notes, Seraphin's grandson Eddie has the notation "very heavy – died between 45 & 50." Although Seraphin listed Catherine Muller as his mother when he was married in Baltimore (she raised him), she outlived her daughter Catherine, who died at age 44 (ordinal num-

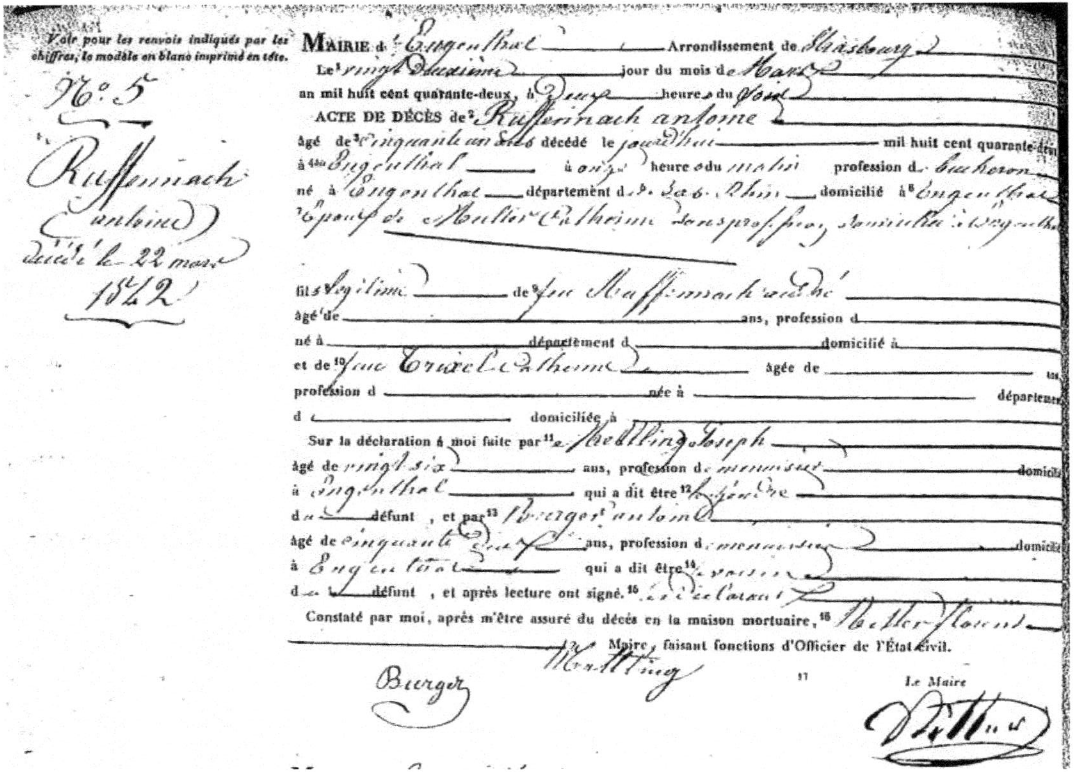

Commune d'Engenthal – 1842 Death Record of Antoine Ruffenach

Antoine Ruffenach (id1156) was the husband of Catherine Müller (id1157) and father of Catherine Ruffenach (id1147)

Translated Data

Death: 22 March 1842
of
Ruffenach, Antoine
(id1156) (a34)
age: 51 (imp 1791)
Bucheron
Spouse of:
Müller, Catherine
(id1157) (a35)
Legitimate son of:
the late
Ruffenach, André
(id1227) (a68)
and
the late
Drixel, Catherine
(id1228) (a69)

Witnesses:
1. Mettling, Joseph
age: 26
menisuer (?)
2. Burger, Antoine
age: 52
menisuer (?)

bering) when Seraphin was about nine. So what constitutes "very heavy" to a nine year old?

■ 45 ■

Seraphin (I) Oberlé and Elizabeth Stiltz

Like his father Joseph, Seraphin initially worked as a day laborer (*journalier*), at least through 1834. He later became a *bucheron*[39] like his older brothers, and was known to be working in this capacity at least by 1838[40]. By that time, the population in Engenthal had finally crossed 1000.

On 20 October 1837, Seraphin I married Elizabeth Stiltz id1146 in Engenthal. Seraphin and Elizabeth's mothers had both died by this time, and Elizabeth's father had since married his third wife Catherine Reixal. Seraphin and Elizabeth had six children, beginning with Marie Louise id1163 on 10 September 1838 and ending with Augustin id2259, born on 16 December 1848.

Children & Grandchildren of Seraphin (I) Oberlé & Elisabeth Stiltz

- Marie Louise Oberlé id1163, (born 10 September 1838)
- Marguerite Oberlé id1165, (born 27 March 1841)
- Josephine Oberlé id1166, (born 6 July 1842), had one child with an unknown father ("pere inconnu" reported on birth record):
  François Antoine Oberlé id1994, (born 18 JUL 1866)
- Madelaine Oberlé id1153, (born 5 February 1844)
- Marie Anne Oberlé id2277, (born 2 February 1846)
- Augustin Oberlé id2259, (born 16 December 1848)

Elizabeth died on 12 October 1849 at age 37, leaving Seraphin with six young children ranging in age from 9 months to 11 years old, and he obviously needed help caring for them. So far, I have located no information to confirm who helped to raise these children, but his mother Marie Anne Schreiber and mother-in-law Cecile Ruffenach were both deceased by this time, and his older sisters were, for various reasons, not obvious choices[41].

Seraphin's choice of a second wife may provide a clue, however.

---

[39] A "forestry worker," – incorporating what we would call lumberjack, sawyer, and some transportation skills.

[40] This is documented in his daughter Marie Louise's birth record of 10 September 1838, as well as those of his subsequent children.

[41] For instance: Elizabethe Oberlé id1167, his nearest sibling, born 27 May 1808, had by this time conceived a child out of wedlock (who died in its first year), and she doesn't seem to appear in any Engenthal records after 1836.

Seraphin (I) Oberlé and Catherine Ruffenach

On 21 September 1850, less than a year after his first wife's death, Seraphin married Elizabeth's cousin Catherine Ruffenach, leading one to speculate that it may have perhaps been Catherine (and/or her mother Catherine Müller) who helped raise his children. In any case, Seraphin and Catherine had their first child, Rosine id1148, on 17 July 1851. The Engenthal birth records list four more children born there and, in conversations with his grandson Tom Jelks, Seraphin II mentioned a (presumably younger) sister named Eugenie[42], but I could find no record of her birth in Engenthal.

Signatures of Seraphin Oberlé and his wife Catherine Ruffenach

Children & Grandchildren of Seraphin (I) Oberlé & Catherine Ruffenach

- Rosine Oberlé id1148, (born 17 July 1851)
- Therese Oberlé id1149, (born 3 September 1853)
- **Seraphin [II] Oberlé** id25, (born 17 July 1855, died 27 May 1931). Seraphin is our family's direct ancestor, and will be discussed in more detail beginning on page 52 below.
- Marguerithe Oberlé id1150, (born 21 September 1857, died 24 June 1927); never married.
- Armand Oberlé id1151, (born 15 May 1859, died 17 January 1943), married Josephine Ruffenach id3599 (Josephine's relationship to her mother-in-law Catherine is unknown) and had eight children:

Signature of Armand Oberlé

Marie Therese Oberlé id3600, (born 2 Aug 1884, died 29 Oct 1961)
Marie Oberlé id3601, (born 11 Aug 1885, died 31 Aug 1961)
Emilie Oberlé id3602, (born 25 Nov 1887, died 14 Oct 1957), married Jules Schaeffer id3608 with whom she had seven children.
Michel Armand Oberlé id3603, (born 29 Sep 1890, died 18 Nov 1960), married Cecile Rubine id3609, but had no children.

---

[42] My father's first cousin Thomas Oberle (Tom) Jelks id182 visited Eugenie Oberlé in Karlsruhe (about 54 miles northeast of Strasbourg across the Rhine River) during the US occupation at the end of World War II in 1945, at which time she was in her eighties and apparently never married. When or why she and possibly others moved there is unknown. Also see the anecdote about her on page 78.

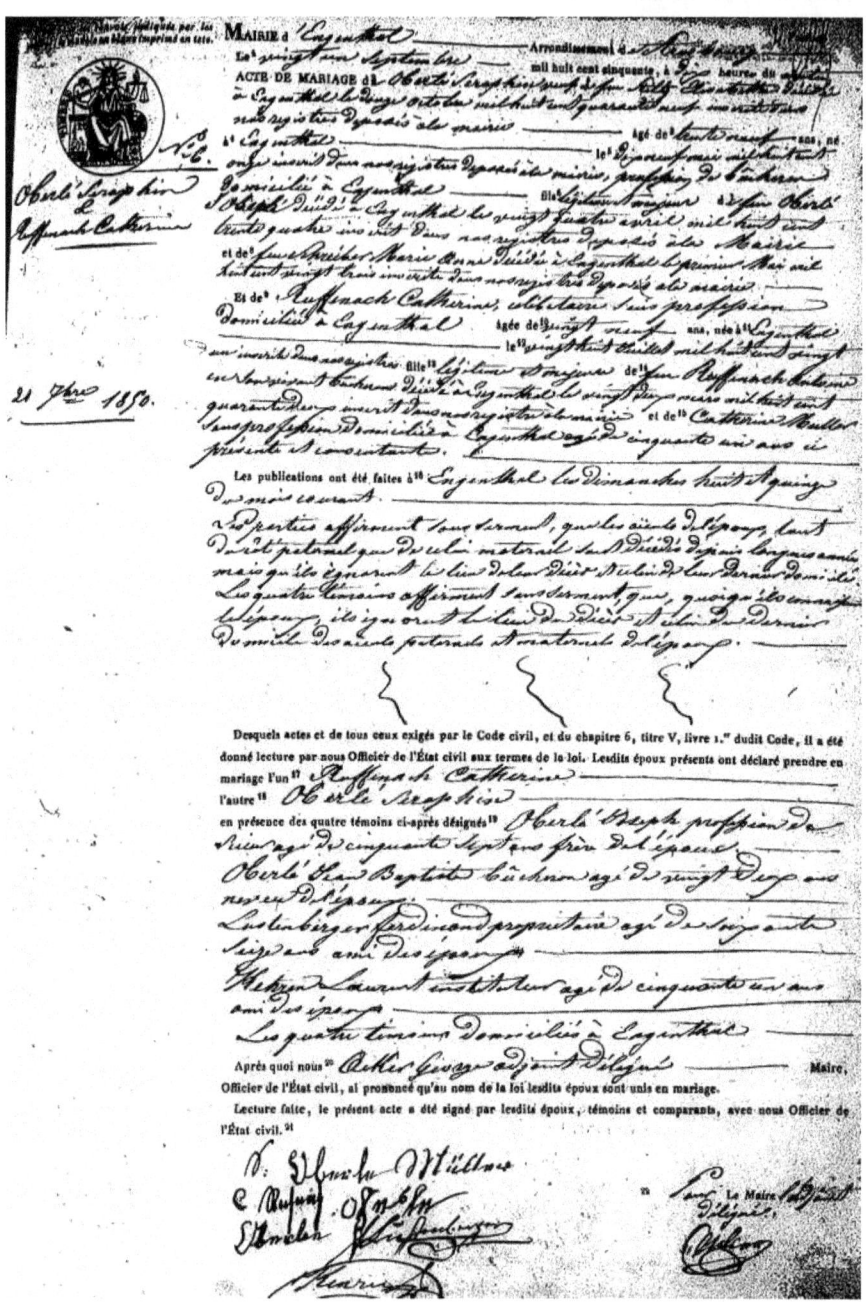

Commune d'Engenthal – 1850 Marriage record of Seraphin Oberlé & Catherine Ruffenach
A translation of the key elements of this marriage record is shown on the next page.

Children & Grandchildren of Seraphin (I) Oberlé & Catherine Ruffenach (continued)

Children of Armand Oberlé (continued)

Alexandrine Oberlé id3604, (born 22 Jun 1892, died 21 Jun 1972), married Joseph Christoph id3610, with whom she had at least four children, including a set of twins.

Victor Oberlé id3605, (born 23 Mar 1894, died 16 Feb 1968).

Virgile Oberlé id3606, (born 9 Oct 1898, died 9 Jul 1972).

Emile Joseph Oberlé id3607, (born 5 Nov 1903).

- Alexandrine Oberlé id1152, (born 5 May 1861, died 26 April 1886). Alexandrine is the last child of Seraphin and Catherine for whom I have found a birth record.
- Eugenia Oberlé id1894, (born between March 1862 and November 1864, presumably in Engenthal; died after 1945)

Unfortunately, Seraphin's second wife Catherine also died in Engenthal on 15 November 1864[43], leaving him with a total of seven children under the age of fifteen and possibly several older daughters. My great-grandfather, Catherine's son Seraphin II, was nine years old at the time his mother died.

After Catherine's death, it seems reasonably certain that her mother Catherine Müller raised the children. Many years later, when Seraphin II provided information to St. James the Less parish in Baltimore at the time of his marriage, he listed his mother's name as "Catherine Müller," not "Catherine Ruffenach." It seems unlikely that he didn't know Catherine Müller was his grandmother – he more likely just assumed that his mother Catherine's surname was the same as his grandmother's[44].

Marriage 21 SEP 1850
between
Oberlé, Seraphin (id708)
(husband of the late
Elisabeth Stiltz, who
died 15 October 1849)
age 39
Forestry Worker
Parents:
Oberlé, Joseph (id1154)
d 24 April 1834
and
Schreiber, Marie Anne (id1155)
d 1 May 1823
and
Ruffenach, Catherine (id1147)
age 29
Parents:
Ruffenach, Antoine (id1156)
d 22 March 1842
and
Catherine Muller (id1157)
Age 50

Witnesses:
1. Oberlé, Joseph (id1230),
   profession ??
   Age 57
   Brother of groom
2. Oberlé, Jean-Baptiste (id1189),
   Forestry Worker
   Age 22
   Nephew of groom
3. Lustenberger, Ferdinand,
   Landlord
   Age 76
   Friend of groom
4. Hebron, Laurent,
   School Teacher
   Age 51
   Friend of groom

Seraphin I id708 died in Engenthal on 7 January 1890 at the age of almost 79. His death was reported by his son Armand, as shown in the record below. It is possible that the family may have moved at some time after his death, since this is the last record of a family member I have been able to locate in En-

---

[43] See an image of her death record on page 53.
[44] This is not as implausible as it seems – at the age his mother died, he would have had no reason to give much thought to the fact that women in Alsace didn't take the surnames of their husbands.

genthal. Based on Eugenie's presence in Karlsruhe at the end of World War II, one might guess that at least some of the family relocated there for economic reasons, but I have no direct evidence of this.

Commune d'Engenthal – 1890 Death Record of my 2nd great-grandfather Seraphin Oberle.

Note that records after the 1871 Prussian conquest were in German, and married women now began to be referred to by their husband's surname. His mother's name is given as "Maria Anna Oberle geboren Schreiber."

Our Oberle Ancestors

Diagram of our Lothringian and French Oberlé Ancestors

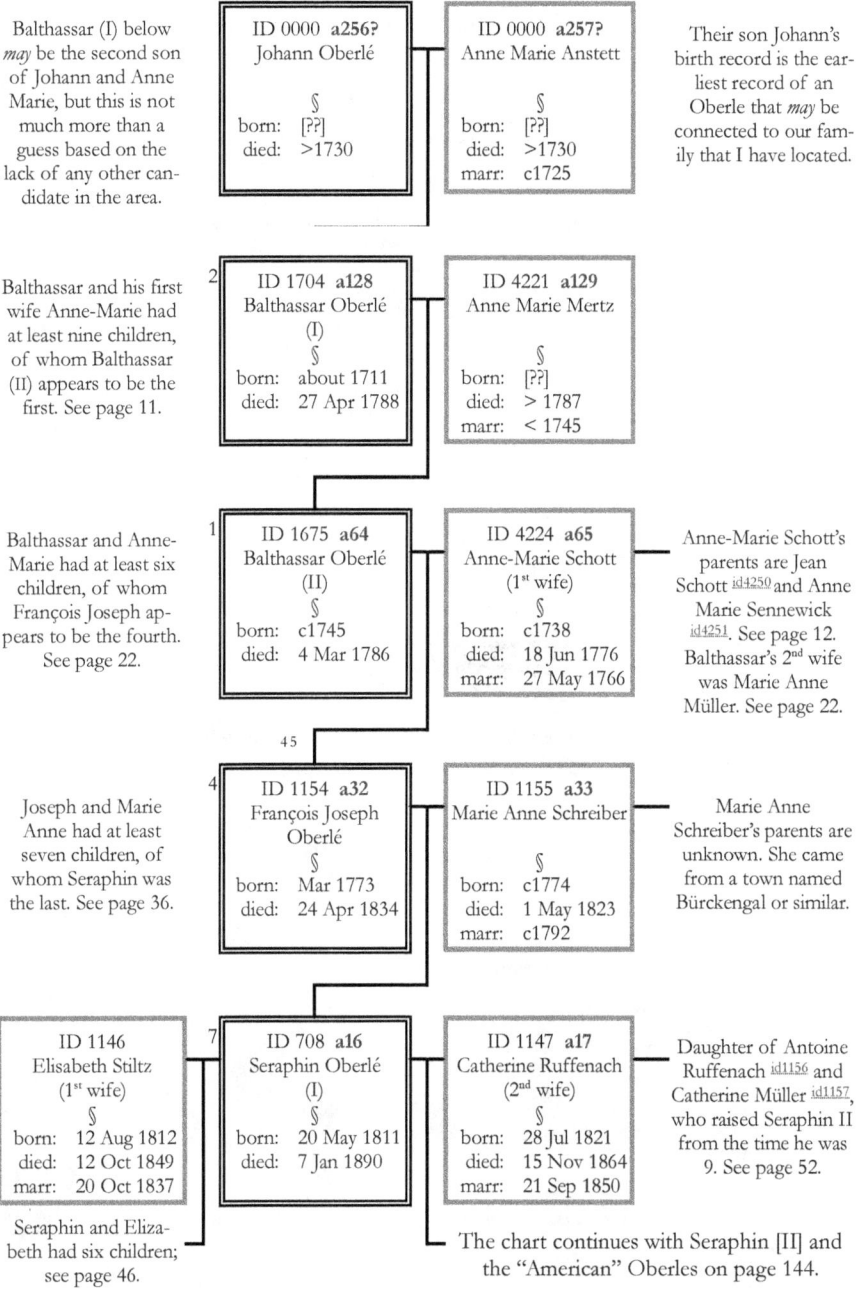

---

[45] The connection between Balthassar (II) id1675 and François Joseph Oberlé id1154 is based on strong circumstantial evidence, but isn't proven. See the appendix beginning on page 165 for more detail.

Seraphin [II] Oberlé – Our Last Ancestor in France

My great-grandfather Seraphin's birth record is shown below. His mother Catherine would have four more children over the next eight years.

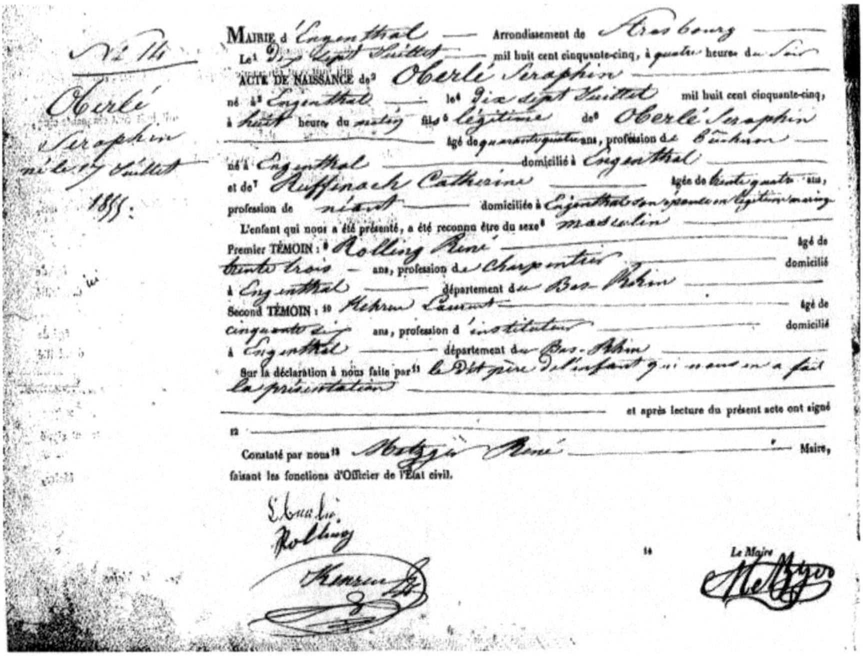
N° 14
Oberlé
Seraphin
né le 17 Juillet
1855.

Mairie d'Engenthal — Arrondissement de Strasbourg
Le dix-sept Juillet mil huit cent cinquante-cinq, à quatre heures du soir
Acte de naissance de Oberlé Seraphin
né à Engenthal le dix-sept Juillet mil huit cent cinquante-cinq,
à huit heures du matin fils légitime de Oberlé Seraphin
âgé de quarante-quatre ans, profession de Bûcheron
né à Engenthal domicilié à Engenthal
et de Ruffinach Catherine âgée de trente-quatre ans,
profession de néant domiciliée à Engenthal son épouse en légitime mariage
L'enfant qui nous a été présenté, a été reconnu être du sexe masculin
Premier Témoin : Rolling René âgé de trente trois ans, profession de Charpentier domicilié à Engenthal département du Bas-Rhin
Second Témoin : Hehron Laurent âgé de cinquante six ans, profession d'instituteur domicilié à Engenthal département du Bas-Rhin
Sur la déclaration à nous faite par le dit père de l'enfant qui nous en a fait la présentation
et après lecture du présent acte ont signé
Constaté par nous Metzger René Maire, faisant les fonctions d'Officier de l'État civil.

Oberle
Rolling
Hehron
Le Maire
Metzger

Commune d'Engenthal – 1855 Birth record of Seraphin Oberlé (II).

This Seraphin id25 was my great-grandfather, the first of our Oberle ancestors to come to America.

Translated Data

Birth 17 JUL 1855
of
Oberlé, Seraphin
(id25)
Parents:
Seraphin Oberlé (note that, by now, his signature is simply "Oberle")
age 44
Forestry worker
(id708)
and
Catherine Ruffenach
age 34
no profession
(id1147)

Witnesses:
1. Rolling, Rene
age 33
Carpenter
2. Hebron, Laurent
age 56
School Teacher

As recounted earlier, Seraphin's mother died when he was barely nine years old; the record of her death is shown below.

Voir pour les renvois indiqués par les chiffres, le modèle en blanc imprimé en tête.

N° 21.

Ruffenach Catherine
Décédée le 15 Novembre
1864.

MAIRIE d'Engenthal Arrondissement de Strasbourg
Le quinze Novembre mil huit cent soixante-quatre, à dix heure du matin
ACTE DE DÉCÈS de Ruffenach Catherine
âgée de quarante quatre ans décédée à Engenthal
le quinze Novembre mil huit cent soixante quatre, à six heures du matin
profession de néant née à Engenthal département du Bas-Rhin
domiciliée à Engenthal, épouse en secondes noces de Oberlé Seraphin bûcheron domicilié à Engenthal
fille légitime de feu Ruffenach Antoine
âgé de ans, profession de sagar de son vivant
domicilié à Engenthal
et de Muller Catherine âgée de soixante six ans,
profession de néant domiciliée à Engenthal
Sur la déclaration à nous faite par Oberlé Seraphin
âgé de cinquante quatre ans, profession de bûcheron domicilié
à Engenthal qui a dit être l'époux
de la défunte, et par Kalbrachs Joseph
âgé de trente neuf ans, profession d'instituteur domicilié
à Engenthal qui a dit être voisin
de la défunte, et après lecture ont signé.
Constaté par nous Metzger Rene Maire, faisant fonctions d'Officier de l'État civil, après nous être assuré du décès en la maison mortuaire,
Oberle
J. Kalbrachs
Le Maire
Metzger

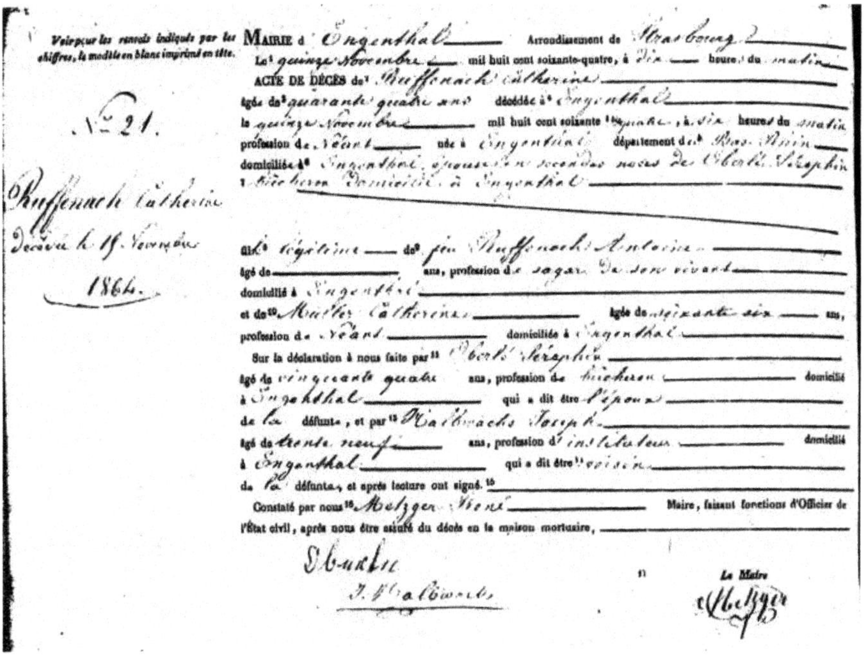

Commune d'Engenthal – 1864 Death record of Catherine Ruffenach Oberlé.
My great-great-grandmother Catherine id1147 died when my great-grandfather Seraphin id25 was nine years old.

Translated Data

Death 15 NOV 1864
of
Ruffenach, Catherine
(id1147)
age 44
Second wife of
Seraphin Oberlé
Legitimate daughter of
the late Antoine Ruffenach
Her profession: de sagar da son vivant (translation questionable)
and
Catherine Müller
age 66
(id1157)

Reported by
Seraphin Oberlé
age 54
Forestry Worker
(id708)
and
Joseph Kalmbachs
age 39
Teacher

As Seraphin grew up, more "interesting times" began clouding France, and this time Alsace was, unfortunately, very much in the thick of the changes.

The Franco-Prussian War

The early history of the border area of Alsace and Lorraine where our ancestors lived was covered in the "Lothringian History" section,[46] and left off with both provinces in relatively peaceful circumstances. Aside from the "interesting times" discussed on page 31 when my third great-grandparents Joseph and Marie-Anne Oberlé began their family, the effects of political activity on the western side of the Vosges Mountains – including the French revolution and the disruptions caused by the on-again/off-again Napoleonic era – were relatively minor, at least in comparison to those of the major portions of France and the Germanic areas east of the Rhine. Seraphin's parents and grandparents had been living under relative economic and political stability for 79 years, during which time the town of Engenthal's population of 510 had almost doubled.

In 1869 Engenthal, like most of the neighboring towns in the Bas-Rhin region of Alsace, was fairly self-sufficient. The area's farmers produced cereal grains, and a variety of fruits and vegetables. In addition, they also raised some livestock – mostly pigs and poultry.

Then, as now, Alsace did supply its well-known wines and lumber products outside the local area, but the sale or trading of most food products beyond the nearby towns was relatively limited by lack of any suitable means of maintaining freshness – roads were generally not paved, and salt-curing had not yet been supplemented by any form of refrigeration.

Almost two decades earlier, some enterprising Alsatian farmers saw an opportunity for expanding trade, and began what would be a fifty year – and ultimately unsuccessful – effort to gain a foothold in the production of beer. This seemed to make economic sense: Alsatian wine varieties had an excellent reputation outside the province, and it appeared that corn production could easily be increased to meet their targets. Thus, by 1869, Alsatian beer had already begun to be distributed to markets on both side of the Rhine, although the native population's drink of choice remained the local wines.

Relative to modern expectations, life in Engenthal certainly couldn't have been considered ideal, but the population was well-fed, living in relative freedom, and in what for the time were fairly good conditions. Education beyond a few years of formal schooling was unusual for the time, but the average literacy level was actually higher than in many other larger cities such as Paris. As French subjects for several generations, the residents of Alsace, who mostly spoke German dialects in their day-to-day life, were also reasonably fluent in French and, as we have seen, all of their official records were in that language. And as far back as the late eighteenth century, the final "e" in our family's name was more often than not the decidedly French "é."

---

[46] ... which begins on page 3

By 1869, my great-grandfather Seraphin (II) had already completed the schooling considered typical for that era, and had joined his father Seraphin (I) as a *bucheron* (a forestry worker/lumberjack or, as he himself would tell his grandchildren in Baltimore many years later, a *Holzhacker*).

In 1870, however, when Seraphin was about fifteen years old, our ancestors' universe changed dramatically when the Prussians decided to create a unified Germany. And of course that meant adding enough new territory – such as the whole of France – to make their new empire a realistic counterbalance to the neighboring Holy Roman Empire. But the Prussians were quite sensitive to their growing international reputation as bullies, so some dissembling was deemed to be in order.

To collapse and over-simplify some European history, Otto von Bismarck, the Prussian chancellor[47], pulled a few dirty tricks designed to maneuver Emperor Napoleon III into declaring war on Prussia – thus making France appear to be the aggressor. This younger Napoleon, being a lot less politically savvy than Bismarck, and certainly far less so than his illustrious heritage might have suggested, fell for Bismarck's ruse completely, and obtained a declaration of war on 19 July 1870.

Not very long after this declaration, a group of French forces were soundly defeated at Wissenbourg on 5 August 1870. Interestingly enough, the force that actually invaded Alsace, although led by Prussian commanders, consisted mostly of members of the Third Royal Bavarian Division of the Uhlan Light Cavalry, an elite force that was distinguished by their *Chapkas* (mortar-board helmets with ostentatious plumage) and long lances carrying their unit's colors (as illustrated in the drawing on the left).

The very next day, just a bit over 40 kilometers[48] from our ancestors' home town of Engenthal, the Battle of Wörth[49] was an even more resounding defeat, leading to more than eight thousand French troops being killed or wounded[50] – in perspective, this represented about eight times the entire population of Engenthal at the time.

---

[47] He was almost universally known in diplomatic circles and the contemporary press (non-Germanic, of course) as "The Iron Chancellor."

[48] This is about 25 miles. The location is 10 kilometers north of Strasbourg in the present day tourist and shopping destination of Haguenau, frequented by both French and German visitors.

[49] ... or "Woerth", also known as the "Battle of Reichshoffen."

[50] This number, representing thirteen percent of the French force, is likely understated, since there were close to twelve thousand more "missing" after the conflict; although some may have deserted, the French troops in this battle were given high marks by thr Prussian/German victors, so large scale desertions don't seem to have taken place. The Germans, by the way, suffered over nine thousand casualties, but reported only about one thousand four hundred missing.

A closer examination of the numbers reported for the Battle of Wörth that had been fought in such close proximity to Engenthal allows us to infer much more about the impacts on the Oberlé family and their Alsatian neighbors. The casualty figures and percentages given in most sources suggest that the combatants numbered between eighty and ninety thousand French and Germanic troops. Since armies at the time had no choice but to "acquire" their food and drink[51] from local "resources," this in effect meant that there were roughly eighty-five thousand uninvited guests sponging off the local food supply – this in an area that typically supported a population of only about one thousand.

There are no sources I have located that specifically discuss the impact of these additional mouths on the local population, but it certainly must have been felt. The "friendly" French likely didn't "purchase" all they consumed – which might have mitigated some resentment – and the Prussian forces certainly didn't. It was also likely the case that many residents were precluded from practicing any of the professions that required them to venture from the safety of the towns, e.g. as farmers, vintners or – of more immediate interest to our family – lumberjacks. It should be noted that this fighting was taking place just about a month before the grape harvests were to begin.

The Battle of Mars la Tour[52], another resounding French defeat, followed ten days later on August the sixteenth. On the first of September, Emperor Napoleon III himself led some of the French forces to engage the Prussians in the Battle of the Sedan, and proved that his military prowess was even less noteworthy than his political acumen.

The following morning, Napoleon III surrendered himself and his troops to Crown Prince Friedrich Wilhelm, Emperor William I's son.

It isn't often that an enemy captures the opposing head of state before reaching that country's capital, and it can be surmised that this event, coupled with the magnitude of the carnage so close to their village, must have raised the stress level of our ancestors.

Napoleon III surrenders his Sword and Colors to Friedrich Wilhelm

---

[51] As Napoleon III's more famous and talented grandfather General Bonaparte supposedly explained when later discussing the reasons for the failure of his invasion of Russia in 1812: "An army marches on its stomach."

[52] This is also known as the Battle of Vionville, about one hundred miles west-northwest of Engenthal.

Engenthal and the surrounding areas in Seraphin's universe were now firmly in Prussian control. The provinces of Alsace and Lorraine were once again known respectively as Elsass and Lothringen. Less than a year later, after more humiliation, the French government formally surrendered control of their entire country on 10 May 1871.

The Oberlés were now German – in itself not as traumatic as might be supposed since, as mentioned earlier, the Alsatians living between the Vosges Mountains and Rhine River generally were fluent to some degree in both languages – but still inconvenient for a number of reasons.[53]

The German's first census of our ancestor's village showed a population of about 1,500 residents, and it remained at that level for many years, but I haven't found any documented explanation for the almost fifty percent population increase in the first six months of fighting. It seems quite plausible, of course, that there was likely heavy migration of those living in the more rural areas – particularly farmers whose crops may have been commandeered to feed the combatants – to the relative safety of even a small town like Engenthal, but it is difficult not to wonder if perhaps some of those "missing in action" after the various battles may have swelled the population.

The most significant change in the lives of the young men of Seraphin's age in Engenthal and all of Alsace, however, was the Prussian proclivity for drafting[54] able-bodied men into military service. I have yet to locate any documentation to prove that Seraphin became a member of the Prussian army – voluntarily or involuntarily – but there is little reason to doubt the family legends, and they certainly fit nicely with what facts we do know.

*Left
Seraphin [II] Oberlé circa 1874
in Wassellone, Alsace*

When Seraphin entered military service is unclear, but it can be assumed that it was between late 1874 and mid-1876, most likely around 1874 when he was about 19 years old.

---

[53] Local records, for instance, were now required to be in German, and you'll note that there is no longer an acute accent on the final "e" in the 1890 death record of Seraphin's father shown on page 50.

[54] "Drafting" is somewhat of a euphemism given their methods. It isn't as if the French didn't have the same proclivities – it's just that not only were the Prussians more efficient, they were now much closer.

He was still in the general area in about 1874, since the photograph on the previous page was taken in the Commune of Wasselonne[55] around the time he was likely conscripted[56]. Since photographs of this type would not have been typical for someone of Seraphin's background, it could be speculated that the photograph might somehow be related to his conscription.

What is certain is that, by at least 1878, Seraphin was located more than eight hundred miles to the north – in or very near the North Sea port town of Emden, where he met his future wife.

In 1874, Seraphin's older half-brother Augustin id2259 [57] would have been almost thirty, so it is quite possible that he may have also been conscripted – perhaps even earlier than Seraphin was. In any case, I was able to find no records of Augustin at all in Engenthal after this period

I also haven't been able to determine if Seraphin's younger brother Armand id1151, who would have been about fifteen in 1874, was eventually conscripted as well. It is known that, by 1883, Armand had married Josephine Ruffenach id3599 in Engenthal where they lived with their children into the next century.

World War II – Seraphin's grandsons return to Alsace

Seventy years after Seraphin left Engenthal, two of his grandsons passed through Alsace during the final year of World War II and participated directly in the liberation of both Alsace and Lorraine from the Nazis.

Tom Jelks id182 [58], the son of Seraphin's daughter Anna id24, who wrote a book about his experiences (see page 111), and Francis Oberle id197 [59], the son of Seraphin's son Joseph id81, whose experiences are discussed in Appendix VIII on page 274, were both in same area of Belgium during the Battle of the Bulge and were never far from each other during the liberation of Paris as well as the subsequent marches across Alsace and Lorraine towards Germany.

Although they both passed quite near their Grandfather's birthplace, the two never encountered each other during their European service, nor were either of them in Engenthal itself, although Tom did manage to meet a younger sister of Seraphin's during the subsequent post-war occupation.

Aside from possibly having one or two return trips to visit his family in Alsace[60], Seraphin [II] himself never returned to live in France.

---

[55] We know this from the photographer's inscription on the rear of the photograph. Wasselonne, east of Engenthal, can be seen in map D of the appendix beginning on page 157.

[56] Based on his later comments to his family, it seems safe to assume that it was not his choice to join the military, so the use of the word "conscription" will be used unless and until some further evidence is discovered to contradict this.

[57] Augustin was the only son of Seraphin (I)'s first wife Elisabeth Stiltz.

[58] Tommy was my father's first cousin.

[59] Francis was my father's younger brother.

[60] See page 66 for a discussion of his possible return visits.

Sneaking into America (The Long Way)

The Seaport of Emden

By at least the beginning of 1878 if not earlier, Seraphin II was serving as a Prussian soldier in the North Sea town of Emden in Ostfriesland. Shown in the map below, Emden is on the mouth of the Ems River where it joins the Dollart, a bay of sorts dividing Germany from the Netherlands. Although the Dollart is quite shallow at low tide, Emden had by 1870 become a major North Sea freight shipping port with a newly expanded shipbuilding yard, and its occupation and defense was important for Prussian control of its empire, as it would be for the Germans during several subsequent wars. This explains the significant presence of troops there, as both Ostfriesland and the Netherlands were part of the Prussian Empire while Seraphin was there.

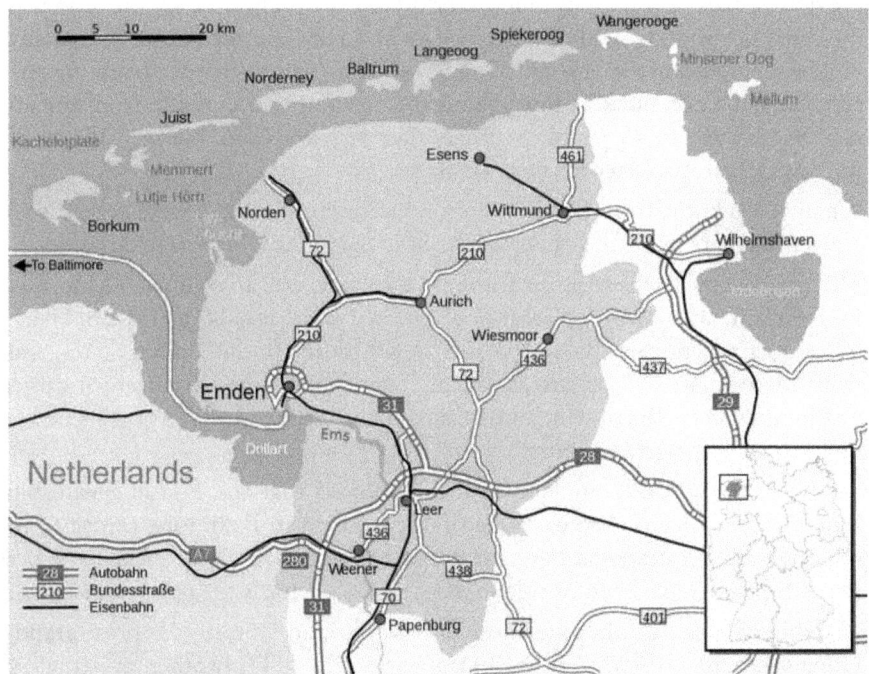

Modern Map showing the Town of Emden in Ostfriesland, across from the Netherlands

In stark contrast to Engenthal, Emden was a bustling and vibrant town, with a cosmopolitan population of 12,588 in 1870. Many of the city's buildings were faced with locally produced and widely exported red brick, unlike the largely wooden construction Seraphin was used to in Alsace. Another difference – and apparently an important one to him – was that Emden was as heavily Dutch Reformed Lutheran as Dabo and Engenthal had been Roman Catholic – a factor that later became relevant to our family's history.

The Kiwiet Family

Some family stories suggest that the Kiwiets may have originally been from Holland, and our earlier Kiwiet ancestors probably were, given that Emden was part of that country during the Napoleonic period. Kiwiet is certainly a Dutch surname. A large Dutch immigration in the seventeenth century resulted in a city that, by Seraphin's time, might even have been mistaken for a Dutch one – with numerous canals, bridges, and dikes.

Based on the research I have done, I am doubtful that any records of our Emden ancestors will be discovered. On September 6, 1944, shortly before 6:30 pm, and reportedly in retaliation for the German bombing of the civilian center of Dover, England, 181 Lancaster and Halifax bombers of the Royal Air Force dropped thousands of high explosive and liquid fire bombs on the city center of Emden. Although there had been more than seventy previous attacks on the city since World War II began in 1939, this one was the most devastating, with the explosions and resulting fires destroying many buildings and homes in the city. Due to the excellent emergency planning and system of air raid bunkers throughout the town, the loss of life from the attack was limited to 49 people, with another 109 wounded, but virtually all of the town's historical records were destroyed.

What we do know from family stories, however, is that there were at least two Kiwiet brothers living in Emden at the time Seraphin Oberle arrived there.

The first brother, whose given name isn't known, was a wealthy and successful merchant who owned at least one ship that made regular trips from Hamburg[61] to Emden, then Baltimore and New Orleans in the United States, and from there to Rio de Janeiro in Brazil. The bulk of the ship's return cargo was lumber from Brazil which was transported both to Emden (for its newly built paper mill) and Hamburg.

Seraphin's grandson Tom Jelks said he believed that the Kiwiet Steamship Line had an office on the east side of Light Street in Baltimore, across from the original First National Bank of Baltimore, and their ships docked at Fell's Point. So far, I have been unable to discover any records to support this.

The other Kiwiet brother we know of was our ancestor, my 2nd great grandfather Gerhard id1725 who, although not as wealthy as his brother, nonetheless had a good business as a cap maker.[62]

Gerhard Kiwiet & Josephine Dirkson

Gerhard was married to Josephine Dirkson id1726, about whom I've discovered no information. The couple is believed to have had two sons and three

---

[61] Hamburg is about 140 miles east of Emden.

[62] This and some other information in this section is based on genealogy notes made by another of Seraphin's grandsons, his oldest son Seraphin's youngest child Joseph Edward id195, known as "Eddie" (see page 80) that were provided by one of Eddie's children.

daughters. One of the daughters, born in May of 1855, was my great-grandmother Sarah Johanna id26. The only information we have about any of her siblings is that at least one of her sisters also made her way to the United States,[63] but it isn't known if she was older or younger than Sarah.

Family stories suggest that Sarah was an ice-skater[64], perhaps even competitive or professional, but I've been unable to discover any other details about Sarah's childhood.

During the 1865-1880 period, it is very likely that Gerhard's brother, or any others involved in the business of sea transportation, would have had considerable contact with the German/Prussian military, and Tom Jelks recalls hearing stories that Gerhard himself often entertained troops.

Whether Seraphin was ever involved in such "entertainment," however, is unknown, but Gerhard's daughter Sarah was working as a servant in the household of one of the Prussian officers. This, according to family lore, is how she met the dashing soldier she would eventually marry. Although there is only one known photograph of Seraphin in his younger years (see page 57), it is apparent even from those taken much later that he was a striking man. Marge Ford id193 said he had "piercing blue eyes" – certainly the type of man who might have attracted a young figure skater!

Another anecdote about the Kiwiet family was one that Sarah related to at least two of her grandchildren. She told of a brother or (more likely, it would seem) a cousin who was being groomed to take over her uncle's shipping business by working an apprenticeship in all of the on-board jobs. At about age 16, while climbing up in a ship's rigging at sea, he apparently fell overboard, and his body was never recovered.

Seraphin [II] Oberle & Sarah Johanna Kiwiet

We don't know exactly when Seraphin first met Sarah, but what is certain is that, by September of 1878, they had not only become acquainted, but had conceived a son, who was born in Emden on 20 June 1879.

It isn't known what transpired in the next two years, nor do we have answers for many intriguing questions about Seraphin's subsequent ongoing relationship with Sarah and her family.[65] By the early part of 1881, however, my great-grandparents had evidently decided to leave for the United States. First, though, their two year old son needed to become a Catholic like his father!

---

[63] When Marge Ford id193 was young, Sarah told her about a sister who emigrated to New Orleans and married someone named Schaeffer (spelling unknown). Marge once attempted to locate the sister (her great-aunt) when she visited that area, but given such a common surname, was unsuccessful.

[64] Sarah used the term "Schnittschuhlaufen," according to Tom Jelks. The literal translation of this typically German word for ice-skating is roughly "cut + shoe + run."

[65] We can assume Sarah's parents weren't thrilled with having a grandson out of wedlock, but what form that disappointment took isn't known. We also don't know when (or even if) Seraphin eventually received his discharge from Prussian military service.

On 19 June 1881, Seraphin Kiwiet [id60] was christened at St. Michael Katholische Kirche in Emden. St. Michael's, which had been built in 1775, was at the time the only Roman Catholic church in the area. The picture on the right shows the church as it looks today. The record transcription lists the mother as "Dora Kiwiet"[66]. The father's name is given as Seraphin Oberle from Engenthal, born 1850,[67], whose occupation was "Schuhmacher."

Regarding this profession, my father's cousin Thomas Oberle Jelks told me that *"one of the immigration requirements for entering the U.S. at that time was that every man must have a trade. Since Holzhacker (wood chopper) was not a recognized trade, Seraphin chose shoemaker as his trade and purchased the tools and practiced the trade. He made my grandmother's shoes and he made my shoes when I was a toddler, high shoes with buttons like hers."* This would seem to indicate that Seraphin had already learned this profession by 1881, and that perhaps he and Sarah

Emden – St. Michael Katholische Kirche

had been planning to go to the United States for some time. Or, perhaps, this was a profession he adopted after being discharged from the military.

The Migration to Baltimore

Almost immediately after their son's christening, Seraphin and Sarah traveled to Baltimore, but without their new son Seraphin, leaving him in the care of Puckel Simelcha[68] with Sarah's family in Emden.

Again according to stories passed down from those in the family who knew them, they traveled on the family freighter, and were the only two passengers

---

[66] Unfortunately, I have only been able to view a transcription of this record, and cannot find the original, so it isn't clear whether the transcriber misread Sarah as Dora, but this seems likely, as the remaining information matches too closely to what we know for this to be coincidence. The full reference for the listing is Geburtsbuch, 109,16 St. Michael Kirche Emden <Quelle> 1800 10 Maye Henricus Kroeger, 53 Anny. Note the last name recorded was Kiwiet, not Oberle!

[67] Sic. As his birth record (see page 52) shows, he was actually born on 17 July 1855.

[68] Tom Jelks recalled his Grandmother Sarah using this name, but I've been unable to uncover any information about who it was, or whether it means something like "aunt" or "uncle.". "Puckel" means "hump" in Swedish, however, and this may relate to Seraphin's recollections given on the next page.

on board. It would seem then, although we don't know for certain, that the decision to settle in the United States came down to an arbitrary choice between Baltimore and New Orleans – a choice that may have been informed by the Kiwiet sailors' knowledge of the various cities they regularly visited. It's quite tempting for all of Seraphin and Sarah's descendants to wonder how different our lives might have been had the pair decided to head for Rio de Janeiro instead.

At the time, the United States kept very scrupulous records of those entering the country on passenger vessels, and most of these survive; they did not, however, keep records of those on freighters, which arrived at different docks and whose occupants were generally assumed to be crew who would only remain temporarily. From July to September 1881, 95 German-flag freighters arrived in Baltimore, but I haven't located enough data to identify the Kiwiet ship. In any case, there are no extant records of my great-grandparents' arrival, which tends to support the family stories that they came on a family freighter, and simply walked away from Fell's Point into their new life.

Upon their arrival, the couple soon found a place to live, possibly on Jenkins Lane[69] in east Baltimore and began attending St. James the Less Church. Sarah arranged to become a Catholic (according to family stories, this was a condition Seraphin II set out for bringing their son Seraphin III to the United States, and possibly even for marriage)[70].

On 29 November 1881, Seraphin and Sarah were married as Catholics at St. James. As mentioned earlier, Seraphin listed his mother's name on the registry as "Catherine Muller," which is incorrect. Although she raised him, Catherine Müller was actually his grandmother and Catherine Ruffenach his mother.

Seraphin III comes to America

The couple's son Seraphin III remained in Emden, however, and was by now almost two and a half years old. According to his daughter Marge Ford, Seraphin III always had a phenomenal memory for details, and described looking out a ship window in Germany when he was a baby. He also recalls being carried around by someone with a hunchback (or at least very stooped – see footnote 68), and believed that was one of his mother's Kiwiet relatives.

Sarah departed for Emden in about February of 1882, at which time she would have been in the very early stages of pregnancy, although she may not have been aware of that at the time. At the time, the United States kept no

---

[69] This later became known as Jenkins Alley, west of what is now the Jones Falls Expressway. They were certainly living there by 1884, when they were listed in that year's Baltimore City Directory. Seraphin's profession was listed on page 906 as a laborer.
[70] Like many converts, Sarah apparently became a far stricter Catholic than Seraphin ever was. All of their surviving grandchildren I spoke to seemed to agree on this. One has to wonder at what seems an incredible leap of faith on Sarah's part to have gone to America in 1881 with Seraphin before they were married and without her child; certainly the story is more complex than I suspect we'll ever know.

1711-1975 HISTORY

records of those leaving the country but, again, it seems likely that she would have traveled on the Kiwiet ship, which would explain the delay between her marriage and the return voyage.

Sarah and her son Seraphin arrived back in the United States sometime in mid summer of 1882[71], possibly on the 6th of July, at which time she would have been entering her third trimester. Given her pregnancy (see below) as well as the conditions aboard even the best ships of the day, this must have been an interesting voyage to undertake with a son who was not quite three years old, even though he was apparently a very alert child.

Again, there is no record of Sarah arriving back in Baltimore, and it is tempting to assume that this trip may also have been on a family ship. But I suspect this may not be the case, since I was able to locate a passenger manifest for a ship arriving in New York, in which the following two entries appear:

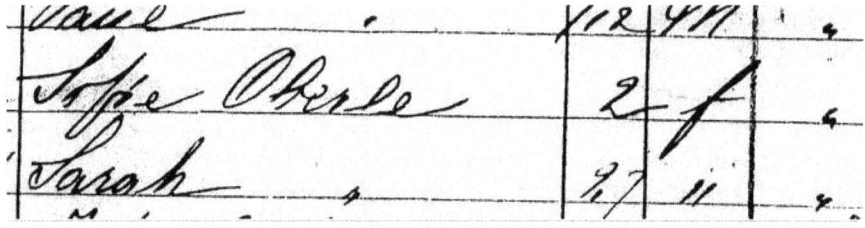

Port of New York – 1882 Segment of passenger manifest page for the ship Salier
The Salier arrived from Bremen on 6 July 1882.

The list shows a Sarah Oberle, age 27, who arrived with a child on the Salier[72] from Bremen on 6 Jul 1882. As can be seen, she is about the right age, but this Sarah's child's name seems to be "Sophie Oberle, age 2." This would certainly be the correct age for her son Seraphin, and although this might be the customs agent's interpretation of what he heard, the manifest seems quite legible, and clearly lists the gender as "f" (which still might not mean much).

This manifest did not specify the passengers' U.S. destinations, but the book "Germans to America"[73] lists them as bound for Baltimore. I have never been able to find any trace of a Sarah and Sophie Oberle in the United States[74], so these two might indeed be our "Sarah and Seraphin." If Sarah realized by then that she was pregnant, and no family freighter was scheduled to leave for several weeks or months, she may have opted for commercial passenger travel on the first available ship and departed from Bremen.

---

[71] The year of the child's arrival is further confirmed by Seraphin III's statement on the 1930 census that he had immigrated in 1882.

[72] A then state-of-the-art ship, the S/S Salier was built in 1874 at Hull, England by Earle's Shipbuilding Engineering Co., and was operated by the Norddeutscher Lloyd company of Bremen, Germany. It was rated as: 3,083 Gross Burden (Displacement), 353 ft Length.

[73] ...created from departure manifests in German records. This reference work is readily available.

[74] Of course, the 1890 U.S. Censuses were mostly destroyed, so this might not mean a lot given their ages. This "Sarah and Sophie" (or whatever the names are) would have been 45 and 20 on the 1900 census.

Barely a month later, on 14 September 1882, Sarah gave birth in Baltimore to her second son, Francis J. (Frank) Oberle id45, the first Oberle in our family to be born in the United States and, therefore, the first Oberle to be a citizen.

By 1887, Seraphin and Sarah had moved from Jenkins Lane to 306 N. Washington Street (by Orleans Street), and they later moved to Homestead Street, likely in the 1890s. Anna Oberle, their third child, told her son Tom Jelks:

> *"they used to look from the house on Homestead Avenue (sic) to the big white house on the hill - wishing they could move there some day. That was the house on Gorsuch Avenue, and eventually we did move there."*

There is some indirect evidence that Seraphin may have returned to visit his family in 1896, several years after his father had died there. This will be discussed in conjunction with his 1905 trip beginning on page 66.

By 1898, and at the time of both the 1900 and 1910 Censuses, the family resided at 539 Gorsuch Avenue[75], which is in the Waverly district of the city.

1900 US Census: National Archives Set t623 roll 612 page 054b (bottom of page)

1900 US Census: National Archives Set t623 roll 612 page 055 (top of page)

Baltimore – 1900 U.S. Census page segments showing family of "Lewis" Oberle

In the 1900 U.S. Census, the first surviving census after his arrival, Seraphin Oberle (II) id25 is recorded as "Lewis J.," and his oldest son Seraphin id60 as "Lewis H." It is tempting to dismiss this, but the birth dates match our family, and the names and dates for the remainder of the household match as well. Since "Lewis H." doesn't sound like something that "Seraphin" could be mistaken for, it doesn't seem likely that this is a census taker's mistake, but

---

[75] Unfortunately, virtually all records for the 1890 census were lost in a fire, so I haven't been able to determine exactly when they moved from Homestead to Gorsuch Avenue. See Map on page 95.

there doesn't seem to be any other explanation[76]. Furthermore, he lists himself, Sarah and his son Lewis H. (Seraphin III) as coming from Germany in 1881, and subsequent children as being born in Maryland. The name of the seventh child is given as "Tracey" rather than Theresa, but Tom Jelks said she was always called "Treesy" by the family, so this doesn't tell us anything.

Seraphin returns to Engenthal

Sometime in 1905 when he was fifty years old, Seraphin made what appears to be a second trip back to Germany, presumably to visit his family. As can be seen in the passenger manifest for the S.S. Cassel shown on the following page, his return from Bremen took place on August 23, 1905. Seraphin traveled alone and, on the manifest, we can see that he had $70[77] with him when he arrived back in Baltimore after the relatively speedy thirteen day voyage.

The S. S. Cassel

The Cassel, a modern (built in 1901) steamer of the Köln class, traveled mainly to Baltimore and Galveston, and represented a significant improvement in passenger comfort over earlier vessels. Even steerage class, which could accommodate 1,500, was well lit and significantly roomier than had been the norm in the nineteenth century. Although the Cassel carried large amounts of cargo as well as passengers, it was capable of reaching a top speed of 13 knots, reducing the time it took to travel from Bremen to Baltimore to less than two weeks and was thus reasonably competitive with the dedicated passenger ships of the day.

Another entry to note on this manifest is Seraphin's statement that his previous residence in the United States was from 1896 to 1905, clearly suggesting that he may also have left the country in 1896, although I have been unable to locate any evidence of that in existing passenger manifests.

The date of his 1896 journey is unknown, but likely began in or after April of that year. Since his son Tommy's id23 birth took place on December 21st, his conception would likely have been in late March, and Seraphin would have to have left Baltimore after that date.

---

[76] Could he have been attempting to insure that the name "Seraphin Oberle" didn't appear in any federal government records? As far as I can determine, he never applied for naturalization, which required little more than a token effort and the passage of several years in those days. Later censuses show their correct names and the younger "Lewis" (Seraphin III) and both of his eligible brothers all registered for the World War I draft. See page 102.

[77] An amount of $70 in 1901 (four years earlier) would be equivalent to almost $1900 in 2012. Hmmm.

Port of Baltimore – 1905 Alien Passenger Arrival Manifest for the S.S. Cassel

Segments of two Manifest pages for the S.S. Cassel, showing Seraphin's arrival in Baltimore from Bremen on 23 August, 1905

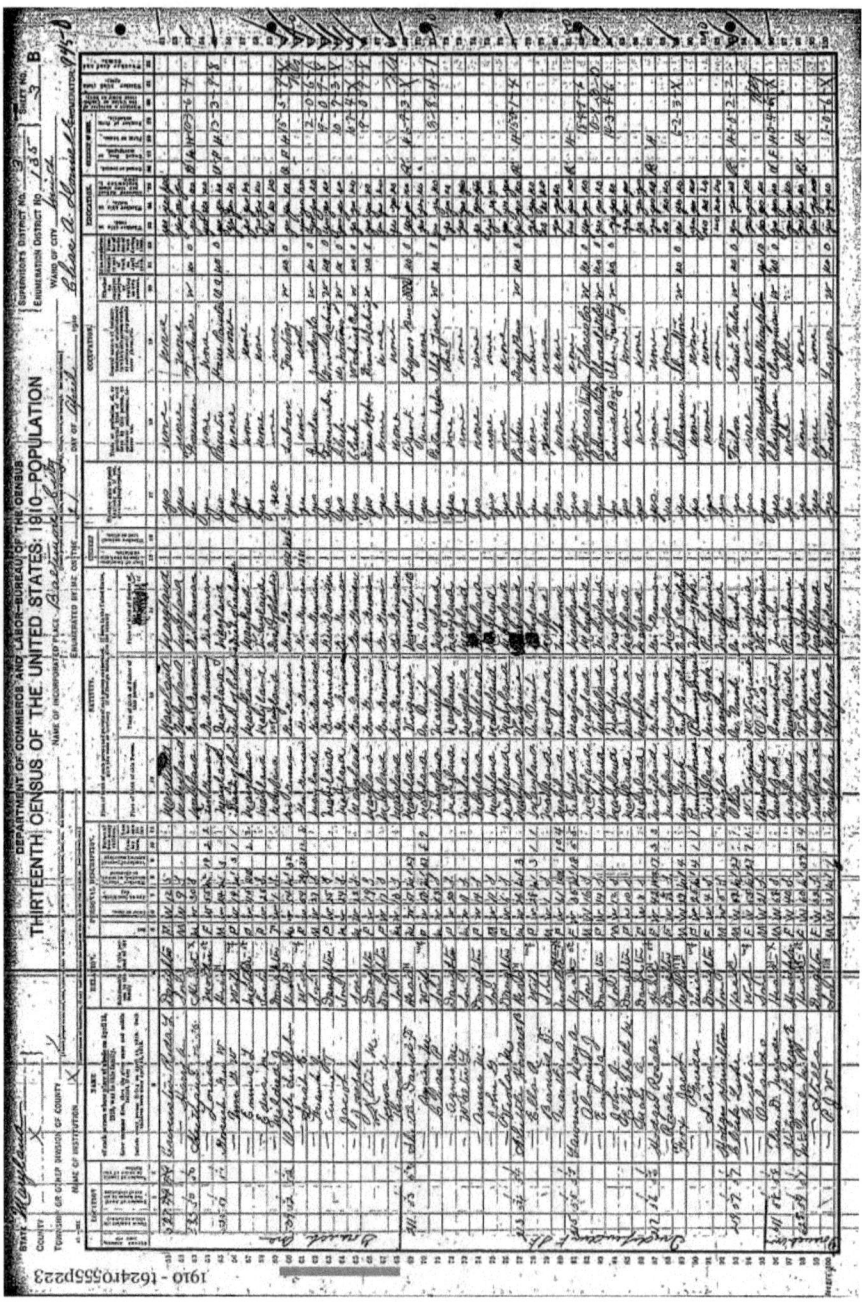

*Baltimore – 1910 U.S. Census showing family of Seraphin Oberle (II)
NARC Series t624 Roll 555 Page 223. This Seraphin id25 is my great-grandfather*

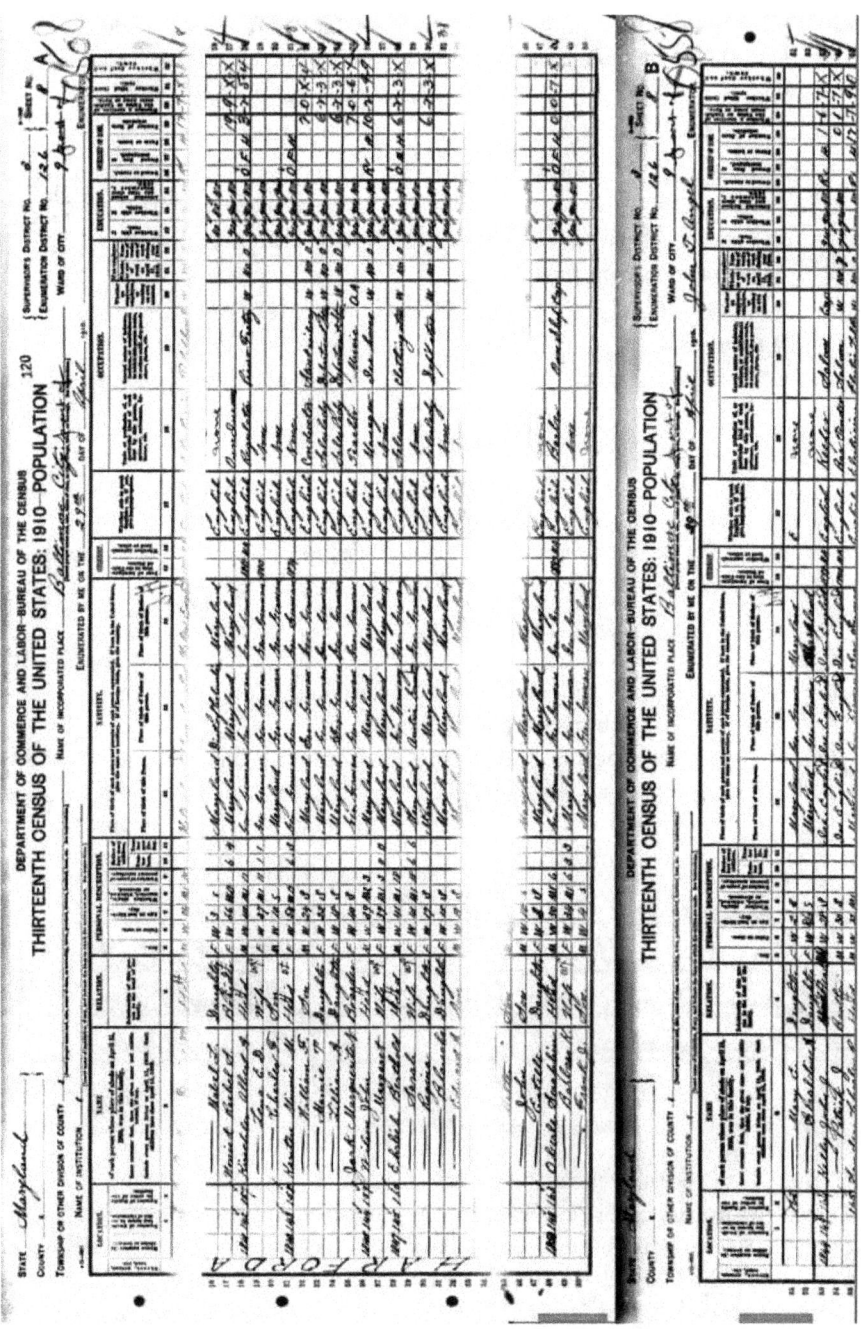

Baltimore – 1910 U.S. Census segments showing family of Seraphin Oberle (III) NARC Series t624 Roll 555 Page 120a/b. This Seraphin id60 is my grandfather's older brother.

1711-1975 History

In the 1910 U.S. Census, shown on page 68, my great-grandfather Seraphin II lists both himself and Sarah as coming from Germany. Note that Seraphin's name is spelled "Serayelin" in the published index, making it hard to locate.

The children listed as living with them in 1910 at 539 Gorsuch Avenue are Frank J., Annie T., Jacob, Joseph, Katie M., Teresa A., and Thomas.

By that same year, Seraphin and Sarah's oldest son, Seraphin III, now married to Barbara (Nickol) id61, lived in the 1800 block of Harford Road with their children Frank J. id63, Mary E. id164, and their new daughter Geraldine A. id194. See the census image on page 69.

In the 1920 U.S. Census, Seraphin II lists both himself and Sarah, now living at 1114 Gorsuch Avenue, as coming from Germany. The only family members still living with them were their married (but separated) daughter Anna Jelks and their grandson Thomas Jelks id182, who is quoted frequently as a source in this book. See the census image on page 71.

Seraphin III (shown as "Searphin" in the NARC index) and Barbara were now living at 1277 East North Avenue with their earlier children as well as their new children (i.e. born in the previous decade) William S. id187, Margaret id193 (Marge Ford, who is also quoted in this book) and Edward id195. See the census image on page 72.

Frank was now married to his first wife Catherine Grandy, and living with their son Joseph F. X., who was 8 years old, at 1418 Gittings Avenue in Baltimore. Frank listed both his parents as coming from "B....(illegible), Ger" (presumably an abbreviation for "Germany"). Catherine, his wife, also reports that both her parents came from "B... (illegible), Ger." See the full image on page 73. The illustration below magnifies the illegible "B...." from that image, which I can't interpret.

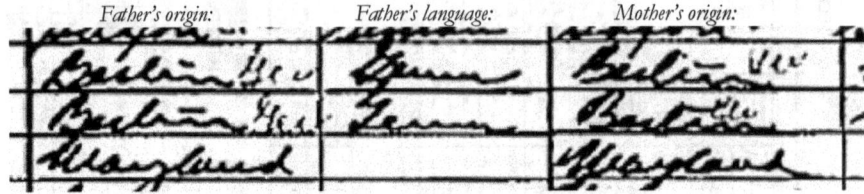

Baltimore – 1910 U.S. Census: closeup of sheet for Frank Oberle's family (see page 73)
This shows illegible columns in the rows for Frank id45, his wife Catherine id46, and their son Joseph id179.

If the "Ger" doesn't mean Germany, the word might be "Baltimore," but this seems unlikely, not only because it is incorrect, but also because with all other entries, a state name is given rather than a city name. The word might also be "Berlin," which suggests some other intriguing possibilities (e.g. that Frank's parents' trip to the United States may have been quite a circuitous one), though this seems highly doubtful.

*Baltimore – 1920 U.S. Census showing family of Seraphin [II] Oberle
NARC Series t625 Roll 662 Page 269. This Seraphin id25 is my great-grandfather*

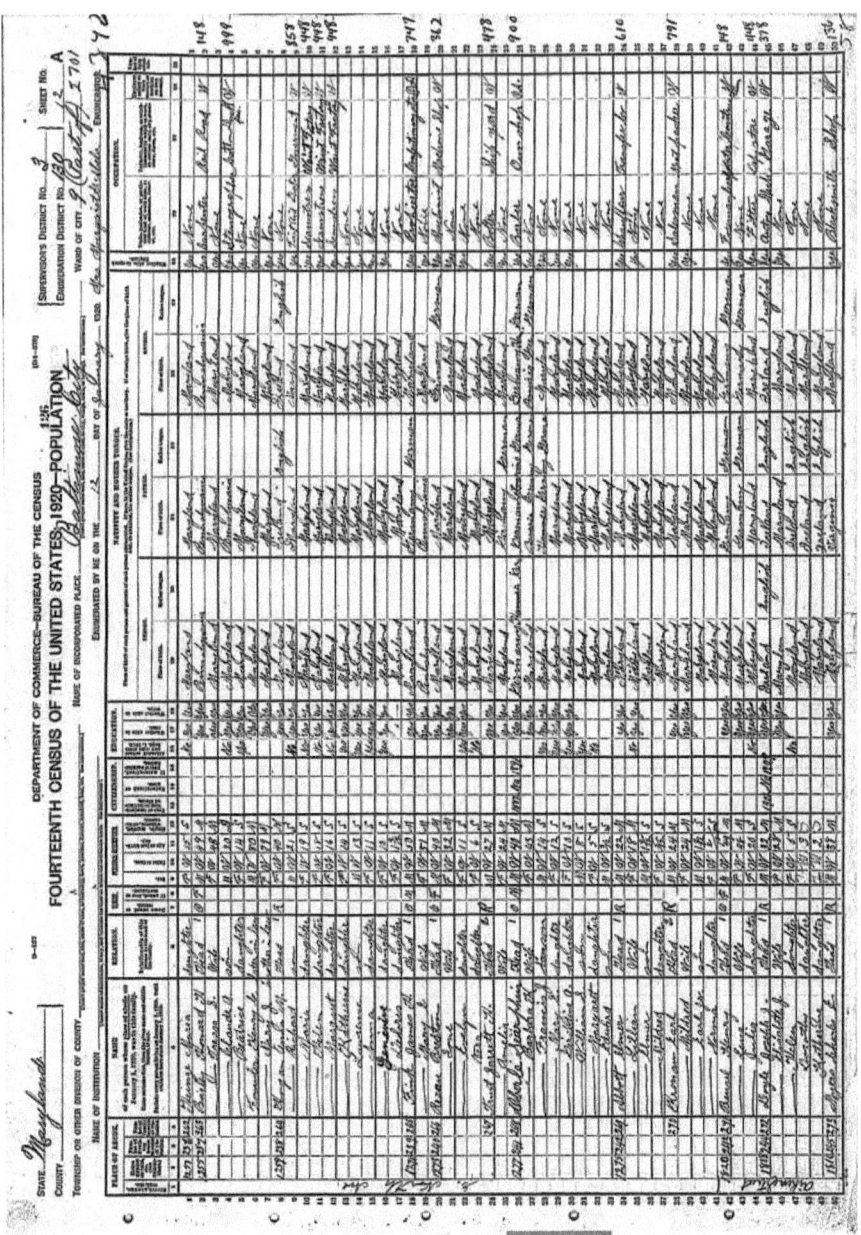

Baltimore – 1920 U.S. Census showing family of Seraphin [III] Oberle
NARC Series t625 Roll 662 Page 12a. This Seraphin idGO is my grandfather Joseph's older brother.

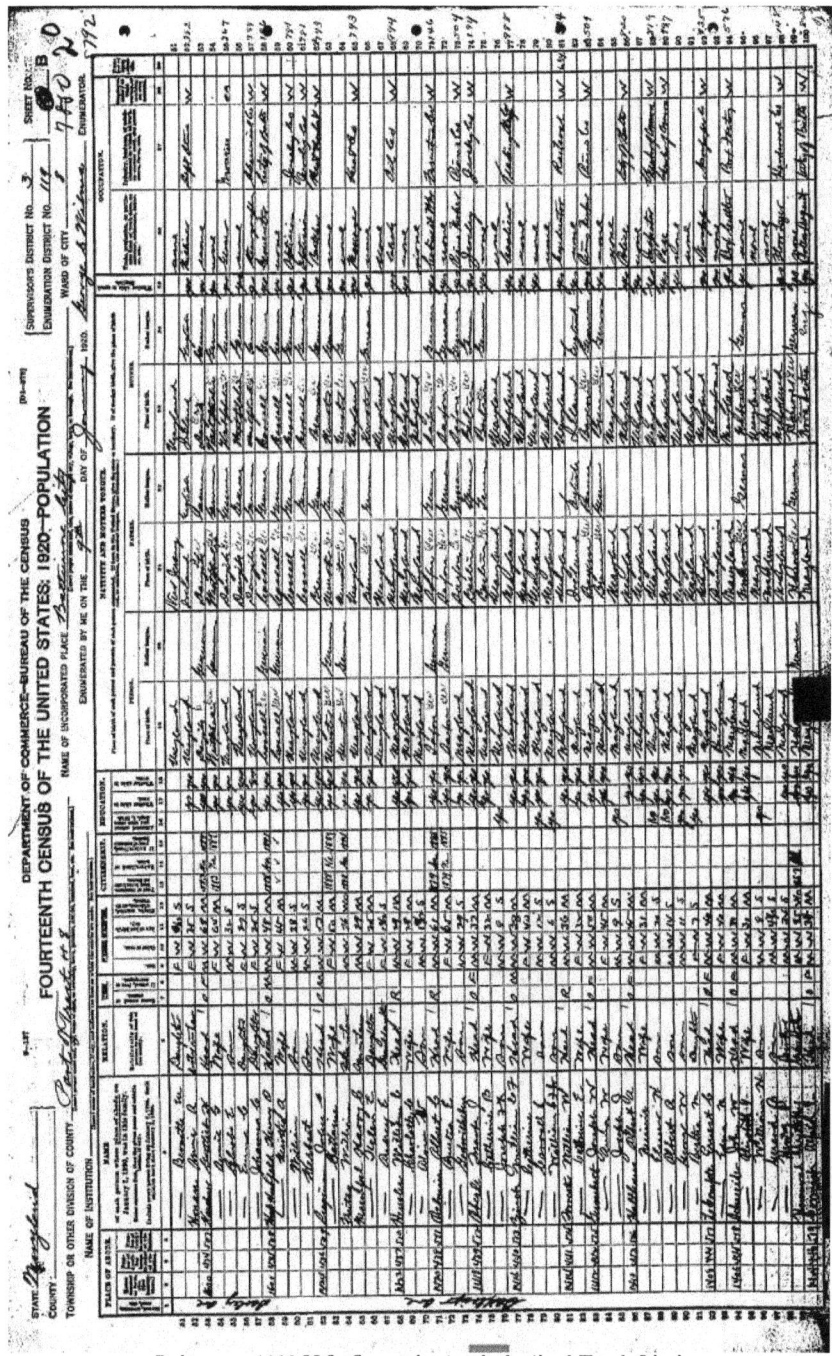

Baltimore – 1920 U.S. Census showing the family of Frank Oberle
NARC Series t625 Roll 657 Page 253. Frank Oberle id#5 is my grandfather Joseph's older brother.

*Baltimore – 1930 U.S. Census showing family of Seraphin (II) Oberle
NARC Series t626 Roll 853 Page 215. This Seraphin id25 is my great-grandfather*

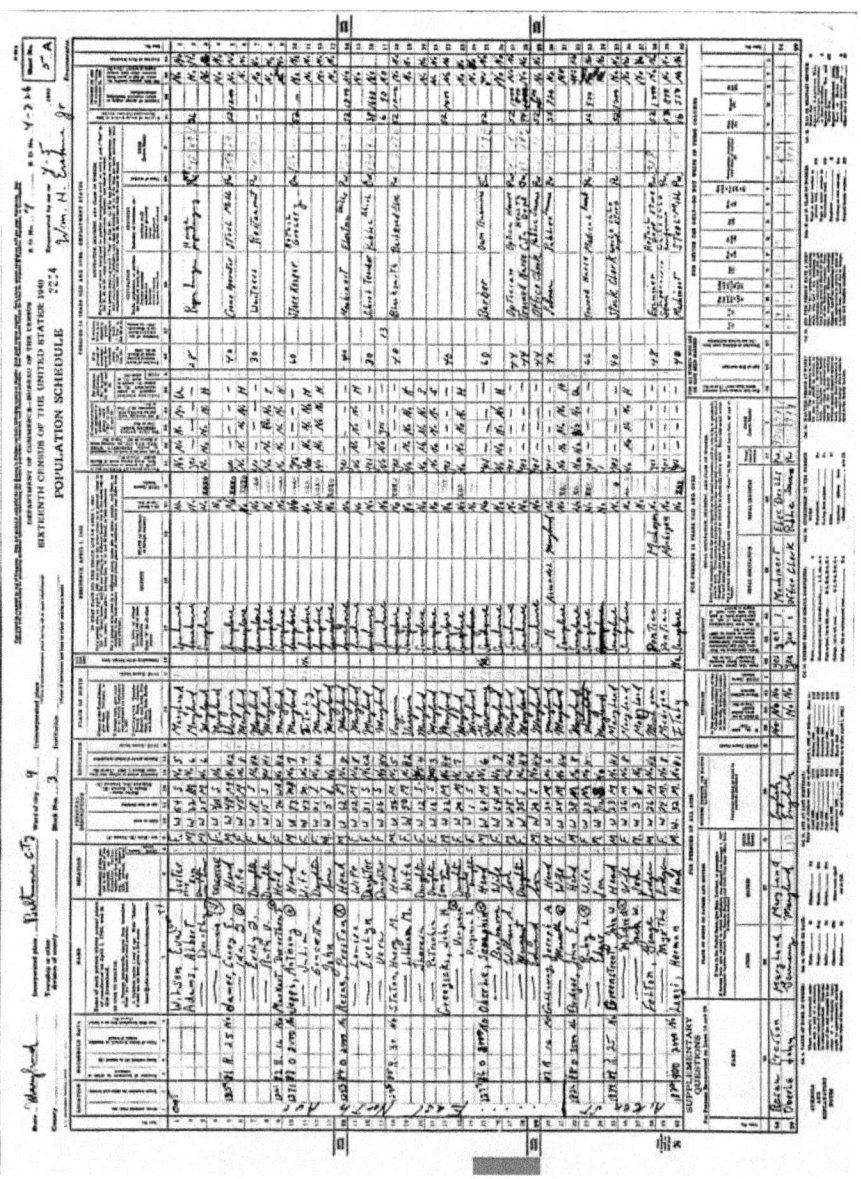

*Baltimore – 1930 U.S. Census showing family of Seraphin (III) Oberle
NARC Series t626 Roll 853 Page 54. This Seraphin id60 is my great-uncle.*

Seraphin's Employment in Baltimore

During his youth in Engenthal, Seraphin II, like many men in his family, had worked as a *bucheron* (French for forestry worker or, as he told Tom Jelks, a *Holzhacker*, the German word for wood cutter – what we would today call a lumberjack). As we shall see later, he was apparently also exposed to the Alsatian tradition of wine making, but there is no record that he ever practiced that as a profession in Engenthal.

As mentioned earlier, he began working as a shoemaker in Emden in order to develop a recognized trade so he and Sarah could immigrate into the United States which, as it turned out, wasn't necessary due to their entry from a commercial vessel. So far as anyone recalls however, although he kept his cobbler (shoe making) tools with him until the end of his life and sometimes made pairs of shoes for his wife and grandchildren to wear, he was actually never employed in that profession in the United States.

Baltimore – 1920 Photo of Workers at the Stieff Piano Company Factory
My great-grandfather Seraphin (II) worked here. The photo is from the Maryland Historical Society.

In Baltimore, he worked in several factories as a laborer making things as varied as mattresses and pianos. He worked at the Charles M. Stieff Piano Factory on Aiken Street about two blocks south of North Avenue in Baltimore until it closed as a result of the great depression. The Company was in a large three-story brick building with "Stieff Piano Co" painted on the side in large white letters, and remained something of a Baltimore landmark even after it closed. There is no indication that Seraphin was a skilled artisan, but there were probably many opportunities to exercise his wood cutting skills.

The Stieff Piano building remained standing but unoccupied until April 1968 when, two days after Martin Luther King Jr. was assassinated, rioters in Baltimore set the building on fire[78], and it was subsequently razed.

---

[78] Along with many other buildings of course.

Seraphin's final job, which he took after the Stieff layoff, was with a Slaughter House on Twenty-Fifth Street between Kirk Ave and Harford Road[79]. His job, as Tom Jelks describes it, required removing hair from animal hides, and Seraphin referred to the place disparagingly as "the Hair Factory." Due to the nature of the work, he was often nauseous when he came home, and hated the job. He remained there for only a short time before retiring for good.

Sometime between the 1910 and 1920 censuses, the family moved down the street to 1114 Gorsuch Ave., but no one was able to tell me why they did this.

Seraphin regularly made his own wine at home (a skill he seems to have picked up as a young man living in Engenthal-le-Bas, which was and is still today in the heart of Alsatian wine country), but his granddaughter Marge Ford id193 said that he never offered wine to a woman, even though he entertained often[80].

According to Tom Jelks:

Baltimore – Seraphin and Sarah in their later years

> "I used to go down in the cellar with Grandpop when he made wine. He had a big old wooden wine press, and I would help him to turn the screw on the press to squeeze the juice out of the grapes. Then for each gallon of juice, he would add two pounds of sugar in a big stone crock. After several weeks he would siphon it into bottles and let it age. I do the same thing, except I don't have a press and I use a Hydrometer to tell me how much sugar to use – more modern. I am sure he brought his wine making knowledge with him to America."

---

[79] I haven't been able to identify the name of this business, but it isn't there now.
[80] My grandmother Katie Goldrick called him on this while dating his son Joseph, and he obliged her from then on. This anecdote will be related later when discussing Katie.

Tom Jelks id182 related stories to me that when my grandfather Joseph Oberle began working, he would occasionally give his father Seraphin five dollars and Seraphin would send this to his younger sister Eugenie in Alsace before Sarah would find out; this often led to shouting matches between Seraphin and Sarah. As mentioned in footnote 47, Tom would later have an opportunity to visit his great-aunt Eugenie during the post-World War II occupation.

Marge Ford said that the kids "feared him," although "Sarah didn't put up with his crap." Marge said that her grandfather had a reputation as a womanizer, helped by the fact that he always looked a lot younger than he was.

Baltimore – Seraphin II circa 1925

The story she tells of Seraphin's last days is that he was apparently hitting on some woman in a bar (and he was 74 at the time!), and ended up getting into a fight with the woman's husband. During a fall (while fighting), Seraphin hit his head on a railing.

Marge said that her grandfather Seraphin went downhill rapidly after the incident and died soon afterward on 27 May 1931. The photo to the left, from his late daughter Anna's collection[81], shows Seraphin in about 1925.

Sarah died less than six years later on 10 January 1937. She was laid out in their home on Gorsuch Avenue, and when it came time for the funeral, her coffin was lifted out the side window and carried down to St. Bernard's Church, since that was so close that carrying the coffin was easier than attempting to use a hearse.

Sarah was buried on the 13th of January in Section N, Lot 30 at Holy Redeemer Cemetery off Bel Air Road in Baltimore with her husband Seraphin.

---

[81] … and provided to me by her son Tom Jelks, who is mentioned several times in this document.

As can be seen in the photograph to the right, the monument has become slightly tilted over the years. Thomas, Jacob, and Annie each have separate stones that are flat to the ground, and Annie's continues to sink below ground level, making it sometimes difficult to locate.

Helena, Adalbert, Johann, and Simon, being infants, are in a single grave in the same plot with a shared stone (shown below).

The Lot Detail Report from Holy Redeemer Cemetery suggests that the plot wasn't purchased until two years after Helena's death in 1892, so that her body must have been originally buried elsewhere – another mystery for someone to uncover.

Baltimore – Oberle headstone at Holy Redeemer Cemetery

Baltimore – Oberle Infants' Stone in Lot 30 of Holy Redeemer Cemetery

Many of Seraphin and Sarah's descendants and their families are also buried in Holy Redeemer. Among these are:

StEd-329: Their son Seraphin (III) id60, his wife Barbara id61, his son Francis id63 with wife Dorothy id64 and daughter Alvina Cypher id65, and his daughter Geraldine Hartnett id62.

LL-400: Their son Francis J. (Frank) id45 and his wives Katherine id46 and Barbara id47.

SH-103: Their grandson Cornelius id196, his wife Rosalie id242 and their son Thomas id56. (see photos on page 142)

Not all Oberle graves in Holy Redeemer are our relatives, however; some are from another unrelated Oberle family living in Baltimore[82], and several of these have first names in common with those in our family.

---

[82] The Sulpician priest Fr. Vince Oberle from this family was on the faculty or St. Charles College in Catonsville Maryland when I was a student there in the 1960s. He also served as the school's treasurer.

Children & Grandchildren of Seraphin (II) Oberle & Sarah Johanna Kiwiet

Seraphin and Sarah had a total of twelve children; consistent with the statement on the 1900 census that Sarah was the "mother of 12, 8 living." A photograph of Seraphin and Sarah's family from that time is shown on page 83.

Seraphin and Barbara Oberle

- Seraphin (III) Oberle id60, (born 20 June 1879, died 14 November 1955), married Barbara K. Nickol id61, (born 1876, died 25 August 1949). Seraphin, a barber by trade, was the only child not born in the United States (see page 63). He and Barbara had six children:

Francis John (Frank) Oberle id63, (born 15 March 1906, died 18 May 1950), married Dorothy Trabert id64 and had one child Alvina Mary id65 Oberle.

Mary Elizabeth Oberle id124, (born 16 October 1907, died 29 April 2004), became Sister Alvina of the Sisters of St. Francis of Philadelphia..

Anna Geraldine Oberle id62, (born 21 August 1909, died 12 January 1992), married Joseph Hartnett and had two children.

William Seraphin (Bill) Oberle id187, (born 15 November 1911, died 26 August 1995). Bill married Nina Burke id670 (born 3 September 1918) and had six children. See photos of Bill on page 82 and as part of my parents' wedding party on page 126.

Mary E. (Sr. Alvina) Oberle

Margaret Rita (Marge) Oberle id193, (born 5 October 1914), married Daniel Aloysius Ford id192 and had seven children. Marge is mentioned often as a source.

Joseph Edward (Eddie) Oberle id195, (born 30 September 1919, died 11 March 2004), married Marie Madsen id671 (born 16 January 1922, died 22 August 2010) on November 8, 1947 and had four children.

Eddie and Marie Oberle

- Francis Joseph (Frank) Oberle id45, (born 14 September 1882, died 10 JAN 1960), and was the first of Sarah and Seraphin's children to be born in the United States. He married Katherine Grandy id46, (born 4 November 1887, died 15 September 1926), and the couple had one child:

Joseph Francis (Joe) Oberle id179, (born 17 September 1911, died 24 June 2001), who became a Redemptorist priest.

Francis Joseph (Frank) Oberle

Katherine Grandy died when their son was 15, after which Frank married Katherine's sister Barbara M. id47, (born 11 November 1893, died 16 MAR 1929); they also had one child:

Gerard George (Jerry) Oberle id180, (born 12 March 1929). Like his older brother, he became a Redemptorist priest as well, and spent many years as a missionary in Brazil.

Barbara Grandy Oberle died a few days after Fr. Jerry's birth, and he was raised by Margaret A. Schirmer id178 (13 September 1881 - 11 September 1958), his mother's cousin, who lived with the family.

The future Fr. Jerry Oberle, Frank Oberle, and Fr. Joe Oberle

- Anna T. (Annie) Oberle id24, (born 21 March 1884, died 5 April 1971), married Albert Preston Jelks id175 (3 January 1882 - 7 April 1948) and had one son:

Thomas Oberle Jelks id182 born 19 May 1916, died 4 November 2011. Tom Jelks is often referred to as a source in this document. In 1944, sixty-seven years after his grandfather had left the eastern hills of the Vosges Mountains, Tom was part of a machine gun crew advancing up the western slopes of the same mountains in pursuit of the Nazi forces during World War II. His book about his years in the military is mentioned on page 111.

According to her nephew Fr. Jerry Oberle id180 (her brother Frank's son), Aunt Annie,

Tom Jelks in early 2011

upon the death of her long separated husband id175, said that *"it was too bad he died so late —otherwise I could have gotten remarried when I was young enough to do so."*

- Jacob (Jake) Oberle id30, born May 1885, died in the Spanish Flu epidemic on 21 April 1918.
- **Joseph Oberle** id81, (born 1 December 1887, died 19 August 1954). Joseph is our family's direct ancestor, and will be discussed in more detail beginning on page 98 below.
- Helena Oberle id27, (born 21 September 1889, died 7 October 1892).
- Katherine (Kate) Oberle id177, (born before December 1890), married John G. Johnson and had a daughter Helen (21 Oct 1919-24 Dec 2007).
- Adalbert Oberle id601, (born 20 November 1891, died 23 November 1891)
- Theresa Oberle id174, (born before October 1892), married Harry Strasinger; they had no children.
- Johann Oberle id28, (born 27 December 1895, died 27 December 1895)
- Thomas (Tommy) Oberle id23, (born 21 December 1896, died 20 February 1915). Tommy died of tuberculosis at age 18. As Marge Ford tells it, *"Tommy liked to ride his bicycle, and went out one day when it was quite cold and he then became very cold and sweaty, after which he went and laid down on the ground. Realizing that he was sick, the family then put him outside on a second floor porch to rest. Within a few days, he had died."*
- Simon Oberle id29, (born 28 October 1899, died 28 October 1899)

Frank Oberle with Fr. Joe Oberle circa 1938

Bill and Nina Oberle and family in 1954

One of my daughters in Esopus NY with Fr. Jerry Oberle in 2005

Baltimore – Oberle Family Portrait, circa 1900.
Left to right, standing: Kate id177, *Annie* id24, *Jake* id30, *Seraphin (III)* id60 *& Frank* id45
Seated: Theresa id174, *Sarah* id26, *Joe* id81, *Seraphin (II)* id25, *and Tommy* id23

Joseph Oberle, Katherine Grandy Oberle, Tom Oberle, Katherine Goldrick Oberle, Jake Oberle, Tressa Oberle, Anna Oberle, Frank Oberle kneeling holding Joseph Oberle (later Fr. Joe Oberle CSsR)

Four of the Oberle brothers and two sisters:
Tommy died in 1915, and Jake in 1918. "Tressa" was Theresa's nickname; this picture is
from about 1912 – photo supplied by Tom Jelks from his mother Anna's albums.

The next immigrant nationality to join our ancestry was Irish, represented by the Boyle and Goldrick families discussed below.

Ireland in the Nineteenth Century   (The Goldrick & Boyle Families)

My paternal Grandmother Katherine Goldrick Oberle <u>id80</u> was the daughter of two Irish immigrants who arrived in the United States during the nineteenth century and married in Baltimore. Her father was Martin Goldrick, and her mother was Catherine Boyle.

Home Counties of Martin Goldrick and Catherine Boyle

From the earliest days of the American colonies, and continuing through the first decades of nineteenth century, those leaving Ireland for the "New World" left for the same reasons as those from other countries who had made the same journey. The incentives to leave Ireland became far stronger, however, as the economic conditions there began significantly declining. This was in spite of shipboard conditions generally deplorable enough that the

U.S. Congress felt compelled in 1848 to specify minimum requirements for food, water and ventilation as well as requiring that ceiling heights in the passenger areas be at least six feet – with penalties for non-compliant ships.

U.S. Congress – 1848 "Passenger Bill of Rights" passed on May 17th.

By the time the potato famine had taken hold, starvation had become commonplace across Ireland[83], and the Irish left their country in great numbers, often walking many miles to reach a port from which they could leave. In 1835, Gustave de Beaumont, a well-traveled French sociologist was visiting Ireland. He wrote:

> "I have seen the Indian in his forests, and the Negro in his chains, and thought, as I contemplated their pitiable condition, that I saw the very extreme of human wretchedness; but I did not then know the condition of unfortunate Ireland ... In all countries, more or less, paupers may be discovered; but an entire nation of paupers is what was never seen until it was shown in Ireland."

Some of the Irish left for Great Britain and Australia, but the majority came to North America, settling in Canada and the United States.

The map of Ireland shown above indicates the approximate locations from which our Goldrick and Boyle ancestors emigrated. My Great Grandfather Martin Goldrick id170 was born in County Sligo, and his future wife Catherine Boyle id171 was born in County Donegal, likely in the town of Letterkenny.

The Goldricks of County Sligo, Ireland

The inscription on his tombstone[84] indicates that my great-grandfather Martin G. Goldrick id170 was a native of County Sligo in Ireland and that he was age 52 at his death on October 4, 1896. This implies he was born between October 5, 1844 and October 6, 1845, and therefore probably sometime in 1845.

The origins of the surname *Goldrick* don't seem to be universally agreed upon by researchers, and the sources I've examined give quite different meanings. The most plausible sources suggest that *Goldrick* and its sometime variants *MacGoldrick* and *MacGolrick* are anglicized versions of *Ó Góilín*, an older family from County Cork. One source elaborates upon this to say that the Gaelic *Mag Ualghairg* (also anglicized as *Golden*, *Goulding*, and *MacGoldrick*) is a branch of the *O'Rourke* clan of County Leitrim.[85] Yet another source suggests that the name Gold(e)rick is Teutonic for "golden ruler". In any case, the name is certainly an Irish (not Scottish) name, albeit an uncommon one, leading to the conclusion that Martin's records would be relatively easy to locate, but this hasn't proven to be the case.

The County Sligo Research Center[86] confirms that the name *Goldrick* is common to that County, but the variant most often used is *Mac Goldrick*, and it is

---

[83] A full discussion of the famine and its effects is far beyond the scope of this history. For an interesting account, visit the web site http://www.historyplace.com/worldhistory/famine/index.html.
[84] See photograph on page 93. A photograph that may be of Martin Goldrick is shown on page 196.
[85] "The Surnames of Ireland"; Edward MacLysaght; Irish Academic Press, Dublin, Ire and Portland OR; 6th Edition; Copyright © Edward MacLysaght, 1999; ISBN 0-7165-2366-3
[86] County Sligo Heritage Genealogy Centre; Aras Redden, Temple St., Sligo, County Sligo, Ireland; Phone (071) 43728 e-mail heritagesligo@tinet.ie.

under that name that all variants are indexed in their databases. Other research I've done indicates that another area usually associated with the *Goldrick* name is the northeast part of County Leitrim near Lough Melvin on the border of County Fermanagh. County Leitrim is just east of County Sligo, and south of County Donegal in the northwestern part of Ireland. See the map on page 85. It seems reasonable, however, to accept Martin's tombstone inscription as correct.

In my father's Baby Book, Martin's father (and my 2nd great-grandfather) is listed as James Goldrick id1907 (see the page to the right). Since no maternal great-grandmother's name is present, it seems safe to assume my grandmother never knew her, and possibly never knew either of her Goldrick grandparents. This might further suggest that her Goldrick grandparents never came to the United States; in any case, I have never been able to locate any arrival or census information for them.

In the indexes of Irish records for County Sligo, only twelve birth records for boys named Martin Goldrick/MacGoldrick are listed for the time frame in which he was likely born, and none of these show a father's name of James[87]. Although there are a number of possible explanations for this[88], it seems that, without stumbling upon some new evidence, tracing our Goldrick ancestors may be impossible.

Baby Book of Cornelius Oberle
Note the misspelling of her mother Catherine's name.

The only Irish record I have located for a Martin Goldrick is a tithe dated 13 March 1835[89]. Based on the infrequent occurrences of the name Goldrick or Goldrich[90] in any Irish records, the possibility that this tithe record may be

---

[87] James was a very common first name for the Goldrick/MacGoldrick families there however. It should be noted that there is a 29 Jun 1868 marriage record for a Martin McGoldrick, born 1843, son of James McGoldrick, to Margaret Crowel, daughter of Denis Crowel. I am assuming this is not our Martin.

[88] The two most likely to me would be that my Grandmother was mistaken when she listed her grandfather's name as James, or that Martin may have been born elsewhere (County Leitrim?) and relocated to Sligo before emigrating.

[89] Parish of Shancough; Diocese of Elphin; County. Sligo: Tithe Applotment 13 March 1835; Commissioner: Burton Phibbs; FHL Film 256,655; Carrownacluane. Entry number 214 on this page is for Martin Goldrick.

for Martin's uncle or grandfather needs to be investigated[91]. I have been unable to locate Martin Goldrick in the 1870 United States Census.

The Boyles of County Donegal, Ireland

The Gaelic name Ó *Baoighill*, or its Anglicized forms *O'Boyle*, and later *Boyle*, translate to "having profitable pledges," although to be honest, it isn't clear to me what that means. Nonetheless, it is apparently a common family name in County Donegal in northwest Ireland. The initial O' began to disappear in the 16th century, but is now beginning to appear again in Ireland[92].

In January of 1848, possibly in Glenswilly, part of the Irish civil parish of Conwal and just outside the town of Letterkenny[93] in County Donegal, my 2nd great grandparents Edward Boyle id1715 and Margaret Kelly id1716 had a daughter Catherine id171 (right). On the 1900 Census (see next page), at which time she was a widowed head-of-household, Catherine reported that she immigrated into the United States forty-eight years earlier in 1852. Because she would have been four years old at the time, she would presumably have traveled with her parents or possibly some other adult.

Catherine Boyle, circa 1862

I have not been able to discover any further information about this family, but the immigration year suggests they were not part of the main wave of the Irish famine exodus to the U.S. (1845 to 1850) or, if they did leave Ireland during that period, may not have come here directly. Thus far, however, I have found no record of a Boyle family with an appropriately aged daughter in any passenger manifests or indexes.

---

[90] Other records I've located include a Martin *Golrich*, who emmigrated from Sligo to New York on the Foundling on 30 June 1816, and Terence *Golrick*, who arrived on the Helen in September 1815, also from Sligo. Neither of these would seem to be ours, but their existence suggests that the spelling Goldrick varied quite a bit.

[91] Note that the International Genealogical Index (IGI) lists a Martin Goldrick, born in Sligo, son of James Goldrick and Mary Conway, but his birth date is given as 15 November 1867, making him a generation older than our Martin, who was born in about 1845. Now if this Martin had an older brother James – this line should be examined more closely since, due to the uncommon name, any Sligo Goldricks may likely be related to us.

[92] This is mentioned to establish that the name we should be looking for in Irish records when searching for our ancestors is almost certainly *Boyle*, and not Ó *Baoighill* or *O'Boyle*, as some have speculated.

[93] This is "informed speculation," based on the concentration of surnames in Donegal, but my cousin recalled his father Francis id197 mentioning the town name of Letterkenny, lending it more credence.

[94] My Grandmother Oberle wrote the names of her grandparents in my father Cornelius's baby book. See a copy of the relevant entries on page 88.

Baltimore – 1900 U.S. Census segments showing Catherine (Boyle) Goldrick's Family
This shows Catherine's immigration in 1852 and residence in the U.S. for 48 years.[95]

The 1864 Boyle Photo album[96] has pictures with inscriptions of photographers in Boston and Liverpool as well as in Baltimore, so it is possible that the Boyles originally arrived at some location other than Baltimore, or that Catherine may have been brought to the United States by another family.

Baltimore – 1870 U.S. Census segment showing the Holland Family
Catherine Boyle [id171] *(line 5) can be seen living with the Holland Family as a servant*

By the time she was 21, though, Catherine was working as the older of two female servants living with the Holland family[97] in Baltimore. They don't appear to be related to our family, but there is a picture of one of their children in the Boyle photo album, possibly with his mother or the other housekeeper.

---

[95] See National Archives Series t623 Roll 0612 Page 260. I had originally thought the year was 1857, but now believe it says 1852 (with the bottom of the 2 directly on and obscured by the line of the form.) This makes more sense and adds up nicely with the 48 years she says she has been in the U.S.

[96] See the appendix on page 175, which describes the contents of the album, and provides reproductions of all the photographs it contained when I discovered the album in my parents' basement.

[97] National Archives Series m593 Roll 0574 Page 031a; see image above.

The Hollands were living with just one child in the 1860 census[98], so Catherine must have begun working for them after 1860 (i.e. when she was between 12 and 22 years old).

Martin Goldrick and Catherine Boyle

I haven't uncovered where or how Martin and Catherine met[99], but they were probably married between late 1870 and mid 1872. Their first child, Mary Goldrick id557, known to most of the family as "Aunt Mamie," was born in August 1873 and eventually married William Rinn id536, father of the William Rinn, M.D. id538 who provided (or more likely returned) the Boyle photo album mentioned earlier to my Grandmother Oberle.

Martin[100] and Catherine eventually had another daughter (Margaret id546) and three sons (James, Martin, and Edward id184, id554 & id551) before finally giving birth to my grandmother Catherine (Katie) on 10 March 1884.

Catherine Boyle Goldrick, circa 1915

Martin Goldrick and Catherine Boyle Goldrick lived at 406 27th Street in Baltimore. My Dad said that he remembered being told that his grandfather Goldrick was a gardener and florist. According to the 1890 Baltimore City Directory, a Martin Goldrick was working as a gardener in the Waverly district of Baltimore – so this was probably our Martin.

On 4 October 1896, at age 52, Martin Goldrick died and was buried at Old Saint Mary's Cemetery in Govans west of York Road. I've been unable to determine the cause of his early death.

As mentioned above, Catherine was listed as head-of-household on the 1900 U.S. Census[101], and was living with her five children, daughter-in-law Grace and one granddaughter Margaret (the latter two being her son James' wife and daughter).

---

[98] National Archives Series m653 Roll 0460 Page 459
[99] Although it must certainly have been in the United States, since Catherine immigrated at about four years old.
[100] The photograph on page 196 is possibly of my great-grandfather Martin Goldrick, since a copy was found in my Uncle Joe's effects as well as in my father Cornelius' effects.
[101] See National Archives Series t623 Roll 612 Page 260 – segments of this page are shown on page 90.

Baltimore – 1910 U.S. Census showing the family of Catherine Boyle Goldrick

By the 1910 Census[102], Catherine was living at 706 23rd Street, with only her daughters Mary ("Aunt Mamie") and Katherine id80 (my paternal grandmother, now spelled with a "K"; see page 96 regarding this change) in the

---

[102] National Archives Series t624 Roll 555 Page 136; see the image above.

household. The younger Katherine listed her profession as "stenographer" in this census, and gave her age as 26, which would imply a birth year of about 1884 (see the discussion on page 96).

Catherine Boyle Goldrick died on 14 September 1927 at age 79, and was buried with her husband Martin at Old Saint Mary's Cemetery. A picture of the Goldrick plot (Section F-211) and markers at Old St. Mary's is shown to the right. Close-ups of the upper and lower portions of the obelisk showing Martin and Catherine's origins and ages at death are shown below.

As a point of interest, it should be noted that there is another Goldrick plot at Old St. Mary's for Johanna Goldrick (1830-1868) and Jas. W. P. Goldrick (1858-1883). Since Goldrick is an uncommon name, even in the "old country," it seems possible (even likely) that they may be related to our family, but I have been unable to obtain any further information about them. According to my grandmother's entry in my father Cornelius' baby book, her grandfather's name was James Goldrick, but this couldn't be him because of the dates. Johanna would have been about fourteen when Martin Goldrick was born, so she isn't likely to be his mother, but could conceivably be an older sister.

 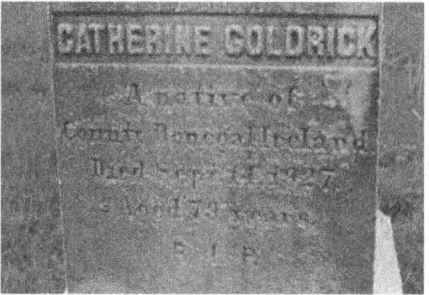

Close-ups of portions of my 2nd great-grandparents' tombstone at Old St. Mary's Cemetery.

Children & Grandchildren of Martin Goldrick & Catherine Boyle

The following section will provide only a brief commentary on Martin and Catherine's children and grandchildren.

- Mary G. (Aunt Mamie) Goldrick id557, (born August 1873), married William Rinn and had a son William A. Rinn, Jr., M.D., the psychiatrist who is mentioned in the appendix about the Boyle Photo Album

- Margaret A. Goldrick id546, (born December 1875, died 21 October 1944), married Darby Dunn id547 and had three children:

  John M. Dunn id548, (born about 1908)

  Julia A. Dunn id549, (born about 1909)

  Francis Leonard (Leonard) Dunn id550, (born 3 March 1915; died 19 Mar 1994). Leonard married Mildred Kraft id1908 and had four children.

- James Daniel (Jim) Goldrick id184, (born 27 June 1876, died 19 October 1955), married Grace and had one daughter: Jim apparently must have looked like his nephew (my father) Cornelius; see Katie Goldrick's remarks on page 116

1949 – Mildred Dunn

  Mary Margarite (sic) Goldrick id185, (born about 1898)

- Martin J. Goldrick id554, (born 11 March 1877), married Anna A. (Nannie) Zabienski id555 and had six children:

  Margaret Goldrick id556, (born about 1905, died before 2003)

  Carl F. Goldrick id1290, (born about 1906)

  Catherine Goldrick id1291, (born about 1908)

  Mary L. Goldrick id1292, (born about 1910)

  Elisabeth Goldrick id1293, (born about 1914)

  Martin Louis Goldrick id186, (born about 1916)

- Edward Vincent Goldrick id551, (born February 1880), married Nellie M. O'Connell id552 and had three children:

  Loretta Goldrick id1979, (born about 1908)

  Martin Goldrick id553, (born about 1912)

  James Goldrick id1980, (born about 1915, died 2 December 1987)

- **Catherine Philomena Gertrude Goldrick** id80, born 10 March 1882, died 9 April 1975. Catherine, later Katherine, is our family's direct ancestor, and will be discussed in more detail beginning immediately below.

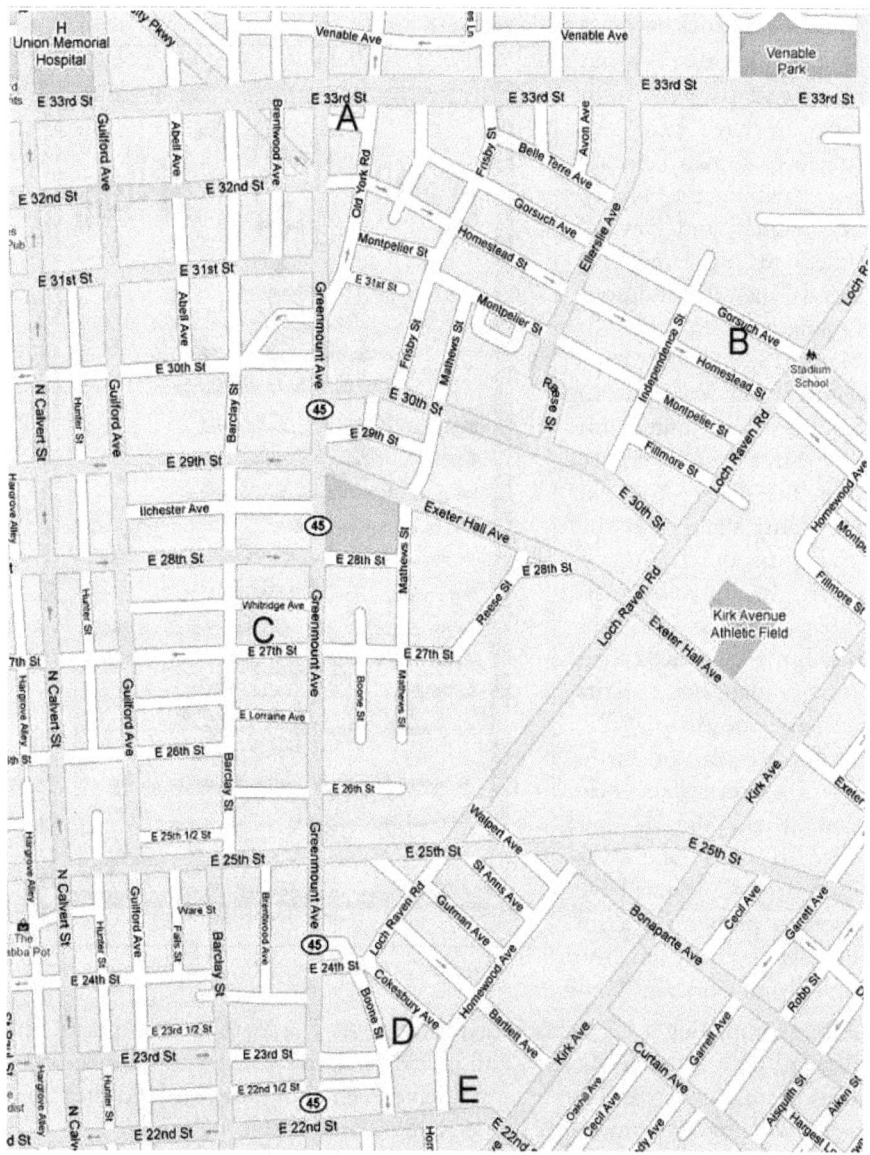

Map of areas where the Oberles and Goldricks lived from 1900 to 1926

Key: A: 539 Gorsuch Ave (Seraphin [II] Oberle Household – 1900 & 1910)
 B: 1114 Gorsuch Avenue (Seraphin [II] Oberle Household – 1920 & 1930)
 (Homestead Street is south of and parallel to Gorsuch Avenue.)
 C: 406 27th Street (Katherine Boyle Goldrick Household – 1900)
 D: 706 23rd Street (Katherine Boyle Goldrick Household – 1910)
 E: 812 22nd Street (1930 – Joseph Oberle & Katie Goldrick Household – 1930)

Union Memorial Hospital, where I was born, is in the upper left of the map.

Catherine Goldrick becomes Katie with a "K"

My grandmother's given name and date of birth seem to have been the subjects of many discussions within the family. My father and several others in the family insisted that Grandmom Oberle was born on 10 March 1882, but her baptismal certificate from Saint Ann's Church on 22nd Street in Baltimore (see the illustration on the right) states that she was born on 10 March 1884. It's possible, although not likely, that her baptism was delayed long enough that her parents felt the need to "fib" about her year of birth, but it seems more likely that, if she did tell her children that she was born in 1882, it may have been to perpetuate a fib of her own when she first began working.

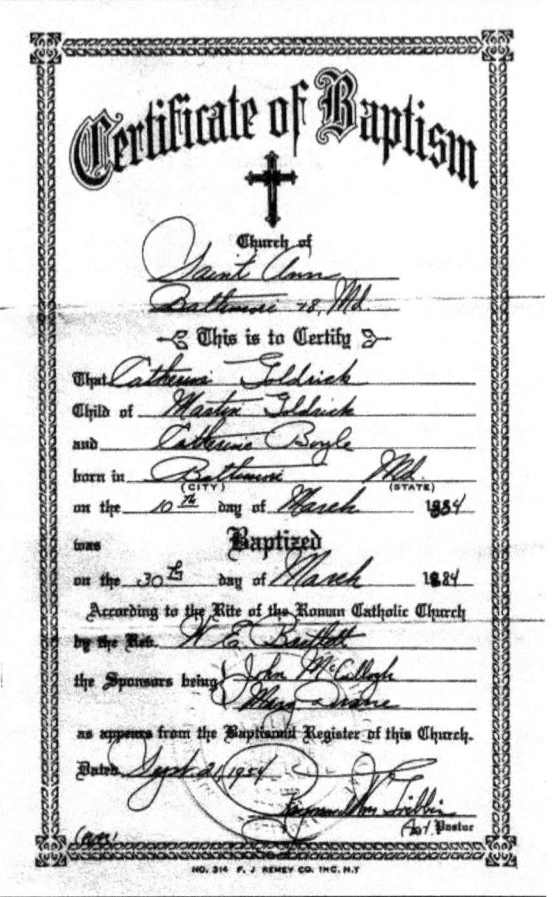

Catherine Goldrick's Baptismal Certificate from St. Ann's

After completing high school in about 1900, Katie took a job with the Richardson Insurance Agency, and quickly became secretary to a vice-president of that corporation. She would have been about 16 years old then, and was still living at her mother's home at 406 27th Street in Baltimore.

At 10:48 am on the morning of 7 February 1904, a fire alarm went off at the John E. Hurst & Company on German Street in downtown Baltimore. The fire, which appeared at first to be relatively insignificant, quickly engulfed most of the downtown area and the docks of the inner harbor. With the aid of fire equipment from seven additional cities, including some heroic efforts by Philadelphia fire fighters to save the docks, the fire was finally contained after twenty-eight hours, although it took several weeks to completely extinguish all of the fire's remnants.

Family stories say that, as a result of her role with the insurance agency, Catherine (probably *Katherine* by then – more about that change in the next paragraph) Goldrick became the first female permitted into the destroyed areas of downtown Baltimore. A March 1884 date of birth would have made her just under 21 years old at the time. Given that she must have had some proven experience in order to take part in on-scene activities, it seems likely that she had been working for the insurance company for at least a few years and, if so, we should consider that her superiors may have believed she was almost 23 years old. It is also interesting to note that her future husband was born in 1887, and she would therefore seem to have had some good reason for making her age seem even closer to his than it actually was.

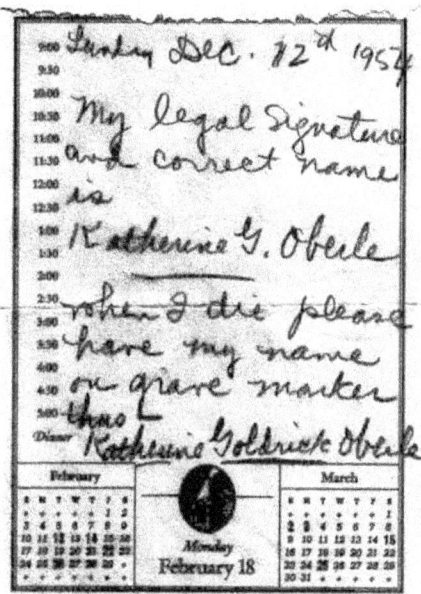

The discussion about Grandmom's given name has always been whether it was spelled with an initial "C" or "K." As late as the 1900 U.S. Census, after her father died and her mother Catherine was head-of-household, Grandmom, then listed as age 15, was still known as Catherine – spelled with a "C."

She clearly wanted to be known as Katherine, however. It isn't known how old she was when the nicknames Katie or Kaddie[103] began to be used. My mother knew her name as "Katie" from the time she met my father, so the "K" was well established by the late 1930s. Nonetheless, four months after Granddad's death in 1954 she still apparently felt compelled to write the note on the left for her children, which was still in my father's possession at the time of his death in October 2004.

Her grave marker at New Cathedral Cemetery, marked as she wished after her death in 1975, is shown on the right. Note the 1884 birth year, which is consistent with the Baptismal Certificate shown earlier!

Katie is shown in a photograph below with her future husband Joe Oberle.

---

[103] The Oberle side all called her Katie; her Rinn and Dunn nieces and nephews called her "Aunt Kaddie."

The notations on the photograph, which was in Anna Oberle Jelks' photo album, identify her as "Katie Goldrick," so it must have been taken prior to her marriage.

Katie Goldrick and Joe Oberle circa 1911 or 1912

Katie was not known for being shy. Tom Jelks said that every Sunday, the extended family would come for a visit to the Gorsuch Avenue home, and Seraphin would go down in the cellar and bring up a glass of his homemade wine[104] for each of the men.

While Katie and Joe were going together, they visited and Seraphin served wine to each of the men. Katie asked him "how come only the men get wine?" In his usual gruff tone, he said "You Vant Vine?" Katie responded, "Yes." Seraphin looked at her for a bit and then went down again and brought up a glass of wine for her. According to Tom, Katie was the only woman ever to get served wine at Seraphin's house, and he always included her from then on.

Joseph Oberle & Katherine Goldrick

My Granddad Joseph Oberle grew up at 1114 Gorsuch Avenue in the Waverly section of Baltimore. Although this part of Baltimore is thoroughly urban today, it wasn't unusual for families in the area to own livestock in the late nineteenth and early twentieth centuries. One of Joe's recurring chores when he was young was to milk the Oberle's cow each morning; according to family stories, Joe and the cow never got along well, and he was quite uncomfortable with the early morning visits to the back yard. Granddad also helped his mother Sarah occasionally when she churned butter from the milk.

My father reported that, later in life, Granddad refused to eat any butter at all. My Dad didn't know for sure, but said he always suspected that there was a cause-effect relation between this distaste and his father's childhood chores.

Granddad's formal education ended with only two years of Academic High School at Loyola College in Baltimore. Several small reproductions of pages from Loyola's year-end commencement booklets shown on the following page suggest that he was an excellent student.

---

[104] See page 77 for Seraphin's wine "recipe" (sort of).

LOYOLA COLLEGE, 1901-1902. 67

In the Class of Second Academic
THE GOLD MEDAL
was awarded to
JOSEPH C. HIMMEL.

Premium . . . . CLARKE J. FITZPATRICK.
Distinguished . . . . J. Walter McNeill,
                              Edward L. Koontz.
Honorably Mentioned . . . . . J. Readmond Guy,
                              Raymond J. Jenkins.

In the Class of English Composition.

Cross of Honor . . . . EDWARD L. KOONTZ.
Distinguished . . . . J. Walter McNeill,
                              Clarke J. Fitzpatrick,
                              William F. Schwartz,
                              Raymond J. Jenkins,
                              Joseph C. Himmel,
                              Andrew J. Groeninger.
Honorably Mentioned . . . . . J. Readmond Guy.

In the Class of Third Academic
THE GOLD MEDAL
was awarded to
ROMAN F. WELZANT.

Premium . . . . CHARLES E. ROACH.
Distinguished . . . . Joseph F. Oberle.
Honorably Mentioned . . . . . Emil G. Reitz.

1901-1902 Loyola College (H.S.) Booklet, page 67

---

68 LOYOLA COLLEGE, 1902-1903.

In the Class of Higher Algebra
THE SILVER MEDAL
was awarded to
VICTOR I. COOK.
Honorably Mentioned.
William T. Connor,   Charles E. Roach.

MODERN LANGUAGES
French.

Premium . . . . HARRY A. PREVOST.
Distinguished . . . . Francis J. Loughran.
Honorably Mentioned.
Edward L. Koontz.   John F. Clary.

German.

Premium . . . . JOSEPH C. HIMMEL.
Distinguished.
William M. Kennedy, Godfrey F. Kaspar,   Joseph F. Oberle,
Victor I. Cook,   Edward H. Burke,   John T. Griffin,
Clarke J. FitzPatrick, Charles C. Conlon, Francis J. Ayd,
Joseph J. Kocyan,   William T. Connor,   Bernard J. McNamara.
Honorably Mentioned.
Walter F. X. Cunningham,   Thomas J. Toolen,   Leo Lochman.

1902-1903 Loyola College (H.S.) Booklet, page 68

LOYOLA COLLEGE, 1902-1903. 69

ACADEMIC CLASSES.

In the Class of First Academic
THE GOLD MEDAL
(The Gift of MISS ANNIE HOLLOHAN, in memory of Rev. John S. Hollohan, S. J.)
was awarded to
CLARKE J. FITZPATRICK.

Premium . . . . VICTOR I. COOK.
English Composition.
Cross of Honor . . . . VICTOR I. COOK.
Distinguished.
Clarke J. FitzPatrick,   Walter J. McNeill.
Honorably Mentioned.
Moorhouse X. Millar,   Edward L. Koontz.

In the Class of Second Academic
THE GOLD MEDAL
(The Gift of the REV. JAMES A. CUNNINGHAM)
was awarded to
CHARLES E. ROACH.

Premium . . . . WILLIAM J. WELSH.
Arthur J. Smith,   Joseph F. Oberle.
Distinguished.
English Composition.
Cross of Honor . . . . CHARLES E. ROACH.
Distinguished.
William J. Welsh, Arthur J. Smith, Joseph F. Oberle.

George L. Strohaver was promoted to this class at the mid-term examination; his promotion is equivalent to the honors of the class from which he passed.

1902-1903 Loyola College (H.S.) Booklet, page 69

LOYOLA COLLEGE, 1902-1903. 71

MATHEMATICS.
In the Class of Geometry.
THE SILVER MEDAL
was awarded to
GEORGE F. STROHAVER.

Premium . . . . CLARKE J. FITZPATRICK.
Distinguished.
Arthur J. Smith,   Joseph C. Himmel.
Honorably Mentioned.   Francis J. Loughran.

In the Class of Algebra, Section A.

Cross of Honor . . . . JOHN L. STEWART.
Premium, *ex aequo.*
Francis A. Warner,   Eugene I. Higgins,   Bernard Link.
Distinguished.
Joseph F. Oberle,   William L. Galvin,
John Griffin,   Edward K. Hanlon
William H. Welsh.

In the Class of Algebra, Section B.

Premium . . . . JOSEPH A. WOENY.
Distinguished . . . . Joseph W. Tewes.
Honorably Mentioned.
John T. Hamberry,   John Kmieciak.

In the Class of Arithmetic.

Premium . . . . HORACE BRADLEY.
Distinguished . . . . V. Leonard Keelan.

MODERN LANGUAGES.
In the Class of German.

Premium . . . . EMIL G. REITZ.
Distinguished.
Charles E. Roach, George F. Strohaver, William H. Welsh,
Arthur J. Smith,   L. Frank O'Brien.

1902-1903 Loyola College (H.S.) Booklet, page 71

Upon graduation, Joe began working for the Citizen's Bank of Baltimore; he and his brother Jake were both employed there as telephone operators and runners by March 1905.

Although Joe and Katie didn't live very far from each other while growing up, and both were in Saint Ann's Catholic parish, it isn't known when or how they first met, or when they became engaged.

By 1910, however, they seemed to have been at least an unofficial couple. The picture on the right shows the two of them taken, oddly enough in light of their clothing, at an oceanfront boardwalk photography shop. Such photos were provided to the customers in the form of postcards, which were common souvenirs at the time.

Atlantic City – Postcard of Katie and Joe

Another early postcard of Joe and Katie

On the fifteenth of April in 1913, Joe and Katie were married at St. Ann's Church. They purchased the house at 812 22nd Street down the street with a $4,000 mortgage, so they continued to live, at least for a time, in the neighborhood where they grew up.

Their first child, Joseph id201, was born on March 1st 1914 – the year the Panama Canal was completed. "Aunt Mamie" Rinn, Katie's oldest sister, made a christening dress for the new baby that was subsequently used not only by him, but also by his siblings and several later generations.[105] On the 13th of November 1915, Katie gave birth to their second child Katherine id202 [106], who immediately became known as "Sis" – the only name I ever heard her called.

---

[105] Including, I am told, by me. I have pictures of my cousin Nan (Joe's daughter) and my Father in the outfit, and my Mother says that several of my Miller cousins wore it for their baptisms as well. My cousin Nan still has this gown.

[106] Unlike her Mother, she was born with a "K." Katherine was almost universally known (in the family) as "Sis."

By that time, the U.S. banking industry was undergoing one of its periodic consolidations. The original First National Bank of Baltimore was liquidated in 1916, and its assets acquired by the National Mechanics Bank. Since 1863, the United States Government had "chartered" a number of the most stable regional banks to become "National Banks," with authority to issue currency. The third of these charters began in 1902, and the Citizen's National Bank, where Granddad worked, had begun issuing their first series of these in 1909.

On June 28th 1914, while Katie was still pregnant with her second child Katherine, Archduke Francis Ferdinand, heir presumptive to the crown of the Austro-Hungarian Empire, was assassinated in Sarajevo. By 1916, the resulting "war to end all wars" (World War I) had spread across Europe, involving England, Russia, and several other countries not at that time usually associated with Europe. There were a significant number of Americans participating as volunteers with the French and English forces in a variety of roles, but up until late 1916, the United States had limited its official participation to providing supplies and materiel to support the western allies.

This changed on 6 April 1917, when the U. S. declared war on Germany, and began preparing to send troops. The Selective Service Act of 1917 was passed, and a schedule for registration was published. Joseph's birth date required him to register for the draft on June 5th of that year. On March 17th, he had just become Assistant Cashier for the Citizen's National Bank.

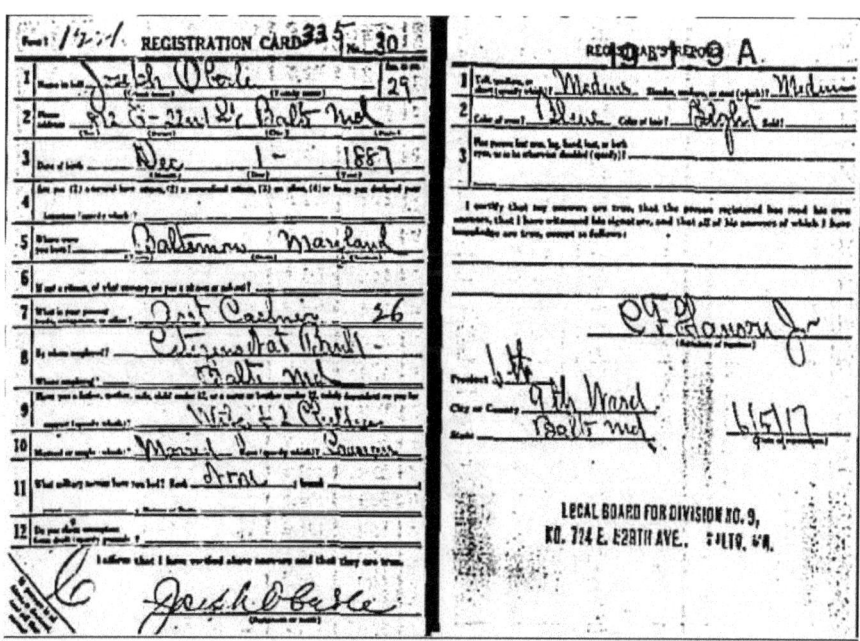

Joseph Oberle's World War I Draft Registration Card of 5 June 1917

A third draft registration, for all males aged 18-45, was set for 12 September 1918. Joe's older brother Jake had died suddenly in the 1918 "Spanish Flu" (aka "Swine Flu") epidemic, but his other older brothers Seraphin and Frank registered during this cycle, and their draft cards are shown below:

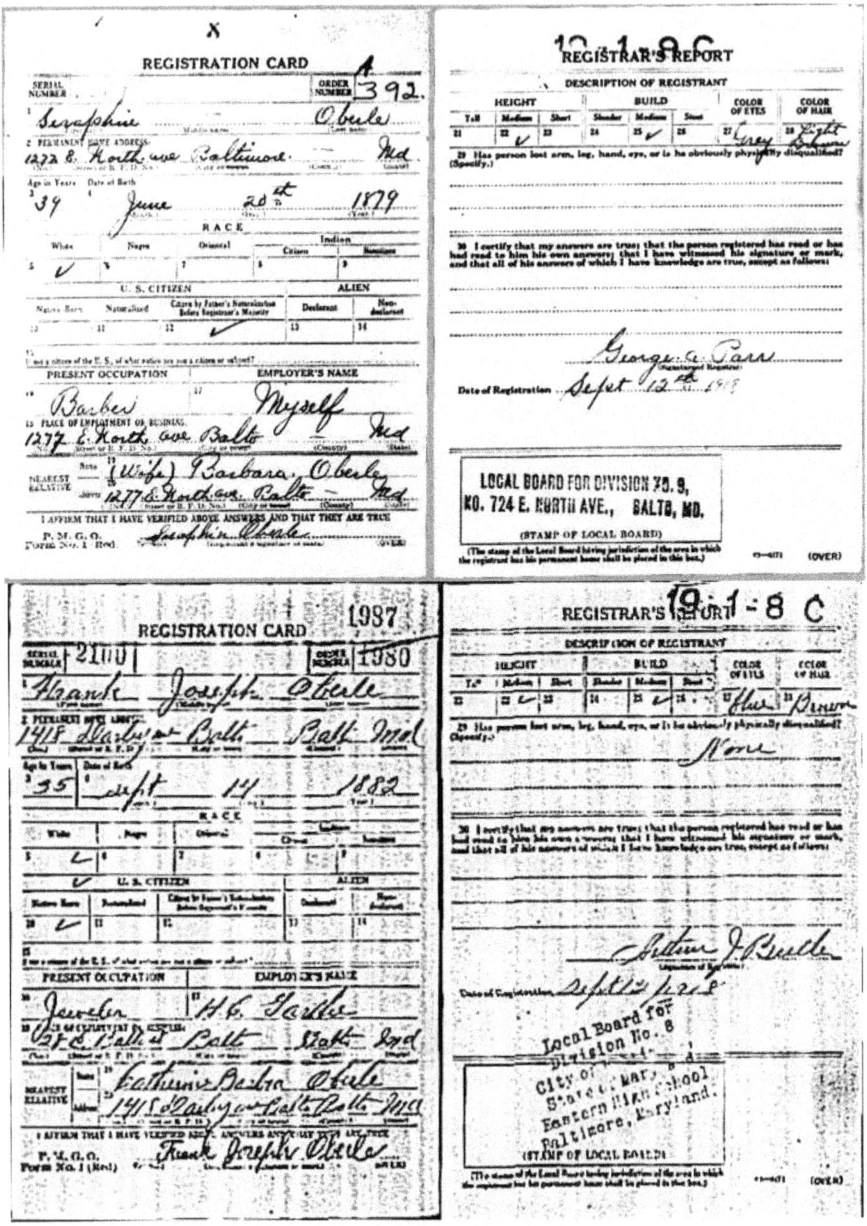
REGISTRATION CARD

SERIAL NUMBER — ORDER NUMBER A 392.

1 Seraphine Oberle

2 PERMANENT HOME ADDRESS: 1272 E. North ave Baltimore Md

Age in Years 39 — Date of Birth June 20th 1879

RACE: White ✓

U. S. CITIZEN: Citizen by Father's Naturalization Before Registrant's Majority ✓

PRESENT OCCUPATION: Barber — EMPLOYER'S NAME: Myself

PLACE OF EMPLOYMENT OR BUSINESS: 1277 E. North ave Balto Md

NEAREST RELATIVE: (Wife) Barbara Oberle, 1277 E. North ave. Balto Md

I AFFIRM THAT I HAVE VERIFIED ABOVE ANSWERS AND THAT THEY ARE TRUE

Seraphin Oberle

P. M. G. O. Form No. 1 (Red) (OVER)

REGISTRAR'S REPORT

DESCRIPTION OF REGISTRANT

Height: Medium ✓ — Build: Medium ✓ — Color of Eyes: Grey — Color of Hair: Light Brown

29 Has person lost arm, leg, hand, eye, or is he obviously physically disqualified? (Specify.)

30 I certify that my answers are true; that the person registered has read or has had read to him his own answers; that I have witnessed his signature or mark, and that all of his answers of which I have knowledge are true, except as follows:

George A. Parr (Signature of Registrar)

Date of Registration Sept 12th 1918

LOCAL BOARD FOR DIVISION NO. 9, NO. 724 E. NORTH AVE., BALTO, MD.

(STAMP OF LOCAL BOARD)

(The stamp of the Local Board having jurisdiction of the area in which the registrant has his permanent home shall be placed in this box.) (OVER)

REGISTRATION CARD 1987

SERIAL NUMBER 2100 — ORDER NUMBER 1980

1 Frank Joseph Oberle

2 PERMANENT HOME ADDRESS: 1418 Darley ave Balto Balt Md

Age in Years 35 — Date of Birth Sept 14 1882

RACE: White ✓

U. S. CITIZEN: Native Born ✓

PRESENT OCCUPATION: Jeweler — EMPLOYER'S NAME: H. C. Tarthe

PLACE OF EMPLOYMENT OR BUSINESS: 21 E Balto st Balt Balto Md

NEAREST RELATIVE: Catherine Barbara Oberle, 1418 Darley ave Balto Balto Md

I AFFIRM THAT I HAVE VERIFIED ABOVE ANSWERS AND THAT THEY ARE TRUE

Frank Joseph Oberle

P. M. G. O. Form No. 1 (Red) (OVER)

REGISTRAR'S REPORT 19-1-8 C

DESCRIPTION OF REGISTRANT

Height: Medium ✓ — Build: Medium ✓ — Color of Eyes: Blue — Color of Hair: Brown

29 Has person lost arm, leg, hand, eye, or is he obviously physically disqualified? (Specify.) None

30 I certify that my answers are true; that the person registered has read or has had read to him his own answers; that I have witnessed his signature or mark, and that all of his answers of which I have knowledge are true, except as follows:

Arthur J. Beutle (Signature of Registrar)

Date of Registration Sept 12 1918

Local Board for Division No. 8, City of Baltimore, State of Maryland, Eastern High School, Baltimore, Maryland.

(STAMP OF LOCAL BOARD)

(The stamp of the Local Board having jurisdiction of the area in which the registrant has his permanent home shall be placed in this box.) (OVER)

Seraphin and Frank Oberle's World War I Draft Registration Cards of 12 September 1918

My grandfather Joseph's draft card tells us that he had bright hair, blue eyes, and was of medium height and build. He was never drafted, however, and was still at home when Katie had their third child (my father) Cornelius id196 on September 25th that year. Joe was evidently doing very well, as evidenced by the promotion to Assistant Cashier, a relatively high management position for a twenty-nine year old tenth grader who began as a telephone operator.

In 1919, Joseph was appointed Cashier of the Citizen's National Bank of Baltimore by the bank's Board of Directors. The picture on the next page, from one of the bank's annual reports, shows the office space he and his staff occupied.

Babe Ruth Strikes Out

In his capacity as a bank officer, Joseph often escorted important clients to ball games and introduced them to players and other sports figures, and this was supposedly how he obtained the baseball with Babe Ruth's autograph that was displayed in his home when my cousins and I were children. My parents later displayed this ball in their home and my Mother continued to do so in the independent living apartment she moved to after my Dad's death.

When I decided to photograph the ball in 2009, however, it seemed to be a lot cleaner than I recalled, and when I compared my photos with ones taken by my Dad back in 1998, many other differences became apparent.

My photograph of the baseball taken in April of 2009 at my Mother's apartment in the retirement community where she was then living.

It was quite obviously not the same ball that had been displayed at my parents' home in Bel Air.

Dad's Photo of Babe Ruth Baseball taken on 15 March 1998

Note: differences in formation of "e" (fifth letter) in "Sincerely";
Note: the descender of the "y" in "Sincerely" crosses the "R" in "Ruth" in a different location;
Note: different flourish at bottom of first "B" in "Babe";
Note: different width on bottom of second "b" in "Babe";
Note: different tilt on "e" at end of "Babe";
Note: different spacing between "e" in "Babe" and "R" in "Ruth";
.... and the kicker ....
Note: the different direction of the stiches on the side of the signatures (arrows down on original; up on current ball).

1998 to 2009 – The Vanishing Babe Ruth Baseball

This discovery was annoying, but tempered by the fact that further examination of my Dad's photograph suggested that that ball may not have been genuine either, as it had some anachronisms of its own. *Sic transit gloria Babe...*

In 1921, about two years after his appointment as Cashier, the Citizen's National Bank issued the last of the large size United States currency in what was known as the "Third issue of the Third Charter Period (series 1902)." In his role as Cashier, Joseph's signature can be found on all the notes from this and subsequent National Bank Note issues. Examples of these and other notes signed by Granddad can be found in Appendix V, beginning on page 203.

Office of Cashier/Vice-President in the Citizen's National Bank Building

The photograph to the right is from 1919, and shows Katie holding her son Cornelius id196 ("Cornie"), with her daughter Katherine id202 ("Sis") and oldest son Joe id201 standing.

On the following page is a set of pictures taken in about 1920, and showing all of the family members.

The first three pictures were taken in the back yard of the home at 812 22nd Street in Baltimore.

The location of the other pictures is unknown. In the absence of any indication to the contrary, I am assuming that these photographs were all taken by Joe and/or Katie themselves.

Baltimore – 1919 Photo of Katie and her Kids

Left:
Baltimore – circa 1920: Cornie, Sis, & Joe Oberle

Right:
Baltimore – circa 1920: Cornie, Joe, & Sis

Left:
Baltimore – circa 1920: Cornie, Joe, & Sis

Right:
Baltimore – circa 1920: Katie, Cornie, Sis, & Joe

Left:
Baltimore – circa 1920: Sis, Cornie, Joe, & Joe Jr.

Right:
Baltimore – circa 1923: Cornie & Sis

1711-1975 HISTORY

The U.S. Census of 1920[107], showing the family living at their home on 22nd Street in Baltimore, is shown on the following page:

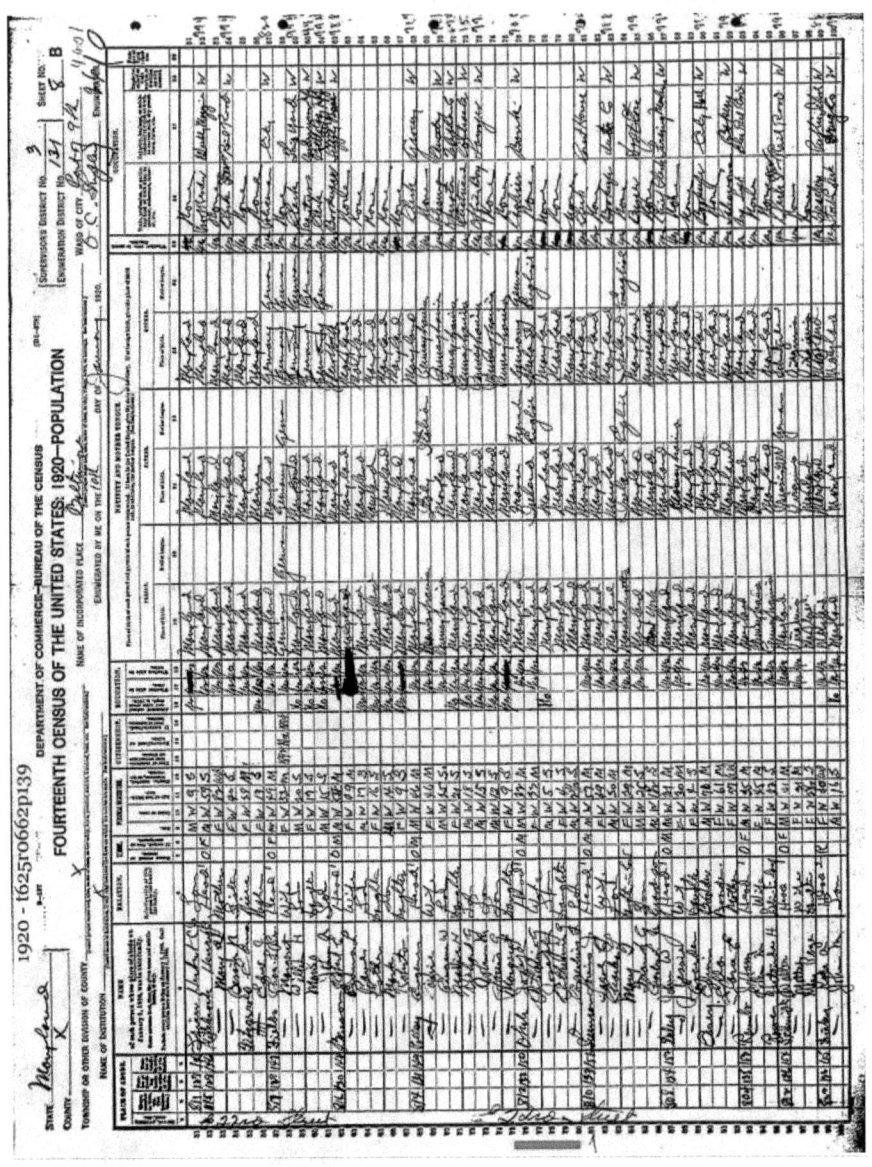

Baltimore – 1920 U.S. Census showing family of Joseph Oberle

My grandfather Joseph [id81] says here that his father Seraphin came from France, and his mother from Germany.

---
[107] National Archives Series t625 Roll 662 Page 139

On February 20th of 1923, Katie gave birth to their fourth and last child, Francis id197, at their home on 22nd Street. Francis was premature, and weighed less than four pounds, which at that time meant that his chances of survival were not very good. The attending physician advised Grandmom to "let him go," but she shooed the doctor away, picked the baby up, and began to breast-feed him. He lived for another seventy-four years. The stubborn streak she was known for apparently extended to most areas of her life.

Now that Joe and Katie had four children, and his career was established, they built a new home[108] in the exclusive area of Pinehurst, north of Baltimore – quite a ways north of their old neighborhood.

When they moved into the new home at 213 Midhurst Road on May 6, 1926, their son Joseph was twelve years old, Katherine (or Sis, as she was known) ten, Cornie eight, and Francis a little over three.

Baltimore – 1926: the new home at 213 Midhurst Rd. on move-in day.
Joe and Katie Oberle move into the new family home with their four children on May 6th

An early photograph of the house is shown above. On the side porch, from left to right[109] are my Dad Cornelius id126, Granddad's older brother Frank id45, Granddad id81, Uncle Joe id201, Grandmom (seated) id80, and Aunt Sis id200.

---

[108] The home was purchased for $16,750.00 and was the first "detached" home in the family. That amount equates $214,831.57 in 2012 dollars, but was a substantial price for a home in 1926.

[109] This is an educated guess on my part as to the identities of the folks on the porch, but older family members I've contacted seem to believe it is reasonable.

Before the move from 22nd Street to Midhurst Road, the three oldest children had been attending St. Ann's school in Baltimore, but beginning in the 1926-27 school year, they began attending Immaculate Conception Parochial School in Towson.

In 1928, the National Mechanics Bank (charter #1413), which had earlier assumed the assets of the shuttered First National Bank of Baltimore, merged with Citizen's National Bank of Baltimore, and renamed the combined entity the First National Bank of Baltimore.

Granddad remained Cashier of the newly formed First National Bank of Baltimore after the merger, and on 10 July 1929, when the first of the new, smaller, currency was issued, he signed all these as well.

Because of the Bank's solidity and Joseph's now senior position, the family was relatively unaffected by the stock market crash of 1929 and the subsequent depression.

A picture of Joe and Katie's family in the 1930s, but without their oldest son Joe, is shown above right.

*Baltimore – mid-1930s: The Oberle Family
Francis, Granddad, Cornelius, Grandmom and Sis*

Granddad Oberle driving his 1931 Dodge with "Sis" and "Cornie."

On the 1930 Census, the first taken after their move to Midhurst Road, Joe's age was reported as 46, not quite consistent with a late 1887 year of birth. Katie's age was given as 44, even less consistent with either an 1882 or 1884 year of birth. The ages of the children were closer to reality, given as 16, 14, 12 and 7 respectively.

See an image of this census sheet on the next page.

Baltimore – 1930 U.S. Census showing family of Joseph Oberle
National Archives Series t626 Roll 846 Page 109

Joe and Katie's oldest son Joseph Jr. and their daughter Katherine were now teenagers, and their son Cornelius was not far behind. The youngest, Francis, had just reached school age. Through the 1930s, the family remained well off compared to the many who were suffering the effects of the great depression. By the end of the decade, however, the inevitability of our involvement in the growing European war began to be apparent to intelligent Americans.

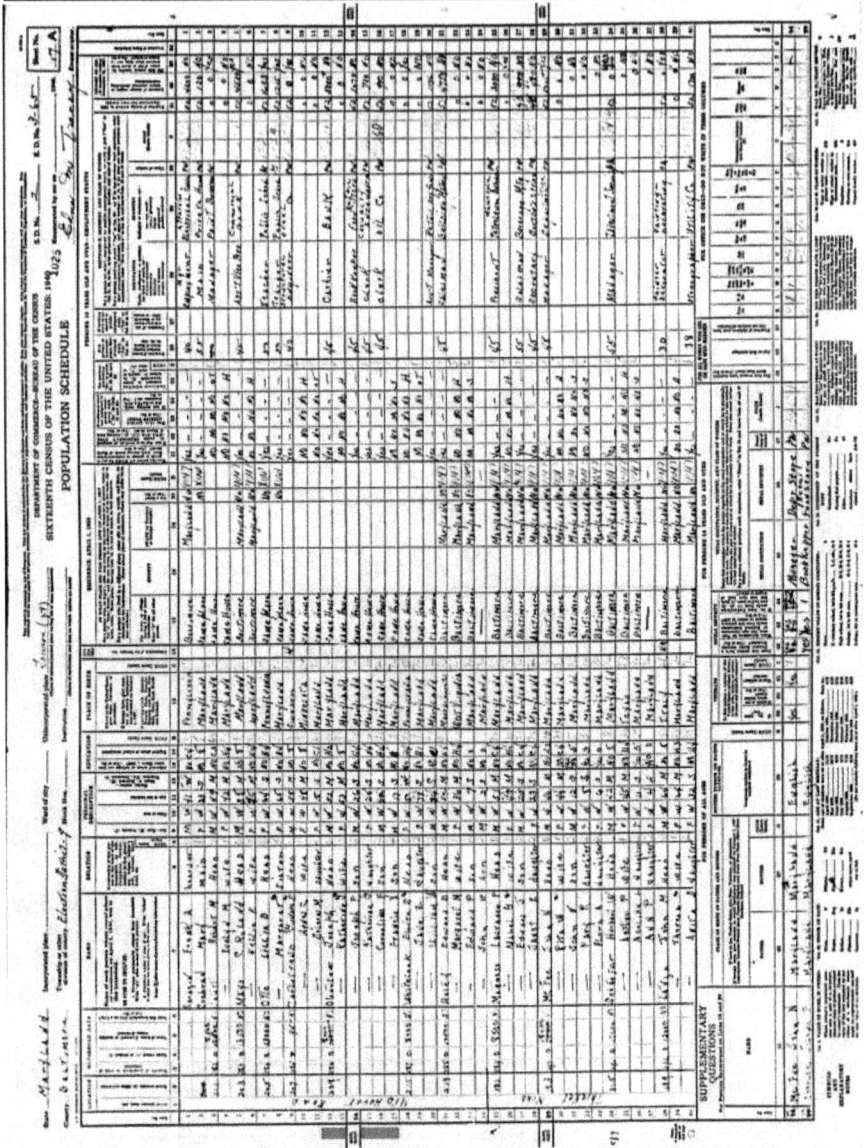

Baltimore – 1940 U.S. Census showing family of Joseph Oberle
National Archives Series t627 Roll 1505 Page 17a

By 1940, the U.S. Census (above) shows that the three oldest Oberle children had completed high school, and were working full time.

Joe & Katie's Family during World War II

When the attack on Pearl Harbor precipitated the direct involvement of the United States, Joe and Katie's son Cornelius was already in the military – later to be joined by Joe and Francis as the war progressed. Joe was stationed in Washington, D.C. area, and Francis eventually served during the Allied sweep through Belgium and France. My father Cornelius' service in the Pacific and Francis' experiences in Europe will be discussed later in this book.

Much has been written about the conditions in both theaters of operation. Of particular interest to our family is the book "Memoirs of a Combat Infantry Soldier" (shown to the left), by my Dad's first cousin Thomas Oberle Jelks id182, a career military infantryman and officer who also served in Europe during World War II. There is, therefore, no need to describe these years any further here, except to mention what was then known colloquially as the "Old Men's Draft."

Due to concerns about the progress of the war, preparations were made to draft older individuals into the military, and a fourth draft requiring the registration of all males born between 28 April 1877 and 16 February 1897 was established. Granddad was 54 years old when he filled out the draft registration form below. He was (again) not drafted.

Tom Jelks Book Cover

The only wartime correspondence among Joe, Katie, and their children that has survived (at least that I'm aware of) consists mostly of short "V-Mails" written by Katie or her daughter Katherine (Sis), and has significant passages describing the activities, fates and fears of friends and neighbors who were also overseas. But, all the Oberle boys survived World War II safely.

Joe, Katie, Joe, Jr. and Sis in back yard at Midhurst Road

The photograph on the left, in the garden behind the house at 213 Midhurst Road, seems to have been taken at a family gathering shortly before World War II, and shows Joe and Katie seated with their children Joe and Katherine ("Sis") standing behind them.

My Grandmother's garden was quite elaborate, with a trellised entryway and stone benches along a winding path (unfortunately I've been unable to locate any photographs that do it justice). Although she was only 12 years old when her father Martin died, his horticultural influence seemed to have left its mark.

The picture on the right, also taken in the garden behind the house on Midhurst Road, shows Joe, Katherine ("Sis") and Francis, and appears to have been taken on the same day as the one shown above[110]. These pictures were both taken by my father Cornelius.

Joe, Jr., Sis and Francis in back yard at Midhurst Road

---

[110] Joe and Sis are wearing the same clothing in both.

The Post-World War II Years

In January of 1945, shortly before World War II ended, Granddad was elected as Vice-President of the First National Bank (see clipping below), and remained in that capacity until his retirement due to illness in February of 1953.

J. D. Harrison New President First National

By J. S. ARMSTRONG
[*Financial Editor of The Sun*]

James D. Harrison was elected president of the First National Bank of Baltimore at the annual meeting of the board of directors yesterday. He succeeds Morton M. Prentis who was made vice chairman of the board. Albert D. Graham continues chairman of the board and chief executive of the bank.

James W. McElroy was moved up from vice president to first vice president, replacing Mr. Harrison in the latter position.

Joseph Oberle was promoted from cashier to vice president and was succeeded as cashier by Harper R. Clark, formerly an assistant cashier.

Mr. Harrison started his banking career in 1908 at Danville, Va., where he served as cashier of the American National Bank. He came to Baltimore in 1923 as vice president of the former Citizens National Bank, becoming senior vice president of the First National when that bank was formed in 1928 out of the merger of the Citizens and Merchants banks.

Mr. Prentis started in the banking business with the Third National at St. Louis and later joined the former National Bank of Commerce at Norfolk. He served as a national bank examiner for eight years and became manager of the Baltimore Federal Reserve Branch when it was opened in 1918. Mr. Prentis was elected vice president of the Merchants National in 1922 and became its president two years later, continuing as president of the First National when the merger occurred in 1928.

Entering the banking business in 1910, Mr. McElroy served with several local banks and with the Federal Reserve until 1923 when he became associated with the Merchants National. He later became a vice president of that bank and continued to serve as a vice president of the First National when the consolidation took place. Mr. McElroy is a former president of the Maryland Bankers Association and has been active in the affairs of the American Bankers Association.

Mr. Oberle started with the Citizens National in 1905 and after serving in various positions with that bank was made assistant cashier in 1917, advancing to cashier in 1919 and continuing in that post with the First National.

Mr. Clark, new cashier of the First National, has been in the banking business 22 years, serving as assistant cashier since 1940.

Baltimore Morning Sun: 11 Jan 1945

In addition to his position with the First National Bank, Granddad was also on the Board of Directors of the St. James Savings Bank and was secretary-treasurer of the Maryland Bankers' Association.

It is said that a person's eyes are the only place in the human body where the condition of the blood vessels can be clearly observed. An alert ophthalmologist can spot signs of incipient diabetic conditions, hypertension, and even evidence of recent minor stroke activity while examining a patient – even one with no other apparent symptoms. This was the case with Granddad, whose eye doctor, during a routine examination, told him "Joe, I don't like what I see in your eyes," and urged him to see a specialist – a warning that Granddad shrugged off.

He suffered a major stroke a short time later, and became confined to bed at home. On Thursday 19 August 1954, the day he died, we went to Midhurst Road to visit him and Grandmom. When we arrived, there was an unusual number of cars outside the house, so my Dad Cornelius went in alone. He then came back outside and told us that Granddad had just died.

Joseph Oberle, Banker Here, Dies At 67

Joseph Oberle, former vice-president of the First National Bank and widely known in financial circles here, died yesterday following a long illness, at the age of sixty-seven.

Mr. Oberle became cashier of the First National in 1928, when that bank was formed by the merger of the Citizens' National Bank and the Merchants' National, and was elected to the vice-presidency in January, 1945.

He had been cashier of the Citizens' National since 1919, having been with that bank since March, 1905, when he was eighteen.

• • •

MR. OBERLE is survived by his wife, Mrs. Katherine Goldrich Oberle; a daughter, Mrs. Katherine Miller; three sons, Joseph, Jr., Cornelius and Francis, and six grandchildren.

He lived in the 200 block Midhurst road. Funeral services will be held Monday in the Immaculate Conception Church, Towson.

JOSEPH OBERLE

Funeral services for Joe Oberle, retired vice president the First National Bank, were held Monday at the Church of the Immaculate Conception, Towson. Mr. Oberle died last Thursday at his home, 213 Midhurst road, after a long illness. He was 66 years old.

The Rt. Rev. Msgr. Joseph M. Nelligan, pastor, offered the High Mass of Requiem. Present in the sanctuary were the Rev:, Thomas J. Mardaga and Martin A. Schwalenberg.

Born in Baltimore, Mr. Oberle attended St. Ann's Parochial School and was graduated from Loyola College. He joined the staff of the old Citizens National Bank as telephone operator in 1905. In 1919, after holding a number of posts, he became cashier. When the bank was merged with the Merchants Bank in 1928 to form the First National Bank, Mr. Oberle retained his position. In 1945 he was elected vice president, a post he held actively until his retirement in February last year.

For many years he was active in the Maryland Bankers Association, serving as secretary-treasurer. In 1951 he became secretary-treasurer emeritus. He was president of the International Permanent Building and Loan Association of Baltimore and a director of the St. James Savings Bank.

He was also an active member of the Church of the Immaculate Conception and a member of the Holy Name Society.

Mr. Oberle is survived by his wife, Katherine Goldrick Oberle; a daughter, Mrs. Katherine Miller; three sons, Joseph, jr., Cornelius and Francis, and six grandchildren. All of Baltimore.

Burial was in New Cathedral Cemetery.

Obituary

Joseph Oberle

Funeral services for Joseph Oberle, 66-year-old retired vice president of the First National Bank, who died on Thursday, will be held at 10 A.M. Monday, at the Church of the Immaculate Conception in Towson.

Mr. Oberle, who lived at 213 Midhurst road, joined the predecessor of the First National Bank in 1905, shortly after his graduation from Loyola College.

He was elected vice president in 1945, a position he held until his retirement eight years later.

Mr. Oberle was active in the Maryland Bankers Association, serving as its secretary-treasurer. He was president of the International Permanent Savings and Loan Association and a director of the St. James Bank.

He was also an active member of the Church of the Immaculate Conception and a member of the Holy Name Society at the Towson church.

Mr. Oberle is survived by his wife, Katherine Goldrick Oberle; a daughter, Mrs. Katherine Miller, of Baltimore, and three sons, Joseph, Cornelius, and Francis, of this city.

Joseph Oberle (ID81)
Born 1 DEC 1887
Died 19 AUG 1954
Age at Death: 66y 8m 18d

Baltimore – 1954 Obituaries of Joseph Oberle
Various discrepancies in these are described in the following text.

The first obituary shown above lists his age as 67 and says that he was 18 years old in March of 1905; these facts are consistent with each other, but Granddad was actually only 17 when he started at the bank (and wouldn't have turned 18 until December of 1905). It also refers to Katie's name as "Goldrich" rather than "Goldrick."

Whoever annotated the top of the third obituary from the Baltimore Sun (apparently my father Cornelius) gave the date as Sunday August 21 (Sunday was actually August 22). It is therefore likely that this was from an early (Saturday afternoon) edition of the Sunday paper.

As was still the custom at the time, Granddad's wake and viewing were held at the house on Midhurst Road. His funeral was held at the Church of the Immaculate Conception in Towson, where he and Grandmom had been parishioners since 1926.

Katie and Joe in their garden in the early 1950s.
This, the last known photograph of the two, was taken by my father Cornelius.

Grandmom continued to live in the house on Midhurst Road, attended most days by her long-time housekeeper Mamie Stewart[111] until Mamie's death in 1955, and Granddad's 1940 Dodge remained unused in their garage until my cousin Ric Gonce id398 acquired it when the house was sold in 1974.

---

[111] Mamie, for whom I have fond memories, was the only person who was ever able to get me to eat tomatoes without disguising them as pizza, soup, or spaghetti sauce, since she prepared them fried and covered with sugar – something I only later learned was a traditional old "southern Negro" recipe.

As she grew older, Grandmom began showing signs of senility and eventually needed to be moved from Midhurst Road into a nursing home after several falls. The senility (probably what we now know as Alzheimer's) progressed after the move. Once, when my father Cornelius visited her there and asked if she knew who he was, she replied, "Of course; you're my brother – Jim" (James Goldrick id184 who

Katie Goldrick Oberle shortly before her death

had died in 1955). On 9 April 1975, Grandmom passed away and was buried with Granddad at New Cathedral Cemetery.

Many of the household items that Grandmom passed in her will[112] to her children and grandchildren are still in the family. Granddad's pocket watch, for instance, shown on the left, was passed to me with an exhortation from Grandmom in her Will to "keep the same for good luck."[113] Much of their silver service, furniture, and other items are still in use.

My inheritance – and still working!

---

[112] Copies of Joseph and Katherine Oberle's Wills and Codicils, as well as other related documents, are provided in the appendix beginning on page 219.

[113] See page three of her will, shown on page 232.

My Grandmother's death certificate, listing the cause as "generalized arteriosclerosis," is shown below.

STATE OF MARYLAND
DEPARTMENT OF HEALTH AND MENTAL HYGIENE
CERTIFICATE OF DEATH

1. DECEASED NAME: KATHERINE G. OBERLE
2a. DATE OF DEATH: APRIL 9, 1975 — 2b. HOUR: 12:25P
3. SEX: FEMALE — 4. RACE: WHITE — 5. DATE OF BIRTH: MARCH 10, 1884 — 6. AGE: 91
7a. BIRTHPLACE: MARYLAND — 7b. CITIZEN OF WHAT COUNTRY: U.S.A. — 8. WIDOWED [X] — 9. BALTIMORE CITY OR COUNTY OF DEATH: BALTIMORE CO.
10. CITY OR TOWN OF DEATH: TOWSON — 11. NAME OF HOSPITAL, NURSING HOME OR OTHER INSTITUTION: Dulaney Towson Nursing & Convalescent Home — 12a. USUAL OCCUPATION: Housewife
13a. STATE: MARYLAND — 13b. COUNTY: BALTIMORE — 13d. INSIDE CITY LIMITS: YES [X] — 13e. STREET ADDRESS: 213 Midhurst Road
14. FATHER'S NAME: MARTIN GOLDRICK — 15. MOTHER'S MAIDEN NAME: KATHERINE BOYLE
16a. WAS DECEASED EVER IN U.S. ARMED FORCES? NO — 16b. SOCIAL SECURITY NO.: 220-48-7270 — 17. INFORMANT: Dulaney Towson Nursing & Convalescent Home
18. CAUSE OF DEATH: IMMEDIATE CAUSE (a) ARTERIOSCLEROTIC HEART DISEASE; DUE TO, OR AS A CONSEQUENCE OF (b) GENERALIZED ARTERIOSCLEROSIS
21a. I certify that I attended the deceased from October 22, 1968 to April 9, 1975
Signature: T. C. Lewis[illegible] — ATTENDING PHYSICIAN [X]
22a. PHYSICIAN'S NAME: DR. THADDEUS STWINSKI — 22b. ADDRESS: 206 W. Pennsylvania Avenue Towson, Md. 21204 — 22c. DATE SIGNED: 4/10/75
23a. BURIAL, CREMATION, REMOVAL: Burial — 23b. DATE: 4/12/75 — 23c. NAME OF CEMETERY: New Cathedral Cem. — 23d. LOCATION: Baltimore Md. — 23e. DATE REC'D BY REGISTRAR: APR 14 1975
24. FUNERAL DIRECTOR: George J. Conce, 4001 Ritchie Hy. Baltimore

VALID ONLY WITH IMPRESSED SEAL
I HEREBY CERTIFY THAT THE ATTACHED IS A TRUE COPY OF A RECORD ON FILE IN THE DIVISION OF VITAL RECORDS.
APR 14 1975
DATE ISSUED
STATE REGISTRAR OF VITAL RECORDS
WARNING: IT IS ILLEGAL TO DUPLICATE THIS COPY BY PHOTOSTAT OR PHOTOGRAPH.

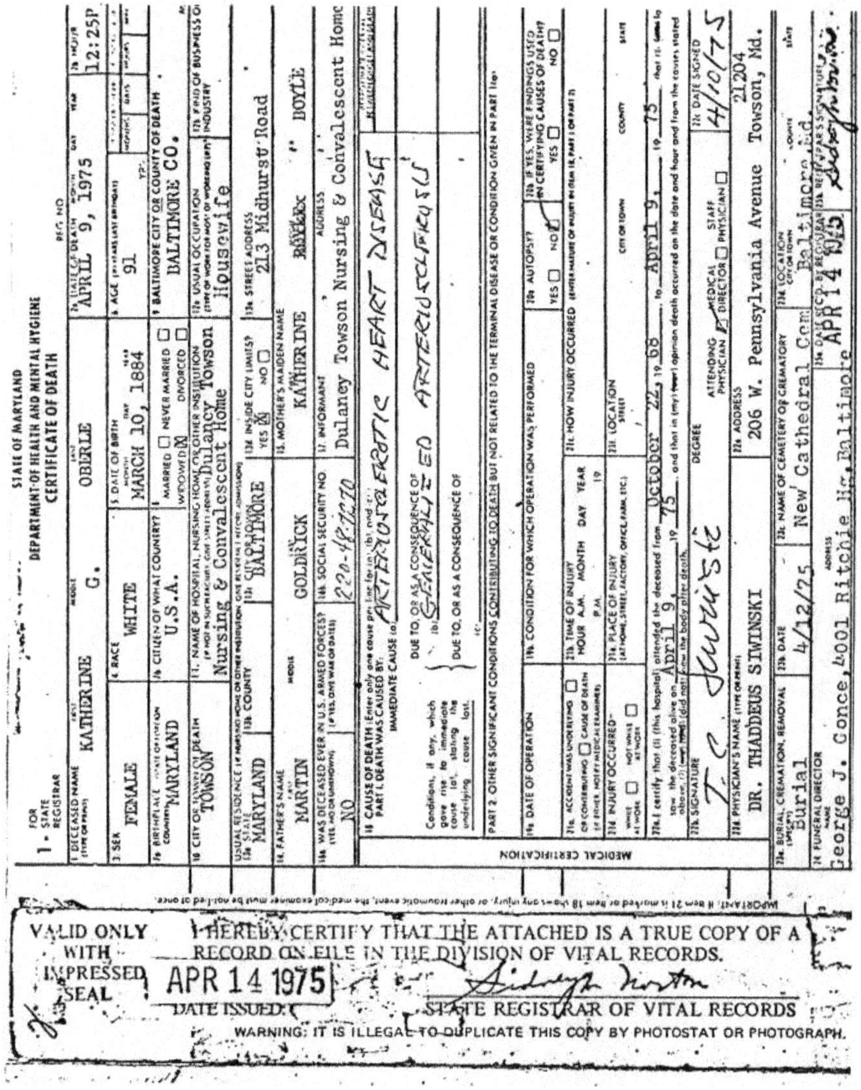

Baltimore – 1975 Death Certificate of Katherine G. Oberle

Mrs. Oberle mass set for today

A mass of Christian burial for Mrs. Joseph Oberle, Sr., widow of a banking executive, will be offered at 10 A.M today at Immaculate Conception Church, Baltimore and Ware avenues in Towson.

Mrs. Oberle, who was 91, died Wednesday at Dulaney Towson Nursing & Convalescent Home after a long illness. Before moving there six years ago, she lived at 213 Midhurst road.

A native of Baltimore, she attended local parochial schools and worked as a secretary for several years for what was the Richardson Insurance Agency before her marriage to Mr. Oberle in 1913.

Mr. Oberle, who was once a vice president of the First National Bank of Maryland, died in 1954.

The former Katherine Goldrick was a member of St. Ann's Church, where she sang in the choir for a number of years. Her hobbies included opera and gardening.

Mrs. Oberle is survived by three sons, Cornelius F Oberle, of Stamford, Conn., Francis X. Oberle, of Westminster, and Joseph Oberle, Jr., of Baltimore; a daughter, Mrs. Katherine G. Miller, of Baltimore; 12 grandchildren, and six great-grandchildren.

Burial Saturday For Mrs. Oberle

A mass of Christian burial for Mrs. Katherine Goldrick Oberle, 91, wife of the late vice president of the First National Bank of Maryland, will be offered at 10 A.M. Saturday at the Church of the Immaculate Conception in Towson.

Mrs. Oberle died yesterday at the Dulaney-Towson nursing home after a long illness. She lived for many years at 213 Midhurst road.

Church Choir Soprano

Born in Baltimore, Mrs. Oberle attended parochial schools.

Prior to her marriage to Joseph Oberle in 1914, she was secretary to a vice president of the Richardson Insurance Agency for 14 years.

A soprano, Mrs. Oberle for many years sang in St. Ann's Choir. Both she and her husband, who died in 1954, were members of the Baltimore Opera Company.

Mrs. Oberle was also an avid gardener and was particularly proud of her roses.

Survivors include three sons, Joseph Oberle, Jr., of Baltimore; Cornelius F. Oberle, of Stamford, Conn., and Francis X. Oberle, of Westminster; a daughter, Mrs. Katherine G. Miller, of Dundalk; 12 grandchildren and 6 great grandchildren.

actually 15 April 1913

OBERLE
On April 9, 1975, KATHERINE GOLDRICK, beloved wife of the late Joseph Oberle, and dear mother of Joseph Oberle, Jr., Mrs. Katherine G. Miller, Cornelius F. and Francis X. Oberle. Also survived by 12 grandchildren and six great-grandchildren.

Friends may call at the Dulaney Valley home of Lemmon—Mitchell—Wiedefeld, Inc., 10 West Padonia road (at York road) Timonium—Cockeysville, on Thursday from 7 to 9 P.M. and on Friday from 3 to 5 and 7 to 9 P.M. Mass of Christian Burial in Immaculate Conception Church, Towson, on Saturday at 10 A.M. Interment in New Cathedral Cemetery.

```
 1913
  -14
 1899
-1884  YOB
   15  age
```

Viewing was at L-M-W but funeral was handled by my uncle George Gonce

Baltimore – 1975 Obituaries of Katherine G. Oberle

My Oberle Grandparents were married on 15 April 1913; the obituary above left states the correct year, but the one on the upper right gives the year as 1914.

Also, note that, if she had worked for the Richardson Agency for fourteen years prior to her marriage, Grandmom could have been no older than sixteen when she began working – and possibly younger – tending to confirm the suspicions of "age-fudging" discussed on page 96.

Baltimore – Graves of Joseph and Katherine Goldrick Oberle at New Cathedral Cemetery[114]

Children and Grandchildren of Joseph Oberle & Katie Goldrick

- Joseph Francis (Joe) Oberle id201, (born 1 March 1914, died 22 February 1990), married Catherine T. (Nancy) Borig id202 (born 13 November 1915, died 7 July 2000) and had three children and several grandchildren. My Uncle Joe is discussed in more detail beginning on page 259.

- Katherine Gertrude (Sis) Oberle id200, (born 7 August 1915, died 29 January 1996), married Norbert Joseph (Bud) Miller id199, (born 16 June 1910, died 20 June 1993) and had five children and several grandchildren. My Aunt Sis is discussed in more detail beginning on page 266.

- **Cornelius Francis (Cornie) Oberle** id196, (born 25 September 1917, died 10 October 2004), married Rosalie Gertrude Gonce id242 (born 26 December 1919) and had four children, of which I am the oldest, and numerous grandchildren. Grandmom always spelled Dad's nickname "Corny," although everyone else, including my Dad, used "Cornie." He was the last of Joe and Katie's children to die – on the day before his 63rd wedding anniversary.

- Francis Xavier Oberle id197, (born 20 February 1923, died 26 November 1997), married Gladys Helen (Bookie) Maroney id198 (born 26 November 1929, died 7 August 1996) and had one child and one grandchild. My Uncle Francis is discussed in more detail beginning on page 274.

---

[114] This is Section VV, Lot 575 at New Cathedral Cemetery in Baltimore. There are four graves on this lot, but two of them are unused. The deed for these graves is in my possession.

1711-1975 HISTORY

Rosalie Gonce and our Gonce Ancestors

My mother Rosalie Gertrude Gonce id242, shown to the right in 1926, was born on 26 December 1919 to Charles Richard Gonce id43 and Anna Gertrude Hulshoff id44 of Baltimore. My grandfather Charles was a direct descendant of Justice id2577 and Magdalen id2858 Gonce, who were living in Maryland at least as far back as 1760 – prior to the American Revolution. My maternal grandmother's Hulshoff ancestors, whose history I've traced back to 1665, didn't arrive in the United States until November of 1855. Histories of both the Gonce and Hulshoff families are provided in separate books[115], so further details are not given here.

Rosalie Gonce as a child in 1926

Cornelius Oberle and Rosalie Gonce

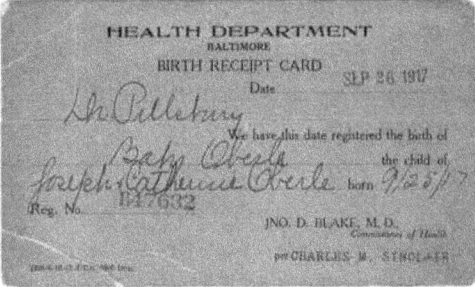

Receipt for original birth report of Cornelius Oberle

As mentioned earlier, my father Cornelius Oberle id196, known almost universally as "Cornie," was born on 25 September 1917 at 3:50pm, the third child of Joseph Oberle id81 and Katherine[116] Goldrick id80. He was delivered at my grandparents' first home on 22nd Street by Dr. Pillsbury, and weighed 9½ pounds.

As can be seen in the initial report of his birth (illustration to the left), Dad's name hadn't been settled on by the time Dr. Pillsbury filed the required birth notification with the city of Baltimore.

---

[115] Imaginatively enough, these are titled "Our Gonce Ancestors" (ISBN: 9-780615-923147) and "Our Hulshoff and Kerchner Ancestors" (ISBN: 9-780615-923147).

[116] Note that Dr. Pillsbury spelled my grandmother's name with a "C."

His baptism took place on the 8th of October at St. Ann's Church in Baltimore where his parents had been married almost four and a half years earlier.

A variety of photographs of my Dad as a child with his siblings and/or parents are scattered throughout the section covering my grandparents; these pictures are on pages 104, 105, and 108.

In October 1923, Cornie began grammar school at the neighborhood parochial school run by St. Ann's Church, but after the family's move to Midhurst Road, was transferred to the parish school of Immaculate Conception in September 1926 when he began the fourth grade.

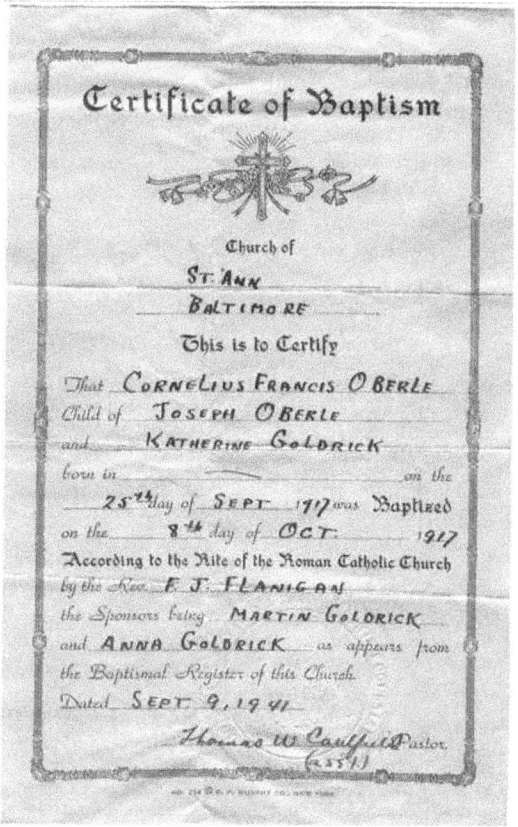

Duplicate Baptismal Certificate obtained for Catholic approval of his wedding in 1941.

After graduating from Immaculate Conception school in June of 1930, Dad began attending Towson Catholic High School in September of that year, graduating in June 1934.

During his high school years, he worked part time at the local pharmacy/soda shop, but by 1935, he had a "real" job as an assistant bookkeeper at Jas. A. Gary & Sons, Inc. in Baltimore. In October 1936, he applied to attend night school at Johns Hopkins University (see a copy of his application on the next page.)

Cornie in about 1927 (age 10)

> **THE JOHNS HOPKINS UNIVERSITY**
>
> **Application for Admission to The College for Teachers; The Evening Courses in Business Economics; The Night Courses for Technical Workers.**
>
> 1. Name of applicant (in full) *Cornelius Francis Oberle*
> 2. Year and place of birth *1917 – Baltimore, Md.*
> 3. Home address *413 Midhurst Road*
> 4. Name and address of parent or guardian *Joseph Oberle (Father)*
>   (For applicants under 21 years of age.)
> 5. Institutions in which preparatory training was obtained, and number of years spent in each:
>
> | | NAME | LOCATION | DATES OF ATTENDANCE | DIPLOMA OR DEGREE | DATE RECEIVED |
> |---|---|---|---|---|---|
> | Grade School | *School of Immaculate* | *Towson* | | | |
> | High School | *Towson Catholic High School* | *Do.* | | | |
> | Normal School | | | | | |
> | College or University | | | | | |
> | Summer Session | | | | | |
>
> *6. State to what extent you have studied the following subjects:
>
>   a. Mathematics *2 yrs Algebra – 1 yr plane Geometry – 1 yr Accounting*
>
>   b. Physics *none*
>
>   c. Chemistry *none*
>
>   d. Drawing *2 yrs Mechanical*
>
> 7. Present occupation
>
>   a. Position and place of employment *Asst Bookkeeper Jas. J. Gary + Son Inc Balto*
>
>   b. How long in present position? *one year*
>
> *8. What positions other than the present one have you held?
>
> 9. a. Do you wish to become a candidate for the degree of Bachelor of Science? *no*
>
>   b. Do you wish to become a candidate for the Statement of Completion in the Business Economics course? *yes*
>
> 10. I recognize the right of the University to exclude at any time a student whose conduct or academic standing renders undesirable his or her presence in the institution.
>
> Date *October 2, 1936*
>
> Approved _____ Signature *Joseph Oberle Parent*
>   *Signature of applicant, if of age; otherwise, parent or guardian*
>
> * Sections that are starred should be filled in only by students in The Night Courses for Technical Workers.
>
> N. B.—This is not an application for matriculation. Students who wish to be matriculated should secure a special form from the Registrar.

Cornelius Oberle – October 2, 1936 application to Johns Hopkins University

In 1937, having been accepted at Hopkins, Dad began attending business and accounting courses after work most evenings.

In this same year, he joined a church-sponsored youth group called the Catholic Students Mission Crusade, which was founded and run by the Josephite order of priests in 1924 under the auspices of The Catholic University of America in Washington, D.C.

Ro and Cornie after a 1938 CSMC Social Event

Although its stated purpose was to instill a "missionary spirit" among young lay Catholics, it had a less publicized intent of encouraging Catholic youth to fraternize with other Catholics in order to stem the increase in inter-faith marriages that had been taking place during the early years of the twentieth century [117].

In the case of my parents and many of their friends, this objective was realized. My mother Rosalie, whose father Charles had died unexpectedly in June of 1936, joined the group, and shortly thereafter met my father at one of the organization's social functions. My parents quickly became known as a couple, and had their first date on January 28th of 1938. They dated each other almost exclusively from that time forward.

Interestingly, although the formal organization had long since ceased to exist, many of the surviving couples who had become my parents' friends during these functions were still meeting socially some sixty-five years later. Although my parents had moved away from the Baltimore area in the mid-1960s, they easily rejoined this group of friends when they retired back to Bel Air, Maryland over twenty years later.

By 1938, Dad had obtained a better position working as an accountant for the American Oil Company (later known as Amoco – now part of British Petroleum); he and my mother began discussing marriage a short time later.

The situation in Europe was becoming more serious by this time, and the United States government instituted a draft in 1940 in order to be prepared for the eventuality that the U.S. might be drawn into a war. My father was an early draftee, receiving his initial notice on 27 January 1941, and was inducted into the Army on the 19th of February in 1941 for a term of two years.

After basic training, he was sent to Edgewood Arsenal in Aberdeen Maryland for advanced training in the chemical corps [118]. As is typical of the military, the command structure was busy preparing for the previous war. Thus, they were hard at work designing up-to-date gas masks for our troops, as described in the newspaper article on page 125 (Dad is on the right).

---

[117] The records of this organization are still extant on microfilm. The Josephite Fathers Microfilm MJOS 18.200: "Catholic Students' Mission Crusade Minutes [trnscrpt] 1924-1942", is now housed at Notre Dame University outside South Bend, Indiana.

[118] As the military might be expected to do with someone having an accounting and tax background ... At the time, the military was working on protection from chemical agents; after the war, they began a more controversial program to develop chemical agents.

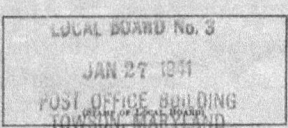

January 27th, 1941
(Date)

NOTICE OF SELECTION

To __Cornelius Francis Oberle,_____, Order No. __324__

You have been selected for training and service under the Selective Training and Service Act of 1940. You will receive an Order to Report for Induction—such induction to take place on or about __February 10th-15th_____, 19 41, when adequate facilities are expected to be available.

This notice is given you in advance for your convenience, and is not an order to report. Persons reporting to the induction station in some instances may be rejected for physical or other reasons. It is well to keep this in mind in arranging your affairs, to prevent any undue hardship if you are rejected at the induction station. If you are employed, you should advise your employer of this notice and of the possibility that you may not be accepted at the induction station. Your employer can then be prepared to replace you if you are accepted, or to continue your employment if you are rejected. The Order to Report for Induction will specify a definite time and place for you to report.

W. Barrie
Member of Local Board

D. S. S. Form 148

Order received to report 8:30 A.M. February 19, 1941

The handwriting on the letter is clearly my father's.

WOMEN MAKE NEW GAS MASK AT EDGEWOOD

By EARLE R. POORBAUGH
Sunday American Staff Correspondent.

EDGEWOOD ARSENAL, Edgewood, May 24.—Authorities here today, for the first time, broke through the veil of secrecy surrounding the Army's newest gas mask, and permitted this writer to see and examine the newest gas protective device.

According to the authorities, the new mask is the most modern, and most efficient in use by any army, any where.

MANY IMPROVEMENTS.

Differing from its predecessors in many ways, the new mask makes use of optically neutral glass eye pieces, rather than the transparent plastic formerly used, and permits its wearer to converse, even over a telephone, and to give commands.

Another new feature of the mask is the placing of the canister of purifying chemicals upon a shoulder, permitting greater freedom of movement for the wearer.

Production of the new mask, and of the Army's better known service masks is entrusted to the nimble fingers of several thousand Maryland women.

The women are turning out a production which, according to authorities, is completely satisfactory.

FINEST MASKS.

The masks the Maryland women are making are the finest and most modern in use by any Army, anywhere, according to Army officers on duty at this Arsenal.

Material for the masks arrives at Edgewood from widely separated points in the country.

The plant, which is supervised by Mr. R. D. Kulp of Aberdeen, with Mr. Phillip E. Fisher of Baltimore as assistant, soon routes the various parts into one long, continuous production line.

First step in the assembly of the masks is fixing the metal tabs to the moulded rubber face piece. Later the tube will have straps of cloth attached, and will hold the mask in place, over the face of the wearer.

MASK TRAVELS ON.

The grotesque looking eye pieces of the older mask, are next put into place, some by hand, others by machines, especially designed here at Edgewood.

Mrs. Margaret Ritter of 403 North Streeper street, and Miss Marie Koen of Street, Md., operate one of a battery of such machines which crimp the metal ring and glass-like eye pieces into place in the mask.

With the eye pieces in place, the mask travels on, to have an escape valve inserted, wired and taped into place, by the flying fingers of a large group of women, of whom Mrs. Jeanette Kelly of Belair road, aged nineteen, is the youngest.

None of Mrs. Kelly's co-workers would admit being the oldest of the group, but Mrs. Eleanor DuVall of 511 Scott street and Mrs. Madeline Seldomridge of 2505 Eastern avenue, both proudly proclaimed the fact they were grandmothers. Mrs. DuVall admitted four grand-daughters and a grandson, while Mrs. Seldomridge could boast only a granddaughter.

Thirty per cent of the employes here are inspection employes, according to Mr. Fisher, and each mask is so rigidly inspected by so many different persons, that any attempt at wilful, or any accidental damage, is sure to be detected. Supervising this important part of the work is Mrs. Marie Klug of 230 Elmora avenue.

MAKE CARRIERS.

The carriers for the masks are made here at Edgewood, and batteries of sewing machines hum 24 hours a day turning them out in satisfying quantities.

Typical of the skillful women who operate these machines is Mrs J Beacham of 632 South Potomac street, whose children, Naomi, fifteen; Audrey, eleven, and Kay, ten, she is proud of "mamma" and the part she is playing in equipping Uncle Sam's rapidly expanding Army.

Brig. Gen. Ray L. Avery, Commanding General of the Edgewood Arsenal, in commenting upon the work done by the gas mask assembly plant, said "each employe here is investigated before he is employed, and only those who can pass a careful investigation receive appointments.

"They work hard and honestly, and they are as much interested in

THE NEW —AND THE OLD
Mask on left, worn by Lieut. Richard O. Gordon, is the Army's latest now being produced at Edgewood. Pvt. Cornelius Oberle wears former style mask.

the success of our endeavors as we are. They are fine, loyal employes."

The actual output of masks here is "satisfactory."

duced daily? Well that, according to Lieutenant Norton, public relations officer, is a secret, but it is

PARENTS! GIVE YO
NEWSPAPER ROUTE T

TODAY, scores of successful men of Baltimore that they once were carriers for The Baltimore News American.

They rate this boyhood business experience as an addition to their scholastic education—too valuable ambitious youth to miss!

Guided by able counselors, News-Post and Ame *money and cultivate health and good habits.*

This training will prove invaluable to YOUR SC him join our staff of carriers?

APPLICATIONS from boys, 13 and considered. If interested phone th Manager of The Baltimore News-P American, LExington 0100, Extensio

BALTIMORE AMERICAN - SUNDAY, MAY 25, 1941   Page 16--L

Dad was then assigned to his first active unit, the 5th Air Force[119] at Hunter Field, which was adjacent to Stewart Army Base outside Savannah, Georgia.

Granted a weekend pass after seven months of service, Cornelius returned home and married Rosalie at Blessed Sacrament Church on Old York Road in Baltimore – on the corner of Springfield Avenue just a few houses away from where my mother lived – on Saturday, October 11, 1941.

In the picture below, taken outside of Blessed Sacrament Church after their hastily arranged wedding, the bride and groom are marked #2 and #1 respectively. The wedding party, from left to right, included Dad's older brother Joe id201 (#4), Mom's sister Jean id248 (#3), Dad's younger brother Francis id197 (#5), and Dad's cousin Bill id187 (#6). Others I can identify include Dad's father Joseph id81, (#7), Dad's sister Katherine id200 ("Sis", #9), and Mom's youngest brother George id245 (#8).

Baltimore – 1941 Wedding Party of Ro and Cornie at Blessed Sacrament Church

Since Dad needed to report back to Hunter Field on Monday, there was no time for a honeymoon, but my mother traveled with him on the train back to Savannah the next morning, where they spent Sunday night at "The Georgian Tourist Home" run by Mrs. Skeffington, located at 401 West 37th Street. My Mom returned to Baltimore on Monday.

---

[119] This was the "Army Air Force," which had not yet become a separate branch of the services.

Savannah, Georgia – Mrs. Skeffington's "The Georgian Tourist Home"

Cornelius and Rosalie – World War II

When Dad returned to duty after the wedding, he was expecting to placed on active reserve on February 19th at the completion of his tour. A little more than a month later, however, the Japanese attacked Pearl Harbor on December 7, 1941, putting all of the military on active duty for an indefinite period.

Very shortly thereafter, his unit was put on standby for deployment to the Pacific Theater. In January, Rosalie returned to Savannah by train for a make-do honeymoon before his departure. Once again, they obtained a room at Mrs. Skeffington's guesthouse and, for a few days, toured the city of Savannah.

Some pictures from this visit are shown immediately above and on the following page:

1711-1975 History

Savannah, Georgia – January, 1942: Ro and Cornie Oberle

The impromptu honeymoon didn't last for long, and was made slightly less than entertaining by Dad having to check in daily to see if his unit's transportation was ready for the trip to California. On the afternoon of January 15th, he sent the postcard below to his parents.

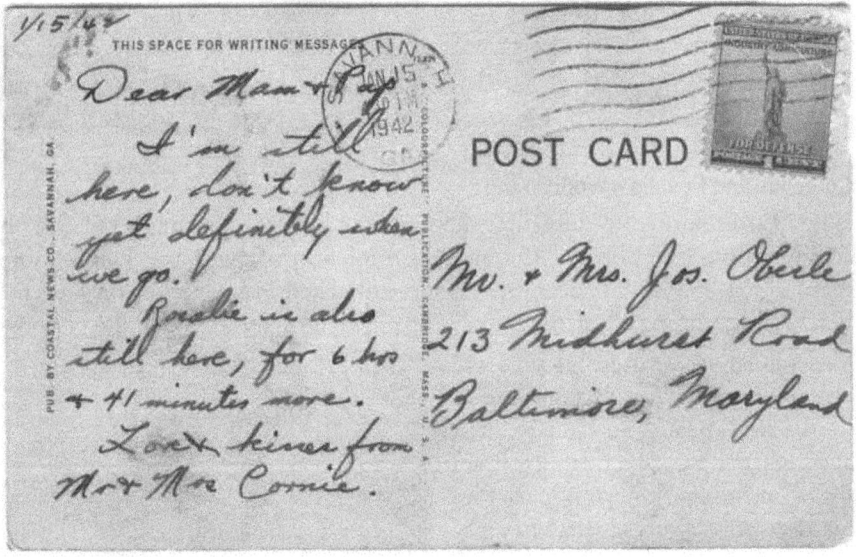

Rosalie left that evening on an overnight train back to Baltimore, and this was the last time she and Cornie would see each other until the end of the war.

Shortly thereafter, Dad's unit left Savannah on a troop train bound for California where they joined the thousands of other troops preparing to leave for the Pacific Theater.

Dad left by ship for Australia on January 31st 1942, arriving there on February 25th to await further assignment, which came within thirty days.

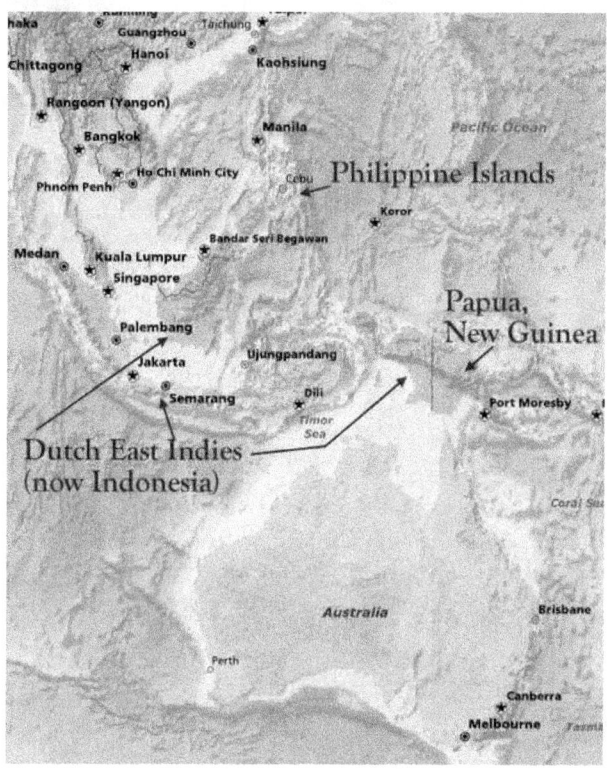

Dad's Pacific Theater Assignments in WW-II

He would not be returning to the United States for more than three years. By March of 1942, at about the same time the Japanese invaded the Dutch East Indies (now known as Indonesia), he was stationed in Papua, New Guinea.

Dad served as a chemical technician in the 894th Chemical Company. This group, which was attached to the 5th Air Force Air Operations Group (AOG), was responsible for handling the chemical ordinance[120] then being used in the various campaigns to drive the Japanese out of the Pacific Islands. Dad was assigned to Unit No 1 of this company, eventually becoming the NCOIC for his unit's operations.

The island of New Guinea, shown in the map above, is directly north of Australia, and lies just south of the equator. Papua, New Guinea occupies the eastern half of the island, and is separated from the west by a wide, forbidding, and virtually impenetrable mountain ridge called the Highlands.

Much has been written about the Pacific campaigns of World War II; there is even a good deal of published history of the 5th Air Force's activities on New Guinea during the period my father served there. It seems redundant, therefore, to do anything other than provide a short overview of this period.

---

[120] Including large quantities of the newly invented chemical known as Napalm. See page 134 for more details.

Under other circumstances, the coastal areas of Papua New Guinea would be considered a tropical paradise (see photograph to the right) and, most likely, a plum assignment. Given the workload, the equatorial temperatures, the daily exposure to interesting chemicals and (oh, by the way) the presence of the Japanese on the western half of the island[121], however, most of the island's charms were lost on the members of the 894th Chemical Company, who spent most of their days in the open sun.

A few months after the Allies invaded the Philippines in October of 1944, the 894th followed the 5th Air Force there. Although the remaining Japanese in the northern part of the island

Papua, New Guinea – Modern-day shoreline

didn't surrender until September 1945, Dad and others in his unit followed the force that then left to invade parts of the Dutch East Indies in early 1945.

With the end of the war finally appearing to be in sight, some of the longest serving soldiers were beginning to be rotated back to the U.S., and on April 14 1945, Dad left Australia with part of his unit on a troop transport

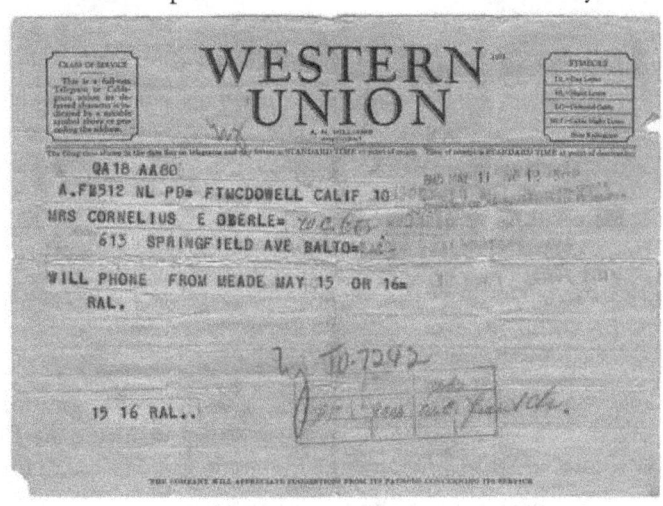

ship bound for San Francisco. He arrived there on the 9th of May, and was processed through Ft. McDowell. He sent the telegram above once his rail

---

[121] The western half of the island was part of the Dutch East Indies, which the Americans took care to refer to as only the "East Indies." They had nothing in particular against the Dutch, but the native population had been attempting for years to achieve their independence (which they did in 1945), so some political sensitivity was required.

transportation back to Baltimore was confirmed, and returned to Fort Meade[122].

20 March 1942 and 24 July 1942 Promotion Records for Cornelius Oberle

---

[122] He brought with him a collection of currency from the various countries he visited that includes pre-war notes, Japanese occupation bills, and post-liberation bills printed by the U.S. for the post-occupation governments; this collection is stored in my safe deposit box

Discharges for the soldiers returning from both the European and Pacific theaters were not immediate, however. The Army didn't feel comfortable beginning this process until after the Japanese accepted the Allies' terms of surrender on August 14, 1945.

Nevertheless, by June of 1945, my parents had moved in to their first apartment together at 721 Radnor Avenue in Baltimore. Dad was finally discharged on the 1st of October that year after serving four years and seven months.

Dad's Discharge and Qualification Records are shown on the next two pages.

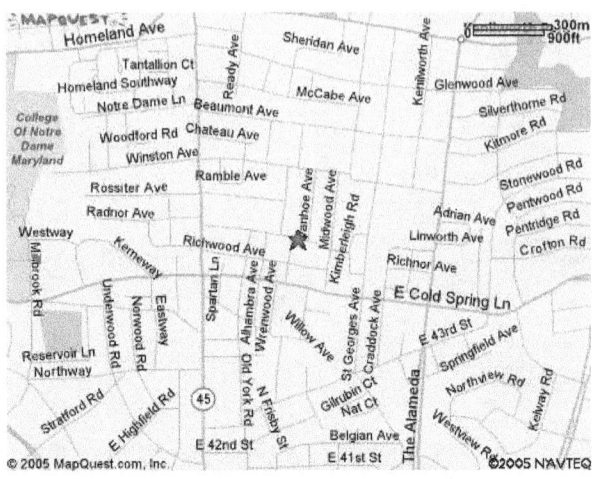

Map showing my parents' home at 721 Radnor Avenue

In November of 1945, Dad returned to work at the American Oil Company, and my parents were finally able to begin married life. In 1947, they purchased their first home at 3918 Rexmere Road for ten thousand dollars.

Our 3-bedroom Baltimore row house at 3918 Rexmere Road

Ft. Meade, MD – 1945 Report of Separation for Cornelius Oberle
The "Enlisted Record and Report of Separation" is the Military's official Discharge Form

Like many returning soldiers, Dad had tentatively begun settling back into civilian life with my Mom while he was still officially in the employ of Uncle Sam, who wasn't prepared to handle the large influx of these veterans, but not quite ready to declare that they were no longer needed.

Ft. Meade, MD – 1945 Separation Qualification Record for Cornelius Oberle

The official record shows my father's qualifications for handling interesting "weapons of mass destruction," likely not related to his eventual lymphoma, since his older sister died of the same cause, but likely not pleasant either.

Shortly after moving in to the new home, Dad was able to return to Johns Hopkins University at nights, and completed his degree there. A copy of his application to return to Hopkins is shown below:

THE JOHNS HOPKINS UNIVERSITY

Application for Admission to The College for Teachers; The Evening Courses in Business Economics; The Night Courses in Technology

1. Name of applicant (in full) **Cornelius** (First Name) **Francis** (Middle Name) **Oberle** (Last Name)
2. Date and place of birth **September 25, 1917, Baltimore**
3. Home address **721 Radnor Ave., Baltimore 12, Md.**
4. Name and address of parent or guardian .... (For applicants under 21 years of age)
5. Institutions in which preparatory training was obtained, and number of years spent in each:

	NAME	LOCATION	DATES OF ATTENDANCE	DIPLOMA OR DEGREE	DATE RECEIVED
Grade School	St. Ann's Parochial – Balto. Catholic School	Towson, MD	Sept 1930		
High School	Catholic High School	Towson, MD	June 10, 1935	Diploma	June 10
Normal School	None				
College or University	Hopkins		1937		
Summer Session	None				

*6. State to what extent you have studied the following subjects:
   a. Mathematics ....

   b. Physics ....

   c. Chemistry ....

   d. Drawing ....

7. Present occupation **Accounting Clerk**
   a. Position and place of employment **American Oil Company, Baltimore**
   b. How long in present position? **Three Years Prior to Military Service. Returning After 4 Yrs. 2 Mos. Service**

*8. What positions other than the present one have you held? ....

9. a. Do you wish to become a candidate for the degree of Bachelor of Science? **Not at Present**
   b. Do you wish to become a candidate for the Statement of Completion in the Business Economics courses? **Not at Present**

10. I recognize the right of the University to exclude at any time a student whose conduct or academic standing renders undesirable his or her presence in the institution.
    Date ....
    Approved .... Signature **Cornelius F. Oberle**
    Signature of applicant, if of age; otherwise, parent or guardian

*Sections that are starred should be filled in only by students in The Night Courses in Technology.

N. B.—This is not an application for matriculation. Students who wish to be matriculated should secure a special form from the Registrar. They are not required to file this general application blank.

Cornelius Oberle – Post-World War II application to Johns Hopkins University

Settling into Civilian Life

The new row houses on Rexmere Road were still in the Catholic parish of Blessed Sacrament, where my mother grew up, and where she and Dad were married. Our house was a three-bedroom home at the top of the hill[123] and, like most houses in that area, was reached from the street by a lengthy concrete staircase.[124] The houses were served by an alley at the level of the back yards, where regular deliveries of milk, bread and eggs were made, and where the huckster Paul would come with his truck several times a week to sell fruits and vegetables to the neighborhood Moms.

During the first year or so, the top floor of the house was rented to another young family – the Popes – who, like my parents, had one small child.

Baltimore – 1948: Sally Pope & the author.
The back yard at 3918 Rexmere Rd. Note the bread truck in the alley and the clothesline above.

In 1948, by which time my younger brother had been born[125], the Popes had moved on, and Dad had accepted a new job at the Lord Baltimore Press as an accountant.

Over the next year, the upstairs portion of the house was reworked, and Rosalie's brother-in-law helped finish the basement to add new living space. On May 13, 1949, Ro and Cornie had a daughter, Mary Agnes id258.

Baltimore – 1949: Tommy and his big brother   *Baltimore – 1950: Tommy and his big brother*   *Atlantic City – 1951: Rosalie and her children*

---

[123] See the photograph on page 132.

[124] The phone number was Tuxedo 6455; curiously similar to the Tuxedo 4855 Dad grew up with.

[125] I was born in November 1946, and my brother Thomas Steven id56 was born in December 1947.

Baltimore – 1951 photographs of me and my siblings Tommy and Mary on Rexmere Road

Baltimore – 1953: The author and his grandmother Katie   *New York State – 1953: Cornelius and his children*   *Philadelphia – 1956: The author and his sister Mary*

On June 14th 1955, Dad graduated from Johns Hopkins University. My Grandfather had passed away the year before, but my Grandmother Oberle was able to attend. The picture on the right shows her, Dad, and my barely pregnant Mom after the ceremony, with me peeking out disinterestedly from between my parents.

Baltimore – 1955: After Dad's graduation from Johns Hopkins

A week later, on 21 June 1955, the new baby, whom they named Martha id42, was stillborn. She was buried, along with an earlier stillborn infant from June

22, 1951, in the plot of her maternal grandparents at Holy Redeemer Cemetery in Baltimore.[126]

In the fall of 1955, Dad's Hopkins degree opened new opportunities, and he left the Lord Baltimore Press to begin working for the Mathieson Company, located in what was then the tallest building in Baltimore (known appropriately as the Mathieson Building – now the Bank of America Building).

He was to stay with Mathieson for the next thirty years – through its merger with Olin (at which time it became the Olin-Mathieson Chemical Corporation and, later, as simply the Olin Corporation) until his retirement in 1986.

A few months after Martha's burial, Rosalie was again pregnant. In February of 1956, she was rushed to Union Memorial Hospital with serious complications related to the pregnancy, and doctors immediately removed the baby in order to save her life. Nonetheless, she was in critical condition for several days and, at only a little over two pounds, the baby was not expected to live. She remained there for several weeks after the birth, and her son remained in intensive care for much longer, but both survived.

Various relatives cared for my sister and me during this period, and when our new little brother finally came home, Mary Agnes and I spent time with my Mom's Aunt Rose (Hulshoff) and Uncle Frank Easter in Philadelphia (see earlier photo), where I was introduced to subways for the first time.[127]

During my Dad's years with Olin, the family moved several times – first to Staten Island, New York in 1963 and, later, to Huntington, Connecticut.

Not long after being settled in Connecticut, their second son Tommy died. They purchased their four grave plot at Holy Redeemer Cemetery in Baltimore where he was buried.[128]

Dad reached sixty-five in 1982, but was asked to remain with Olin for a while longer due to several projects he was involved in. Finally, however, he retired and on 23 August 1985 they received the deed for their new and last home at 1318 Vanderbilt in Bel Air Maryland.

During their time in Connecticut, they often traveled, and they continued to do so after they retired to Bel Air. Most of these trips were to visit grandchildren in Arizona and, later, Illinois. Photos of them taken during some of these visits are shown on the next page.

Their last visit to Illinois was in 1999, after which travel became impractical due to my Dad's failing health, but he nonetheless continued volunteering to prepare tax returns for "old people" through the St. Vincent de Paul Society, as he had done for many years.

---

[126] There are no headstones for these infants, but their burials are recorded in Holy Redeemer's Cemetery Lot Detail Reports for section BHR.V.70

[127] At the time, this was far more interesting than having a new brother.

[128] See the photograph on page 142.

Tucson – 1975: Ro and Cornie at Colossal Cave   *Legend City – 1982: Cornie and Ro on water slide*

Illinois – 1990 visit to new granddaughter   *Illinois – 1999 last visit together to Buffalo Grove*

Bel Air – 2004: Cornie and one of his great-grandsons

The photograph on the left is from what is probably the last set of pictures made of Dad, and was taken at his home in Bel Air in the summer of 2004 holding one of his great-grandsons.

By this time, Dad had suffered through several bouts of cancer ranging from skin melanomas (perhaps related to the earlier years working in continuous sunlight in Papua) to the lymphoma that finally took his life. Note the severe bruising on his hands in the picture above left, which was a constant during his last few years. Dad died on the 10th of October 2004, the day before what would have been my parents' sixty-third wedding anniversary.

Dad was buried at Holy Redeemer Cemetery. By this time, he had four grandchildren (there are now five) and eight great-grandchildren (now thirteen). His death certificate and obituaries are shown on the next two pages.

Mom remained in the home on Vanderbilt Road for another fourteen months after Dad's death but, in January 2006, relocated to a "senior living facility" in Illinois to be near her oldest son's and her second granddaughter's families.

By late 2010, her condition had deteriorated to the point where she needed to be moved to the facility's long-term care unit.

Lincolnshire – 2010: Rosalie with her new great-grandson. Taken on 27 May at the Sedgebrook Rehabilitation Center.

Her health continued to decline and she passed away on March 3, 2013. She was returned once again to Maryland for her funeral and burial next to her husband. Her death certificate is shown on page 143.

To Be Continued:

There has been minimal discussion of Mom and Dad's children, since Genealogical convention suggests that a period of seventy years or so should pass before presenting any specific family history. Since that admittedly arbitrary guideline has already been passed, further history will be left for another generation to prepare.

Bel Air – 2004 Death Certificate of Cornelius F. Oberle

Page 6B : Tuesday, Oct. 12, 2004 : The Sun

Death/Lodge Notices 215

OBERLE, Cornelius F.
On October 10, 2004 CORNELIUS F.; beloved husband of Rosalie Gonce Oberle; dear father of ▓▓▓▓▓ ▓ ▓▓▓▓▓ and his wife Som and ▓▓▓▓▓ ▓ ▓▓▓▓▓; devoted brother of the late Joseph Oberle, Jr., Francis X. Oberle and Katherine G. Miller. Also blessed with four grandchildren and seven great grandchildren.
Friends may call at Gonce Funeral Service, P.A., 4001 Ritchie Hywy on Wednesday from 3 to 5 and 7 to 9 P.M. Further visiting in St. Margaret Church, 141 Hickory Ave., Bel Air, MD on Thursday from 10 to 11 A.M. followed by Mass of Christian Burial at 11 A.M. Interment in Most Holy Redeemer Cemetery. Those who wish may contribute to the Centennial Campaign of St. Margaret Church.

Tombstone of Cornelius Oberle (1917-2004) and his wife Rosalie (1919-2013)

Opposite side of Tombstone showing their son Thomas Steven Oberle (1947-1969)

Cornelius F. Oberle

Cornelius F. Oberle of Bel Air died Oct. 10 at Lorien Nursing Home after a long battle with Lymphoma. He was 87.

Mr. Oberle was born Sept. 25, 1917 in Baltimore.

He graduated from Johns Hopkins with a bachelor of science degree in business administration and certification at a certified public accountant. He retired from Olin Corporation in 1985 where he had worked as an accountant in data processing.

He served as staff sergeant in the Army from 1941 to 1945 during World War II.

He was a member of St. Margaret Church in Bel Air and the Seniors Computer Club. He was a Boy Scout Leader in the 1950s for Blessed Sacramount Church Troop 119 and later a leader in New York and Connecticut. He gave of his time every year to assist the elderly with their income tax filing free of charge.

He is survived by his wife of 63 years, Rosalie Gonce Oberle; two sons, ▓▓▓▓▓ ▓ Oberle of Illinois and ▓▓▓▓▓ ▓ Oberle of Florida; daughter-in-law, Som Oberle of Illinois; granddaughters, ▓▓▓▓▓ ▓▓▓▓▓▓, ▓▓▓▓▓▓▓ ▓▓▓▓▓▓▓ and ▓▓▓▓▓▓ ▓▓▓▓▓ all of Illinois; a grandson, ▓▓▓▓▓ ▓▓▓▓▓ of Heidelberg, Germany; great grandchildren, ▓▓▓▓▓ ▓▓▓ ▓▓▓▓▓▓ ▓▓▓▓▓▓▓ of Illinois, ▓▓▓▓▓▓▓ ▓▓▓▓▓▓ of Illinois and ▓▓▓▓▓▓, ▓▓▓▓▓▓▓▓, ▓▓▓▓▓▓▓ and ▓▓▓▓ ▓▓▓▓▓ of Illinois.

Mr. Oberle was predeceased by two brothers, Joseph Oberle Jr. and Francis X. Oberle; and a sister, Katherine G. Miller.

Visitation will be today (Oct. 13) from 3 to 5 and 7 to 9 p.m. at Gonce Funeral Service in Baltimore. Services will be held Oct. 14 at St. Margaret Church in Bel Air. Interment will be in Most Holy Redeemer Cemetery following the service.

Donations may be made to Centennial Campaign of St. Margaret Church, 141 Hickory Ave., Bel Air, Md., 21014.

Obituaries and photos of Cornelius and Rosalie Oberle's headstone

Lincolnshire, Illinois – 2013 Death Certificate of Rosalie Gonce Oberle

Chicago weather conditions prevented the local funeral home from being able to transfer Rosalie's body back to Baltimore for her funeral and burial until March 11th.

1711-1975 History

Three Generations of Oberles from Seraphin (II) to Cornelius and his Siblings

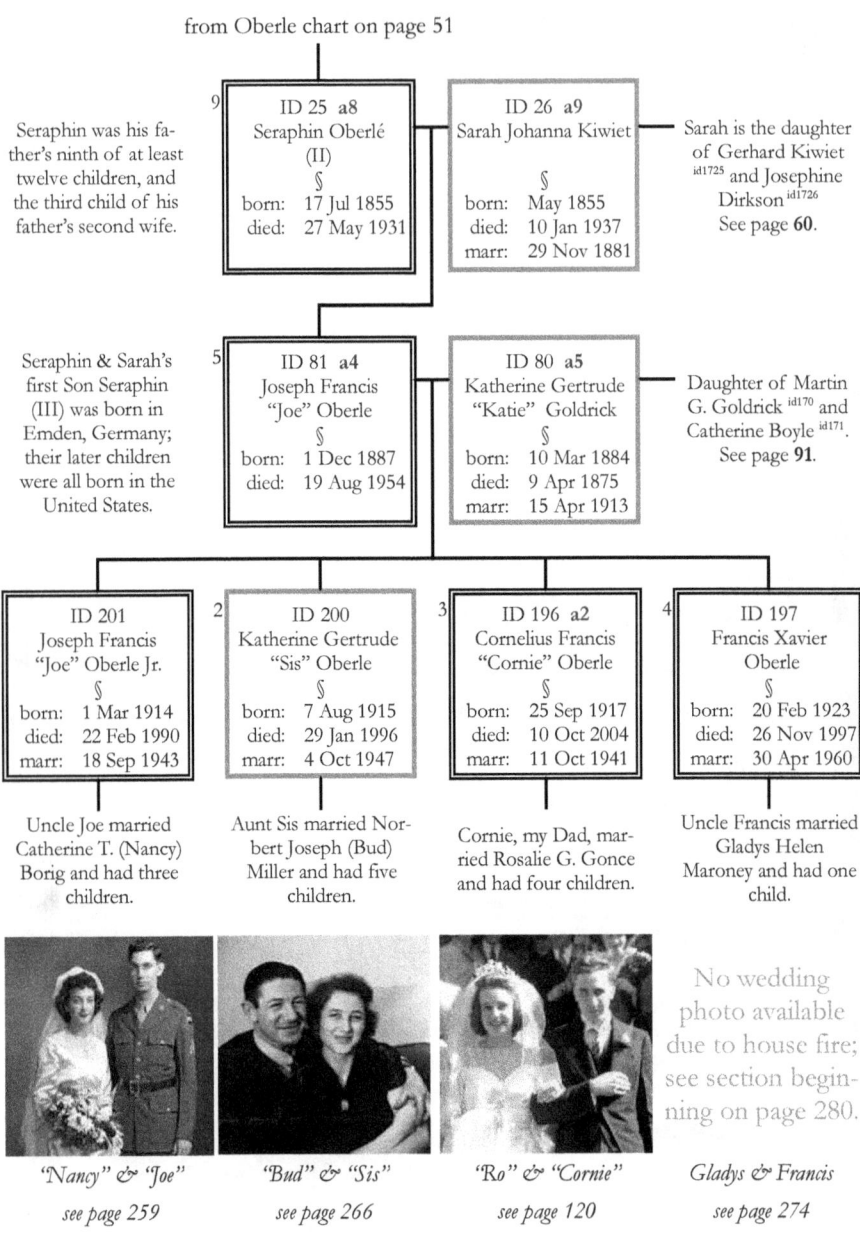

from Oberle chart on page 51

Seraphin was his father's ninth of at least twelve children, and the third child of his father's second wife.

ID 25 a8
Seraphin Oberlé (II)
§
born: 17 Jul 1855
died: 27 May 1931

ID 26 a9
Sarah Johanna Kiwiet
§
born: May 1855
died: 10 Jan 1937
marr: 29 Nov 1881

Sarah is the daughter of Gerhard Kiwiet [id1725] and Josephine Dirkson [id1726]. See page 60.

Seraphin & Sarah's first Son Seraphin (III) was born in Emden, Germany; their later children were all born in the United States.

ID 81 a4
Joseph Francis "Joe" Oberle
§
born: 1 Dec 1887
died: 19 Aug 1954

ID 80 a5
Katherine Gertrude "Katie" Goldrick
§
born: 10 Mar 1884
died: 9 Apr 1875
marr: 15 Apr 1913

Daughter of Martin G. Goldrick [id170] and Catherine Boyle [id171]. See page 91.

ID 201
Joseph Francis "Joe" Oberle Jr.
§
born: 1 Mar 1914
died: 22 Feb 1990
marr: 18 Sep 1943

ID 200
Katherine Gertrude "Sis" Oberle
§
born: 7 Aug 1915
died: 29 Jan 1996
marr: 4 Oct 1947

ID 196 a2
Cornelius Francis "Cornie" Oberle
§
born: 25 Sep 1917
died: 10 Oct 2004
marr: 11 Oct 1941

ID 197
Francis Xavier Oberle
§
born: 20 Feb 1923
died: 26 Nov 1997
marr: 30 Apr 1960

Uncle Joe married Catherine T. (Nancy) Borig and had three children.

Aunt Sis married Norbert Joseph (Bud) Miller and had five children.

Cornie, my Dad, married Rosalie G. Gonce and had four children.

Uncle Francis married Gladys Helen Maroney and had one child.

No wedding photo available due to house fire; see section beginning on page 280.

"Nancy" & "Joe"
see page 259

"Bud" & "Sis"
see page 266

"Ro" & "Cornie"
see page 120

Gladys & Francis
see page 274

Appendix I ::
Languages of
Our Oberle
Ancestors

A short discussion of the Lothringer Platt, Elsässisch, Church
Latin, French, and German languages, and an introduction to the
handwriting of the period.

Signature of (François) Joseph Oberlé
Taken from the birth record of his son Seraphin on 20 May 1811.
See page 32.

The Languages of Our Ancestors

Our existing knowledge of the Oberle family's history in the eighteenth and nineteenth centuries is derived almost exclusively from vital records of that period[129]; it is therefore appropriate to spend a few paragraphs discussing the various languages of the area, which are *Lothringer Platt*, *Elsässisch*, *French*, *German*, and *Church Latin*[130].

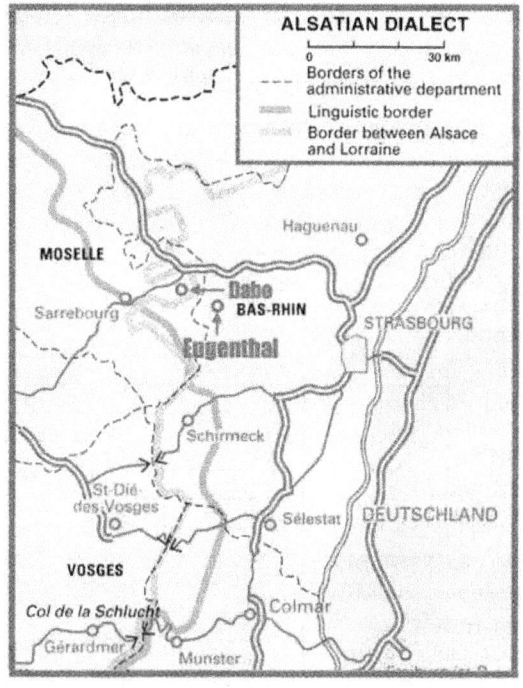

Elsässisch

The language spoken in Dabo, Engenthal, and most of Alsace in the eighteenth century was *Elsässisch*, a dialect derived from early High German. While mainstream German was also derived from High German, it evolved along a different path. The Alsatian and German dialects were thus similar, but not identical, and the natural boundaries of the Vosges mountains in the west and the Rhine River to the east precluded significant homogenization until the late nineteenth century. The map above right shows the areas where *Elsässisch* dominated.

Lothringer Platt

It can be seen from the linguistic borders on the same map that *Lothringer Platt*, mentioned earlier as the German dialect spoken in much of Lothringen, was not the language of Dabo, since the linguistic borders didn't match up with the administrative and political borders. Further, since the only extant records from Dabo are church records in Latin, we needn't concern ourselves with *Platt*.

Medieval (Church) Latin

Until the time of Napoleon's conquest at the end of the century, vital records in Alsace were mostly kept by church authorities, and were thus usually in Latin. As used by the church, Latin had changed quite a bit from the time of

---

[129] That is, civil and religious records of births, deaths, and marriages.

[130] Church Latin was used only in recording vital events in parish registers, and was not spoken by the general populace.

APPENDIX I – LANGUAGES OF OUR ANCESTORS

the "classics" (e.g. Cicero, Horace, et al.), and had been "contaminated" by more than seventeen hundred years of contact with other languages[131]. The interpretation of pre-Napoleonic civil vital records in Alsace (when such records have even survived) is made more difficult by the unusual variant of German script[132] used by the recorders.

The 18th century records from the Catholic Paroisse de Dabo in Moselle, Lorraine and the Mauri Monastery in Wangenbourg illustrated in this book are also in Medieval Church Latin. The following chart, although no substitute for a dictionary, is provided to assist when attempting to interpret the Latin records illustrated in this book should suffice:

Number	Latin root[133]	English	Latin
1/1st	prim*	January	Januar*
2/2nd	secund*	February	Februar*
3/3rd	terti*	March	Mart*
4/4th	quarti*	April	April*
5/5th	quint*	May	Mai*
6/6th	sext*	June	Jun*
7/7th	septim*	July	Jul*
8/8th	octav*	August	August*
9/9th	non*	September	Septembr*
10/10th	decim*	October	Octobr*
11/11th	undecim*	November	Novembr*
12/12th	duodecim*	December	Decembr*
13/13th	decim* tert*	Year	annum | o
14/14th	decim* quart*	Month	mensis
15/15th	decim* quint*	Day	die
16-18th	*similar format*	Husband	maritus
19/19th	decim* non*	Wife	uxor
20/20th	vigesim*	Groom | Bride	sponsus | a
30/30th	trigint*	Widow (er)	vidua | us
40/40th	quadrigesim*	Late (deceased)	mortu*
50-80th	*similar format*	Witness	testator
90/90th	nonagesim*	Married	conjug*
100th	cent*	Baptised	baptisat*
1000th	millesim*	Farmer	agricol*

---

[131] Although efforts were being made by philosophical, legal and engineering disciplines, as well as the universities who trained them, to return Latin to its more formal roots, this effort hadn't yet been successful. See the book *Le Latin ou l'empire d'un signe* ("Latin or the Empire of a Sign") by François Waquet (translated by John Howe), Verso, 2001, © Verso; translation © John Howe. ISBN: 1-85984-615-7, particularly chapter 5, for further reading.

[132] See the section "Reading 18th and 19th Century French and German Handwriting" on page 150 of this Appendix.

[133] Because of the many different forms a word can take in Latin, only the roots are shown. Also note that the numbers from thirteen to nineteen are sometimes written in the reverse order of what is shown in the table; for instance, *decima octava* (18) could also be written as *octava decima*.

French

Although twentieth-century civil governments have developed a reputation for meticulous record keeping, this habit had not yet formed in the eighteenth century. Furthermore, the early French records were completely handwritten, making them sometimes quite difficult to decipher. Napoleon changed all that, and rather quickly, when he took power at the end of that century. Vital records began to be kept religiously (but by civil authorities – pun intended), penalties were established for failure to report vital events, and pre-printed forms were introduced that greatly reduced the difficulties with interpreting handwriting variances. With Napoleonic-era records, it is clearly evident which scribble is, for instance, the mother's name, even if the name itself is illegible. Luckily for the study of our Engenthal ancestors, the French record-keeping regimen lasted until my great-grandfather Seraphin Oberlé left Alsace for the last time. The drawback for the Alsatians was that the records were now all kept in French; for us, however, a modern French dictionary is far more useful when reading these records than a classical Latin dictionary (based on Cicero, Horace, et.al.) is for the pre-Napoleonic records.

The following charts provide English and French equivalents for the words that are key to understanding the French vital records relevant to our ancestors:

Number	Chiffre
1	une
2	deux
3	trois
4	quatre
5	cinq
6	six
7	sept
8	huit
9	neuf
10	dix
11	onze
12	douze
13	treize
14	quatorze
15	quinze
16	seize
17	dix-sept
18	dix-huit
19	dix-neuf

Number	Chiffre
20	Vingt
30	Trente
40	quarante
50	cinquante
60	Soixante
70	Soixante-dix
80	quatre-vingts
90	quatre-vingt-dix
100	Cent
1000	Mil

English	French
?	vaitur
?	lesairin
?	sejeur or sijeur
?	lavier
?	sagar (see pg 53)

APPENDIX I – LANGUAGES OF OUR ANCESTORS

English	French
Husband	Mari
Wife	Femme
Wife	Épouse
Groom	Marié
Bride	Mariée
Spouse (m)	Époux
Spouse (f)	Épouse
Widower (m)	Veuf
Widow (f)	Veuve
Late (deceased)	Feu
Witness	Témoin
Friend	Ami
Neighbor	Voisin
Teacher (Gr 1-8)	Instituteur
Landlord	Proprietaire
Forestry Worker	Bucheron
Carpenter	Charpentier
Day Laborer	Journalier
Weaver	Tisserant

English	French	
Cobbler	Cordonnier	
Worthless (Sic)	Neant[134]	
Year	**an**	
Month	mois	
Day	jour	
Week	semaine	
January	Janviere	
February	Fevriere	
March	Mars	
April	Avril	
May	Mai	
June	Juin	
July	Juillet	
August	Aout	
September	Septembre	7bre
October	Octobre	8bre
November	Novembre	9bre
December	Decembre	10bre

German

For our Oberle ancestors, there are very few records in German. Late records, such as that of the death of the first Seraphin Oberle, who didn't die until his son Seraphin had already departed for the United States, are in German because of the Prussian conquest of Alsace in 1871. Other records, which might have had relevance to our family's history (such as records of the Kiwiet family), seem to have been destroyed during World War II.

Reading 18th and 19th Century French and German Handwriting

For the most part, sloppiness on the part of individual clerks presents more of a problem in reading many of the documents presented in this book than older letter forms do, since learning to interpret the written characters doesn't take all that long to master.

There are, however, specific issues with certain of the older letterforms, primarily because they look like the same letterforms used to represent different letters today.

The best, or perhaps most relevant, example of this is the final letter "e" in the name "Oberle" which, to the modern reader unfamiliar with the handwriting of this period, appears to be an "n," making the name "Oberle" look something like "Dberln."

---

[134] Although the dictionaries give the translation "worthless," that is not quite the slur that it would be in English. In context, it simply means "has no formal employment."

Although I've provided transcriptions and/or translations of key elements in the forms reproduced here, the following table[135] provides examples of eighteenth and early nineteenth written letter forms for all the letters of the alphabet. These may be of help to those wishing to look for more information than what I have provided.

Commonly used written forms of printed letters

A	
a	
B	
b	
C	
c	
D	
d	
E	
e	
F	
f	

[135] Compiled and adapted from several Family History Library Research Outlines.

APPENDIX I – LANGUAGES OF OUR ANCESTORS

Commonly used written forms of printed letters

G	*cursive letter samples*
g	*cursive letter samples*
H	*cursive letter samples*
h	*cursive letter samples*
I	*cursive letter samples*
i	*cursive letter samples*
J	*cursive letter samples*
j	*cursive letter samples*
K	*cursive letter samples*
k	*cursive letter samples*
L	*cursive letter samples*
l	*cursive letter samples*
M	*cursive letter samples*
m	*cursive letter samples*

Commonly used written forms of printed letters

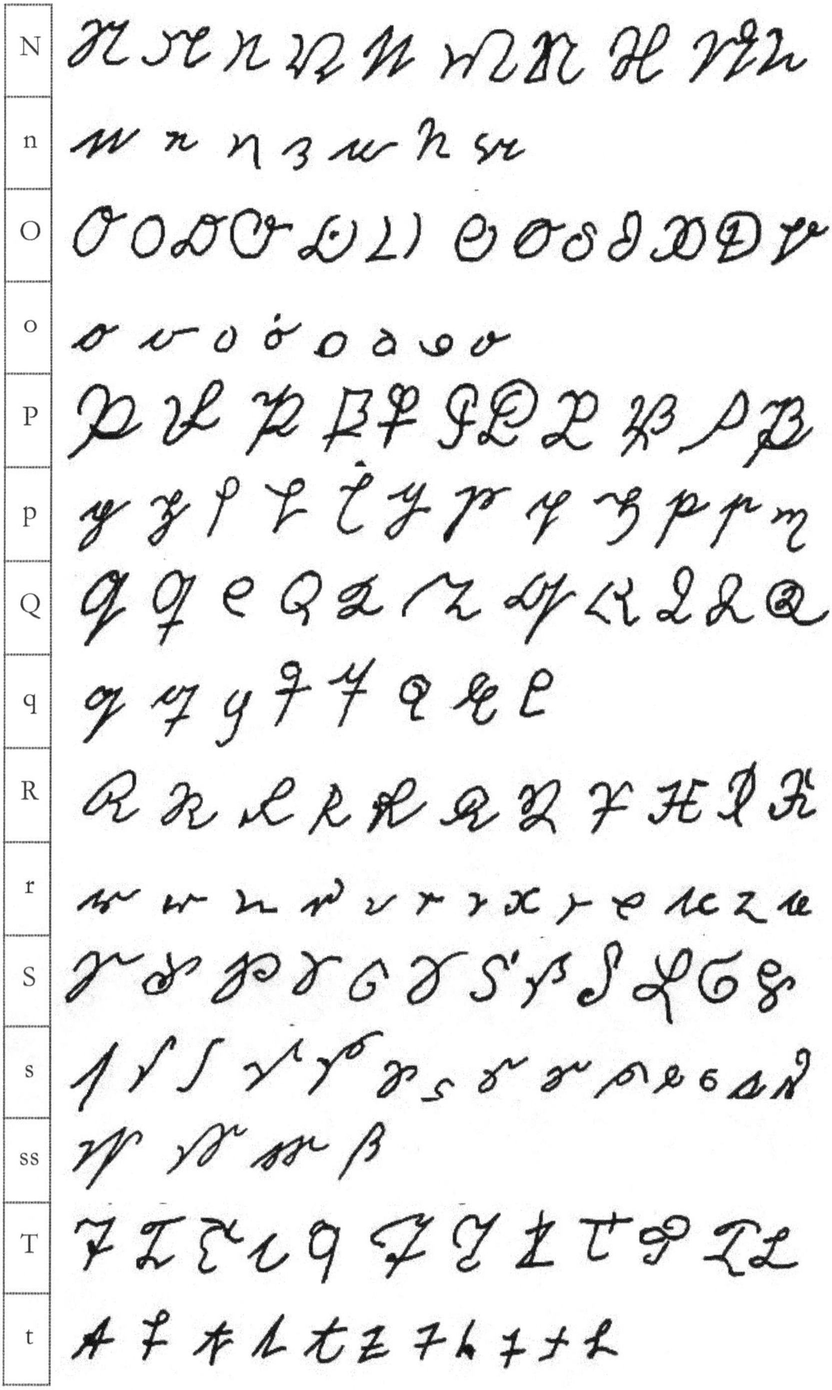

Commonly used written forms of printed letters

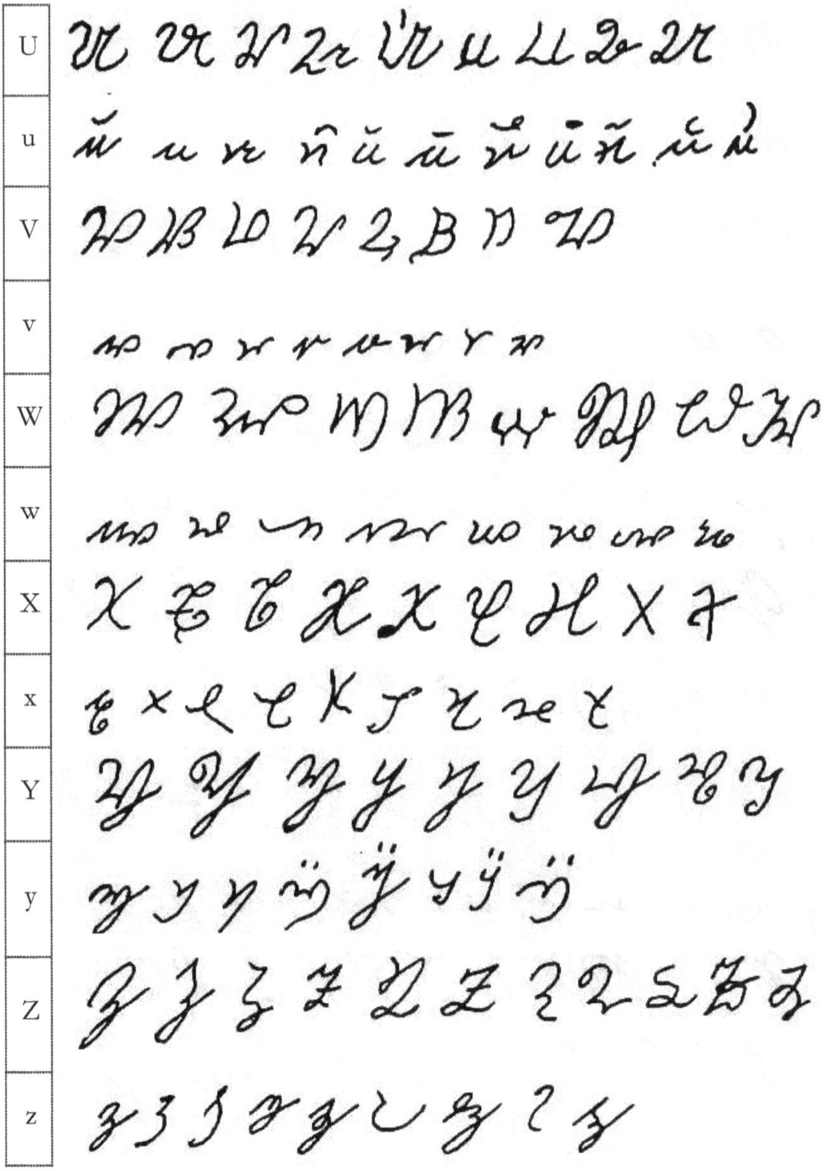

APPENDIX II ::
GETTING THERE

Scene by the D224 Roadside in Romanswiller between Wasselonne and Engenthal

Driving from Strasbourg to Engenthal

Engenthal-le-Bas, the town from which our direct ancestor Seraphin left for Emden and then the United States, is located west and slightly north of Strasbourg, which is the nearest major city. This appendix provides instructions for driving to the area where our Oberle ancestors lived during the eighteenth and nineteenth centuries. Although there is a daily bus service, an automobile is a much preferable way to explore the area.

The instructions below begin at Strasbourg, since that is an easy destination to locate, whether by flying there directly, or by driving from Frankfurt, Germany. It's more fun to cross the Rhine on a small ferry rather than a bridge.

Exit the A350 beltway around Strasbourg onto the A351, then merge with major highway N4. Follow N4 through Ittenheim, Furdenheim, and Marlenheim to Wasselonne

The photo to the right shows the N4 road sign marking the entrance to Wasselonne. This is the town where the photograph of Seraphin seen on page 57 was taken in 1874.

Shortly there will be an intersection with the D260 highway, with signs pointing west on that route for Romaswiller, Cosswiller, Wangenbourg, and Dabo. Below that, the sign indicates that the route goes through the town (Centre Ville). Follow this route through town and turn on to the D224 highway west to Romanswiller.

Remain on highway D224; the picture to the right shows the D224 road marker as you enter the town of Romanswiller.

APPENDIX II – GETTING THERE: FROM STRASBOURG TO ENGENTHAL

Shortly after leaving Romanswiller, there is a junction with the D143 highway, a smaller alternative route to Obersteigen and Dabo. The instructions given here assume you remain on the D224 road.

Before nearing the actual towns of Engenthal or Wangenbourg, there is a large roadside welcome sign on D224 shown to the right.

As you reach the junction of D224 and D218, you may turn south (left) to proceed to the Mairie (Town Hall; see page 32 for a photograph) at the top of the hill or north (right) past the lower part of Engenthal and on toward Obersteigen. Engenthal can also be entered from the north by turning left off D218, a route I recommend in

order to get a feel for the part of the town where our ancestors lived. This also leads up to the Mairie, tourist center, castle ruins, and other sites.

The five segment maps on the next few pages will provide sufficient information to be able to reach Engenthal-le-Bas, Obersteigen, or Dabo from Strasbourg in a rental car. Gasoline is available in the town of Wasselonne.

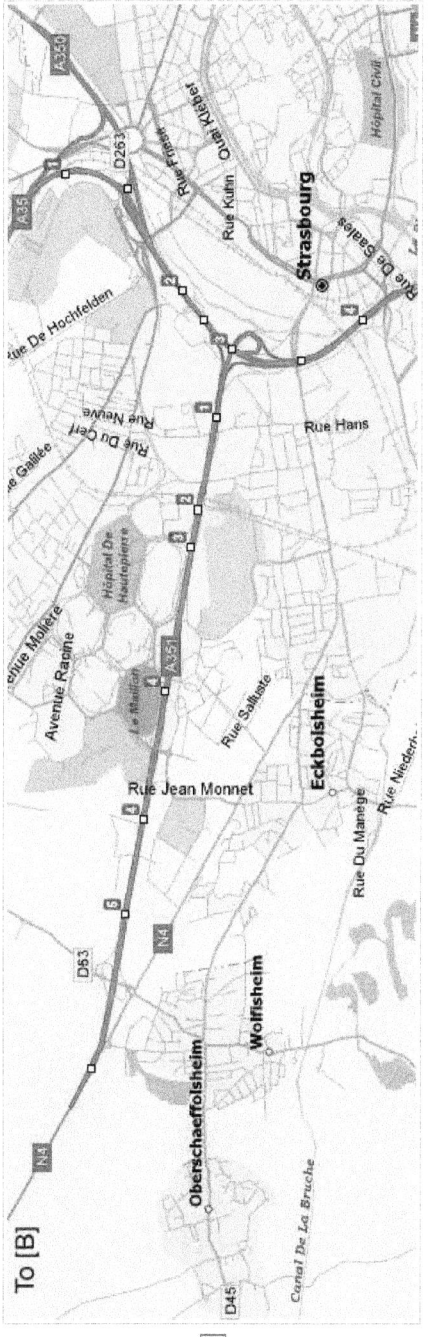

Driving from Strasbourg to Engenthal-le-Bas - Summary:

Map [A] (above): Proceed on highway A 351 west from the A350 Strasbourg beltway, then merge with major highway N4.

Map [B] (top/left of next page): Follow N4 through Ittenheim and towards Furdenheim.

Map [C] (bottom/right of next page): Follow N4 through Furdenheim and Marlenheim.

Map [D] (top/left of following page): Continue on the N4 to Wasselonne, then turn onto the smaller D224 highway and continue through Romanswiller.

Map [E] (bottom/right top of following page): Continue on highway D224 until reaching Engenthal-le-Bas.

APPENDIX II – GETTING THERE: FROM STRASBOURG TO ENGENTHAL

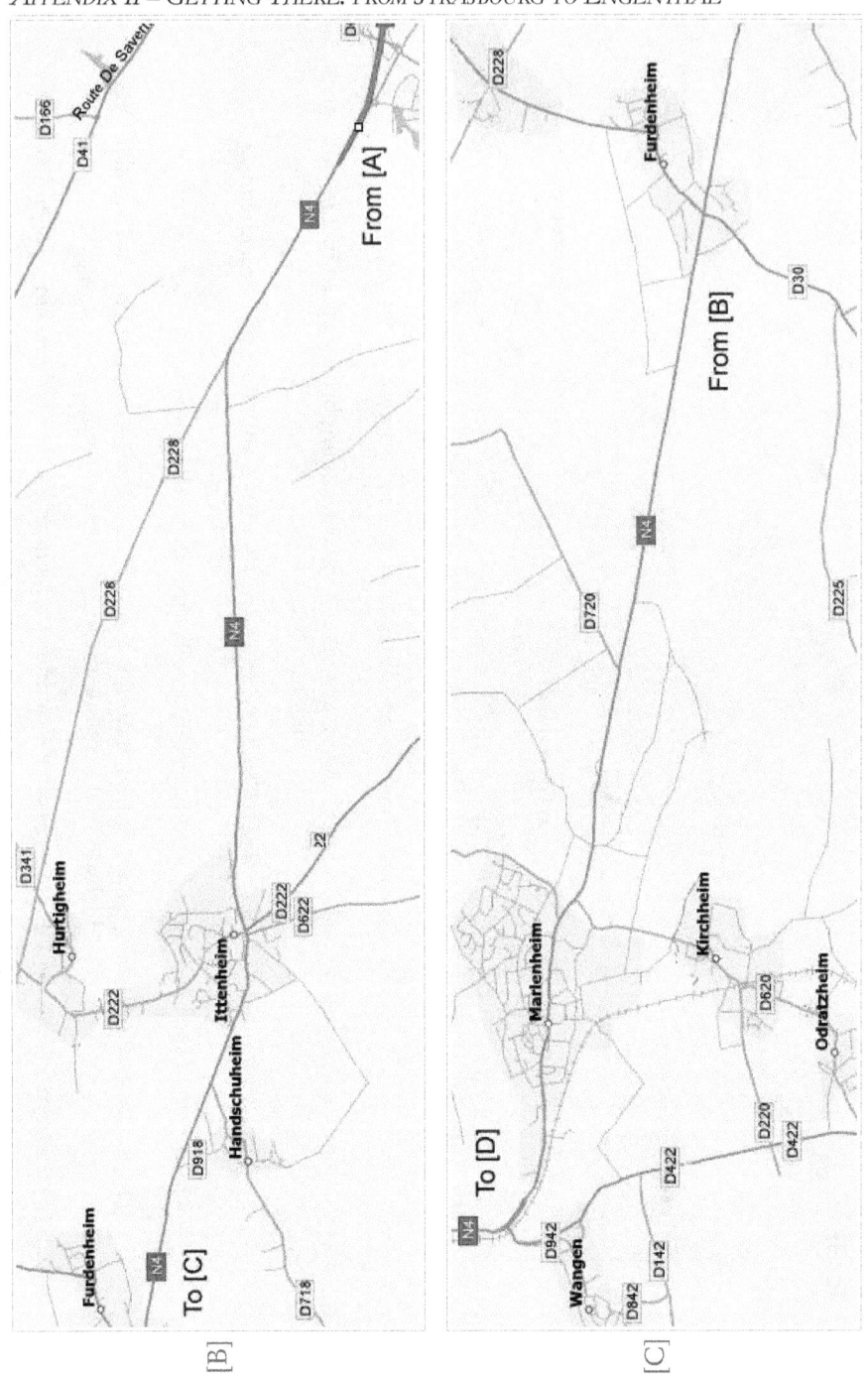

OUR OBERLE ANCESTORS

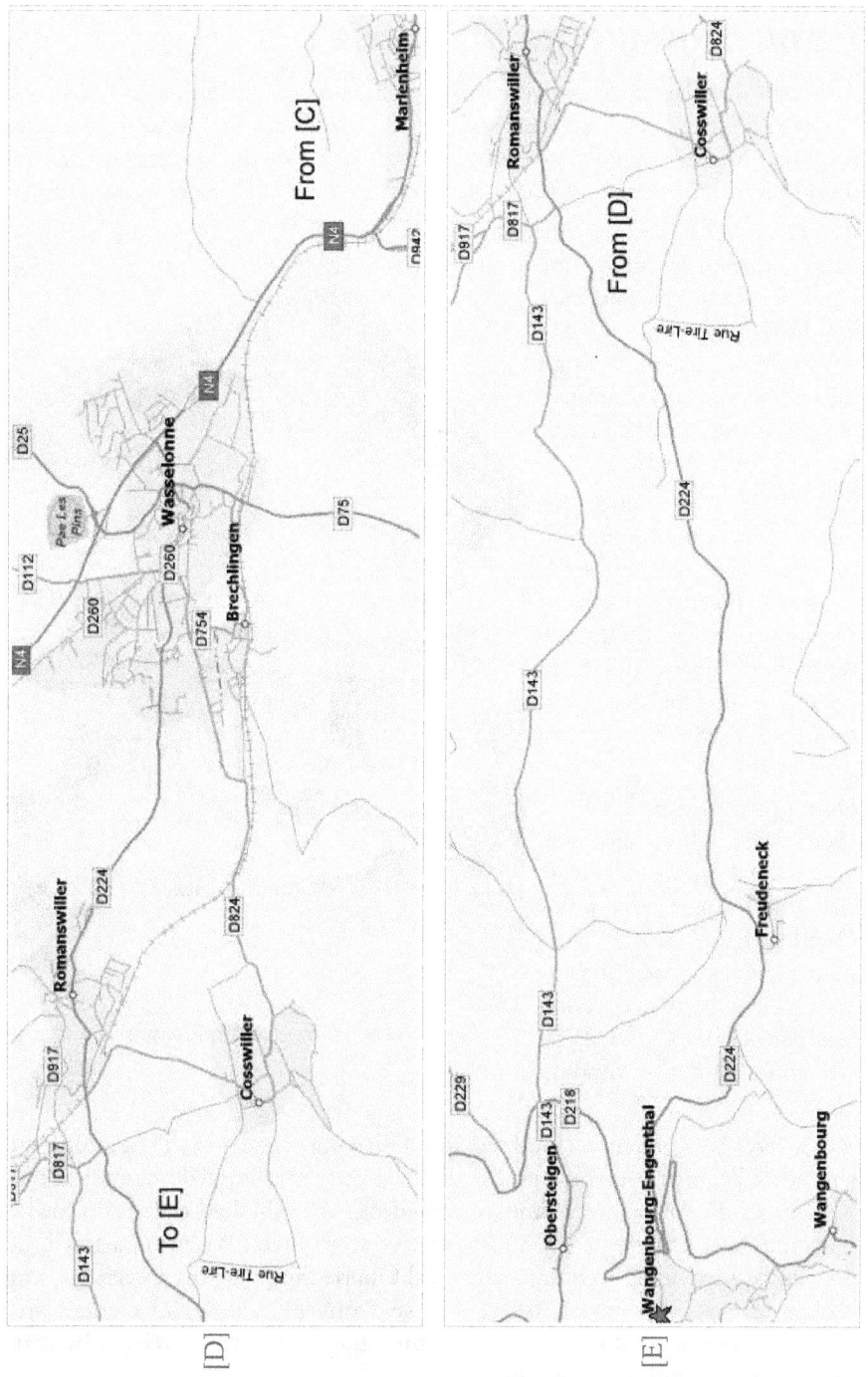

Family Remnants in Alsace?

Although there are very distantly related remnants of our family in Dabo, the last of the Oberles in Engenthal seem to have left long ago. Indeed, given the reuse of burial locations in the area, very few Oberle headstones can be found there, and none that I have been able to directly connect to our family.

But the Oberle name is still quite common in Alsace; my Uncle Francis reported seeing the name on several businesses while passing through the area as his unit was chasing the Nazis out of France during World War II.[136]

His 377th Anti-Aircraft Artillery Battalion was known to have passed very near the town of Kilstett, north of Strasbourg, where the Hotel-Restaurant Oberle has been operating on the Rue Nationale (D468) for several generations.

During our visit in 2004, we spent two nights there, and had several meals. We were also able to meet quite a few Oberles from Kilstett and their relatives in neighboring Gambsheim and even compare family trees with them, but could find no common ancestry.

Kilstett, Alsace – Oberle Hotel & Restaurant in 2004

A few days later, when we inquired about viewing records at the Mairie in the southeastern town of Rhinau, the clerk on duty mysteriously requested that we wait in the lobby for a time. It turned out that she had called the town's mayor, Albert Oberle, to let him know we were there. When he arrived, he was also quite willing to discuss the local Oberle family with us, even copying quite a few records himself for us to take. Ironically, although we could find no connection to that Oberle family either, they are distantly related by marriage to my second daughter's husband!

---

[136] This is mentioned on page 277.

Appendix III :: Connecting Balthassar to François Joseph

This Appendix discusses a weak link in the chain of our ancestry between my 3rd great-grandfather François Joseph Oberlé and Balthassar Oberlé, who I believe to be my 4th great-grandfather, and attempts to justify my belief that they are son and father.

Signature of Balthassar [III] Oberlé

This Balthassar <u>id1691</u> is the half-brother of our ancestor François Joseph Oberlé. Their generation seems to be the first generation of males that we can prove could sign their names, although there is evidence that their father Balthassar [II] <u>id1675</u> could also sign his name.

Is Balthassar Oberlé really our Ancestor?

Names of those in the first three generations of our Oberlé ancestors presented in the chart on page 51 this book are based on the contention that our earliest proven ancestor, François Joseph Oberlé id1154, was the son of Balthassar (II)[137] Oberlé id1675. Since I have located no incontrovertible evidence that proves this relationship, it therefore seems appropriate to present the arguments that support this conclusion.

Balthassar (II) Oberle was born in about 1745 in Dabo and, following the death of his first wife Anne-Marie Schott id4224, who I show as the mother of François Joseph Oberlé id1154, married Marie Anne Müller id1676 (see page 16 & ff). They are the parents of a third Balthassar Oberlé id1691 who, along with his wife Marie Elisabethe Dieda id1689, can be proven to be the ancestors of roughly half the Oberlés living in Engenthal-le-Bas during the nineteenth century. The remaining Oberlés in Engenthal can be definitively traced to our own ancestor François Joseph Oberlé id1154 and his wife Marie Anne Schreiber id1155. What isn't proven is that Balthassar III and our ancestor Joseph are half-siblings, with Balthassar II being the father of both. I believe, however, that there is enough circumstantial evidence to consider this a reasonable conclusion until some records turn up to prove or disprove it.

Naming Conventions

Although not strictly observed, the traditional Germanic way of naming male children was as follows:

- 1st Son: gets his paternal Grandfather's (Father's Father) Name
- 2nd Son: gets his maternal Grandfather's (Mother's Father) Name
- 3rd Son: gets his Father's Name
- 4th Son: gets his Father's eldest brother's Name

This tradition was even less strictly observed by the Alsatians, but occurred often enough that it should be kept in mind when examining records of children born in this era.

The one factor I'm aware of that might argue *against* the second Balthassar id1675 being François Joseph's father is that the naming conventions described above don't seem to be followed.

The first of Balthassar (II)'s sons that I have been able to identify was Antoine id4236, whose paternal grandfather would therefore have been Balthassar (I). This, if correct, would not fit the traditional pattern. Antoine's paternal grandfather had a brother named Antonius id4305, which fits the tradition for a fourth son, not a first son. It is possible, therefore, that the tradition was fol-

---

[137] As mentioned earlier in the book, I have assigned Roman Numerals to the sequential Balthassars and Seraphins in our family tree in order to make it clear which of these I was discussing at any moment. In this case, the first Balthassar lived from about 1711 to 27 April 1788, and his great-great grandson, the fifth sequential Balthassar, lived from 21 September 1860 to 11 January 1861.

lowed, but that there are two earlier sons of Balthassar (II)'s that I haven't identified. So far, therefore, Antoine's name doesn't provide any useful or conclusive resolution to the question.

Balthassar (II)'s second son, who I believe to be François Joseph Oberlé id1154, would not fit the naming pattern at all, since his maternal grandfather would have been named Jean (Jean Schott id4250). Antoine, discussed above, named a son François Joseph id4241. Since this is the only child[138] of his I could locate, and our François Joseph was his younger, not older, brother, it wouldn't fit the naming pattern even if we could assume that Antoine had three older brothers.

Balthassar II's third son was Balthassar III id1691, however, which does fit the traditional naming pattern, but only if one assumes that François Joseph is, in fact, his second son, and I haven't missed any earlier sons.

Later records of the family suggest, however, that there might have been a different naming convention or, more importantly, no convention in use.

François Joseph Oberlé gave his name to his second son id1230, as did his son (and my 2nd great-grandfather) Seraphin I id708. The first Balthassar id1704 and the second Seraphin id25 each gave their name to their respective first son.

Therefore, I don't find the non-adherence to German naming conventions a compelling reason to discard the theory that Balthassar II is Joseph's father.

Several arguments that do support the theory that Balthassar is Joseph's father, although clearly circumstantial, include the following:

Ages and Gaps

Balthassar III id1691 is about the right age to be either a brother or cousin of François Joseph, and their estimated birth years do not conflict with this theory, but I have been unable to locate a birth or baptismal record for my third great grandfather François Joseph.

I have, however, located birth records for the five other children of Balthassar II and Anne Marie Schott listed on page 16. From her marriage until her death in 1776, the records show that Anne-Marie had children quite regularly but for a gap between March 1772 and February 1774 – a gap that would be filled neatly by the birth of François Joseph. In a vacuum, such a coincidence would not be sufficient to make the assumption that François Joseph was Balthassar's son, but there are no records of other Oberle families having children in that decade, making the attribution much less tentative.

Convergence in Engenthal

As the Engenthal vital records are examined in reverse chronological order (i.e. going from the 1870s back towards 1790), the number of Oberles declines significantly. It therefore seems reasonable to assume that all of them are likely descendents of the two younger Oberle males (Balthassar III id1691

---

[138] This François Joseph was born in Dabo on 29 January 1806

and my 3rd great grandfather François Joseph id1154) known to have moved into the Engenthal area in the late eighteenth century from neighboring Dabo.

The death records for Magdalena Oberle id4238 and Michall Oberle id4225, older relatives who also moved to Engenthal, might help to clarify this if they were legible (see images of these records on pages 168 and 169). So far, however, I have only been able to decipher the dates (3 Frimaire an IX and 28 Frimaire an IX, which I believe equate to 24 November 1800 and 18 December 1800 respectively), and to identify the name Antony Rolling on Michall's record – note that Francois Joseph's daughter Catherine id1160 married a Rolling. From what I've learned to date, I believe Michall and Magdalena Oberle are likely siblings of Balthassar II id1675, and thus an uncle and aunt respectively of our ancestor François Joseph. Both Michall and Magdalena were living in Engenthal at the time of their deaths.

Demonstrated Family Connections

On the marriage record for the younger Balthassar (III) id1691 and Elisabethe Dieda id1689, dated 16 April 1812[139], Joseph Müller, age 40, is listed as the first witness. This would make that Joseph's birth year roughly 1772, which is consistent with his being the Joseph [140] Müller id1161 who is the father of Catherine Müller id1157 and the grandfather of my 2nd great-grandmother Catherine Ruffenach id1147. Catherine Ruffenach is, of course, Seraphin (I) Oberle's second wife, and the mother of my great-grandfather Seraphin (II) who eventually migrated to Baltimore. Although the population of Engenthal at the time was only about 500, this still suggests some close ties, although not necessarily family ones, between Balthassar and Joseph.

The second witness at the younger Balthassar's wedding was Sebastien Demand[141], age 37, which would make Sebastien's birth year 1775, indicating that he is likely the older brother of Catherine Deumant id1210, who is the wife of Joseph Müller above. The idea that the primary and secondary witnesses to Balthassar's marriage are from our own line reinforces the idea that there is a strong connection between Balthassar III's branch and our own branch. The one I have chosen (that they are half-siblings and both sons of Balthassar II) seems to me to be the most likely given the available data.

Images of records mentioned in this appendix are presented on the following pages.

---

[139] This record is reproduced on page 48, with a transcription on the following page.

[140] See page 39.

[141] The spellings Deumant, Demant and Dimant also appear in Engenthal records, but comparison of the various records shows conclusively that these are all the same family.

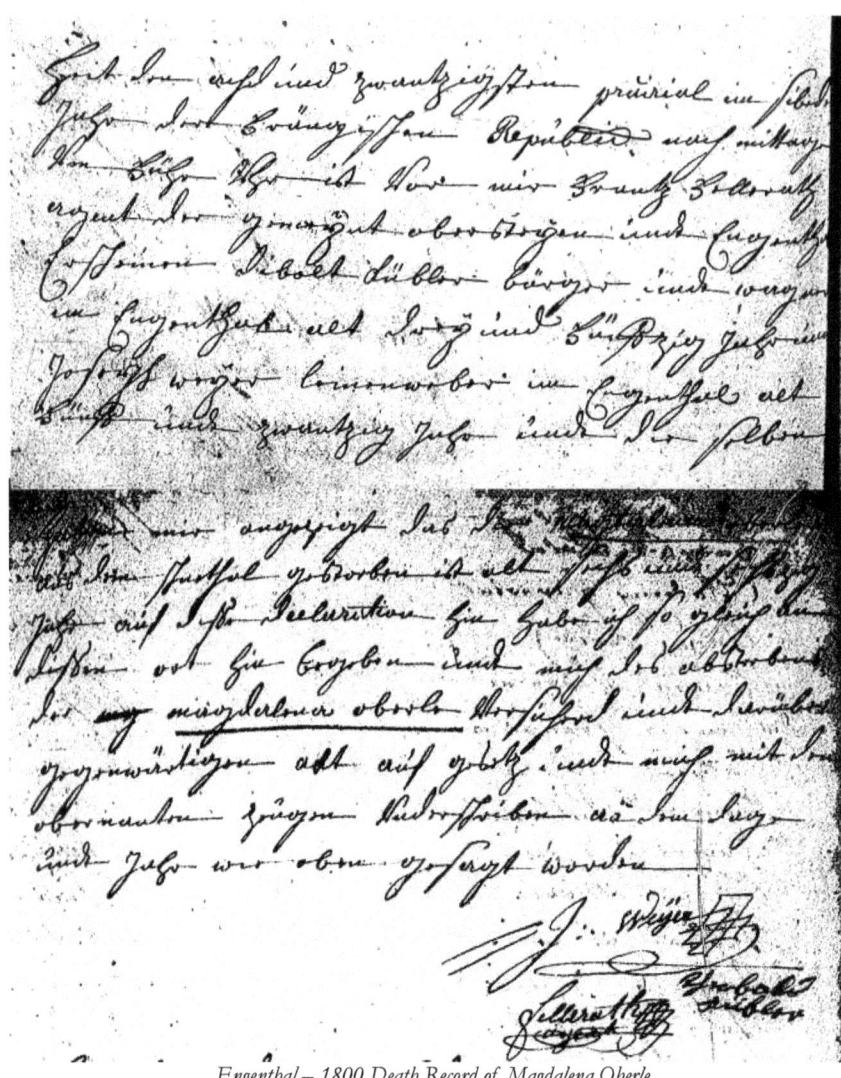

Engenthal – 1800 Death Record of Magdalena Oberle

This is dated 28 Frimaire an IX in the French Revolutionary Calendar[142], which I believe equates to 18 December 1800.

This record begins on the bottom of one ledger page and continues on the top of the next. Magdalena Oberle's name is underlined in the original, and can be seen on the fourth line from the bottom.

This record might also provide information about the Oberle family if it could be deciphered and translated.

---

[142] See a discussion of this calendar on page 41.

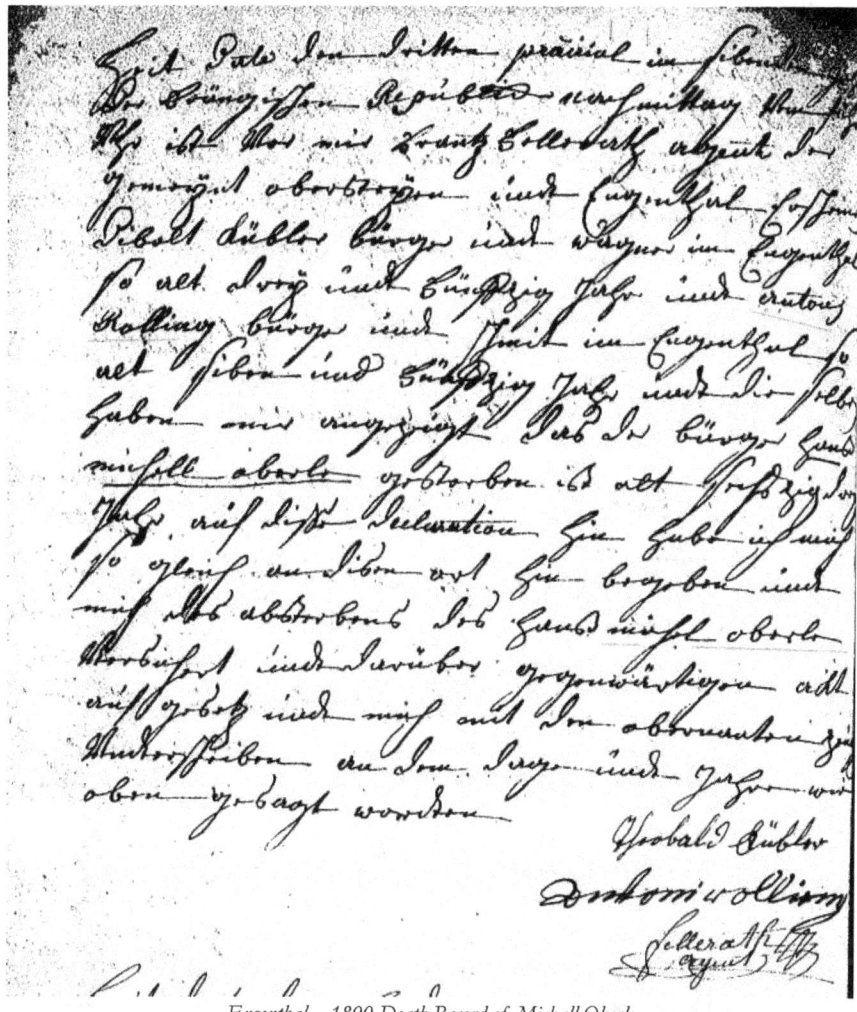

Engenthal – 1800 Death Record of Michall Oberle

This is dated 3 Frimaire an IX in the French Revolutionary Calendar, which I believe equates to 24 November 1800. At the time of this record, preprinted vital records forms had not yet been introduced – that was one of the many improvements introduced by Napoleon Bonaparte's civil government.

Michall Oberle's name is underlined, and can be seen on the tenth line.

In records of this era, one can make out both German and French words. Along with the legibility issues, this makes it particularly difficult to interpret.

If this record could be deciphered, it might provide very useful information to help trace the Oberle line further back into the eighteenth century.

APPENDIX III – CONNECTING BALTHASSAR TO FRANCOIS JOSEPH OBERLÉ

Engenthal – 1812 Marriage record of Balthasar III Oberle and Elisabeth Dieda

Marriage 16 APR 1812
between
Oberlé, Balthassar [III] (id1691)
age: 31
born: 15 April 1781 at Windsbourg
Parents:
the late Balthassar [II] Oberlé (id1675)
and
Marie Anne Müller (id1676)
and
Elisabethe Dieda (id1689)
age: 20
born: 21 Nov 1792 at Windsbourg
Parents:
Joseph Dieda (id1694), laborer
and
Madelaine Saly (id1695)

Witnesses:
1. Joseph Müller,
   profession "Lavier" (??)
   Age 40
   (id1161)

2. Sebastien Deumand,
   profession Day Laborer
   Age 37
   (ID – not assigned)
   (brother-in-law of Joseph Müller above)

3. Florent Stengel,
   profession Day Laborer
   Age 56

4. Dominique Soder,
   profession Day Laborer
   Age 50

To the left is a transcription of the key elements in Balthassar III's marriage record of 16 April 1812, shown on the facing page.

See the text beginning on page 167 for connections between the witnesses listed in this document and the family of our ancestor François Joseph Oberlé.

APPENDIX IV :: THE 1864 BOYLE PHOTO ALBUM

Album belonging to Catherine Boyle

Outside Views of the 1864 Boyle Photo Album

APPENDIX IV – THE 1864 BOYLE PHOTO ALBUM

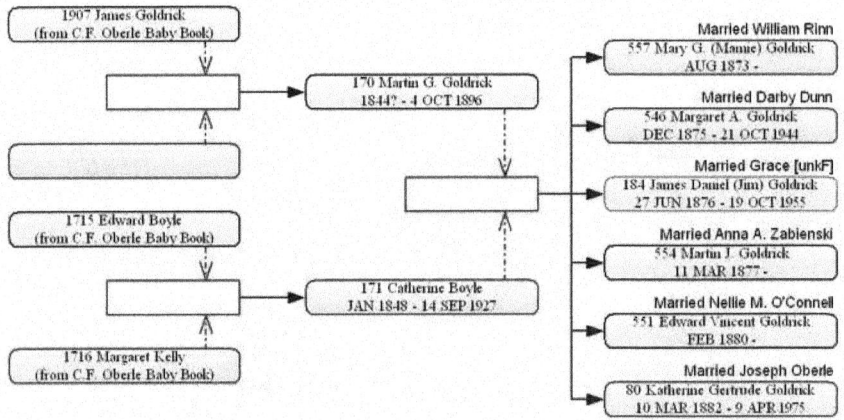

Diagram of our only identified Boyle, Goldrick and Kelly Ancestors

The 1864 Boyle Photo Album

Source of the Album

In their basement, my parents had a box containing a very old photo album that, according to them, was found in my Grandmother Oberle's (Katherine "Katie" Goldrick Oberle [id80]) attic after her house was sold in 1969. My grandmother's maiden name was Catherine Boyle [id171]. Catherine was born in January 1848, and later married to Martin G. Goldrick [id170].

The box itself is actually a Godiva Chocolates box (16 oz), and had apparently contained the photo album for many years. Inside the lid of the box was the following inscription:

> *William A. Rinn, MD*
> *1502 Sherbrook Road*
> *Lutherville, MD 21093*
> *825-3510*
> *Return to above address*

Dr. Rinn [id533] was a cousin of my Father's through his Mother's side of the family and the two of them were good friends during their childhood, although I knew Dr. Rinn only slightly when I was a child.

From the above inscription, and particularly the address, telephone number, and use of a Zip Code, the date of the box itself appears to have been later than 1963 (when ZIP codes were introduced) but earlier than 1969.

Inside the box is a handwritten note on what appears to be a doctor's note page (from a promotional pad supplied by the maker of the drug Tranxene) that says:

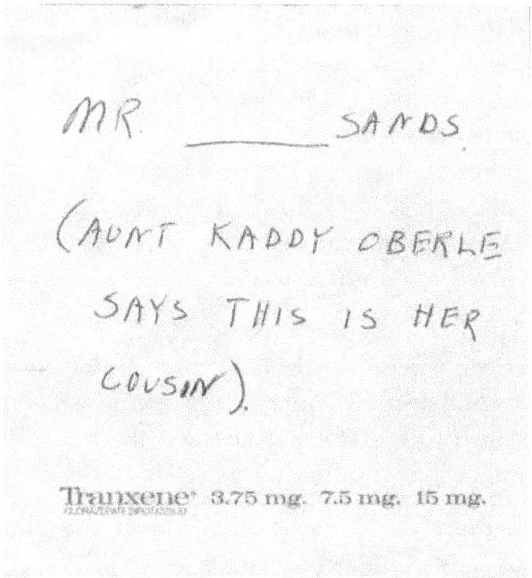

> *Mr. _____ Sands,*
> *(Aunt Kaddy Oberle*
> *says this is her*
> *cousin).*

MR. ______ SANDS
(AUNT KADDY OBERLE
SAYS THIS IS HER
COUSIN).
Tranxene® 3.75 mg. 7.5 mg. 15 mg.

The underscoring and parentheses are as written. The implication from the paper on which the note was written, as well as the name and address on the box, is that Dr. Rinn wrote the note. My parents confirmed that he and that part of the family used to call Grandmom Oberle "Aunt Kaddy" rather than "Aunt Katie", although they couldn't recall why that was. Neither of them had any idea of who Mr. Sands was, although he (or, more likely, one of his ancestors) may be in one of the pictures in the album according to the indexes. It also isn't clear to whom "this" refers – i.e. whether it was someone whose picture is in the album (e.g. Mr. Sands), or the original owner of the album, whose identity isn't proven, but whom I believe is almost certainly Catherine Boyle.

Physical Description of the Album

The photo album measures about 5.75" high, 4.5" wide and 1.5" thick, and appears to have been of very high quality, at least by today's standards. The outer cover seems to be of tooled leather (or possibly a reasonable facsimile thereof), and the buff-colored pages are quite thick, having slots with oval faces into which the photographs were to be inserted. The edges of the pages not only are gold-leafed, but elaborately embossed as well. The leather from the album's outer back spine is mostly missing, although there are several smaller pieces of this in the Godiva box. There are two fairly elaborate metal straps on the rear that clasp to hooks on the front in order to keep the album closed when not in use.

The book as I discovered it was in three pieces, the first consisting of the cover, three front leaf pages, and eight double-sided photograph pages. The second section contains the remaining seven photo pages, and the last contains two blank leaf pages and the rear cover. I could see no marks or other indications on the album itself as to where it was made or by what company.

Because of the poor condition of the album, I have photographed as much of it as I could, and have collected the pictures in this appendix to aid in further research into our Boyle and/or Goldrick ancestors.

Title and Dedication Pages

 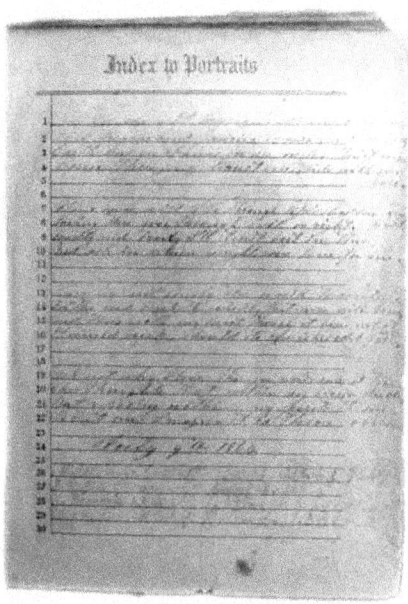

The first page in the album, shown above left, is titled "The Photographic Album." The reverse side of this page is blank.

The third page is titled "Index to Portraits," but the blank printed lines intended for the index entries are filled by a handwritten poem. I have identified the poem, the implications of which are discussed on page 180.

After the poem is the notation "July 9, 1864." This date presents a clue of sorts. If Katie's cousin (Mr. Sands?) owned the book or was one of the subjects, it would be far too early, leading to the assumption that Katie or her cousin more likely inherited the album. The date is not that of the quoted poem (see discussion of the poem on page 180), and I believe the date is confirmed as the date the album was begun by the presence of a tax stamp on the back of one of the pictures (see notes for album photo #18 below).

Finally, at the bottom of the page, and magnified above, are four lines that appear to be an index to the album's contents. As can be seen in the illustra-

Appendix IV – The 1864 Boyle Photo Album

tion, the handwriting is obviously not in the same hand as the one that wrote the poetry portion, and is faint and very difficult to read.

Existing Indexes to the Photographs

There is another handwritten note found in the Godiva chocolate box, which is apparently an attempt by someone (perhaps Dr. Rinn) to transcribe (and possibly add to) the names on the index page above. A comparison of my interpretation of the original index with that provided on the separate sheet is shown below:

Photo Album Index	Index found on sheet in Godiva Chocolate Box
1. Mabel and Mrs. Smith	1. Mabel + Mrs. Smith
There is no listing for pictures 2, 3 or 4 in the Album's index.	(3) Mr. Sands (Koddy's Identification) (4) Grandmother B. + Aunt Bridget.
5. Dela Smith	5. Dela (Delia?) Smith (Boys)
6. E. Kelly	6. E. Kelly
7. Papa	7. Papa ; Kelly's Student
8. Mamma	8. Mamma
9. Aunt B.	9. Aunt B (Bridget?)
10. Aunt M. L	10. Aunt M. Louise
11. Mamie (I see only one "m")	11. Mammie
12. Belle F.	12. Bell F.
13. Uncle John	13. Uncle John
14. Roger	14. Roger (Uncle Roger Boyle?)
15. C. Dowd	*15. C. Dowd.
16. L. Holland	16. L. Holland.
17. E. Boyle	17. E. Boyle.
18. Margaret	18. Margaret.

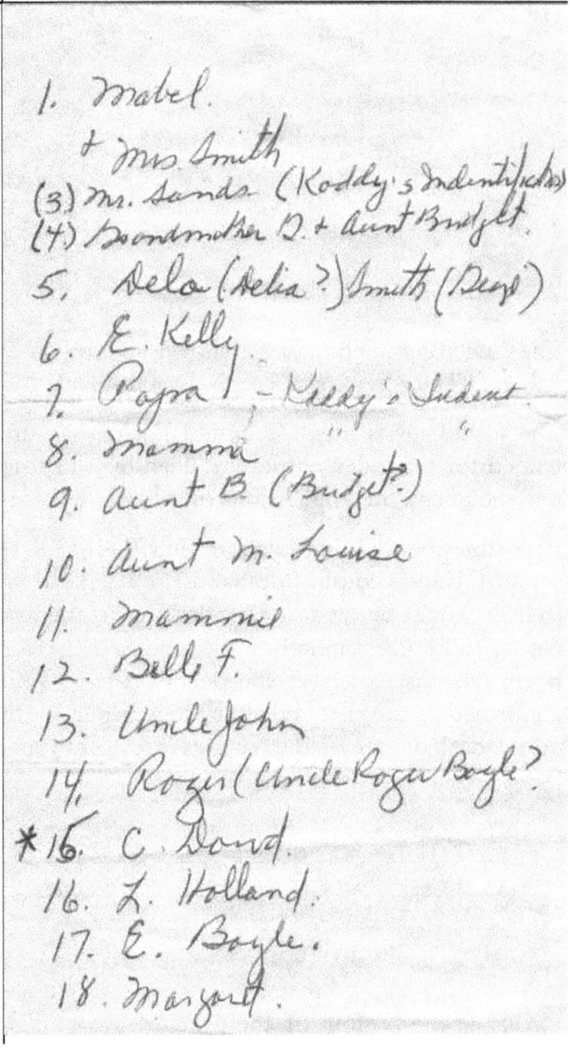

The indexes match almost exactly but for the number of entries (15 vs 17), but neither list corresponds well to the photos after number 1. The transcriber of the separate sheet added notations for slots 3 and 4, which didn't appear in the album's index, and on slot 3, 7 and 8 also made the notation "Kaddy's Indent[143]...," which I am interpreting to mean that these are my Grandmother's identifications to the author of the note as to whose pictures are in those slots. There are nineteen photographs in the album including one duplicate.

Surnames Mentioned in the Indexes

Six surnames are mentioned in the two indexes to the album; these are listed below with a description of how those names fit into the Oberle genealogy.

Boyle My father's maternal grandmother (and my great grandmother) was Catherine Boyle [id171], who was the original owner of this album. Catherine was the daughter of Edward Boyle [id1715] and Margaret Kelly [id1716], and married Martin Goldrick [id170].

Dowd I am not aware of any ancestors with the surname Dowd.

F. There is a "Belle F." listed in the indexes above, so I assume the person's surname begins with F., but I am not aware of any surnames beginning with "F" that are related to our family.

Holland My great grandmother Catherine Boyle [id171] worked for a period of time during her teenaged years as a housekeeper for the family of John and Sarah Holland, and appeared on the 1870 census in their household. As far as I have been able to determine, however, the Holland family is in no way related to ours.

Kelly My great grandmother Catherine Boyle [id171] was the daughter of Margaret Kelly [id1716], who married Edward Boyle [id1715].

Sands I am unaware of any ancestors with the surname Sands. Based on Dr. Rinn's note, my grandmother Katie Oberle's cousin's name is Sands, but I have so far been unable to identify who that is.

Smith I am not aware of any ancestors with the surname Smith.

Locations where the Photographs were taken

Although most of the photographs seem to have been taken in Baltimore[144], the photo in slot 10 was made at a photographer's shop in Liverpool, England, and the one in slot 5 was taken in a Boston studio. Although photo 29 has a Baltimore photographer's identification, "New York" is handwritten on the rear.

---

[143] The word clearly begins with "indent.." as opposed to "ident..." though, but I can't come up with any reasonable interpretation for that.
[144] The photos in slots 18, 24, 25, 26, and 29 are explicitly identified as having been made in Baltimore.

Implications of The Dedication Poem

On the album page intended for an index to the photographs is a poem that I have identified as "Leave me not Lonely" by A. K. Percival, first published on page 229 of the first issue of Ballou's Dollar Monthly Magazine of January 1855. This six-hundred-page collection of fiction, published monthly by Maturin Murray Ballou in Boston for many years, had a cover price of 10¢.

BALLOU'S DOLLAR MONTHLY MAGAZINE.

VOL. I.   BOSTON, JANUARY, 1855.   No. 1.

The poem is transcribed below. I would like to say that it suggests the album owner would have been a romantic adolescent female but, given the era in which this was written, that can't be certain.

> "Leave me not lonely, to sorrow and tears
> Wild dreams and fancies, terrors and fears;
> Earth has no charms for me, unless thou'rt near;
> Come then, my dearest one, bide with me here.
>
> Thine own will I be, through life's shadow and light,
> Loving thee ever, through evil or right;
> Fondly and truly I'll trust but in thee,
> And ask in return, nought save love for me.
>
> Leave me not lonely, the world to contend,
> For "the reed breaketh quickly that never will bend;"
> And thus with my heart, though it bend not at all,
> It would break, should its cherished idol fall.
>
> Ask not why I love thee, for words cannot tell
> The thoughts that within my bosom dwell;
> But reposing upon my spirit's throne,
> Is but one image – it is thine own.

What is clear is that the date written below the poem, July 9th 1864, is likely the date the album was first purchased or used, since the poem had been written at least nine years earlier.

Since, as near as I can tell, Ballou's Monthly was not available outside Boston for its first few years of publication, the availability of the poem (and likely the magazine itself) would indicate that someone connected to our ancestry may have lived in Boston. See Photo #5 in the album.

OUR OBERLE ANCESTORS

Descriptions of the Album's Photos

Because of the condition of the album when I found it, I made no attempt to forcibly remove any photographs to see what, if any, inscriptions were on their backs. The inscriptions I have recorded are all from those photographs that had no other photograph on the backing page. It isn't obvious to me whether these "missing" pictures were ever present, or had been removed or lost over the years.

Each album page measures 4 1/4" x 5 1/2" with a 2 1/16" x 3 3/8" opening with the top edges slightly shorter due to the rounded left and right edges.

Blank white paper glued to back of photograph.

Page 1 Photo – ("Mabel") *Rear of Photo 1*

Album Slot #: 1
Type of Photo: Ferrotype[145]
Size: 2 3/8" x 3 1/2" Ferrotype inserted in a 3 1/8" x 4 5/8" decorative paper sleeve.
Content: Listed in both indexes as "Mabel and Mrs. Smith"
Suspected to be: I haven't identified any Mabel in the Holland or Boyle family, nor have I identified anyone named Smith connected with either family.
Estimated Year: Woman's hair suggests 1860-1870; her collar suggests 1870-1890. Circa 1870-1880??

Album Page

---

[145] Ferrotypes, also incorrectly called Tintypes, were photographs made on very thin coated iron sheets from about 1856 onward. They were gradually replaced by later technologies although they continued to be available until about 1900. One characteristic is that the images are reversed from real-life.

APPENDIX IV – THE *1864* BOYLE PHOTO ALBUM

For comparison purposes, the picture above (not part of the "Boyle Album.") is known to be of Catherine Boyle.
This photo is glued to the backing, so it was impossible to determine if there is any inscription present.

Page 2 Photo – Catherine Boyle

Rear of Photo 2

Album Slot #:   2

Type of Photo: Paper. The picture itself was cut very cleanly and glued onto the flowered background (the lower right is peeling slightly)

Size: Oval glued to 2 $^{1/2}$" x 4 $^{1/8}$" decorative background.

Content: No Name listed in either album index or transcription. This is possibly the owner of the album, since no one felt the need to identify her.

Suspected to be: Catherine Boyle, my great-Grandmother

Album Page

The photo in slot 2 above seems to be the owner of the album – possibly Catherine Boyle herself (she would have been sixteen years old at the time the album was dated – note the slant of the eyes and the set of the mouth when comparing the above photos)

Estimated Year: 1864-1872

OUR OBERLE ANCESTORS

Black Lacquer

Page 3 Photo – (Mr. Sands)

Rear of Photo 3

Album Page

Album Slot #: 3
Type of Photo: Ferrotype
Size: 2 3/8"x3 1/2" with unevenly trimmed corners.
Content: Mr. Sands (Kaddy's Indentifi???)[146]
Suspected to be: Based on Dr. Rinn's note, my grandmother Katie Oberle's cousin's name is Sands, but this person is probably a generation before her cousin. He could conceivably be an uncle (married to a Boyle or Kelly) or similar.

There is a possible inference that can be made from the note that a Sands was in possession of this album at one time and passed it on to the Oberles through Dr. Rinn

Estimated Year: 1870-1880 based on the hair, tie, collar and vest style.

---

[146] Some immigrants came from England and Ireland as "indentured" servants to someone who paid their passage to the United States. Such indentured immigrants would then work for their sponsor for a few years before becoming "free," although often when the immigrant was a relative, the contract period for the indenture was loosely enforced, if at all. If the word is actually "Indent...," the possibility that Mr. Sands, whoever he was, was an indentured immigrant should be mentioned, but it seems very doubtful that he was "Kaddy's Indent...," since the time period of the photograph doesn't fit. I suspect it is more likely that the word actually means that "Kaddy" identified the name of the person.

APPENDIX IV – THE *1864 BOYLE PHOTO ALBUM*

Black Lacquer

Page 4 Photo – ("Grandmother")

Rear of Photo 4

Album Slot #: 4
Type of Photo: Ferrotype
Size: 2 5/8" x 3 11/16", obviously trimmed to fit.
Content: Grandmother and Aunt Bridget per index
Suspected to be: If Catherine Boyle was actually the owner of this album, then Aunt Bridget could be her mother Margaret Kelly's sister (or her father Edward Boyle's sister), and "Grandmother" would be one of my 3rd great-grandmothers.
Estimated Year:

Album Page

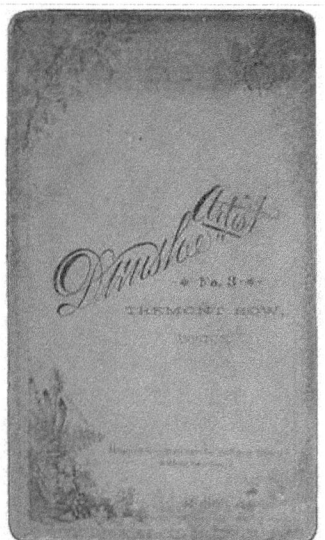

Page 5 Photo – (Unknown Male) *Rear of Photo 5*

Album Slot #:	5
Type of Photo:	Paper, apparently a Carte de Visite
Size:	2 1/2" x 4 1/8" paper with rounded edges (as can be seen in the rear view above.)
Content:	Indexes say "Delia Smith," obviously wrong.
Suspected to be:	I have found no indication, nor is there any family tradition to suggest, that the Boyles came to the United States through Boston (or ever lived there), although Boston was a port of entry (but not as common as Philadelphia, Baltimore, or New York) in the 19th century. Perhaps this is a Kelly or a Sands?
Estimated Year:	1880-1890 based on single top jacket button, and confirmed by the year on the back of the photograph. The Boyles and Goldricks that I am aware of, and certainly those in our direct line, were all living in Baltimore by 1881, further suggesting that this man was possibly "Mr. Sands."

Rear Inscription

Dunshee Artist[147]
No 3
Tremont Row
Boston
Duplicate copies can be had any time within two years.
1881

Album Page

---

[147] The Artist and Photographer E.S. Dunshee was born in Bristol, Vermont in 1823. He worked as an ambrotype photographer in Fall River, Massachusetts between 1853 and 1857, in New Bedford, Rhode Island between 1857 and 1861, and in Boston from 1873 to 1876. He was in Philadelphia in 1880 and died in 1907. His son was also a photographer in Philadelphia.

APPENDIX IV – THE 1864 BOYLE PHOTO ALBUM

Paper Sleeve is glued to photograph and there appears to be nothing on the back.

Page 7 Photo – (Unknown Female)

Rear of Photo 7

Album Slot #: 7
Type of Photo: Ferrotype
Size: 1 5/8"x 2" in a 2 3/8" x 3 7/8" paper sleeve
Content: Young girl. (Both indexes say "Papa")
Suspected to be: If we assume that the photographs may have been moved around in the album since the indexes were created, this could be Delia Smith, who is shown on both indexes as #5.
Estimated Year: Dress style seems to suggest 1870-1890.
:

Album Page

Our Oberle Ancestors

Page 10 Photo – (Unknown Male)

Rear of Photo 10

Album Slot #: 10
Type of Photo: Paper, apparently a Carte de Visite
Size: 2 1/2"x 4 1/4"
Content: Standing heavyset male with Amish-style beard.
Suspected to be:
Estimated Year: 1870-1880, based on the following:
    Props are relatively elaborate
    Long open top coat
:   Photo taken in Liverpool, England, so clothing clues may not match American styles.

Rear Inscription
ISH * DIEN
Photographed
from Life
by
Richard Brown
North
Photographic &
Art Studio
42 Virgil Street
Liverpool

Negatives Kept
Duplicates May be Had
Cartes de Visite colored to
order

Album Page

APPENDIX IV – THE 1864 BOYLE PHOTO ALBUM

Black Lacquer

Page 11 Photo – (Unknown Male) *Rear of Photo 11*

Album Slot #:   11
Type of Photo: Ferrotype
Size: 2 3/8" x 3 1/4"
Content: Sitting young adult male with tie and vest
                Indexes say "Mamie" (obviously incorrect)
Suspected to be:
Estimated Year: 1880-1900 ??
:

Album Page

Page 15 Photo – ("C. Dowd")

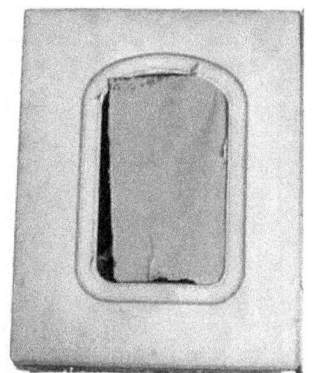

Paper sleeve is loosely attached to the black lacquer back.

Rear of Photo 15

Album Page

Album Slot #:	15
Type of Photo:	Ferrotype
Size:	2" x 3 1/8" obviously trimmed unevenly in a 2 1/2" x 4" decorative paper sleeve.
Content:	Standing adult female. Indexes say "C. Dowd"
	This photo was quite loose in the album and might originally have been in slot 13, which has an empty mask (paper border).
Suspected to be:	
Estimated Year:	1870-1890
	based on
	Simple chair prop
	Severe hair style, pulled back
	Loose sleeves on dress
:	Long wide skirt

APPENDIX IV – THE 1864 BOYLE PHOTO ALBUM

Black Lacquer

Page 16 Photo – ("L. Holland"?) *Rear of Photo 16*

Album Slot #: 16
Type of Photo: Ferrotype
Size: 2" x 3 1/4" hand trimmed
Content: "L. Holland" in both indexes

Neither index has an entry with two names after "Grandmother and Aunt Bridget" above, so the "L. Holland" may not go with this picture, but Holland is the surname of the family with which Catherine Boyle was living (as a servant) at the time of the 1870 census. See census image on page 90.

Album Page

Young boy standing with seated adult female; this is a color picture, but I can't tell how it was hand colored.

Suspected to be: Louis Holland and Claire Johnson.

If this is Louis Holland, the woman is possibly either Sarah Holland (his mother), Catherine Boyle, or Claire Johnson (the younger housekeeper.) Since no name is given, one of the latter two seems more likely and would also explain why only the boy was identified.

Estimated Year: If this picture is of the oldest son Louis Holland, who was born in about 1861, it could be dated in the mid to late 1860s.

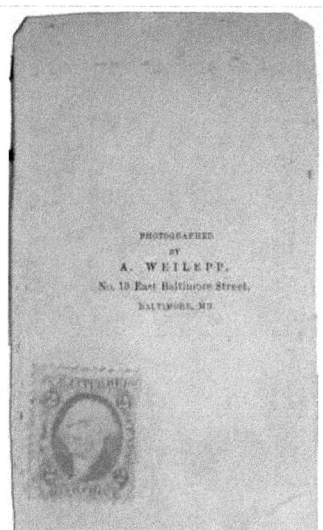

Page 18 Photo – ("Margaret") *Rear of Photo 18*

Album Slot #:	18
Type of Photo:	Paper
Size:	2 3/8" x 4"
Content:	Standing adult female (Index says Margaret)
Suspected to be:	Could this be Margaret Kelly Boyle [id1716] (my great-great grandmother)? The name Margaret comes from the second transcriber rather than the owner of the album (who, if it was indeed Catherine Boyle [id171], wasn't likely to refer to her mother by her given name). Assuming she was about 18-20 when Catherine was born in 1848, she would be about 35-37 in this photograph – this woman looks somewhat younger than I would have expected for a Civil War era 37 year old, but the possibility should be considered.
Estimated Year:	Between 1 AUG 1864 and 1 MAR 1865. [148] According to the first reference, the 2¢ value of the stamp indicates that the picture was prior to 1 MAR 1865; according to the second reference, the 2¢ value of the stamp indicates the cost of the photograph was $0.25 or less.

Rear Inscription

Photographed by
A. WEILEPP
No. 19 East Baltimore Street
Baltimore MD
Note the U.S. Internal Revenue 2¢ stamp

Album Page

---

[148] During the two year period from 1 AUG 1864 to 1 AUG 1866, photographs in the United States were taxed and needed to have a revenue tax stamp affixed; this therefore dates the picture to that time period. See "Dating Old Photographs" and "Uncovering Your Ancestors through Family Photographs." Information on both books is given in the references on page 200 of this appendix.

APPENDIX IV – THE 1864 BOYLE PHOTO ALBUM

Page 19 Photo – (Unknown Male)

Black Lacquer

Rear of Photo 19

Album Slot #: 19
Type of Photo: Ferrotype
Size: 2 ¹/₈" x 3"
Content: Adult Male
Suspected to be:
Estimated Year:
:

Album Page

Page 21 Photo – Archbishop Bayley

Blank

Rear of Photo 21

Album Slot #: 21
Type of Photo: Printed Paper
Size: 2 7/8" x 4 1/2"
Content: A male priest; a commercial print that doesn't have the "look" of a photograph.

Removing this from the album, it can be seen to be what appears as a funeral mass card (although there is no printing on the reverse, it has the black border typical of such cards) for James Roosevelt Bayley, D.D., Archbishop of Baltimore.

Known to be: Archbishop James Roosevelt Bayley
Estimated Year:

Album Page

APPENDIX IV – THE *1864* BOYLE PHOTO ALBUM

This picture backs on to picture #21 and, not wishing to disturb the album's condition, I was unable to see if there is any photographer's inscription on the back of either picture.

Page 22 Photo – (Unknown Females)   *Rear of Photo 22*

Album Slot #:	22
Type of Photo:	Surface seems like other ferrotypes in this album, but it is non-magnetic, so likely a later technology I haven't identified.
Size:	1 1/2" x 2 1/16" glued on to a 2 7/8" x 3 3/8" decorative card.
Content:	Two females leaning heads together.
Suspected to be:	Neither index has an entry with two names after "Grandmother and Aunt Bridget" above, so there is no index match to this picture.
	Although possible that these might be the two oldest daughters of Martin and Catherine Goldrick, I see no resemblance to their youngest daughter (my grandmother) Katie Goldrick, pictured below in 3 head shots.
Estimated Year:	

Album Page

Page 24 Photo – (Unknown Female)

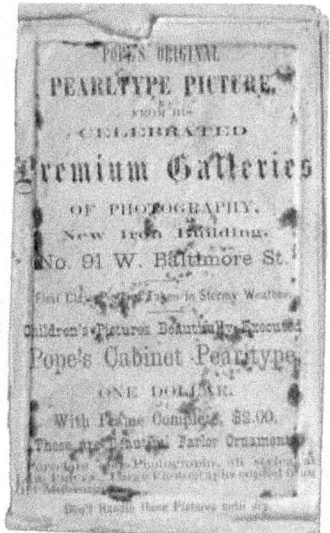

Rear of Photo 24

Album Slot #:	24
Type of Photo:	Ferrotype
Size:	2" x 3 1/4" hand trimmed in a 2 1/4" x 3 7/8" decorative paper sleeve.
Content:	Sitting female
Suspected to be:	
Estimated Year:	

Album Page

A single similar-sized "tintype" (the colloquial but incorrect name for a ferrotype) sold over the internet was the only reference I could locate for Pope's Studios, but I have not had the opportunity to review Baltimore City Directories for the period.

The photo was identified as "circa 1860," although there was no image and the seller didn't explain how that year was estimated. The picture was described as being of "a gentleman with rosy cheeks," implying that the portrait was probably colored.

I suspect that photo was probably not of the same vintage as the ones in this album, since the labeling on the rear of the photograph was slightly different. The company name, for instance, is given as *"JH Pope's Celebrated Premium Gallery, 91 W. Baltimore Street, over the Carpet Store."* It continues *"Pope's Album Pearltypes, Two for 25 cents, Sitting or Standing. Pope's Cabinet* Pearltype, One Dollar With Complete Frame $2.00. These are Beautiful Parlor *Ornaments. Porcelain and Photographs, all styles, at Low Prices. Large Photographs copied from Old Ambrotypes."*

Note that the pictures in this album refer to "Pope's Original Pearltype Picture."

APPENDIX IV – THE 1864 BOYLE PHOTO ALBUM

Page 25 Photo – (Martin Goldrick?)

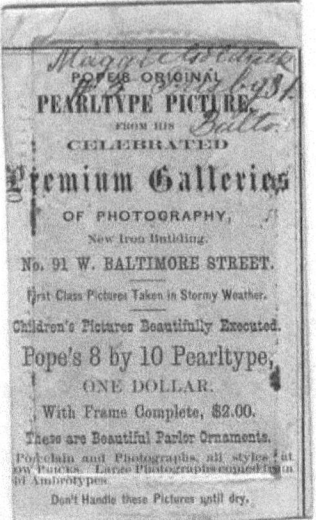

Rear of Photo 25

Album Slot #: 25
Type of Photo: Ferrotype
Size: 2" x 3 1/4" hand trimmed in a 2 1/4" x 3 7/8" decorative paper sleeve.
Content: Sitting Male
Suspected to be: My cousin Angela said her father Joe had a picture of this person in his effects but there was no notation as to who the subject was.

Note the name Maggie Goldrick and the address #5 Frisby Street handwritten on the rear. This may be my great-grandfather Martin G. Goldrick [id170], husband of Catherine Boyle who is likely the original owner of this album.

Estimated Year:

Album Page

Likely candidates for "Maggie Goldrick" are my grandmother's older sister Margaret A. Goldrick (1875-1944) [id546], and her niece Mary Margarite Goldrick (b 1898) [id185], daughter of her older brother Jim Goldrick [id184] and his wife Grace [id539]. Based on the age of the photograph, it seems reasonable to suggest that the photo was produced (or reproduced) for Margaret [id546] sometime before her marriage to Darby Dunn [id547] in about 1906.

The photo in album slot 26 appears to be identical to picture 25 above.

The rear is also identical, except that the label is glued on upside down and doesn't have Maggie Goldrick's name written on it.

Page 28 Photo – (Unknown Male)

Black Lacquer

Rear of Photo 28

Album Page

Album Slot #: 28
Type of Photo: Ferrotype
Size: 2 1/4" x 3 3/8"
Content: Seated Male
Suspected to be:
Estimated Year:
:

APPENDIX IV – THE 1864 BOYLE PHOTO ALBUM

Page 29 Photo – (Unknown Male)

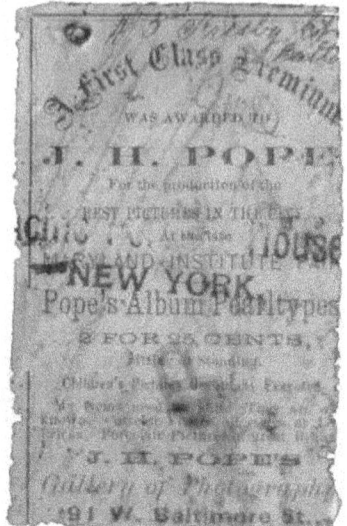

Rear of Photo 29

Album Slot #:   29

Type of Photo: Ferrotype

Size: 2 1/8" x 3 3/8" in a 2 1/4" x 3 7/8" decorative paper sleeve.

Content: Seated male (resembles person in #25, but facial hair is different). There is a single hole punched through the top right side of the photo (can be seen on the top left of the picture of the rear above).

Suspected to be:

Album Page

Estimated Year: The labeling on the rear is slightly different than the other J. H. Pope ferrotypes (numbers 24, 25, and 26), indicating that it is likely a different vintage.

:

Our Oberle Ancestors

Page 30 Photo – (Unknown Female)

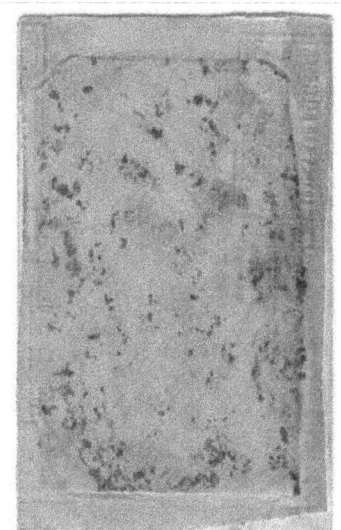

Rear of Photo 30

Album Slot #: 30
Type of Photo: Ferrotype
Size: 2" x 3-1/4" in a 2-3/8" x 3-7/8" decorative paper sleeve.
Content: Standing Female
Suspected to be:
Estimated Year:
:

Album Page

The paper glued to the rear of this picture has what appears to be a transferred (because it is reversed) image of a rubber stamp, suggesting that it might have been in contact with something else while one of the items was drying. The lettering is extremely difficult to make out, but the words "London and Baltimore" can be made out (see below).

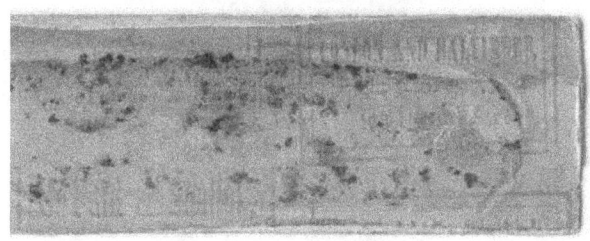

This is a rotated and reversed version of the rear of the photograph illustrated above.

References for Dating Photographs

The following books provide tips for identifying old photographs:

Dating Old Photographs 1840 – 1929; Family Chronicle Publications; Dewey LH/GENEA 779 DATING

More Dating Old Photographs 1840-1929; Family Chronicle Publications; edited by Maureen A. Taylor.

Uncovering Your Ancestors through Family Photographs; Maureen A. Taylor, Betterway, © 2000; ISBN 1-55870-527-9

Windows on the Past: Identifying, Dating, & Preserving Photographs; Diane VanSkiver Gagel; © 2000; Heritage Books, Inc. ISBN 0-7884-1620-0

Unlocking the Secrets in Old Photographs; Karen Frisch-Ripley; © 1991; published by Ancestry. Dewey LH/GENEA 773.999; ISBN: 0-916489-50-7.

APPENDIX V :: JOSEPH OBERLE CURRENCY EXAMPLES

Montage of Series 1929 National Bank Notes signed by Joseph Oberle

Sample Currency signed by Joseph Oberle

This appendix provides examples of United States National Bank Notes signed by my grandfather Joseph Oberle id81, and include bills from both the large 1902 Series (Third Charter Period, Third Issue) and all of the small[149] 1929 Series.

The National Currency Act of 25 February 1863, signed by Abraham Lincoln, provided for a national banking system to replace the myriad of currencies then being issued by state banks with a single standardized national currency. From December 1863 through May 1935, banks across the country could, by depositing specified amounts of United States interest-bearing bonds with the treasury, become "National Banks," and be authorized to issue U.S. Government paper currency.[150]

Two of the signatures on currency thus issued were Federal – those of the Register of the Treasury and the Treasurer of the United States. The remaining two signatures on each bill were the Cashier and President of the issuing bank. Over this seventy-year period, there were six major issues of such currency – four large size issues, and two small size issues. The final group of large bills, those of Series 1902, was issued in several phases, the last of which was signed for the Citizen's National Bank of Baltimore and First National Bank of Baltimore by Joseph Oberle in his role as Vice-President and Cashier.

By the time the smaller Series 1929 bills began to be issued, Joseph Oberle was the Cashier for the larger First National Bank of Baltimore, formed by a merger of Citizen's with the National Mechanics Bank of Baltimore, which itself had previously absorbed the original First National Bank of Baltimore.

Each of the examples reproduced on the following pages is identified with the information from the standard catalogs of United States currency listed below; see these catalogs, which are available in most libraries and the internet, for further details.

Comprehensive Catalog of U.S. Paper Money: Gene Hessler; Sixth Edition; Copyrights 1974 through 1997; ISBN 0-931960-51-7 (or 50-9).

Standard Catalog of United States Paper Money, 19th Edition; Chester L. Krause and Robert F. Lemke; Joel T. Edler, Editor; © 2000 Krause Publications; ISBN 0-87341-930-8; Dewey Decimal Number 769.55.

Paper Money of the United States: Arthur L. Friedberg, Ira S. Friedberg; Coin & Currency Institute, Jul 30, 2010; ISBN 978-0-87184-519-1; The Coin and Currency Institute. Based on original work of their father Robert Friedberg.

---

[149] The "small" size is the size used for today's United States currency.

[150] This was many years before the Federal Reserve system was instituted.

Appendix V – Currency Signed by Joseph Oberle

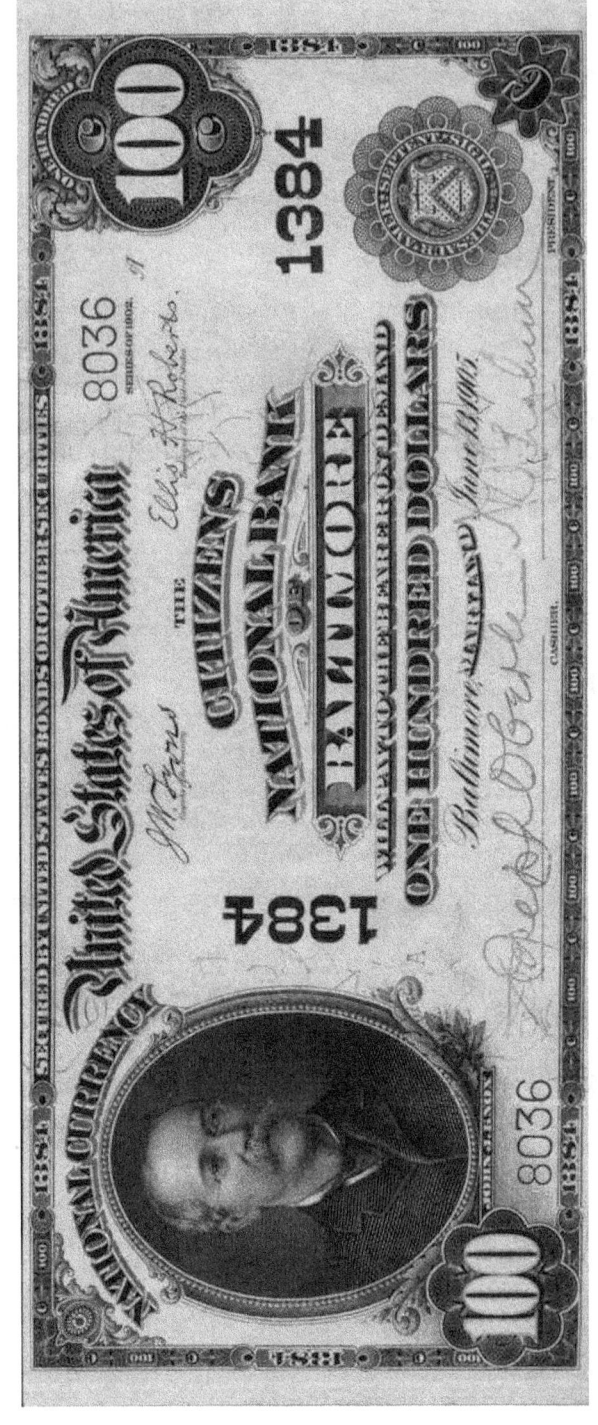

Slightly Reduced from Actual Size of 3.125" by 7.4218" (7.94cm by 18.851cm)

National Bank Note / Third Charter Period / Series 1902 / Second Issue / Blue Seal

The Citizen's National Bank of Baltimore

Hessler Comprehensive Catalog of U.S. Currency Number 1187

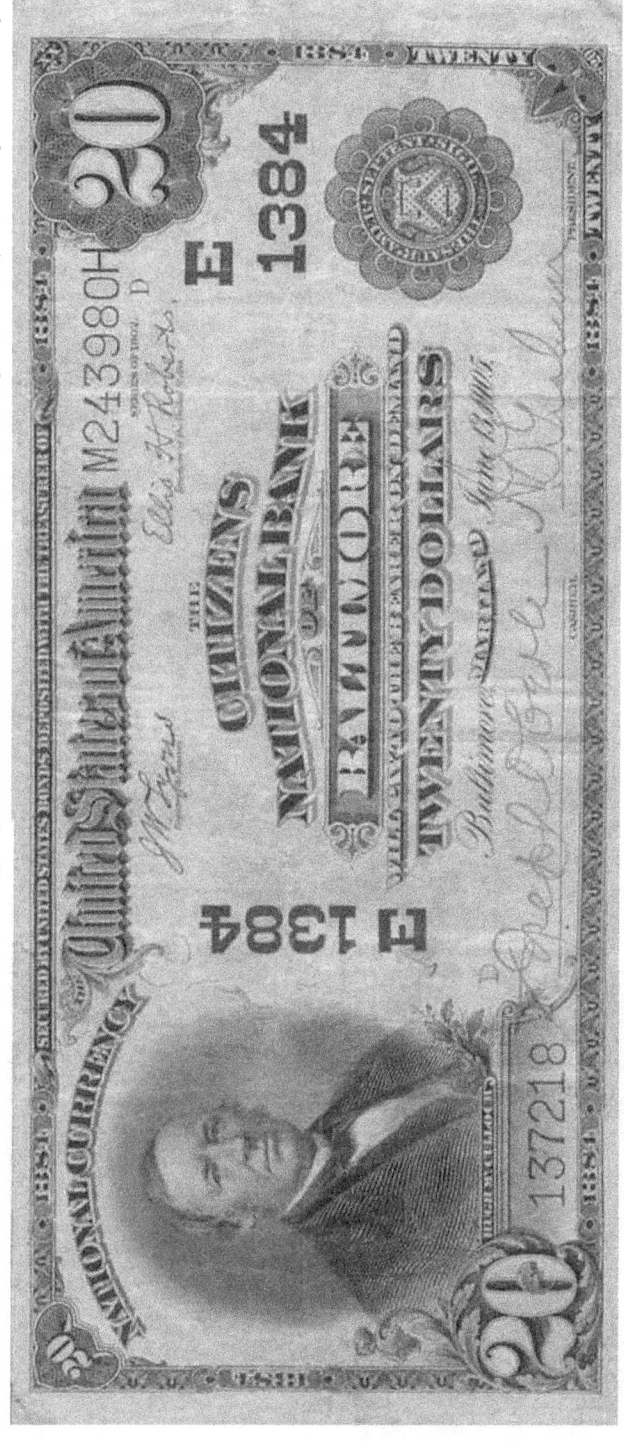

Slightly Reduced from Actual Size of 3.125" by 7.4218" (7.94cm by 18.851cm)

National Bank Note / Third Charter Period / Series 1902 / Third Issue

The Citizen's National Bank of Baltimore

Hessler Comprehensive Catalog of U.S. Currency Number 785; Friedberg Catalog Number FR# 650-663A

Krause-Lemke Standard Catalog of United States Paper Money Number KL# 1302-16

APPENDIX V – CURRENCY SIGNED BY JOSEPH OBERLE

Slightly Reduced from Actual Size of 3.125" by 7.4218" (7.94cm by 18.851cm)

National Bank Note / Third Charter Period / 1902 / Third Issue

The Citizen's National Bank of Baltimore

Hessler Comprehensive Catalog of U.S. Currency Number 552; Friedberg Catalog Number FR# 613-615
Krause-Lemke Standard Catalog of United States Paper Money Number KL# 1216-18

OUR OBERLE ANCESTORS

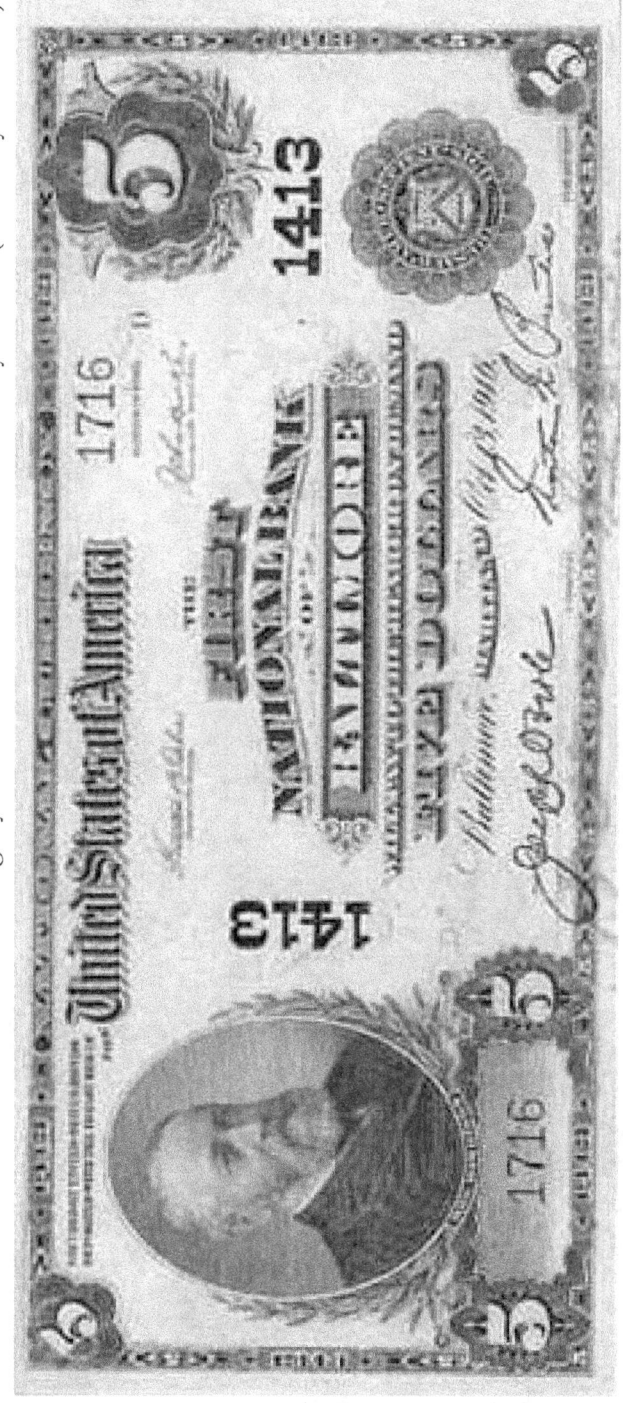

Slightly Reduced from Actual Size of 3.125" by 7.4218" (7.94cm by 18.851cm)

National Bank Note / Third Charter Period / 1902 / Third Issue

The First National Bank of Baltimore

Friedberg Catalog Number Fr# 598-612

Krause-Lemke Standard Catalog of United States Paper Money Number KL# 1155-1169

APPENDIX V – CURRENCY SIGNED BY JOSEPH OBERLE

National Bank Note / Third Charter Period / Series 1929 / Type I / Brown Seal

The Citizen's National Bank of Baltimore

Hessler Comprehensive Catalog of U.S. Currency Number 1249

National Bank Note / 1929 / Brown Seal / Type I

The First National Bank of Baltimore

Hessler Comprehensive Catalog of U.S. Currency Number 1048; Friedberg Catalog Number FR# 1803-1

Krause-Lemke Standard Catalog of United States Paper Money Number KL#1378

History of this Bill

In the latter part of the 1950s, this note was brought into the Union Trust Bank in Towson (north of Baltimore) where, coinzidentally, my Mother's sister Jean Iglehart worked. Because such National Bank Notes were to be taken out of circulation and eventually destroyed, my Father scrambled to gather fifty dollars in cash and take it to Towson before her shift ended so my Aunt could exchange it and keep it in the family.

APPENDIX V – CURRENCY SIGNED BY JOSEPH OBERLE

National Bank Note / 1929 / Brown Seal / Original Issue / Type I

The First National Bank of Baltimore

Hessler Comprehensive Catalog of U.S. Currency Number 852; Friedberg Catalog Number FR# 1802-1

Krause-Lemke Standard Catalog of United States Paper Money Number KL# 1317

National Bank Note / 1929 / Brown Seal / Original Issue / Type I

The First National Bank of Baltimore

Hessler Comprehensive Catalog of U.S. Currency Number 627; Friedberg Catalog Number FR# 1801-1

Krause-Lemke Standard Catalog of United States Paper Money Number KL# 1243

National Bank Note / 1929 / Original Issue / Type I

The First National Bank of Baltimore

Hessler Comprehensive Catalog of U.S. Currency Number 390; Friedberg Catalog Number FR# 1800-1

Krause-Lemke Standard Catalog of United States Paper Money Number KL# 1170

Currency Bequests in Katherine Oberle's Will

A number of examples of currency with Joseph Oberle's signature were passed on to various family members in my Grandmother's will; so far as I am aware, these are still in the possession of their descendants. These can be seen in the Appendix "The Wills of Joseph and Katherine Oberle" where they are marked with a ($) symbol in the right margin: Among these are:

- Item Five, No.13; $5 bill to her son Francis (see page 231)
- Item Six, No.5; $5 bill to her son Cornelius (see page 231)
- Item Eight, No.13; $10 bill to her daughter Katherine (see page 231)
- Item Nine, No.2; $50 bill to her son Joseph (see page 232)
- Item Fifteen; $5 bill to her grandson Thomas Steven (see page 232)
- Item Eighteen; $5 bill to her son-in-law Norbert (see page 233)

This is a shorter list than one might expect since, except for the serial number 1 bill, my Grandparents apparently weren't impressed enough to consider deliberately amassing a collection of these bills.

Most of the bills in our family's collections, therefore, have been acquired from currency collectors on the open market.

The Serial Number 1 Five Dollar Note

Perhaps the most interesting example of currency signed by my Grandfather was mentioned on page 2 of my Grandmother's Will of 26 January 1956, where she describes it as "No. 1 bill issued by the First National Bank with his father's signature." Because of its historical significance – at least to our family – both sides are illustrated on the following two pages.

Although this particular issue of National Bank Notes was first authorized in 1915, the First National Bank itself wasn't formed until 1928, when the Citizen's National Bank of Baltimore took over the National Mechanics Bank[151], at which time, the new bank restored the name to the First National Bank of Baltimore. Thus, in 1928, the First National Bank issued a new series of Notes; the serial number 1 for each of the denominations issued were presented to the new Bank's officers., including Albert D. Graham, James D. Harrison, Morton M. Prentis[152], and our ancestor Joseph Oberle.

On 10 July, 1929, the United States government mandated the new smaller-sized bill be used for all currency, including the National Bank Notes as well as that issued by the federal treasury. Thus, relatively few of the large size First National Bank Notes were ever made, making them somewhat unique.

---

[151] The National Mechanics Bank had taken over the original First National Bank of Baltimore many years earlier.

[152] Morton Prentis' signature can be seen to the right of Granddad's on many of the bills illustrated in this book.

Appendix V – Currency Signed by Joseph Oberle

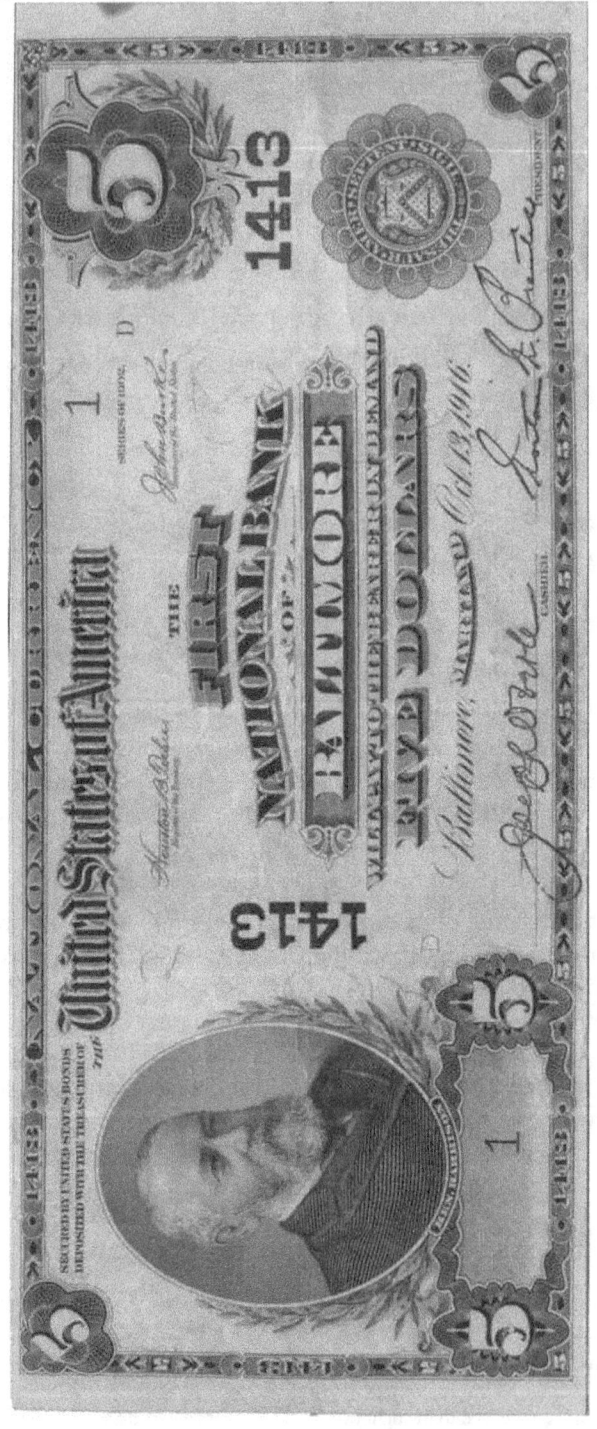

Slightly Reduced from Actual Size of 3.125" by 7.4218" (7.94cm by 18.851cm)

National Bank Note / Third Charter Period / Series 1902 / Blue Seal / Original Issue / Type I

*** Serial Number One Bill ***

Friedberg Catalog Number FR# 598-612

Krause-Lemke Standard Catalog of United States Paper Money Number KL# 1155

OUR OBERLE ANCESTORS

Slightly Reduced from Actual Size of 3.125" by 7.4218" (7.94cm by 18.851cm)

The notation (in pencil) "For Francis" was written by Katherine Oberle, and is reflected in her Will.

Appendix V – Currency Signed by Joseph Oberle

Baltimore – Citizens National Bank Building

Appendix VI :: Wills of Joseph and Katherine Oberle

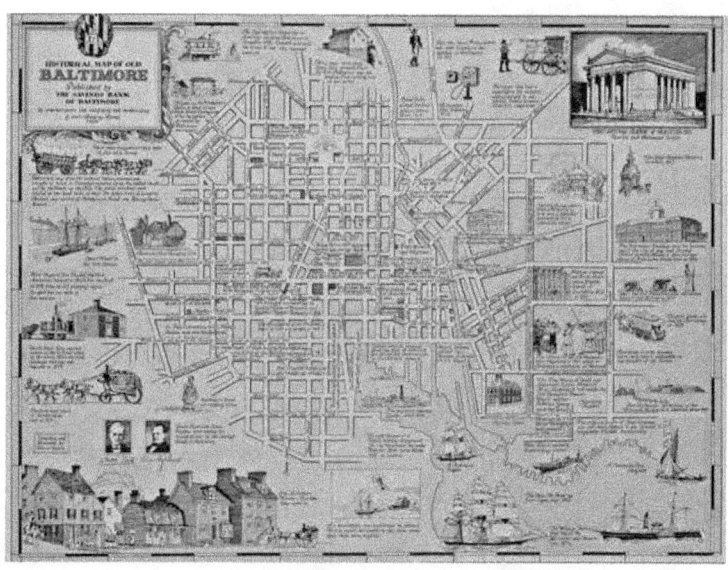

An Early Baltimore Map

The Wills of Joseph and Katherine Oberle

The illustrations beginning on page 221 are reproductions of my paternal grandfather Joseph id81 Oberle's Will and the inventories taken while probating his estate.

The Will itself, made in March 1948, is of little interest, giving everything to my grandmother Katherine id80 should he predecease her, and to his children and their heirs should she predecease him. He does not name any of his children or grandchildren.

Since the Will was executed while Granddad was still an officer of the First National Bank[153], and since the Bank was named as the executor, my assumption is that this was a standard Will prepared by the bank's attorneys for their officers, but I don't know this for sure.

The Estate Inventories taken in the month after Granddad's death in 1954 are more interesting, since they provide some insight into their financial condition at the time of his death. These begin on page 223.

Reproductions of my paternal Grandmother Katherine id80 (Katie) Goldrick Oberle's Will and two subsequent Codicils begin on page 230.

Granddad had died on 19 August 1954, and Grandmom's Will was executed 26 January 1956, a little less than a year and a half later. I don't know of any earlier Will she may have had, although it seems likely that she would have had a reciprocal one with Granddad because of his position. In any case, however, the 1954 Will reflects the fact that she was now a widow and sole owner of all their assets.

Katie's Will is interesting due to the fact that many of the items mentioned as bequests are still owned by various members of the family. Some years later when I had become an adult I received my own bequest, for my "grandfather's silver watch and chain," which she encouraged me to "keep the same for good luck." The chain was no longer present when I got the watch (my parents had the watch remounted on a display stand) but I still have the watch, shown on page 116, and it is still in working order.

Grandmom also distributed several of the National Bank Notes Granddad had signed during his tenure as the bank's Cashier, as well as china, furniture, carpets and silverware.

The First Codicil to Grandmom's Will was executed 3 February 1959, and was driven by several changes in the three years since the Will was written.

In her original will, Grandmom's long-time housekeeper was to receive a cash settlement and a weekly stipend after Grandmom's death; Mamie had since died, and so these bequests were revoked. Three new grandsons had been born since the original will was executed, including my younger brother as

---

[153] He didn't retire until February 1953, and then only because of his heart condition.

well as my two youngest Miller cousins. The codicil provided bequests to these, as well as general bequests to any grandchildren that would be born in the future.

A few of the household items that were listed as bequests in the original Will had since been disposed of in one manner or another, and the first codicil provided for replacement items.

Katie Goldrick Oberle circa 1948

Grandmom's second and final Codicil was executed 19 April 1963. The two major events that prompted this codicil were her son Francis' marriage and the recognition that my brother Tommy's mental deterioration was permanent.

In the original Will, Francis was granted permission to continue residing in the house on Midhurst Road for at least a year after Grandmom's death. Because he had since married and set up his own household, this provision apparently no longer seemed appropriate, and the house became part of her general Estate.

Details of my younger brother Tommy's condition are outside the scope of this document, but because it was becoming untenable for my parents to continue caring for him at home, it was necessary to have him committed to a facility where he could be properly managed. She thus deleted the earlier bequest to him and replaced it with money to assist my parents with his care.

As of this writing, there is one item from Joseph and Katherine Oberle's general Estate that has not yet been distributed, which is a pair of grave plots on their burial site at New Cathedral Cemetery in Baltimore, Maryland. As near as I have been able to determine, these are jointly owned by me, my surviving brother, and my first cousins on the Oberle side of the family. The Deed for this plot, currently in my possession, is shown on pages 240 and 241 of this Appendix.

I, JOSEPH OBERLE, of Baltimore County and the State of Maryland, do make, publish and declare this my Last Will and Testament, hereby revoking any and all wills and codicils heretofore made by me.

FIRST: I direct my Executor, hereinafter named, to pay all my just debts and funeral expenses as soon after my decease as may be practicable.

SECOND: I have heretofore given to my wife, Katherine G. Oberle, all of the household goods, furniture, books, pictures and similar articles of tangible personal property situate in our residence, 213 Midhurst Road, Pinehurst, Baltimore County, Maryland, and I hereby confirm her absolute title thereto.

THIRD: I give, devise and bequeath all of my property and estate of whatsoever kind or character and wheresoever situate to my beloved wife, Katherine G. Oberle, if she survives me. In the event, however, that my said wife shall predecease me, or my said wife shall not be living ninety days after my death, then I give, devise and bequeath all of my property and estate of whatsoever kind or character and wheresoever situate to my child or children, in equal parts or shares, the descendant or descendants of any deceased child of mine to take its or their parent's share, per stirpes and not per capita.

FOURTH: (a) I nominate and appoint The First National Bank of Baltimore, Executor of my estate and I excuse my said Executor from the necessity of giving bond for the faithful performance of its duties.

(b) I hereby confer upon my Executor full power and authority to sell, assign, transfer, convey, exchange, divide, invest, reinvest, mortgage, lease or otherwise deal with or dispose of any part of my estate whether real or personal whenever it may deem such action advantageous to my estate, without application to the Orphans' Court of Baltimore County or any other court for authority in respect thereto.

(c) I also confer upon my Executor full power to compromise any claims against or in favor of my estate for such sums and upon such terms and conditions as it may deem proper, without application to the Orphans' Court of Baltimore County or any other court for the approval thereof.

(d) In any case in which my Executor be required under the provisions of this my will to divide any property or other assets of my estate or any

id 81

id 80

id 80

154

Joseph Oberle's Will of 8 March 1948 — Page 1

---

[154] Per stirpes: the estate is to be divided by descendant branch, and not apportioned equally across individuals.

APPENDIX VI – WILLS OF JOSEPH AND KATHERINE OBERLE

part thereof, I confer upon it full power and authority to make such division in kind and/or to sell such portions thereof, real or personal, as it may deem necessary or proper to effectuate such division; and any division so made by it shall be binding and conclusive upon all persons interested in my estate.

IN WITNESS WHEREOF, I, Joseph Oberle, have hereunto set my hand and affixed my seal this ___8th___ day of March, 1948.

                                              ___Joseph Oberle___ (SEAL)

SIGNED, SEALED, PUBLISHED AND DECLARED by the above named Testator as and for his Last Will and Testament in the presence of us, who, at his request, in his presence, and the presence of each other, have hereunto subscribed our names as witnesses.

John Thayer Tainter	326 St. Paul Place
	Baltimore 2, Maryland
Roger B. Williams	1604 First National Bank Bldg.
	Baltimore, Md.

Joseph Oberle's Will of 8 March 1948 – Page 2 (Signature Page)

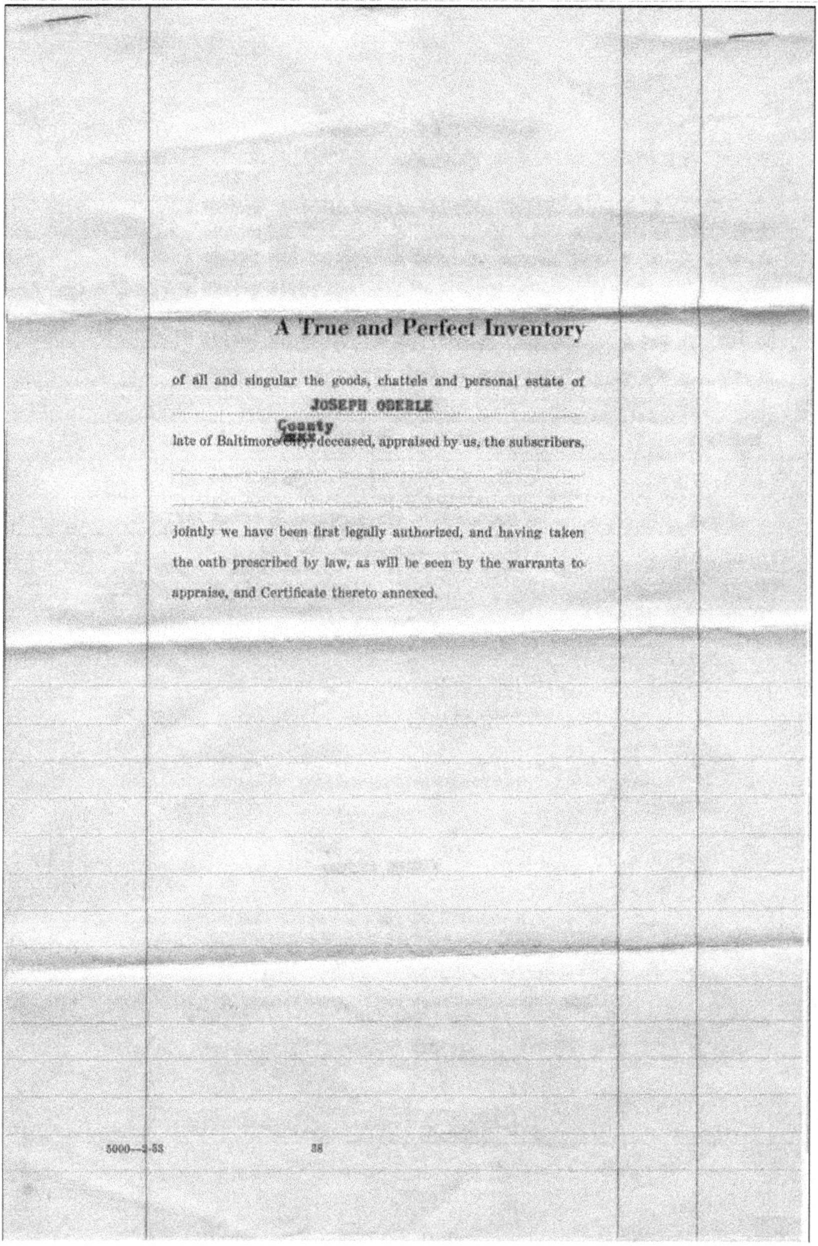

A True and Perfect Inventory

of all and singular the goods, chattels and personal estate of

JOSEPH OBERLE

late of Baltimore ~~City~~ County deceased, appraised by us, the subscribers,

jointly we have been first legally authorized, and having taken the oath prescribed by law, as will be seen by the warrants to appraise, and Certificate thereto annexed.

id 81

155

Joseph Oberle's Inventory Cover Sheet of 28 September 1954 – Page 1

---

[155] Baltimore City is within, but not part of, Baltimore County; these are legally separate entities. Pinehurst was just north of the Baltimore City line.

APPENDIX VI – WILLS OF JOSEPH AND KATHERINE OBERLE

ID

id 81

ESTATE OF JOSEPH OBERLE
INVENTORY

2 shares Central States Electric Corporation, @ 1 common		$ 2.00
9 shares Cities Service Company, common (old) @ 10		90.00
100 shares First National Bank of Baltimore, capital	@ 50½	5050.00
10 shares Monumental Radio Company, common	@ 15¼	152.50
2 shares National City Bank of New York	@ 57¼	114.50
SECURITIES TOTAL:-		**$5409.00**

1940 Dodge Sedan AC-26333   30269250   100.00
     Title D 18181
     New Blk. 8-30-46

TOTAL INVENTORY AS ABOVE: $5509.00

Joseph Oberle's Inventory of 28 September 1954 – Page 1

ID

We, the Subscribers, do certify

that the aforegoing is a true and just inventory, and valuation of all and singular the goods, chattels and personal estate of the said **JOSEPH OBERLE** deceased, so far as the same have come to our sight and knowledge; and as valued and appraised by us in dollars and cents, according to the best of our skill and judgment.

id 81

In Testimony all of which, we

hereunto subscribe our names, and affix our seals, this 28th day of September, 19 54

(SEAL)

(SEAL)

APPRAISERS

Amount of appraisement as above,	$ 5509	00
Cash in the house at the time of deceased's death,	- - -	
Cash in bank at the time of deceased's death,	837	93
Whole amount of inventory.	$ 6346	93

THE FIRST NATIONAL BANK OF BALTIMORE

By:
H. Graham Wood, Vice President and Trust Officer

SWORN to September 28, 19 54 a Notary Public before ~~LEROY C. SHAUGHNESSY, Register of Wills~~ for Baltimore City.

Carroll A. Pagel
-Notary Public-

Joseph Oberle's Inventory Certification Sheet of 28 September 1954 – Page 1

Appendix VI – Wills of Joseph and Katherine Oberle

Estate of Joseph Oberle

Cash on hand — 204.99
To be disbursed:

Reg. of Wills	14.00	
W.C. Pinkerd & Co.	25.00	
Katherine G. Oberle	75.00	
Transfer tax	3.00	
First Nat. Bank	642.25	
Reg. of Wills	71.36	
Reg. of Wills	34.69	865.30

660.31 deficit
Less allowance to Katherine Oberle   75.00
Due by Katherine Oberle   585.31

Note: When tax refund of $75.79 is received, it will be paid to Mrs. Oberle.

Proof

Acct. shows due by Mrs. Oberle	1984.52
Advanced by her to date	1900.00
Still due	84.52
Plus tax refund not yet received	575.79
	660.31
Less widow's allowance	75.00
	585.31

Joseph Oberle's Inventory Accounting Work Sheet – Page 1

Owned		Paid Out	
9/24/54 – Inventory filed	6346.93	50.10 – Filing will	
Income tax refund	575.79	2319.00 – Funeral	
Sale of 2 rights		468.50 – Monument	
National City	.64	10.00 – Jeffersonian	
Dividends – FNB	200.00	25.00 – Appraisal	
Monumental Radio	9.50	4.28 – Transfer taxes	
National City	2.40	1.50 – Notary	
Cities Service	.90	Executor's	
	7136.16	Commission 10% of 7136.16 = 713.61	
Cash advanced	1900.00		
	9036.16	642.25 { Less 10% tax 71.36 / 642.25 }	
		71.36 – 1% tax Register of Wills	
		3591.99	
		34.69 – Paid Inheritance Tax	
	9036.16	3626.68 – Total Paid Out	

```
9036.16
3626.68
5409.48 – Balance of Estate – As Follows.
```

2.00	2 shares – Central States
5050.00	100 shares FNB.
152.50	10 shares Monumental
114.50	2 shares National City
100.00	Dodge
5419.00	

Balance of Estate   5409.48
Owe to Executor   9.52

Joseph Oberle's Inventory Accounting Work Sheet – Page 2

APPENDIX VI – WILLS OF JOSEPH AND KATHERINE OBERLE

```
THE FIRST AND FINAL ADMINISTRATION ACCOUNT OF THE FIRST NATIONAL
BANK OF BALTIMORE, EXECUTOR OF THE ESTATE OF JOSEPH OBERLE, DECEASED.

This accountant charges itself with:
    Whole amount of Personal Inventory filed 9/28/54            $6346.93
    Refund of overpayment 1954 U. S. income tax                   575.79
    Proceeds of sale - 2 rights National City Bank                   .64

And with the following dividends collected:
    First National Bank, Baltimore, due 10/4/54, 1/6 and 4/6/55   200.00
    Monumental Radio Co. due 10/4/54, 1/6/55 and 3/30/55            9.50
    National City Bank, New York due 11/9/54 and 2/2/55             2.40
    Cities Service Co. due 9/7/54                                    .90

                    TOTAL ESTATE TO BE ACCOUNTED FOR:-         $7136.16

And this accountant craves allowance for the following payments
and disbursements:
    Register of Wills for Baltimore County
    9/22/54 Letters, docket costs, recording, certificates     14.10
    9/30/54 Filing Personal Inventory                          22.00
       /55  This account and copy                     8.00
            Petition to pay funeral expenses          1.00
            3 orders to transfer securities           3.00
            1 release                                 1.00
            Report of sale                            1.00    14.00     50.10
Funeral expenses per Order of Court dated
    George F. Gonce - funeral director                        2319.00
    Upan R. Standiford & Sons - monument                       468.50  2787.50
The Jeffersonian - notice to creditors                                   10.00
W. C. Pinkard & Co. - appraisal 213 Midhurst Road                        25.00
Notary fees                                                               1.50
Katherine G. Oberle, widow's allowance                                   75.00
Transfer taxes, postage and insurance                                     4.28
This accountant's commissions, viz:
    10% on $7,136.16                                          713.61
    Less: State tax thereon                                    71.36   642.25
Register of Wills, Baltimore County                                     71.36

                    TOTAL PAYMENTS AND DISBURSEMENTS:-               $3666.99

Maryland inheritance tax, as follows:
    Total estate, as above                          7136.16
    Less: total disbursements                       3666.99
    Estate subject to tax                           3469.17
    Maryland inheritance tax @ 1%                     34.69
    Estate to be distributed                        3434.48

Unto: Katherine G. Oberle - at appraised value:
    2 shares Central States Electric Corporation     2.00
    100 shares First National Bank of Baltimore   5050.00
    10 shares Monumental Radio                     152.50
    2 shares National City Bank of New York        114.50
    1940 Dodge Sedan                               100.00    5419.00

Register of Wills, Baltimore County
    Maryland inheritance tax, as above                         34.69
    Total payments and disbursements                         7120.68
    Cash deficit advanced by beneficiary                     1984.52

                    TOTAL ESTATE ACCOUNTED FOR:-             $7136.16

                                FIRST NATIONAL BANK OF BALTIMORE

                            By:   H. Graham Wood, Vice President

                                EXECUTOR U/M - JOSEPH OBERLE, DECEASED.
```

Audit Statement for Settlement of Joseph Oberle's Estate – 28 September 1954

---

[156] George Gonce's correct middle initial is "J," not "F."; he has an identification number in my genealogy database because he is my mother Rosalie (the wife of Joseph's son Cornelius) Gonce's brother.

STATE OF MARYLAND)
                 (to-wit:
CITY OF BALTIMORE)

  I HEREBY CERTIFY that on this day of , 1955, before me, the subscriber, a Notary Public of the State of Maryland, in and for the City of Baltimore, personally appeared H. Graham Wood, Vice President of THE FIRST NATIONAL BANK OF BALTIMORE, Executor under the will of JOSEPH OBERLE, deceased, and he made oath in due form of law that the matters and facts set forth in the aforegoing First and Final Administration Account are true as therein stated, to the best of his knowledge, information and belief.

  WITNESS my hand and Notarial Seal.

            - Notary Public -

Notary Statement for Settlement of Joseph Oberle's Estate

I, KATHERINE G. OBERLE, of Baltimore County in the State of Maryland, being of sound and disposing mind, memory and understanding, do hereby make, publish and declare this my last will and testament, hereby revoking any and all former wills or other testamentary dispositions that may have been made by me.

ITEM ONE: I direct my executors, hereinafter named, to pay my just debts and funeral expenses as promptly as possible after my death. I direct my executors to have a footstone erected at my grave to duplicate the stone at the grave of my deceased husband, Joseph Oberle. I authorize and empower my executors to expend such sums for my funeral and interment, including the cost of the stone aforesaid, as they may deem fitting and proper, without regard to any limit that may be prescribed by law and without application to the Orphans' Court of Baltimore County or any other court for authority in respect thereto.

ITEM TWO: I give and bequeath to my son, Joseph F. Oberle, Jr., the sum of two hundred dollars ($200.00) in appreciation of his services in settling his father's affairs.

ITEM THREE: I give and bequeath to my grandson, Thomas Stephen Oberle, the sum of one hundred dollars ($100.00).

ITEM FOUR: I give and bequeath to my housemaid, Mamie Stewart, if she is living at the time of my death, the sum of two hundred dollars ($200.00) and the choice of any one easy chair she may desire. In the event that my said housemaid, Mamie Stewart, is living at the time of my death, I direct my executors to pay to her five dollars ($5.00) per week for a period of one year after my death or until the time of her death, whichever event shall first occur.

ITEM FIVE: I give and bequeath to my son, Francis X. Oberle, the following:
1. My three-stone diamond ring.
2. Piano and bench.
3. Record cabinets and contents, any recording machines he wants, all old records in attic, and sheet music and music books.
4. Mahogany cedar chest in dining room.
5. Maple chiffonier in his bedroom, any remaining bedroom furniture he may need and adequate sheets, blankets, pillow cases, etc. for same.

Katherine Goldrick Oberle's Original Will of 26 January 1956 – Page 1

---

[157] The note "[2.3]" indicates that this item was later modified by Item Three of her Second Codicil which is shown later in this chapter.

	ID

    6. Steel engraving of First National Bank (Roche).
    7. Holy communion set used by his father.
    8. Pair religious pictures, "Crown of Thorns" and "Madonna".
    9. Any other pictures in house he may desire.
  10. Secretary desk in living room and any books from any bookcase he may choose.
  11. Any and all remaining stock of liquors, etc. belonging to his father.
  12. Any part or all of flat sterling silverware not bequeathed to others and selection of one-fourth of any china, glassware or crystal, selection to be decided with other families.   [2.2]
  13. No. 1 bill issued by the First National Bank with his father's signature.   ($)
  14. Any bedroom, living room, dining room or kitchen furnishings sufficient to furnish apartment if so desired.
  15. Small gold wrist watch in my box which he found on street when a child.

ITEM SIX: I give and bequeath to my son, Cornelius F. Oberle, the following: id 194

    1. Bookcase in living room and any books he may select.
    2. One 9' x 12' living room or dining room rug, or two 6' x 9' rugs.
    3. Any pictures he may choose.
    4. Selection of tie pins and tie clasps and cuff links.
    5. $5.00 Citizens National Bank note with his father's signature.   ($)

ITEM SEVEN: I give and bequeath to Rosalie Oberle, wife of my son, Cornelius F. Oberle, the following: id 242

    1. Pair mahogany lamp tables and pair bronze lamps.
    2. One cut glass fruit bowl in dining room and selection of one-fourth of any other china, glassware or crystal desired, selection to be decided with other families.
    3. One large Sheffield silver tray and punch bowl and silver ladle.
    4. Glass punch cups in buffet.
    5. Lot of old English Ironstone plates and vegetable dishes (collectors' items).

ITEM EIGHT: I give and bequeath to my daughter, Katherine G. Miller, the following: id 200

    1. Lot of mahogany bedroom furniture, consisting of poster bed, bureau with mirror and dressing table with mirror, two cane seat chairs.   [1.3]
    2. Maple cedar chest in attic.
    3. One 9' x 12' rug or two 6' x 9' rugs, whichever she may choose.
    4. My old-fashioned gold watch.
    5. Trunk and contents in attic.
    6. One cut glass fruit bowl in dining room.
    7. Buffet server and china cabinet and table in dining room and extra leaves for table.
    8. Lot of blue willow ware china and selection of one-fourth of any china, glassware or crystal, selection to be decided with other families.
    9. Picture, copy of Sistine Madonna which belonged to my mother.   id 171
  10. Oblong shaped silver cocktail tray with black handles.
  11. Any pictures she may choose.
  12. Any selection of blankets, pillows, bolsters and bed linen sufficient for bed.
  13. $10.00 bill with her father's signature (First National Bank).   ($)

-2-

Katherine Goldrick Oberle's Original Will of 26 January 1956 – Page 2

APPENDIX VI – WILLS OF JOSEPH AND KATHERINE OBERLE

	ID
ITEM NINE: I give and bequeath to my son, Joseph F. Oberle, Jr., the following: 1. His father's mahogany chiffonier. 2. $50.00 bill of Citizens National Bank with his father's signature. 3. Framed copy of First National Bank Board resolution on occasion of father's death. 4. Any tie clasps or cuff links he may select.	id 201 ($)
ITEM TEN: I give and bequeath to Nancy Oberle, wife of my son, Joseph F. Oberle, Jr., the following: 1. Round tilt-top pie crust table in living room. 2. Walnut corner china case in dining room. 3. One cut glass water pitcher in china case. 4. Entire set pink dogwood dinner dishes and selection of one-fourth of any other china, glassware or crystal, selection to be decided with other families. 5. Selection of one 9' x 12' rug either from dining room, living room or bedroom. 6. Round Sheffield silver tray with grape design border.	id 202 [1.4]
ITEM ELEVEN: I give and bequeath to my granddaughter, Nan Oberle, the following: 1. Plated silver bread tray, grape design border. 2. Bloodstone ring with small chip diamond center.	id 214
ITEM TWELVE: I give and bequeath to my granddaughter, Angela Oberle, the following: 1. Repousse silver olive spoon with initial "O". 2. Small card or bon bon tray, repousse silver border with initial "O".	id 219
ITEM THIRTEEN: I give and bequeath to my granddaughter, Maria Oberle, the following: 1. Repousse silver salad fork with initial "O". 2. Child's fork from flat sterling silver set marked "Jos. Jr."	id 224
ITEM FOURTEEN: I give and bequeath to my granddaughter, Mary Agnes Oberle, the following: 1. One sterling silver bread tray, monogram "K.G.G." 2. Platinum and diamond bar pin. 3. Gold signet ring with initials "K.G.G."	id 258
ITEM FIFTEEN: I give and bequeath to my grandson, Thomas Stephen Oberle, a $5.00 bill of The First National Bank with the signature of his grandfather, Joseph Oberle.	id 56 ($)
ITEM SIXTEEN: I give and bequeath to my grandson, Francis X. Oberle, grandfather's silver watch and chain and I hereby request that he keep the same for good luck.	id 256 158

-3-

Katherine Goldrick Oberle's Original Will of 26 January 1956 – Page 3

---

[158] See the photograph of this watch on page 116.

	ID
ITEM SEVENTEEN: I give and bequeath to my granddaughter, Mary Rita Miller, the following:	id 215
1. My engagement ring. 2. Repousse silver steak knife and fork, which needs mending. 3. My cameo brooch.	
ITEM EIGHTEEN: I give and bequeath to my son-in-law, Norbert J. Miller, a $5.00 bill of The First National Bank with the signature of Joseph Oberle.	id 199 ($)
ITEM NINETEEN: I give and bequeath to my grandsons, Frederick Miller and Girard (Buddy) Miller, my television set.	ids 212 & 211
ITEM TWENTY: I give and bequeath any tools of my deceased husband, Joseph F. Oberle, to my sons, Cornelius F. Oberle and Francis X. Oberle, and to my son-in-law, Norbert J. Miller, to be divided among them equally as they may decide.	ids 196, 197 & 199
ITEM TWENTY-ONE: I give and bequeath twenty-five (25) shares of the capital stock of The First National Bank of Baltimore to each of my four (4) children, namely, Joseph F. Oberle, Jr., Katherine G. Miller, Cornelius F. Oberle and Francis X. Oberle. I suggest but do not direct that each of my children retain said twenty-five (25) shares of stock of The First National Bank of Baltimore or dispose of it only among members of my family.	ids 201, 200, 196 & 197
	159
ITEM TWENTY-TWO: All the rest, residue and remainder of my property and estate, of whatsoever kind or character and wheresoever situate, I give, devise and bequeath in equal parts or shares unto such of my four (4) children, namely, Joseph F. Oberle, Jr., Katherine G. Miller, Cornelius F. Oberle and Francis X. Oberle, as are living at the time of my death, their heirs and assigns, absolutely, the descendants then living of any of my said four (4) children who may then be deceased to take their parent's share, per stirpes and not per capita.	ids 201, 200, 196, & 197
	160
ITEM TWENTY-THREE: In the event that my son, Francis X. Oberle, is living at the time of my death, he shall have the privilege and option of living in my residence, 213 Midhurst Road, Pinehurst, Baltimore County, Maryland, for a period of one year after my death or until said residence	id 196

-4-

Katherine Goldrick Oberle's Original Will of 26 January 1956 – Page 4

---

[159] "remainder" includes two empty graves in their cemetery plot at New Cathedral Cemetery.
[160] Per stirpes: share is to be divided by descendant branch, and not apportioned across individuals.

shall be sold by my executors, whichever event shall first occur, without the payment of any rent to my estate, but he shall be required to pay for gas, electricity and his food and personal expenses.

In the event that any one of my four (4) children desires to purchase my aforesaid residence, 213 Midhurst Road, Pinehurst, Baltimore County, Maryland, from my estate, my executors shall permit such child to credit the whole or such part as may be necessary of his or her one-fourth (1/4) share of my residuary estate on account of the purchase price which may be agreed upon for my said residence.

ITEM TWENTY-FOUR: I authorize my executors to distribute the legacy of any grandchild of mine who may be a minor at the time of my death unto the parents or parent or legal guardian of such child who may be then living to hold the same until such grandchild or grandchildren attain legal age, and a release duly executed by such parents or parent or legal guardian to whom such distribution is made shall be a full and complete acquittance and discharge to my said executors.

ITEM TWENTY-FIVE: (a) I hereby nominate and appoint my son, Joseph F. Oberle, Jr., and The First National Bank of Baltimore the executors of this my last will and testament. I direct that my executor, Joseph F. Oberle, Jr., be excused from the necessity of giving bond as such.

(b) During the administration of my personal estate I hereby confer upon my executors full power and authority to sell, assign, transfer, convey, exchange, divide, invest, reinvest, mortgage, lease or otherwise deal with or dispose of any part of my estate, real or personal, not herein specifically bequeathed, whenever they may deem such action advantageous to my estate, without application to the Orphans' Court of Baltimore County or any other court for authority in respect thereto.

(c) I also confer upon my executors full power to compromise any claims against or in favor of my estate, for such sums and upon such terms and conditions as they may deem proper, without application to the Orphans' Court of Baltimore County or any other court for the approval thereof.

(d) In any case in which my executors be

-5-

Katherine Goldrick Oberle's Original Will of 26 January 1956 – Page 5 required under the provisions of this my will to divide any property or other assets of my estate or any part thereof, I confer upon them full power and authority to make such division in kind and/or to sell such portions thereof, real or personal, as they may deem necessary or proper to effectuate such division; and any division so made by them shall be binding and conclusive upon all persons interested in my estate.

  IN WITNESS WHEREOF, I have hereunto subscribed my name and affixed my seal and have also written my initials in the margins of the other five pages of this my last will and testament this __26th__ day of __January__ 1956.

          Katherine G. Oberle (SEAL)
          Katherine G. Oberle

  SIGNED, SEALED, PUBLISHED and DECLARED by KATHERINE G. OBERLE, the above named testatrix, as and for her last will and testament, in the presence of us, who, at her request, in her presence, and in the presence of each other, hereunto subscribe our names as witnesses.

Harriet R. Brown residing at 313 Eastway Court, Balto. 12,
Dorothy L. Moore residing at 128 W. Lafayette Ave., Balto 17,
Roger B. Williams residing at 3209 N. Charles St Baltimore, 18, Md.

Katherine Goldrick Oberle's Original Will of 26 January 1956 – Page 6 (Signature Page)

This is the FIRST CODICIL to the last will and testament dated January 26, 1956, of the undersigned, KATHERINE G. OBERLE.   id 80

ITEM ONE: I hereby revoke Item Four of my aforesaid will as the legatee therein, my housemaid, Mamie Stewart, has heretofore departed this life.

ITEM TWO: By Item Five of my aforesaid will I gave and bequeathed to my son, Francis X. Oberle, certain articles of tangible personal property marked from 1 to 15 respectively. And, whereas, my three-stone diamond ring,   id 197
marked number 1 in said Item Five, has since been disposed of, in lieu thereof I give and bequeath to my son, Francis X. Oberle, the mahogany chiffonier (chifferobe) which belonged to his father, and I also give and bequeath to my son, Francis X. Oberle, such chairs, tables or other furniture   id 197
in the living room of my residence as he may select.

ITEM THREE: In addition to the dining room pieces given my daughter, Katherine G. Miller, by Item Eight of my said will, I give and bequeath to my   id 200
said daughter the following dining room chairs, namely, two arm and four side chairs of carved walnut with simulated leather seats of red (Victorian type).

ITEM FOUR: I have given to my daughter-in-law, Nancy Oberle, by   id 202
Item Ten of my aforesaid will, the tilt-top table, walnut corner china case, and a set of pink wild rose china (described in said will as "pink dogwood" china). In the event that my said daughter-in-law should decide not to accept said pieces of furniture and china, I give and bequeath the pieces of furniture and china not selected by her unto my four children, or the survivors of them, to be divided among themselves as they may agree.

ITEM FIVE: In my aforesaid will I have bequeathed a legacy to each of my grandchildren who were then living and since the date of the will three grandsons have been born and additional grandchildren may hereafter be born,   id 259
and accordingly, as I am desirous of remembering all of my grandchildren, I   id 213
give and bequeath the sum of fifty dollars ($50.00) to each of my grandsons   id 214
who has been born since the date of my will and is not mentioned therein and also the sum of fifty dollars ($50.00) to each grandchild of mine who may be born hereafter and be living at the time of my death.

ITEM SIX: I direct my executors to pay out of my residuary estate

Katherine Goldrick Oberle's First Codicil of 3 February 1959 – Page 1

all estate and inheritance taxes, and other governmental charges of whatever nature, which may be assessed on account of gifts and transfers of property made by me during my lifetime, if any; and on account of devises and bequests made in my aforesaid will and this codicil thereto; and against any property which I may own jointly with any other person, and on account of the proceeds of any insurance on my life; it being my intention that such gifts, devises, and bequests and such jointly owned property and such insurance proceeds shall pass in full to the persons entitled thereto, free and clear of such taxes and charges, and that my executors shall not demand contribution towards the payment of any such taxes and charges from any person whomsoever.

ITEM SEVEN: In all other respects I hereby ratify and confirm my aforesaid last will and testament dated January 26, 1956.

IN WITNESS WHEREOF, I have hereunto set my hand and seal and have also written my initials in the other page of this first codicil to my last will and testament this 3rd day of February, 1959.

<u>Katherine G. Oberle</u> (SEAL)
Katherine G. Oberle

SIGNED, SEALED, PUBLISHED and DECLARED by KATHERINE G. OBERLE, the above named testatrix, as and for a first codicil to her last will and testament dated January 26, 1956, in the presence of us, who, at her request, in her presence, and in the presence of each other have hereunto subscribed our names as witnesses.

Helen M. Gilder residing at 4314 Sidehill Road, Balto.

Dorothy M. Tayloe residing at 1649 Northgate Rd. Balto. 18

Roger B. Williams residing at 3209 N. Charles St Baltimore 18, Md.

-2-

Katherine Goldrick Oberle's First Codicil of 3 February 1959 – Page 2

APPENDIX VI – WILLS OF JOSEPH AND KATHERINE OBERLE

ID

This is the SECOND CODICIL to the last will and testament dated January 26, 1956, of the undersigned, KATHERINE G. OBERLE, of Baltimore County in the State of Maryland.

    WHEREAS, by the first paragraph of Item Twenty-Three of my aforesaid last will and testament, I devised and bequeathed as follows:- "In the event that my son, Francis X. Oberle, is living at the time of my death, he shall have the privilege and option of living in my residence, 213 Midhurst Road, Pinehurst, Baltimore County, Maryland, for a period of one year after my death or until said residence shall be sold by my executors, whichever event shall first occur, without the payment of any rent to my estate, but he shall be required to pay for gas, electricity and his food and personal expenses";

    AND WHEREAS, my said son, Francis X. Oberle, has since married and established a home of his own;

ITEM ONE: Now therefore I hereby revoke the first paragraph of Item Twenty-three of my aforesaid last will and testament.

    WHEREAS, by Item Five, paragraph 12, of my aforesaid last will and testament, I gave and bequeathed to my son, Francis X. Oberle, "any part or all of the flat sterling silverware not bequeathed to others * * * *";

ITEM TWO: I now therefore hereby revoke that part of Item Five, paragraph 12, as aforesaid, and give and bequeath any part or all of the flat sterling silverware not bequeathed to others to my daughter, Katherine G. Miller.

    WHEREAS, by Item Three of my aforesaid last will and testament, I gave and bequeathed to my grandson, Thomas Stephen Oberle, the sum of one hundred dollars ($100.00);

ITEM THREE: Now therefore I hereby revoke said legacy and I give and bequeath the sum of three hundred dollars ($300.00), in lieu thereof, to my son, Cornelius F. Oberle and Rosalie Oberle, his wife, or the survivor of them, for the use of my grandson, Thomas Stephen Oberle.

ITEM FOUR: In all other respects I ratify and confirm my aforesaid last will and testament dated January 26, 1956 and first codicil thereto dated February 3, 1959.

    IN WITNESS WHEREOF, I have hereunto set my hand and seal this 19th day of April, 1963.

                                                      Katherine G. Oberle (SEAL)

SIGNED, SEALED, PUBLISHED and DECLARED by KATHERINE G. OBERLE, the

ID
id 81
id 197
id 197
id 197
id 200
id 56
id 196
id 242
id 56
id 81

Katherine Goldrick Oberle's Second Codicil of 19 April 1963 – Page 1

above named testatrix, as and for a second codicil to her last will and testament dated January 26, 1956, in the presence of us, who, at her request, in her presence, and in the presence of each other have hereunto subscribed our names as witnesses.

[signature] residing at 6309 Blenheim Rd

[signature] residing at 6302 Blenheim Rd. #10

Katherine Goldrick Oberle's Second Codicil of 19 April 1963 – Page 2

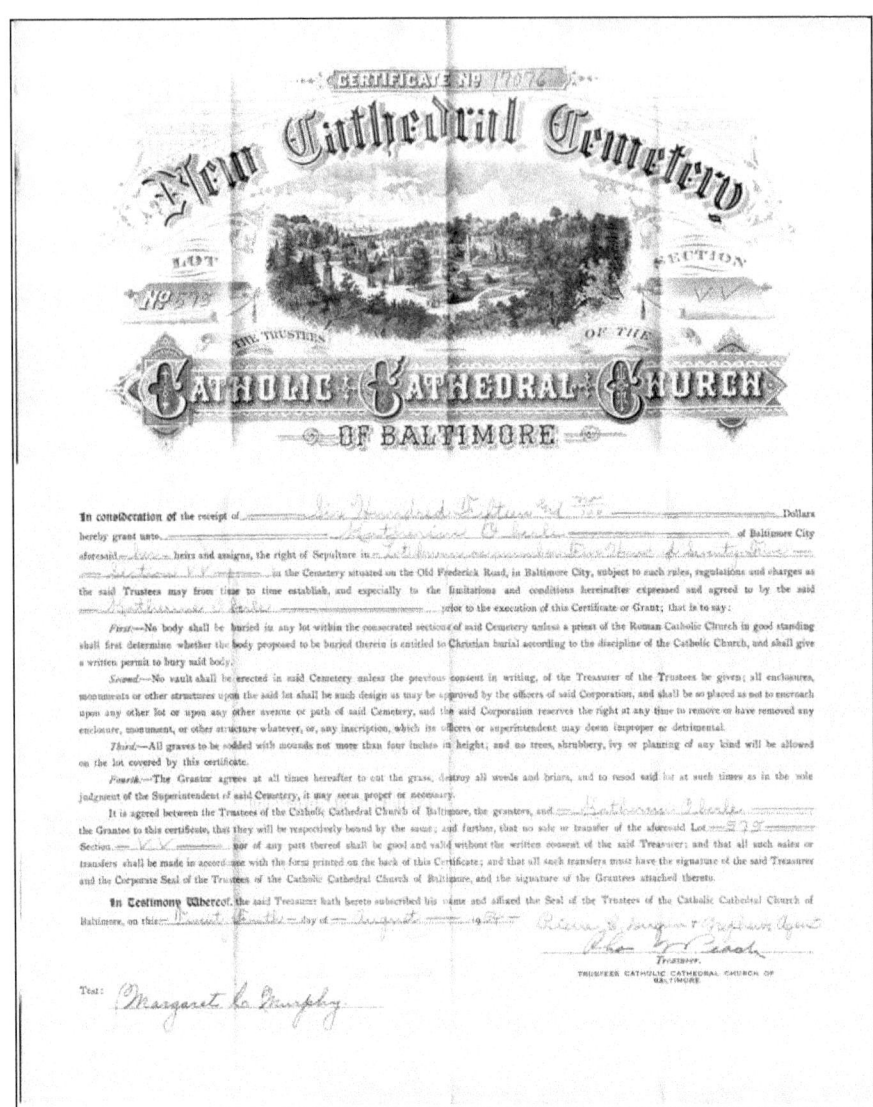

Inside Page from Deed to Lot 575-W in New Cathedral Cemetery in Baltimore, MD

Outside Cover from Deed to Lot 575-W in New Cathedral Cemetery in Baltimore, MD

Appendix VII ::
Descendants of Balthassar Oberlé of Dabo

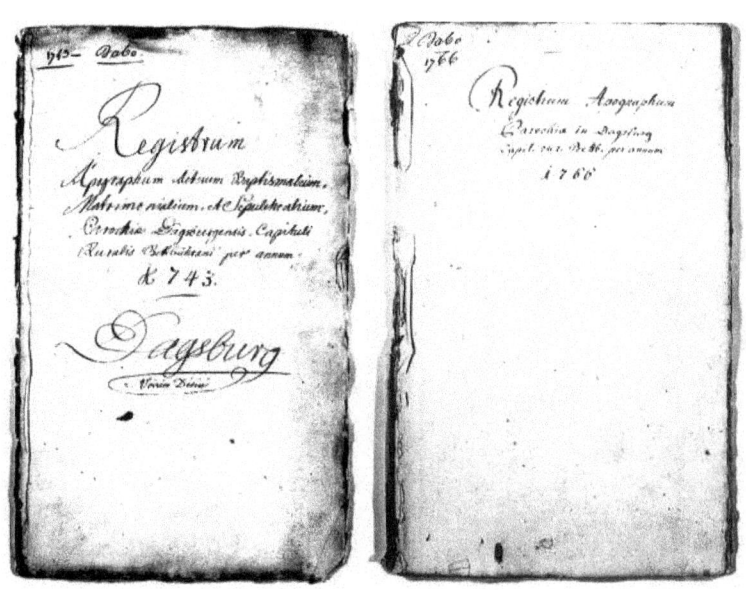

Paroisse de Dabo – 1743 and 1766 Parish Register Covers
Note the name change from Dagsburg to Dabo in the 1766 Register

Descendants of Balthassar Oberle

The table below lists seven generations of the family of Balthassar Oberlé and Anne Marie Mertz. The number preceding each line identifies the generation, and the number at the end of each line is the person's identification number in my genealogical database which is used to reference documents and other material relating to that person. The "a" number preceding the identification number is the Ahnentafel Number showing my direct line to the first Balthassar Oberlé.

As mentioned under "(Suspected) Children of the elder Johann Oberle & Anna-Maria Anstett" on page 8, circumstantial evidence suggests that Balthassar Oberle may be the second child of Johann and Anna Maria, making this couple our earliest *suspected* ancestors.

> A Note about Ahnentafel Numbers ...
>
> *The Ahnentafel (literally, "Ancestor Table) numbering scheme was developed by German genealogists to permit easy identification of particular ancestors in an ancestry tree relative to the person creating the tree. Essentially, the person creating the tree (in this case, me) would be assigned the arbitrary number a1. My father would then be number a2 (my number 1 multiplied by 2), and my mother would be number a3 (my father's number plus 1).*
>
> *My paternal grandparents would be a4 (2 x 2) and a5 (4 + 1), and my maternal grandparents would be a6 (3 x 2) and a7 (6 + 1) and so forth. My four great-grandparents would be 8 & 9, 10 & 11, 12 & 13, and 14 & 15. Anyone's father can be found by doubling his or her Ahnentafel number and adding 1 to that to obtain their mother's number.*

1. Balthassar OBERLE (b.1711;d.1788)..a128   id 1704
++ spouse: Anne Marie MERTZ (m.1744;d.1787)................................a129   id 4221
...2. Pierre OBERLE (b.1748)...id 4222
...++ spouse: Marie Therese SCHMIDT (m.1787)...id 4223
......3. Maria Theresa OBERLE (b.1788)..id 4262
......3. Anna Maria OBERLE (b.1789)...id 4308
......3. Marie Catherine OBERLE (b.1790)..id 4307
......3. Marie Catherine OBERLE (b.1797;d.1842).......................................id 4231
.........++ spouse: Jacques SPENGLER (b.1777;m.1817;d.1842)..................id 4230
...2. Balthassar OBERLE (b.1745;d.1786)...a64   id 1675
...++ spouse: Anne Marie SCHOTT (b.1738;m.1766;d.1776)..................a65   id 4224
......3. Anna Maria OBERLE (b.1767;d.1778)...id 4267
......3. Maria Barbara OBERLE (b.1769)..id 4233
.........++ spouse: François Joseph SCHMIDT (b.1774;m.1800;d.1831)..........id 4232
......3. Antoine OBERLE (b.1772;d.1807)..id 4236

Appendix VII – Descendants of Balthassar Oberle

```
......++ spouse: Marie Anne DILLENSCHNEIDER (m.1805;d.1807)..............id 4237
.........4. François Joseph OBERLE (b.1806;d.1834)...................................id 4241
......3. François Joseph OBERLE (b.1773;d.1834).............................a32  id 1154
......++ spouse: Marie Anne SCHREIBER (b.1774;d.1823).....................a33  id 1155
.........4. Hubert OBERLE (b.1793;d.1848)................................................id 1180
.........++ spouse: Catherine RUSCHMEYER (b.1804;m.1830).......................id 1181
............5. Barthalome OBERLE (b.1831).................................................id 1182
............5. Marie Anne OBERLE (b.1833;d.1865).......................................id 1451
............5. Catherine OBERLE (b.1835).................................................id 1183
............5. Hubert OBERLE (b.1837).....................................................id 1184
............5. Louise OBERLE (b.1840).....................................................id 1185
............5. Louis OBERLE (b.1843)......................................................id 1186
.........4. François Joseph OBERLE (b.1795;d.1854)...................................id 1230
.........++ spouse: Anastasie MÜLLER (b.1798;m.1837)................................id 1256
............5. Aloyse OBERLE (b.1838;d.1840)............................................id 1257
............5. Catherine OBERLE (b.1841)................................................id 1258
............5. Marguerite OBERLE (d.1842)...............................................id 1452
.........++ spouse: Marie Anne RUFFENACH (b.1793;m.1817;d.1836)..............id 1255
.........4. François Antoine OBERLE (b.1799;d.1846)..................................id 1231
.........++ spouse: Françoíse BERLIER (m.1829;d.1830)...............................id 1319
............5. Marie Anne OBERLE (b.1829)..............................................id 1320
.........++ spouse: Marie Anne DEUMAND (b.1801;m.1831;d.1868).................id 1239
............5. François OBERLE (b.1832;d.1837).........................................id 1240
............5. Joseph OBERLE (b.1833;d.1868)...........................................id 1241
............5. Sophie OBERLE (b.1834)...................................................id 1242
............++ spouse: UNKM (children's birth records show "pere inconnu"[161])...........
...............6. Elisabethe OBERLE (b.1863;d.1863)....................................id 1248
...............6. Vendelin OBERLE (b.1863;d.1863)......................................id 1249
............++ spouse: Francois Joseph SPENGLER (b.1830)..........................id 2222
...............6. Joseph SPENGLER (b.1867).............................................id 2223
............5. Seraphin OBERLE (b.1837).................................................id 1243
............5. Elisabethe OBERLE (b.1838)...............................................id 1244
............++ spouse: Jean LINKENHELD (b.1839).....................................id 2214
...............6. Joseph LINKENHELD (b.1861)..........................................id 2233
...............6. Basile LINKENHELD (b.1863)...........................................id 2234
...............6. Leonie LINKENHELD (b.1865)..........................................id 2215
...............6. Josephine LINKENHELD (b.1867).......................................id 2216
...............6. Florent LINKENHELD (b.1869).........................................id 2217
```

---

[161] "Pere Inconnu" is French for "Father Unknown." Several (at least six) of the Oberle girls in Engenthal seem to have had short memories. This might indicate a genetic predisposition to early-onset Alzheimers Disease, but likely had a more interesting explanation. Shhh.

............6. Elisabeth LINKENHELD (b.1871)..id 2218
..........5. François [2] OBERLE (b.1840)..id 1245
..........5. Aloyse OBERLE (b.1842)...id 1246
..........5. Catherine OBERLE (b.1844)..id 1247
..........5. Florent OBERLE (b.1846)..id 2278
........4. Armand OBERLE (b.1805;d.1870)...id 1187
........++ spouse: Marie Anne SPENGLER (b.1800;m.1827).....................id 1188
..........5. Jean-Baptiste OBERLE (b.1828)..id 1189
..........++ spouse: Catherine METTLING (b.1827).....................................id 1236
............6. Basile OBERLE (b.1861)..id 1237
............6. Joseph OBERLE (b.1863;d.1867)...id 1238
............6. Emilie OBERLE (b.1865)..id 1992
............6. Elisabeth OBERLE (b.1869)...id 1993
..........5. Armand OBERLE (b.1830;d.1838)...id 1190
..........5. Marie Anne OBERLE (b.1832)...id 1191
..........++ spouse: Ferdinand STENGEL (b.1829).......................................id 2224
............6. Louis STENGEL (b.1855)...id 2232
............6. Joseph STENGEL (b.1858)..id 2235
............6. Therese STENGEL (b.1860)...id 2236
............6. Louise STENGEL (b.1862;d.1862)..id 2237
............6. Basile STENGEL (b.1864)..id 2225
............6. Aloise STENGEL (b.1866)..id 2226
............6. Marie Louise STENGEL (b.1869)..id 2227
............6. Florent STENGEL (b.1871)..id 2228
..........5. Joseph OBERLE (b.1834)..id 1192
..........5. Therese OBERLE (b.1836;d.1871)..id 1193
..........++ spouse: Joseph LINKENHELD (b.1833).....................................id 2209
............6. Josephine LINKENHELD (b.1862)..id 2242
............6. Elisabeth LINKENHELD (b.1864)...id 2210
............6. Sophie LINKENHELD (b.1866)...id 2211
............6. Louise LINKENHELD (b.1868)...id 2212
............6. Pierre LINKENHELD (b.1870)..id 2213
..........5. Adelaïde OBERLE (b.1839)...id 1194
..........++ spouse: Joseph CLODONG (b.1822;m.1856).............................id 2243
............6. Louis CLODONG (b.1859)..id 2244
............6. Amelie CLODONG (b.1861)...id 2245
............6. Louise CLODONG (b.1864)..id 2246
............6. Françoise CLODONG (b.1866)..id 2247
............6. Armand CLODONG (b.1871)..id 2248
..........5. Armand OBERLE (b.1842;d.1863)...id 1195
........4. Catherine OBERLE (b.1798)...id 1160

APPENDIX VII – DESCENDANTS OF BALTHASSAR OBERLE

..........++ spouse: Louis ROLLING (b.1793;m.1830;d.1864)...............................id 1254
.............5. Seraphin ROLLING (b.1831)..id 2260
.............5. Louis ROLLING (b.1833;d.1855)...id 1556
.............5. Catherine ROLLING (b.1840)..id 2261
..........4. Elisabethe OBERLE (b.1808)..id 1167
..........++ spouse: UNKM [162] (pere inconnu)...
.............5. Veronique OBERLE (b.1836;d.1836)..id 1211
..........4. <u>Seraphin OBERLE</u> (b.1811;d.1890)...a16 id 708
..........++ spouse: <u>Catherine RUFFENACH</u> (b.1821;m.1850;d.1864).....a17 id 1147
.............5. Rosine OBERLE (b.1851)...id 1148
.............5. Therese OBERLE (b.1853)..id 1149
.............5. <u>Seraphin OBERLE</u> (b.1855;d.1931)...a8 id 25
.............++ spouse: <u>Sarah Johanna KIWIET</u> (b.1855;m.1881;d.1937)...........a9 id 26
................6. Seraphin Julius OBERLE , Jr. (b.1879;d.1955)....................................id 60
................++ spouse: Barbara K. NICKOL (b.1876;m.1904;d.1949)......................id 61
..................7. Francis J. OBERLE (b.1906;d.1950)..id 63
..................++ spouse: Dorothy M TRABERT (b.1907;d.1956)..............................id 64
..................7. Mary Elizabeth OBERLE (b.1907;d.2004)..id 194
..................7. Anna Geraldine OBERLE (b.1909;d.1992).......................................id 62
..................++ spouse: Joseph HARTNETT...id 191
..................7. William Seraphin OBERLE (b.1911;d.1995)....................................id 187
..................++ spouse: Nina BURKE..id 670
..................7. Margaret Rita OBERLE (b.1914)...id 193
..................++ spouse: Daniel Aloysius FORD (b.1912;m.1941;d.1974)..............id 192
..................7. Joseph Edward OBERLE (b.1919;d.2004).......................................id 195
..................++ spouse: Marie MADSEN (b.1922;m.1947;d.2010)........................id 671
................6. Francis Joseph OBERLE (b.1882;d.1960)..id 45
................++ spouse: Katherine GRANDY (b.1887;d.1926)...................................id 46
..................7. Joseph F. OBERLE Rev. (b.1911;d.2001)..id 179
................++ spouse: Barbara M. GRANDY (b.1893;m.1928;d.1929)..................id 47
..................7. Gerard George OBERLE Rev. (b.1929)..id 180
................6. Anna T. OBERLE (b.1884;d.1971)...id 24
................++ spouse: Albert Preston JELKS (b.1882;m.1915[Div];d.1948).........id 175
..................7. Thomas Oberle JELKS (b.1916;d.2011)...id 182
..................++ spouse: Helen Agnes KUPINOS (b.1914;m.1938[Div])................id 693
..................++ spouse: Dorothy Jane ESSMAN (b.1924;m.1949;d.2003)...........id 673
................6. Jacob OBERLE (b.1885;d.1918)..id 30
................6. <u>Joseph OBERLE</u> (b.1887;d.1954)..a4 id 81
................++ spouse: <u>Katherine Ger. GOLDRICK</u> (b.1884;m.1913;d.1975)a5 id 80

---

[162] The designations UNKF and UNKM represent "Unknown Female" and "Unknown Male" respectively, and are used in cases where I have not been able to determine the actual name.

.............7. Joseph Francis OBERLE , Jr. (b.1914;d.1990)..............................id 201
.............++ spouse: Catherine T. (Nancy) BORIG (b.1915;d.2000)...............id 202
.............7. Katherine Gertrude OBERLE (b.1915;d.1996)...............................id 200
.............++ spouse: Norbert Joseph MILLER (b.1910;m.1947;d.1993).........id 199
.............7. Cornelius Francis OBERLE (b.1917;d.2004)......................a2 id 196
.............++ spouse: Rosalie Gertr'd GONCE (b.1919;m.1941;d.2013).a3 id 242
.............7. Francis Xavier OBERLE (b.1923;m.1960;d.1997)...........................id 197
.............++ spouse: Gladys Helen MARONEY (b.1929;d.1996)........................id 198
..........6. Helena OBERLE (b.1889;d.1890)...id 27
..........6. Katherine OBERLE (b.1890)...id 177
.............++ spouse: John JOHNSON..id 176
.............7. Helen JOHNSON (b.1919;d.2007)..id 183
.............++ spouse: Carroll L. SPECK..id 2789
..........6. Adalbert OBERLE (b.1891;d.1891)...id 601
..........6. Theresa OBERLE (b.1892)..id 174
.............++ spouse: Harry STRASINGER (b.1895;d.1974)..............................id 173
..........6. Johann OBERLE (b.1895;d.1895)...id 28
..........6. Thomas OBERLE (b.1896;d.1915)...id 23
..........6. Simon OBERLE (b.1899;d.1899)..id 29
.......5. Marguerithe OBERLE (b.1857;d.1927)...id 1150
.......5. Armand OBERLE (b.1859;d.1943)...id 1151
..........++ spouse: Josephine RUFFENACH (b.1864;d.1925)...........................id 3599
..........6. Marie Therese OBERLE (b.1884;d.1961)..id 3600
..........6. Marie OBERLE (b.1885;d.1961)..id 3601
..........6. Emilie OBERLE (b.1887;d.1957)..id 3602
.............++ spouse: Jules SCHAEFFER (b.1885;m.1912;d.1967)...................id 3608
.............7. Marie Julie SCHAEFFER (b.1912;d.2004)...................................id 3612
.............++ spouse: Eugene Marc PETER (b.1912;d.1993)...........................id 3618
.............7. Josephine SCHAEFFER (b.1920;d.2006)....................................id 3611
.............7. Alice Henriette SCHAEFFER (b.1922)...id 3614
.............7. Marguerite SCHAEFFER (b.1923;d.1997)...................................id 3617
.............7. Lucie SCHAEFFER (b.1925;d.1988)..id 3616
.............7. Lina Suzanne SCHAEFFER (b.1926;d.1968)...............................id 3613
.............7. Jules SCHAEFFER (b.1928;d.1950)...id 3615
..........6. Michel Amand OBERLE (b.1890;d.1960).......................................id 3603
.............++ spouse: Cecile RUBINE (b.1884;d.1937)....................................id 3609
..........6. Alexandrine OBERLE (b.1892;d.1972)...id 3604
.............++ spouse: Joseph CHRISTOPH..id 3610
.............7. Paul CHRISTOPH..id 3619
.............++ spouse: UNKF..
.............7. Emile CHRISTOPH..id 3620

APPENDIX VII – DESCENDANTS OF BALTHASSAR OBERLE

..................7. Virgile CHRISTOPH..id 3621
..................7. Jeanne CHRISTOPH..id 3622
...............6. Victor OBERLE (b.1894;d.1968)..id 3605
...............6. Virgile OBERLE (b.1898;d.1972)...id 3606
...............6. Emile Joseph OBERLE (b.1903)..id 3607
............5. Alexandrine OBERLE (b.1861)...id 1152
............5. Eugenia OBERLE (b.1862;d.1945)..id 1894
.........++ spouse: Elisabeth STILTZ (b.1812;m.1837;d.1849)............................id 1146
............5. Marie Louise OBERLE (b.1838)...id 1163
............5. Armand OBERLE (b.1839;d.1841)..id 1164
............5. Marguerite OBERLE (b.1841)...id 1165
............5. Josephine OBERLE (b.1842)...id 1166
............++ spouse: UNKM (pere inconnu)..
...............6. Francois Antoine OBERLE (b.1866)..id 1994
............5. Madelaine OBERLE (b.1844)..id 1153
............5. Marie Anne OBERLE (b.1846)..id 2277
............5. Augustin OBERLE (b.1848)..id 2259
......3. Maria Catherine OBERLE (b.1774;d.1822)..id 1696
......++ spouse: Dominique BURGER (b.1782;d.1863)..id 1697
.........4. Sofia BURGER (b.1807;d.1809)...id 2279
.........4. Hubert BURGER (b.1811)...id 1699
.........4. Sophie BURGER (b.1817)...id 2229
......3. Maria Elisabetha OBERLE (b.1776)...id 4256
...++ spouse: Marie Anne MÜLLER (m.1777;d.1812)..id 1676
......3. Marie Anne OBERLE (b.1778)...id 4235
......++ spouse: Stephane BENTZ (b.1771;m.1799)..id 4234
......3. Maria Cecilia OBERLE (b.1779;d.1848)...................[163] [Duplicate 1]   id 1229
......++ spouse: Antoine SALY (b.1784)...........................[Duplicate 2]   id 1252
.........4. Marie Anne SALY (b.1811)..............................[Duplicate 3]   id 2249
.........4. Françoise SALY (b.1814).................................[Duplicate 4]   id 1253
......3. Balthassar OBERLE (b.1781;d.1829)..id 1691
......++ spouse: Marie Elisabethe DIEDA (b.1792;m.1812)....................................id 1689
.........4. Gaspard OBERLE (b.1813;d.1814)..id 1677
.........4. François Melchior OBERLE (b.1815)..id 1678
.........4. Marie Elisabethe OBERLE (b.1818)..id 1682
.........++ spouse: UNKNOWN (pere inconnu)...
............5. Casimir OBERLE (b.1840)...id 1687
.........++ spouse: Jean AUER (b.1812)..id 2262

---

[163] Maria Cecilia Oberle and Antoine Saly are first cousins; their marriage and two children therefore appear in two different locations, one with Antoine as the spouse and the other with Cecilia as the spouse.

............5. Aloyse AUER (b.1844;d.1844)...id 2263
............5. Francoise AUER (b.1845)..id 2264
............5. Aloise AUER (b.1847)...id 2265
............5. Jean AUER (b.1849)..id 2266
............5. Charles AUER (b.1851)..id 2267
............5. Joseph AUER (b.1854)...id 2268
............5. Caroline AUER (b.1857)..id 2269
.........4. Françoise OBERLE (b.1820;d.1845)..id 1679
.........++ spouse: UNKM (pere inconnu)..
............5. Auguste OBERLE (b.1844;d.1849)..id 1688
.........4. Balthassar OBERLE (b.1822)..id 1680
.........++ spouse: Anne Marie GERSINGER (d.1871)..id 1690
............5. Joseph OBERLE (b.1859)..id 1683
............5. Balthassar OBERLE (b.1860;d.1861)...id 1684
............5. Rosine OBERLE (b.1861)..id 1685
............5. Christine OBERLE (b.1863)..id 1686
............5. Josephine OBERLE (b.1865)...id 1987
............5. Marie Anne OBERLE (b.1866)...id 1988
............5. Louis OBERLE (b.1868)...id 1989
............5. Charles OBERLE (b.1869)..id 1990
............5. Celestine OBERLE (b.1871)...id 1991
.........4. Joseph OBERLE (b.1824)...id 1681
.........4. Caspar OBERLE (b.1827)...id 1692
.........4. Catherine OBERLE (b.1829)..id 1693
.........++ spouse: UNKM (pere inconnu)..
............5. Hubert OBERLE (b.1850)..id 2276
.........++ spouse: Antoine SCHWALLER (b.1819)...id 2219
............5. Catherine SCHWALLER (b.1853)...id 2230
............5. Antoine SCHWALLER (b.1855)...id 2231
............5. Emil SCHWALLER (b.1857)..id 2238
............5. Joseph SCHWALLER (b.1859)..id 2239
............5. Dolphine SCHWALLER (b.1861)...id 2240
............5. Marie Anne SCHWALLER (b.1863)...id 2241
............5. Charles SCHWALLER (b.1865)...id 2220
............5. Clementine SCHWALLER (b.1867)..id 2221
......3. Maria Genoveva OBERLE (b.1785;d.1814)..id 4240
......++ spouse: Hubert SCHWALLER (b.1777;m.1807)......................................id 4239
.........4. Maria Therese SCHWALLER (b.1812)...id 4252
...2. Antonius OBERLE (b.1751)...id 4304
...2. Magdalena OBERLE (d.1800)..id 4238
...2. Anne Marie OBERLE...id 4228

Appendix VII – Descendants of Balthassar Oberle

```
...++ spouse: Johannes Martinus LINGENHELD (sic, m.1778)..............id 4227
......3. Maria Elisabeth LINKENHELD (b.1780;d.1787)......................id 4248
......3. Martina LINKENHELD (d.1781)...........................................id 4249
...2. Catherine OBERLE (b.1759;d.1829).........................................id 1703
...++ spouse: Henri SALI............................................................id 4255
......3. Antoine SALY (b.1784)..................................[Duplicate 2]    id 1252
......++ spouse: Maria Cecilia OBERLE (b.1779;d.1848).....[Duplicate 1]    id 1229
.........4. Marie Anne SALY (b.1811)...........................[Duplicate 3]    id 2249
.........4. Françoíse SALY (b.1814).............................[Duplicate 4]    id 1253
...++ spouse: Jean WEINMANN (d.1829).......................................id 1702
...2. Michel OBERLE (b.1765;d.1800)............................................id 4225
...++ spouse: Odile SCHOTT (b.1771;m.1799)................................id 4226
...2. Joseph OBERLE. ................................................................id 4229
...++ spouse: Francoise GEMMERLE (b.1750;m.1798)....................id 4247
...++ spouse: Catherine DRIXEL.................................................id 4296
......3. Francisca OBERLE (b.1759).............................................id 4264
...2. Joannis OBERLE (b.1763)...................................................id 4309
...++ spouse: Maria Catherine MICHEL (m.1783)..........................id 4258
......3. Catherina Walburga OBERLE (b.1784;d.1786)....................id 4260
......3. Catherina Walburga OBERLE (b.1786)..............................id 4261
......3. Johann Martin OBERLE (b.1789).....................................id 4263
```

The eighth (of which I am a part), ninth and tenth generations have not been listed for privacy reasons although it should be noted that a few of those in the seventh generation are still alive.

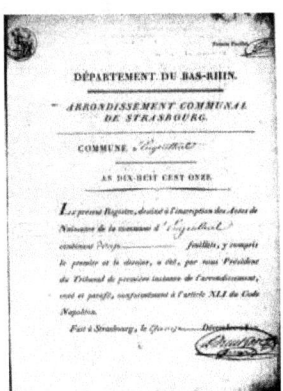

Engenthal – 1811 Birth Register Cover

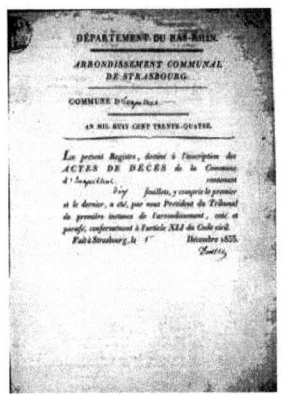

Engenthal – 1834 Death Register Cover

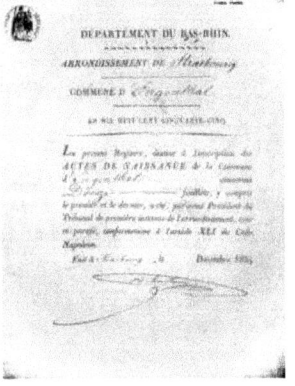

Engenthal – 1855 Birth Register Cover

Appendix VIII :: Ancestors of Joseph Oberle of Baltimore

Baltimore – 1913: Joe and Katie Oberle, with Joe's siblings Tommy and Theresa in the rear. This photograph is believed to have been taken on 15 April 1913, the day of Joe and Katie's Wedding.

Ancestors of Joseph Oberle

The table below lists the known ancestors of Joseph Oberle[164] of Baltimore. The number preceding each line identifies the generation relative to Joseph, who is considered generation 1 in this table (start with the line containing Joseph's name).

His paternal ancestors are listed above him in the table, and his maternal line is listed below him. His father Seraphin Oberle, for instance, can be found by locating generation 2 above, and his mother Sarah Johanna Kiwiet by finding generation 2 below. His four grandparents are numbered 3, his eight great-grandparents are numbered 4, and so on. The id number at the end of each line is the person's identification number in my genealogical database that is used to reference documents and other material relating to that person. The "a" number preceding the identification number is my Ahnentafel Number[165].

```
................7.......Johann OBERLE (speculation)..........................................a256    id ----
..............6. Balthassar OBERLE (b.1711;d.1788)...............................a128. id 1704
................7+....Anna Maria ANSTETT (speculation)............................a257....id ----
...........5. Balthassar OBERLE (b.1745;d.1786).......................................a64...id 1675
..............6+ spouse: Anne Marie MERTZ (m.1744;d.1787).....................a129. id 4221
.........4. François Joseph OBERLE (b.1773;d.1834)..............................a32...id 1154
................7.......Jean-Nicolas SCHOTT (b.1689;d.1737)........................a260. id 4754
..............6. Jean SCHOTT (d.bef 1766)...............................................a130. id 4250
................7+....Anne Claire DILLENSCHNEIDER (b.1693;d.1742). a261. id 4755
...........5+ spouse: Anne Marie SCHOTT (b.1738;m.1766;d.1776).........a65...id 4224
................7.......Frederic SENNEWICK.................................................a262. id 4752
..............6+ spouse: Anne Marie SENNEWICK (d.1748)......................a131. id 4251
................7+....Catherine KERBER......................................................a263. id 4753
......3. Seraphin OBERLE (b.1811;d.1890)........................................a16.....id 708
.........4+ spouse: Marie Anne SCHREIBER (b.1774;d.1823)....................a33...id 1155
...2. Seraphin OBERLE (b.1855;d.1931)..............................................a8..........id 25
...........5. Andre RUFFENACH...............................................................a68...id 1227
.........4. Antoine RUFFENACH (b.abt1788; d.1842)...........................a34...id 1156
...........5+ spouse: Catherine DRIXEL (d.bef 1818)...............................a69...id 1228
......3+ spouse: Catherine RUFFENACH (b.1821;m.1850;d.1864)............a17...id 1147
...........5. Joseph MÜLLER (b.abt 1772).................................................a70...id 1161
.........4+ spouse: Catherine MÜLLER (b.1799)...........................................a35...id 1157
...........5+ spouse: Catherine DUMANT (b.abt 1780;d.1832)..................a71...id 1210
```

---

[164] If it is not obvious, except for his maternal line, this table is identical to what would be created for any of Joe's siblings Seraphin, Frank, Anna (Jelks), Jake, Helena, Kate (Johnson), Adalbert, Theresa (Strasinger), Johann, Tommy, or Simon

[165] That is, an Ahnentafel number based on me as number 1, my father as number 2, and my mother Rosalie Gonce as number 3. See an explanation of Ahnentafel numbers on page 245.

APPENDIX VII – ANCESTORS OF JOSEPH OBERLE

1. Joseph OBERLE (b.1887;d.1954)..a4..........id 81
......3. Gerhard KIWIET..a18...id 1725
...2+ spouse: Sarah Johanna KIWIET (b.1855;m.1881;d.1937)..................a9..........id 26
......3+..spouse: Josephine DIRKSON..a19...id 1726
......3. James GOLDRICK...a20...id 1907
...2. Martin G. GOLDRICK (b.abt 1844; d.1896)...a10.....id 170
......3+..spouse of James Goldrick unknown..a21......id ----
1+ spouse: Katherine Gertrude GOLDRICK (b.1884;m.1913;d.1975)....a5..........id 80
......3. Edward BOYLE. ....a22...id 1715
...2+..spouse: Catherine BOYLE (b.1848;d.1927)..a11.....id 171
......3+ spouse: Margaret KELLY..a23...id 1716

Baltimore – 1913: Anna, Tommy, Katie and Theresa Oberle
This photograph was taken on the same day as the one on page 254, and shows Katie with her new brother and sisters-in-law. These are the only two photographs taken on Joe and Katie's wedding date known to exist.

Appendix IX :: Other Children of Joseph and Katherine Oberle

Since this book was intended primarily for my own descendants, little information about my father's siblings was given in the body of the book (see page 119), and this Appendix is intended to fill that gap sufficiently enough that someone in any of these lines might have a place to begin researching their other lineage.

With assistance from a few cousins, my father's older siblings, Joseph Jr. id201 and Katherine id200, and his younger brother Francis id197, will be discussed in the order of their birth years below.

The United States Censuses that contain references to Joe and Katie's children are included in the body of the book. These include the census sheets for 1920 (page 106), 1930 (page 109), and 1940 (page 110). Some photographs of Joe, Sis, and Francis also appear in the section on their parents which begins on page 98.

Joseph Francis Oberle

The basis for this section about my Uncle Joe and Aunt "Nancy" was provided by their daughter Angela, although I have taken the liberty of adding some related document images and data, as well as reference numbers to my genealogy database. – F.O.

Joseph Jr. id201, the oldest of Joe and Katie's children, was born on March 1st 1914 in his parents' home at 812 East 22nd Street in Baltimore. Joe attended St. Ann's Parish grammar school in Baltimore when he was old enough.[166]

At the age of twelve, after the family's first summer in their new home at Midhurst Road (see page 107), he began attending Immaculate Conception Parochial School in Towson in the fall of 1926. Following his graduation he attended Towson Catholic High School and, during this period, began working part time at Asbill's Pharmacy in downtown Towson in addition to being a starter on Towson Catholic's varsity basketball team.

Baltimore – 1920: Joe Oberle, Jr.

Joe had hopes of studying chemistry and becoming a chemistry teacher, and had saved enough money from his part time job for his first year's tuition at Loyola College. His father effectively vetoed that, however, saying that he could either go to college or continue to live at home, but not both. Joseph Sr., remember, had by this time become part of the senior management of a major bank, and done so with only two years of formal high school education – not enough, apparently, to realize that the United States was rapidly entering a new era with quite different requirements than those he himself had experienced at the beginning of the century.

So, after his High School graduation – at the top of his class – Joe began working full time[167] as a bookkeeper at a local food store.

During his youth, Joe had great affection for and interest in trains, fire engines and ambulances; the interest in trains – both real and miniature – was certainly prominent enough to have influenced both his younger brothers, and they kept a layout with several electric model trains in their basement.

Joe also had a life-long interest in both sports and the arts, and even participated in some amateur plays. His love of opera began at an early age, and he managed to attend many performances for "free" by volunteering as an usher during his teens. He continued to attend the opera throughout his life. Dur-

---

[166] Other photographs of Joe when he was a child appear in the earlier section titled "Joseph Oberle & Katherine Goldrick" beginning on page 98.

[167] FO's note: In 1940, remember, "full time" implied a 45 hour work week – five and a half work days.

ing this period, he also attended college classes part time at, variously, Johns Hopkins McCoy Business College and Loyola College.

Baltimore – 1942: Joseph Oberle

Joe enlisted in the United States Army on August 25th, 1942, at which time he listed his civilian occupation as "Accountant" and his marital status as single with no dependents.

The records show he was seventy-one inches tall[168], weighed one hundred fifty pounds, and had completed four years of college credits.

The picture on the left was taken behind the kitchen at his parent's home on Midhurst Road during a short leave after completing his basic training at Ft. Bragg, North Carolina.

He was then assigned to Fort Belvoir, in the Washington D.C. area, where he remained until the end of the World War II.

In about 1943 Charles Butler, a fraternity brother of Joe's from Hopkins, married Mary Borig and, through him, Joe met Mary's younger sister Nancy. "Nancy's" name was actually Catherine Theresa but, when she was born, her big sister Mary, at less than two years old, was only able to manage calling her "Nana" and this led to Catherine's being known as Nancy from a very early age.

The Borig Family

Richard F. Borig id4332 was born about 1862 in Saxony, and came to the United States in 1882. Within five years, he had married his wife Mary id4333, who herself had emigrated from Bavaria in 1884 when she was about eighteen years old; by 1887 the couple's first child Henry Richard id2314 was born.

Children of Richard F. and Mary Borig

The following section provides minimal details about Richard and Mary's eight children and grandchildren.

- **Henry Richard Borig** id2314, (born 12 March 1887, died February 1967), married Mary J. Greeley id543; he and Mary are discussed in more detail on page 262.
- Frederick George Borig id4320, (born 30 November 1888), married Anna id4321 and had a daughter Eleanore id4330 in about 1918. On the 1910 census, Frederick reports that he was a tinsmith.

---

[168] Military-speak for five feet, eleven inches tall.

- William F. Borig id4322, (born about 1891), married Cecilia id4323 and had a son Millard id4331 in about 1917. According to the 1910 and 1920 census records, William was an insurance agent.
- Annie S. Borig id4325, (born about 1893).
- Clara M. Borig id4326, (born about 1895).
- Hattie Borig id4327, (born about 1900).
- Richard C. Borig id4328, (born about 1902), married Theresa (born about 1906) and had a son Richard F. on 2 Sep 1934. Richard F. married Florence and had a daughter Mary Ann.
- Hilda Borig id4329, (born about 1907) married a man named O'Brien.

The Greeley Family

Patrick Greeley id4313, born about 1810, and his wife Sarah id4467, born about 1810, were married in about 1845 in Ireland. After the birth of their first child John id4468 in 1847, the family emigrated to Baltimore, where they settled in the city's Third Ward, then an area of recent Irish and German immigrants. They likely arrived in 1848 or 1849, since their second child Thomas id4469 was born in Baltimore in about 1850. By 1858, Patrick and Sarah had a total of five children ranging in age from two to thirteen years old.

Patrick and Sarah can be seen with all their children in both the 1860 and 1870 U.S. Census records. A segment of the 1860 census page is shown below, which includes their younger children Mary, Joseph and Bridget.

Page No. 176 787

SCHEDULE 1.—Free Inhabitants in 3 Ward Balto City in the County of Baltimore State of Maryland enumerated by me, on the 25 day of June 1860. Ass't Marshal.

Post Office Baltimore City.

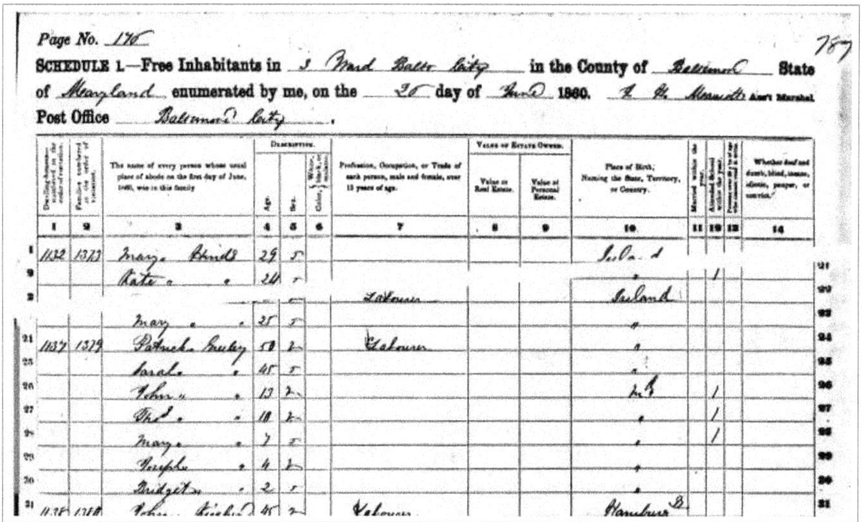

Baltimore – 1860 U.S. Census showing family of Patrick Greeley
National Archives Series m653 Roll 459 Page 787 (extract showing Greeley family)

APPENDIX IX – FAMILY OF JOSEPH AND KATHERINE OBERLE

The third child, Joseph id4313 and his wife Mary id4314, who was born in about 1864, had five children – all girls but the fourth, who was named Horace[169] Greeley id4317. The couple's oldest daughter Mary J. Greeley id543, who lived from 16 January 1887 to 8 October 1961, married Henry Richard Borig. id2314

Henry Richard Borig and Mary J. Greeley

At the time of their marriage, Henry was employed as a meat cutter. Henry and Mary lived with Mary's parents Patrick and Sarah.

In 1917, shortly after the birth of their first two children (Mary and Nancy discussed earlier), the United States instituted a draft to support their anticipated entrance into World War I. Henry's draft card, shown below, describes him as being of medium height and slender build, and with grey eyes and brown hair. So far as can be determined, however, Henry was never selected for service.

Mary had her last child, Henry Jr., in 1919 while she and Henry were still living with her parents.

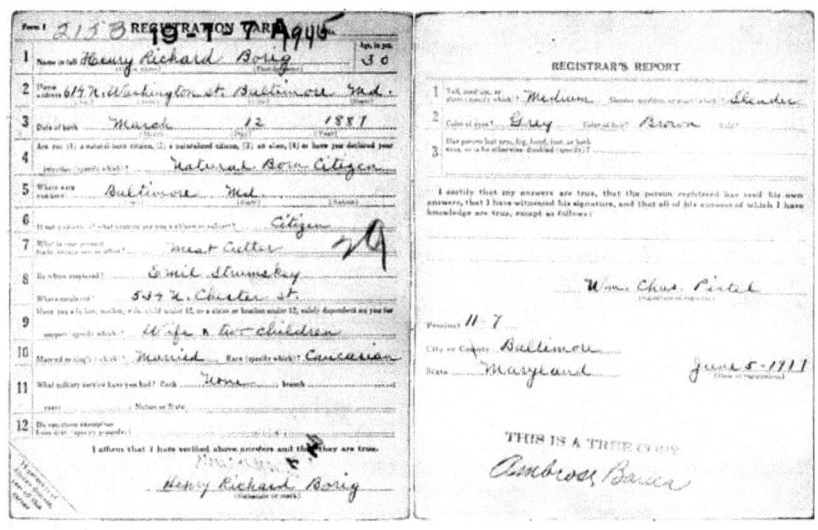

Baltimore – 1917: World War I Draft Card of Henry Richard Borig

A segment of the 1920 census,[170] shown on the following page, shows the families of Joseph Greeley and Henry Borig living at 1735 Eager Street in Baltimore, by which time Henry had become a streetcar motorman.

---

[169] Were Joseph and Mary fans of the New England newspaper editor, politician and reformer Horace Greeley (February 3, 1811 – November 29, 1872) – he of the famous "Go West, young man" quotation?

[170] I have been unable to locate the family in the 1930 or 1940 census records.

DEPARTMENT OF COMMERCE—BUREAU OF THE CENSUS
FOURTEENTH CENSUS OF THE UNITED STATES: 1920—POPULATION
State: Maryland
Name of incorporated place: Baltimore
Ward of city: 7
Enumerated by me on the 5 day of January, 1920

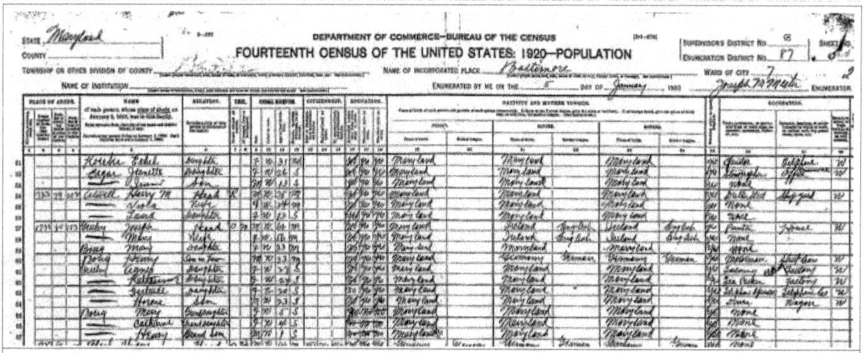

Baltimore – 1920: U.S. Census showing family of Joseph Greeley
National Archives Series t625 Roll 661 Page 111; note the Borig family (his daughter's) living with them.

Like other older men of his generation (he was then 55), Henry was again required to register for the "old man's draft" as progress during World War II bogged down in 1942. His 25 April draft registration form is shown below.

REGISTRATION CARD—(Men born on or after April 28, 1877 and on or before February 16, 1897)
1. Name: HENRY RICHARD BORIG
2. Place of Residence: 2930 CLIFTONPARK TERRACE BALTO MD
3. Mailing Address: Same
4. Telephone: Wolf 6937 J
5. Age in Years: 55
Date of Birth: March 17 1887
6. Place of Birth: Balto. Md.
7. Name and Address of Person Who Will Always Know Your Address: Charles Butler HARFORD County
8. Employer's Name and Address: Baltimore Transit Co.
9. Place of Employment or Business: Equitable Bldg Calvert + Fayette St Balto Md
I affirm that I have verified above answers and that they are true.
D. S. S. Form 1
Henry R. Borig

REGISTRAR'S REPORT
DESCRIPTION OF REGISTRANT
Race: White ✓
Height (Approx.): 5 ft 5 in
Weight (Approx.): 170
Eyes: Gray ✓
Hair: Black ✓
Complexion: Ruddy ✓
Other obvious physical characteristics that will aid in identification: NONE
MARGUERITE A SLADA
Registrar for Local Board 6 BALTO MD
Date of registration APRIL 25 1942
Local Board No. 6 Baltimore

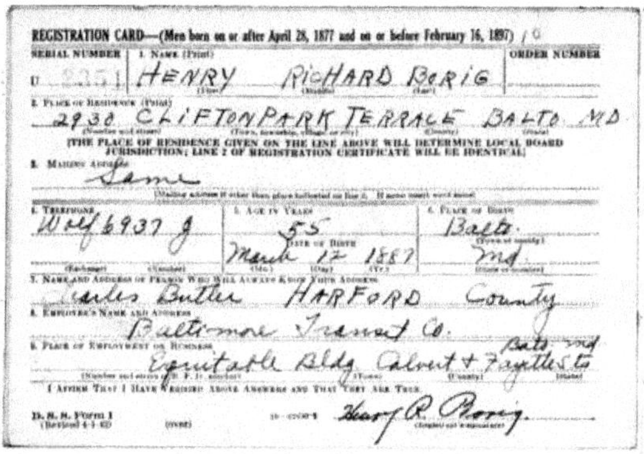

Note that Henry's contact, the "person who will always know your address" was listed as Charles Butler.

Baltimore – 1942: World War II Draft Card of Henry Richard Borig

Mary died on 8 October 1961; Henry lived until February 1967.

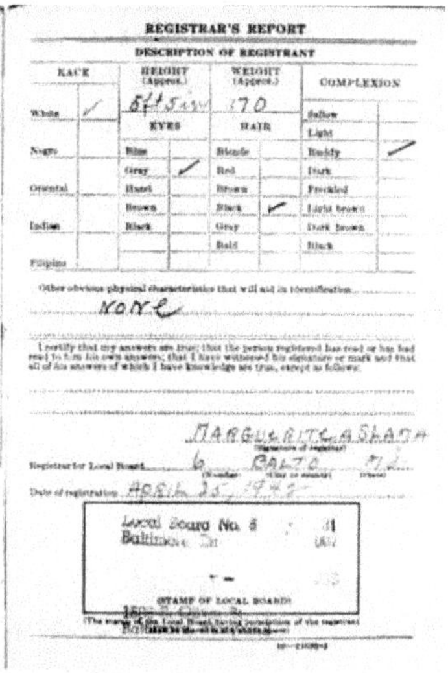

Children of Henry Borig and Mary Greeley

Henry Richard Borig id2314 and Mary J. Greeley id543 had three children:

- Mary Borig id4319, (born about 1914)
- **Catherine T. (Nancy) Borig** id202, (13 November 1915 - 7 JUL 2000)
- Henry L. Borig id544, (20 June 1919 - 9 JUN 1981).[171]
- Francis (Frank) A. Borig id4832, (13 November 1924 – 16 February 1993)

[171] This is not the Henry J. Borig (relationship unknown) who lived from 2 OCT 1918 to 11 AUG 1999.

Joseph Oberle and Catherine Borig

Joe and Nancy were married on 18 September 1943 while World War II was still in progress, and they began living in base housing. In July 19 of 1944, shortly after the D-Day invasion, their first daughter was born.

After the war, the family lived with the Borigs for a time, later moving to an apartment in Catonsville. During this period, they had their second daughter and Joe received his CPA certification.

In 1952, Joe and Nancy bought their first home on 2019 Hillenwood Road in Baltimore and, later that year, had a third daughter.

During the fifties, Joe had a job with some interesting benefits: he worked as an accountant for the local Pepsi Cola Bottling Company where employees each got to bring home a case of soda each week. As his daughter puts it, "All of our dentists are most appreciative."

Some time later he worked for Sweetheart Cup in Owings Mills and then eventually opened his own consulting company.

Baltimore – 2019 Hillenwood Road

In the late 1960s, Joe worked at the American Oil Company in Baltimore. During all of his jobs, he also worked as a tax accountant privately at night at home mostly during tax season.

Joe suffered his first heart attack in the early 1970s, but was able to return to work after a convalescent period. After his retirement he was able to enjoy sports, opera, and books more fully.

His daughter comments:

> "My father was an almost compulsive learner; he surrounded himself with books on every subject and attended classes, notably at Loyola, well into my adulthood. One of his most passionate interests was theology. He used to check our homework and was a very hard task-master who wouldn't let us get away with anything! He was a deeply religious, moral man who never left the house without his rosary in his pocket. I never knew him to miss Mass on Sunday or a holy day, even during a blizzard. Our family would often go to Novenas together, although my mother would go to early Sunday Mass and my father would go at 11 since he sang in the choir."

In 1978, Joe and Nancy were able to visit their second daughter and her family, then living in Heidelberg, Germany where their son-in-law was assigned for military service. As most visitors to Europe do, they also took the opportunity to visit some of the neighboring areas – see the picture on the right taken in Austria.

His final heart attack came on February 22, 1990 on a daily walk to the shopping center; he was taken by ambulance to the hospital where he later died. His daughter writes:

> *"I've always thought God was very kind to allow him to take his last ride in an ambulance since he loved them."*

Joe was buried at the Dulaney Valley Memorial Gardens in Timonium, just north of Baltimore.

Nancy passed away just over a decade later, on July 7th 2000, and was buried next to Joe.

Austria – 1978: Joe and Nancy

Headstones of Joseph and Catherine (Nancy) Oberle
Dulaney Valley Memorial Gardens, Timonium, MD Garden of the Last Supper-240A-1 and 240A-2

Katherine Gertrude Oberle (Miller)

The basis for this section about my Aunt "Sis" and Uncle "Bud" was provided by their daughter Mary Rita, although I have added some related document images and data, as well as reference numbers to my genealogy database. – F.O.

Katherine id200, the second child and only daughter of Joseph and Katie Oberle, was born on the 7th of August, 1915 in the family's home on 22nd Street in Baltimore.

Katherine, known from early childhood by her brothers (and eventually by her parents and extended family) as "Sis," had an uneventful childhood.

Like her brother Joe, she began attending grammar school at St. Ann's parish school in Baltimore, switching to Immaculate Conception School in Towson in September of 1926 after the family's move to their new home on Midhurst Road (see pg 107).

Other photographs of Katherine during her younger years can be seen in the earlier section titled "Joseph Oberle & Katherine Goldrick" beginning on page 98, as well as in her brother's wedding photo on page 126.

Katherine Oberle circa 1919

Katherine graduated from Towson Catholic High School and Strayer's Business College, after which she worked for the Maryland Casualty Company and, later, for Johns Hopkins Hospital doing medical transcription.

The occasion for the studio photograph on the left, believed to have been taken some time around 1934 when Katherine would have been nineteen years old, is unknown.

A friend, Shirley Jacobi id522, introduced her cousin Norbert Joseph Miller id199 to Katherine and, during World War II, the two corresponded while he was stationed at the Homestead Army Air Field in Florida. Katherine also wrote regularly to her brothers overseas (see the example below).

Katherine Oberle circa 1934

1944 – Letter from Katherine Oberle to her brother Cornelius

This letter of September 23, 1944 is somewhat unusual. Although "Sis" wrote regularly to her brothers overseas, most of her correspondence was in the form of V-Mails, where the content was put on standardized printed forms which were then microfilmed on the ships traveling overseas. The individual frames were subsequently printed in theater for delivery to the soldiers. Katherine was able to cram more information into a V-Mail than most, since she actually prepared some of them on a typewriter, but in this longer example, she probably just wished to escape the space and length constraints of the V-Mail format.

APPENDIX IX – FAMILY OF JOSEPH AND KATHERINE OBERLE

The Matchmaker Shirley Jacobi's Family and Margaret Mary Jacobi

The first of the Jacobis to arrive in the United States was Shirley's grandfather Jacob id618, who arrived in Baltimore on the S.S. Ohio on 4 March 1872, just a few months after his eighteenth birthday the previous September.

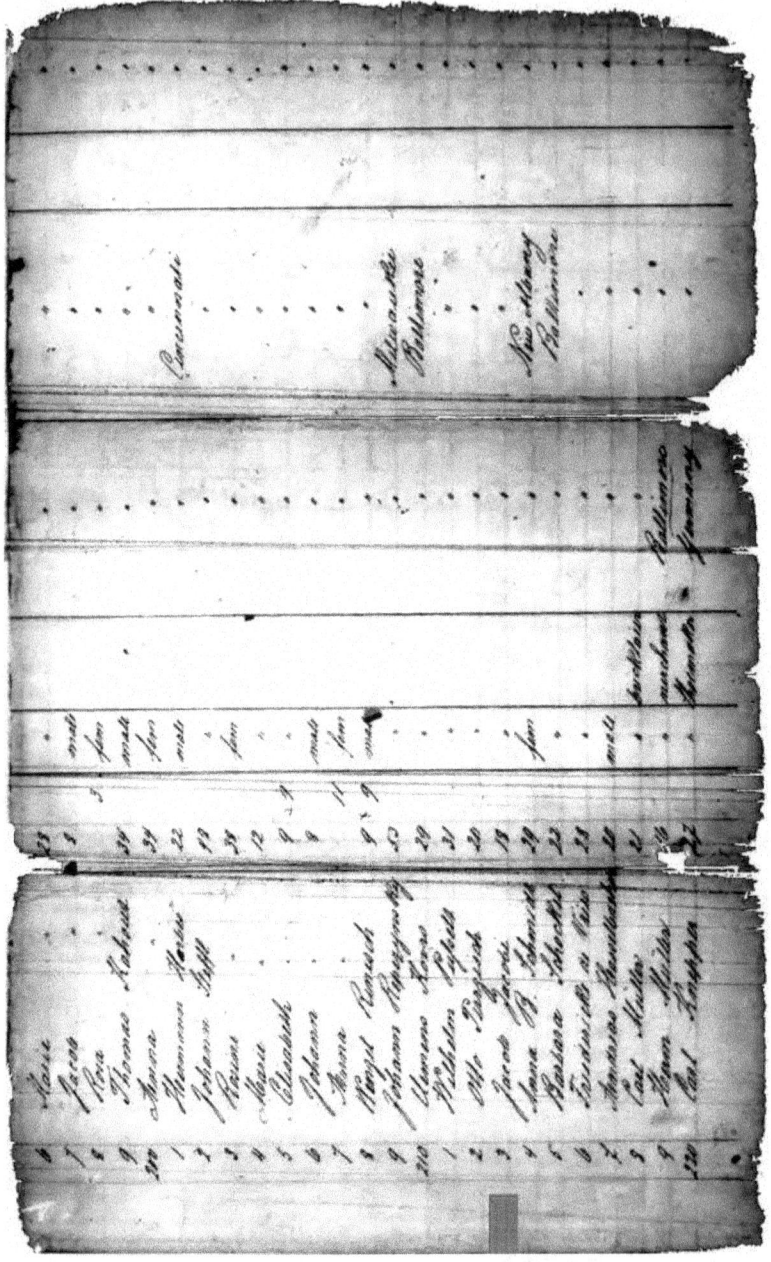

Baltimore – 1872 Passenger Manifest Page for the S.S. Ohio
Jacob Jacobi arrives in the United States on March 4th at age 18

Jacob was the son of Johann Jacobi of Hesse-Darmstadt in Germany. A sheet from the passenger manifest of the S.S. Ohio, shown on the previous page, indicates that he traveled alone to the United States in late 1871.

Within five years Jacob had met and married his wife Barbara id619, born on 24 December 1853 in Maryland to the German immigrants Michael and Margaret Kuemmert.

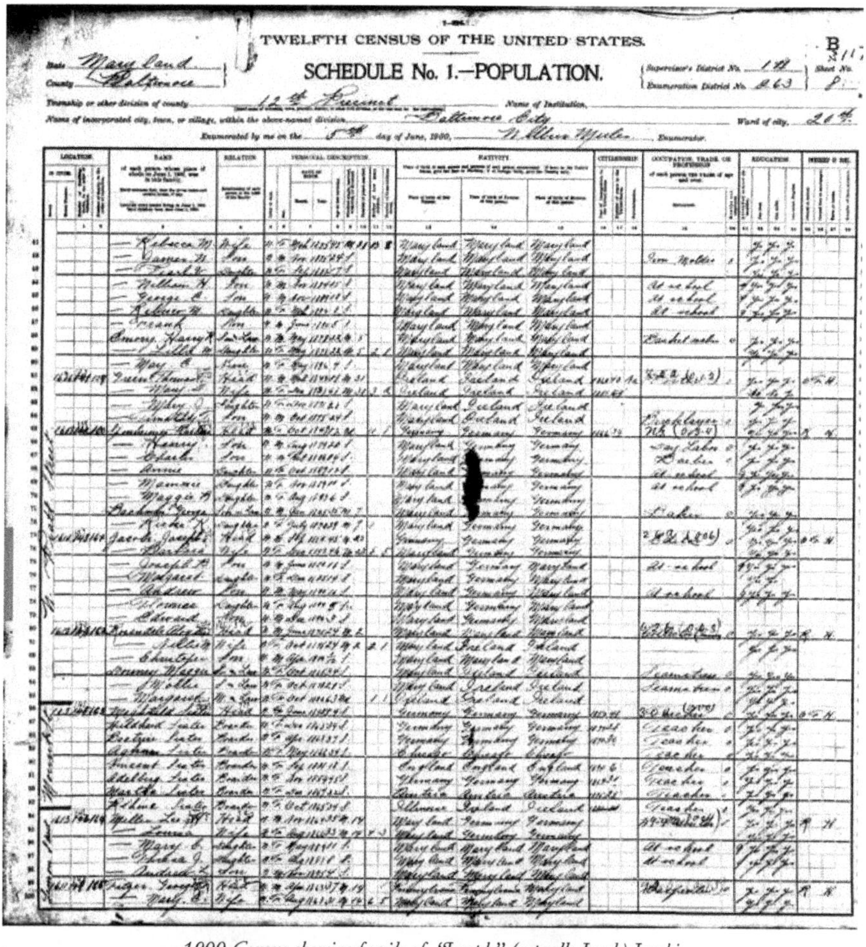
TWELFTH CENSUS OF THE UNITED STATES.

SCHEDULE No. 1.—POPULATION.

State: Maryland
County: Baltimore
Township or other division of county: 12th Precinct
Name of incorporated city, town, or village, within the above-named division: Baltimore City
Ward of city: 21st
Enumerated by me on the 5th day of June, 1900.

1900 Census showing family of "Joseph" (actually Jacob) Jacobi

NARC t623 Roll 617 Page 12

Family stories suggest that Jacob operated a deli or tavern on Pratt Street in Baltimore during his early years, but by the 1880 U.S. Census, Jacob and Barbara[172] were already established in Baltimore with a year old daughter Mary.

[172] Jacob appears in all six U.S. Censuses from 1880 through 1940 (the 1890 Census was lost in a fire), but in the 1880 Census transcriptions he is recorded as "James" and in the 1900 Census, shown above, his name is given as "Joseph." Whether Jacob, like many immigrants, was attempting to assimilate by altering what he perceived as a "foreign" name, or whether these were transcription errors isn't known, but it is quite clear that this is the same person recorded as "Jacob" in later censuses.

Jacob was then working as a printer. The 1900 Census shown above tells more about Jacob's family: Jacob was now the editor of what is believed to have been a local German language (and anti-Prussian) newspaper.

Barbara had by then given birth to eight children – three of whom, including Mary, didn't survive childhood – and reported having been married for twenty-three years. The family was living at 1610 North Pratt Street in Baltimore and Jacob now listed his profession as "Editor."

Children of Jacob and Barbara Jacobi

- Mary Jacobi id4824, born in about 1879. She was no longer listed in the 1900 census and, given her mother's statement then that only five of her eight children were living, must have died at some point in the interim.
- Joseph B. Jacobi id620, born in June 1880, who married Mae G. (surname unknown) was the father of Francis Arnold id2788 and Shirley Ann Jacobi id522, mentioned earlier as the friend of Katherine Oberle's who introduced her to her future husband Norbert.
- Margaret Mary Jacobi id521, born in December 1885. Margaret was Norbert Miller's mother, and is discussed below.
- Andrew A. Jacobi id2782, born in May 1890.
- Florence M. Jacobi id2783, born in August 1894, and married August H. ("Gus") id4831 Miller. Gus is believed to be Francis Joseph id520 Miller's second cousin, although his father's name and relationship is unknown.
- J. Edward Jacobi id2784, born in December 1896.
- Two other children, presumed to have died as infants, are unidentified.

After Barbara passed away on 24 December 1931, Jacob moved in with his daughter Florence and her husband August H. Miller, and was living with them at the time of the 1940 census. Jacob died between 1947 and 1949.

The Miller Family

Joseph A. Miller id615 was born in Germany in April 1864. In about 1884, he married Mary L. id616, with whom he had at least two sons:

According to his responses on the 1900 U.S. Census, Joseph, his wife, and their two sons came to the United States in 1890 and settled in Baltimore.

Children of Joseph A. and Mary L. Miller

- Francis Joseph Miller id520, known as Frank[173], was born about 1886.
- Joseph S. Miller id4825, was born about 1888.

---

[173] In the four censuses from 1900 to 1930, he was listed as "Frank J. Miller," but in the 1940 census was shown as "Francis Miller."

Francis Miller and Margaret Mary Jacobi

Frank married Margaret Mary Jacobi in Baltimore, and in 1910 the couple was living with Frank's parents Joseph and Mary. They had the first three of their five children in Baltimore and, after relocating to the Philadelphia area in about 1916 when their oldest son "Bud" was about six years old, their last two boys were born.

The Miller family can be seen in the 1940 Census below:

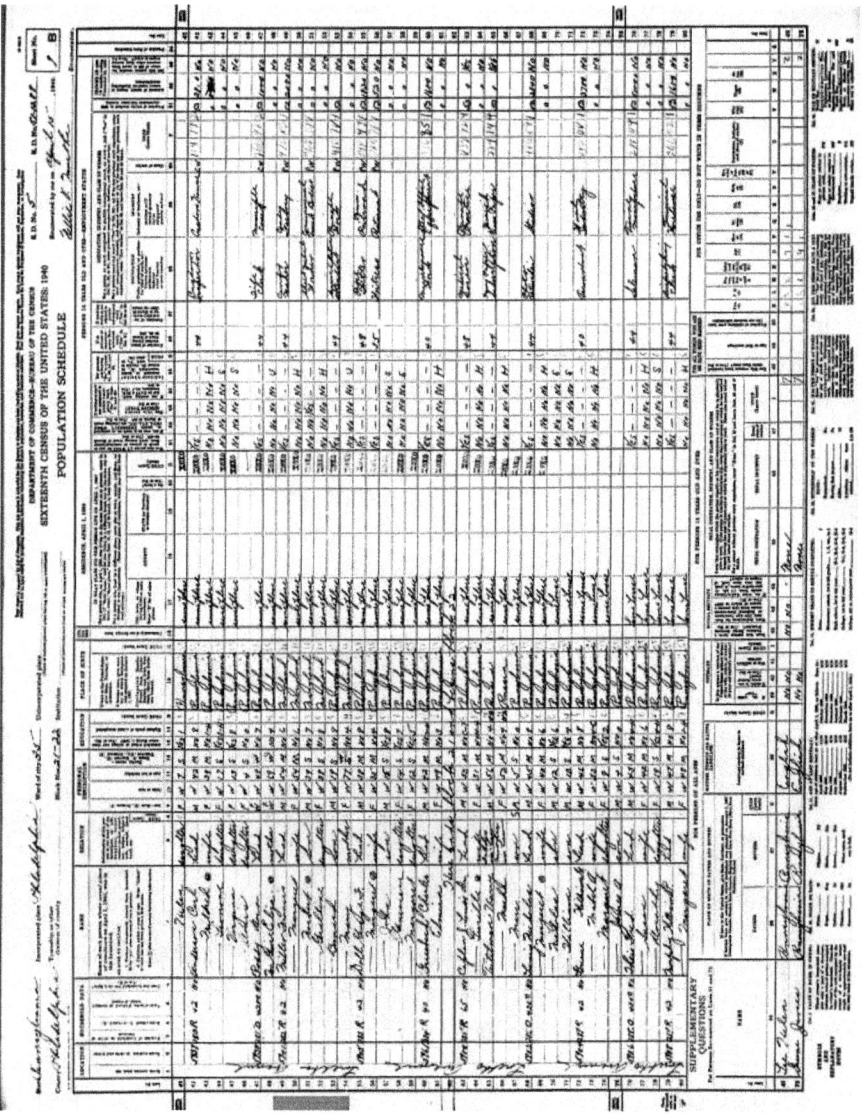

Philadelphia – 1940 U.S. Census showing family of Francis Joseph Miller

Appendix IX – Family of Joseph and Katherine Oberle

By this time, Norbert, then 29, was a sheet metal worker building commercial truck bodies, and his father Francis was a candy maker.

Children of Frank J. Miller and Margaret Mary Jacobi

- Nobert Joseph "Bud" Miller id199, born in Baltimore in 16 June 1910
- Geraldine Miller id4826, born in Baltimore in about 1913
- Cletus Miller id4827, born in Baltimore in about 1915, who eventually married Josephine C. Martino in 1935.
- Francis Miller id4828, born in Philadelphia in 1917, but died of polio in 1921.
- Bernard Miller id4829, born in Philadelphia in about 1921
- Wilfred Miller id4830, who lived for only six weeks. His year of birth is unknown, so the placement at the end of this list has no meaning.

Katherine Oberle and Norbert Miller

As discussed above, Norbert was born on June 10, 1910 to Margaret Mary id521 (nee Jacobi) and Francis Joseph id520 Miller. Although born in Baltimore, Norbert grew up in Philadelphia, Pennsylvania, so would likely not have met Katherine Oberle without his cousin Shirley's introduction. On 6 October 1942, Norbert enlisted in the Army Air Corps. He had already been introduced to Katherine, and they kept in touch throughout the war. When he returned, they continued to see each other.

By early in 1947, Katherine and Norbert had become engaged; among other relatives they visited for congratulatory dinners during their post-engagement "tour" was Katherine's younger brother Cornelius and his wife Rosalie, who had recently had their first child[174]. Because of this, Cornelius, like most photography buffs, had his camera always at the ready, so when his sister visited, he snapped several photographs of his big sister and her fiancee – including the one on the right – as they mugged for the camera while snuggling on the living room couch.[175]

"Bud" Miller and his fiancee Katherine Oberle Taken at Radnor Avenue on 27 February 1947

---

[174] This book's author.

[175] Another photograph from this visit is shown on page 144.

Norbert and Katherine after their Wedding

The new Mr. and Mrs. Miller were married on the 4th of October, 1947 at St. Pius X Catholic Church in Towson, MD. They honeymooned in Niagara Falls, New York.

The couple eventually purchased a new home in the Logan Village Community of Dundalk, Maryland and started a family which came to include one daughter and four sons.

Norbert made his living as a truck mechanic for the Lord Baltimore Laundry and later, following some health problems, managed retail stores.

Norbert also became a deacon in the Catholic Church, being ordained on September 17, 1983. He ministered to the congregation of Christ the King Catholic Church in Dundalk and also to patients at the Johns Hopkins Bayview Medical Center.

The photo on the right shows Katherine and Norbert at the confirmation for one of their grandchildren.

Katherine and Norbert

Bel Air: Katherine visits family

Norbert passed away suddenly on Father's Day, June 20, 1993, of an apparent heart attack. Katherine passed away on January 29, 1996, of complications of Non-Hodgkin's Lymphoma. The couple is buried in Sacred Heart of Jesus Cemetery, 7401 German Hill Rd. Dundalk, Maryland.

Francis Xavier Oberle

This section about my Uncle Francis and his wife was provided by their son Sean, although I have taken the liberty of adding some related document images and data, as well as reference numbers to my genealogical database. A few in-line references to my cousin's sources have also been changed to footnotes. – F.O.

Francis Xavier Oberle id127 was born on 20 February 1923, in Baltimore, Md. He was the youngest of the four children of Joseph F. Oberle and Katherine Goldrick. As recounted on page 107, he was premature and not given much chance to survive. As a boy, he had fascinations with trains, airplanes and astronomy that would last throughout his life.[176]

Baltimore – Francis Oberle circa 1940

However, his main love was music, especially opera and other classical genres, and he was an accomplished tenor and pianist. His childhood dream was to be an opera singer, and he was well known in his youth for his talents. Indeed, some friends signed his high school yearbook "To Orpheus" because of this reputation. Orpheus is a character in Greek mythology known for his ability to charm with his music, a skill he put to use in his famous journey to the underworld. Though Francis never made it to the professional stage, he was a soloist[177] in church choirs until his mid-40s but stopped when his voice began to fail him, likely due to a lifetime of smoking. He played piano his entire life, mostly just for his own pleasure, and he often would do so alone for hours the way others might read, watch TV, or surf the web.

Francis also possibly had a learning disability given his troubles in school – he was held back twice – and there were other hints later in life, including the fact that he had natural artistic talent (music) but poor academic skill (a trait sometimes common in those with such issues and thus the modern preference for "learning differences" as opposed to "learning disabilities"). However, diagnosis and help for such problems were

---

[176] In addition to the photo on this page, there are others in the earlier section titled "Joseph Oberle & Katherine Goldrick" beginning on page 95, as well as in his brother Cornelius' wedding photo on page 121. A photograph of Francis with his father Joseph is on page 286.

[177] FO's note: it was always my impression that musical skills such as my Uncle's – and which have also appeared in some later generations – were almost certainly inherited from our Goldrick or Boyle ancestors. Our grandmother Katie's obituaries allude to her skills in this area, and I recall my father (Cornelius) telling me that she often had solos in various church services.

not common in the 1920s and 1930s, so it is hard to say for sure. In any event, he certainly did not share the mathematics skills of his father and brothers, and he often said that he wished he'd used his GI Bill to get training as a piano tuner rather than in a failed attempt to become an accountant.

One favorite story he would tell of his boyhood involved being invited to play baseball with his older brothers and other neighborhood children. He would say something to the effect of "I somehow made it onto base and around to 3rd." Someone hit the ball and while he was daydreaming, Joe and Cornie began shouting at him, "Go home, Francis, go home," which he did, down the block to his mother, upset and not understanding why they were angry with him and not wanting him to play any longer.

World War II

Following his high school graduation from Towson Catholic on 6 June 1943, Francis was promptly drafted into the army with an enlistment date of 22 June 1943. After basic training at Fort Eustis in Newport News, Va., he shipped out to the European theater, where he served with the 377th AAA[178] Battalion, attached to the 4th Infantry Division.

During the buildup to D-Day in the first half of 1944, he was stationed near Childe Okeford, a tiny village in Dorset, England about 50 miles southwest of Salisbury.

The 377th was armed with 40mm artillery and bi- and quad-mounted .50 caliber machine guns. Francis' accounts of this time include firing at German aircraft and shooting the .50s, mounted on half-tracks, into hedges. Though he never discussed these details, the latter was a tactic used against difficult targets like snipers. The idea was to avoid risking troops by obliterating the enemies in their hiding places.

Normandy to St. Lo – Some Context

The initial objectives of the Allied forces upon landing at Normandy were capturing the port at Cherbourg and gaining control of the town of St. Lo, the junction of the major roads in the area. Both were prerequisites for continuing through France and into Germany. A unique feature of the landscape in Normandy was called *bocage* - the farmlands in the fifty mile stretch from there to St. Lo were divided into small individual pastures, each surrounded by high earthen berms on which were planted very thick hedges. Travel though these areas was by means of sunken lanes between the individual sections.

Due to the preparations taken since occupying the area in mid-1940, the Germans were very confident that the *bocage* would become a shooting gallery, with Allied tanks and infantry being "sitting ducks" while making their way to St. Lo. The large hedgerows would serve as excellent cover to hide them from advancing Allied ground forces. It apparently hadn't occurred to them (Panzer Lehr and elite Waffen SS Divisions) that the Allies were just as hidden from them by the hedgerows as they were from the Allies and, when the totally unexpected volume of Allied bombers began passing overhead, German morale was severely undermined. The German 88mm anti-tank weapons placed in the fields were outclassed by the "Kraut-Mowers" my Uncle Francis described (next page), since the volume of fire they produced didn't rely on the time-consuming need for precision aiming. :FO

---

[178] Anti-aircraft artillery; the acronym was usually pronounced "Triple A."

Four .50s together were quite good at this task, and there are tales of large trees, and whatever was in them, being quickly churned to mulch. This devastating power earned the guns the nickname, "Kraut-Mowers."

He remembered watching in awe as the thousands of Allied aircraft flew overhead during the massive bombing of St. Lo. [179]

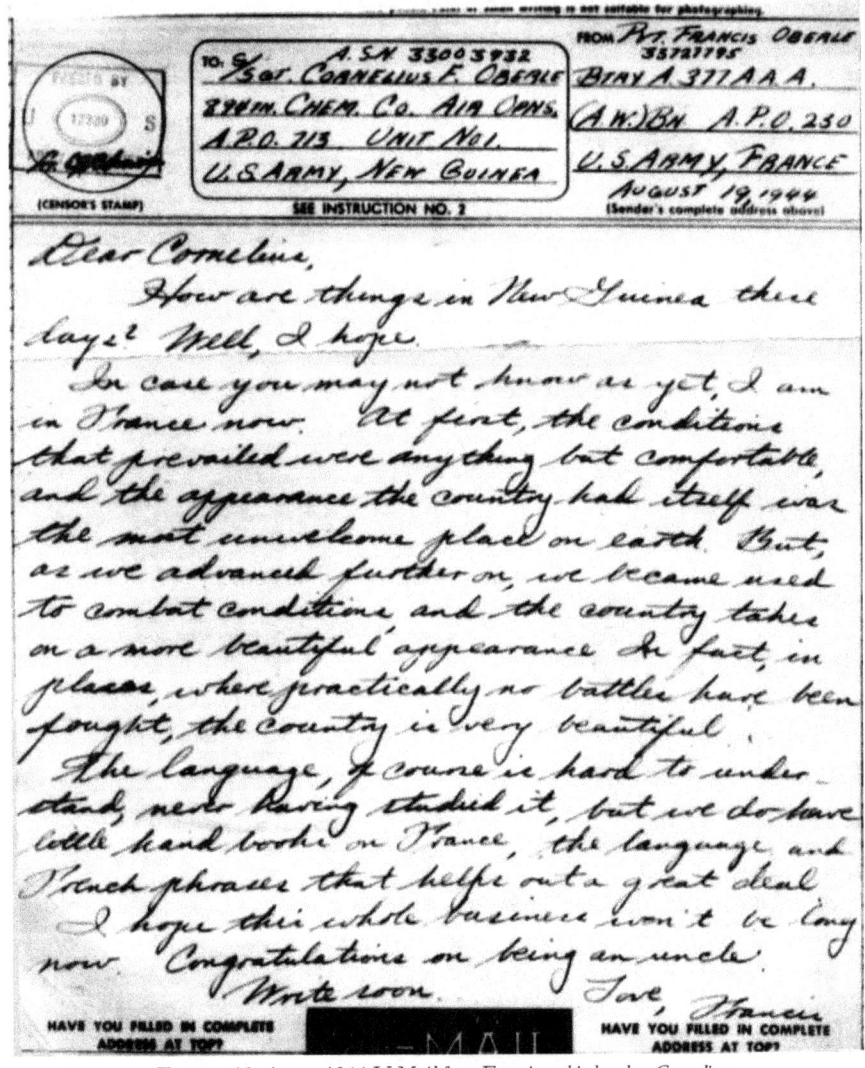

France – 19 August 1944 V-Mail from Francis to his brother Cornelius

Francis' funniest war story involved a cow. The 40mm guns needed to be dug into shallow trenches so they would stay stable when fired. One night, a loose

---

[179] FO's note: A great description and context for this bombing from a local French perspective can be found at http://mynormandy.com/regards-guerre.html.

cow fell into the trench of the gun Francis crewed, and the animal broke off one of the cranks trying to escape. The gun was out of commission for about a week, and the poor cow died. However, the cooks made good of the situation, and Francis and the other soldiers had their best meal of the invasion the following night.

He was present at the celebrations at the liberation of Paris, and he said he kissed French girls just like everyone else did.[180]

During the Battle of the Bulge, he said that the U.S. artillery barrages were so massive and so desperate that even anti-aircraft participated. They received orders to aim as low as possible and in the general direction of the Germans. He doubted that the 40mm shells did much damage compared to larger artillery. The Battle of the Bulge also was the source of his lifelong visceral hatred of being cold. The troops were famously ill-supplied for the unusually harsh winter, which he spent living in a tent.

During the Nazi retreat into Germany, his route took him through Alsace, and he remembered seeing the name Oberle on various shops[181]. He regretted not being able to stop, but the pursuit of the Germans was happening so fast during this time, that he spent most days on a speeding truck.

The Battle of the Bulge – A Respite

The hardships of our soldiers during the Battle of the Bulge, which took place between 16 December 1944 and 28 January 1945, are well documented. But while some Allied troops were completely surrounded by the Germans for the entire period, others on the fringes (like my Uncle Francis) were able to enjoy a short respite during the 1944 Christmas holidays. At that time Francis and his unit were bivouacked on the outskirts of Luxembourg – a scant 83 km (27.6 mi) from the center of the fiercest fighting in Bastogne.

In his mother's V-Mail to my father Cornelius dated 8 January 1945, she related having a letter from Francis (written the day after Christmas) who said that he was given Christmas dinner in a private home in Luxembourg, and was able to attend Mass on both Christmas Day and the prior Sunday.

Uncle Francis remained in the Luxembourg area for another few weeks and, as his mother relates in her 5 February V-Mail to my father, Francis wrote on 18 January that he had gotten a weekend furlough in Luxembourg, and despite "lots of snow," he "ate some ice cream – the first he has had since leaving the USA." :FO

He mentioned being briefly in Berlin following its fall. His discharge papers list the following for his battles and campaigns: "Normandy, Northern France, Ardennes, Rhineland, Central Europe."

In about March 1945 (nine months before discharge, according to his separation papers), because of his ability to use a typewriter and the dwindling need for anti-aircraft troops, Francis was reassigned to the headquarters of the 103rd AAA battery and given a promotion to corporal. He finished the war doing clerical work.

---

[180] FO's note: These celebrations took place mostly on 25 August 1944. In his V-Mail of 14 December 1944 to his brother (my father Cornelius) in the Pacific Theater, Francis wrote "The people there just treated us like kings to show their gratitude and appreciation for having been liberated." The Battle of the Bulge would begin two days after he sent this letter.

[181] FO's note: One of these could very well have been the Oberle Hotel and Restaurant in Kilstett, north of Strasbourg near the Rhine, since his unit passed that area. See page 162.

He arrived back in the United States on 30 November 1945. The next day was his father's birthday, and he was excited that he could find a payphone to give his father the present of knowing that one of his sons was home and safe. He received an honorable discharge on December 5 at Fort Meade, Md.

Post-War Years

Francis lived in his parents' home[182] in the late 1940s and 1950s. At some point, he secured a clerical job with Legg Mason at its main Baltimore building. He would hold this job until the early 1970s.

Stories about Francis during this time mostly come from his nieces and nephews who recalled him entertaining them with his piano playing at family gatherings or otherwise doing what uncles typically do such as taking them to special outings like Orioles games.[183]

It was during this time, despite his lifetime fascination with planes, that he would take his only flight – on a trip involving one of his other interests, astronomy. He flew to the Midwest (perhaps Minnesota) to witness a total eclipse of the sun.

In the late 1950s, he met his future wife Gladys.

The Maroney Family and Gladys "Bookie" Maroney

Gladys Helen (Bookie) Maroney was born on 26 November 1929, in Richmond, Va. She was the third of four children, but the eldest of two daughters. Bookie's father, James Edward (Jim) Maroney, was born in Colorado and was the son of Irish immigrants drawn to the Rockies by the gold mines there. They died when he was a boy, and he made his way east by way of Texas and Tennessee, eventually settling in Virginia. Bookie's mother, Ruth Alleene Perdue, went by her middle name, and she was of old Virginia lineage going back to the first half of the 1600s. Most of Alleene's ancestors likely were English and Scotch-Irish, given their surnames and the settlement-history of the region.

Bookie grew up Methodist but converted to Catholicism during college. She attended Westhampton College, which is the women's school for the University of Richmond, earning a B.S. in chemistry.

The page from the 1940 U.S. Census below shows the Maroney family, with the ten year old Bookie's Dad Jim working as a machinist.

---

[182] FO's note: A picture of this home on 213 Midhurst Road is shown on page 107.

[183] FO's note: The coolest baseball game I ever attended was when Uncle Francis took me to an Oriole's game at Memorial Stadium against the Yankees on 20 September 1958. The then thirty-six year old and supposedly washed-up knuckle-baller Hoyt Wilhelm pitched a no hitter against the team that had earlier traded him away.

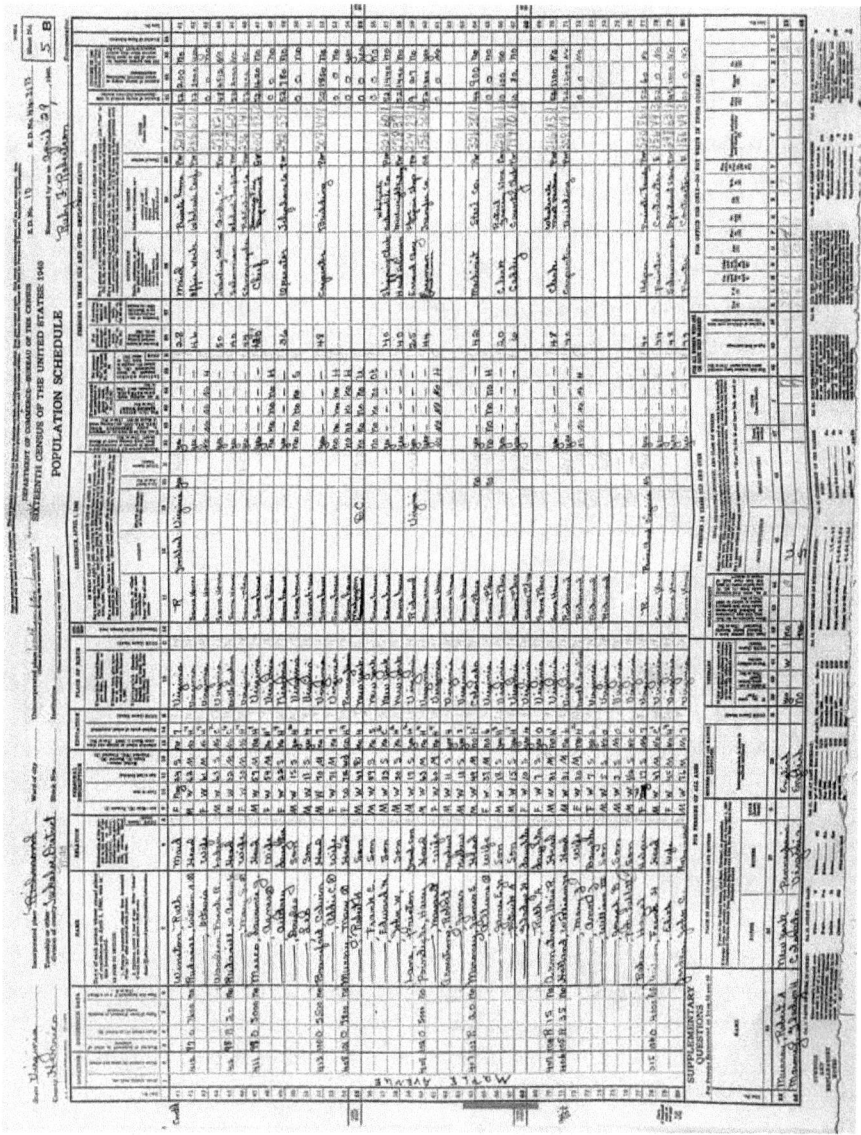

Virginia – 1940 Census showing family of James E. Maroney
National Archives Series t627 Roll 179 Page 90

APPENDIX IX – FAMILY OF JOSEPH AND KATHERINE OBERLE

Bookie received her nickname as a toddler when her grandfather, Spencer Perdue[184], would bounce her on his knee and say, "Bookitiy, bookitiy, bookitty, ride a horse." When she wanted a ride, she would pull on his pants leg and say "Bookie, Bookie," with the oo pronounced as in hoot. At some point in her life, the pronunciation changed to the oo in hook. It was thus possible to know when or where people met her by how they pronounced her nickname.

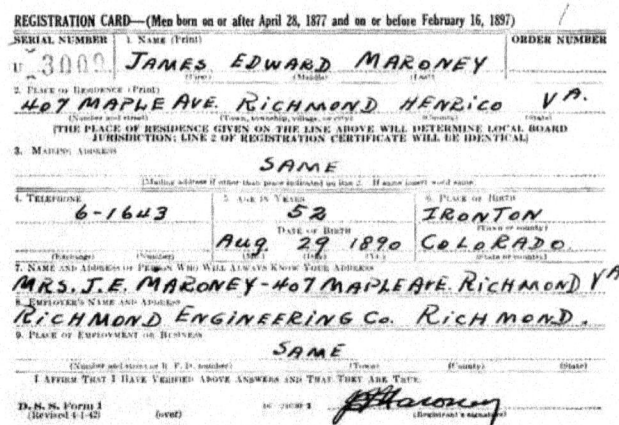

1942 – "Old Man's" Draft Card of James E. Maroney.

Like most men of his generation, Francis' future father-in-law was required to register for the draft even at his then age of 52 because of concerns over the progress of World War II. Like Francis' father Joseph, however, James was never conscripted.

Francis Oberle and Gladys Maroney

The hook pronunciation was in place by the late 1950s when Bookie was living and working in Maryland and met Francis at the home of mutual friends, Lou and Terry Shultz. She previously had moved to the state for a job at the National Institutes of Health in Bethesda as a cancer research chemist, which she held from 1955 to 1957.

Francis and Bookie were married at St. Bridget Catholic Church in the Westhampton area of Richmond on 30 April 1960. The priest was Rev. J. Francis Byrne. Bookie's sister Ruth and Francis' brother Cornelius were the maid of honor and best man. Her uncle Thomas Nuckols gave her away as her father had died in 1957. Their honeymoon was a camping trip in Virginia's Blue Ridge Mountains.

During the early years of marriage, they lived in Owings Mills, Md., with him still doing clerical work at Legg Mason and her employed as a licensed practical nurse at Rosewood Center, a state residential hospital for the severely

---

[184] FO's note: Aleene's parents were living with the Maroneys at the time, as can be seen in the 1930 U.S. Census. James, at age 34, had been a boarder in the Perdue household at the time of the 1920 census, taken in Richmond, where his then 16 year old future wife Aleene was living. Spencer, son of Samuel and Mary, had married Ruth Martin, daughter of John and Cornelia, on 18 April 1899. According to Francis and Bookie's son, Sean, the name Cornelia likely is a misreading of Ruth's stepmother's name, which was Lavinia. Ruth's biological mother (the census doesn't distinguish), Jennie, died in the 1880s.

mentally handicapped located in that community. They soon would move to Carroll County, about 40 miles northwest of Baltimore.

The Mayberry Years

In approximately 1962, Francis and Bookie purchased a four bedroom house in a small village in Carroll County, Md., called Mayberry. The community – between Westminster and Taneytown – had about 20 homes, a church and a small store, which would go out of business by the late 1960s. Historically, it once had a post office, a second store, and a one-room school, but all were closed and converted to homes by the 1960s. The houses lined a country lane called Mayberry Road, rising up a hill on the east side of Mayberry Creek, which was a favorite swimming and fishing place for neighborhood children.

Most of the homes had substantial acreage behind them either dedicated to farming or allowed to remain woodland. The Oberles' three acres thus were on the small side for the community. Nonetheless, beside the house, the lot had eight buildings: three small "barns" (more coops than barns), a corn crib, a tiny pump house for the spring that supplied the home's water, a large detached garage with a loft accessible by a trap door, and two larger buildings that once had been dedicated to the former owners' occupation as a regional canner. One, dubbed "the canning factory," was a large barn-like structure that still contained one long table (there probably were more historically) as well as a winch presumably for lifting heavy loads into trucks that had entered by a large, sliding door at one side. The other, called "the pavilion," was merely a raised wooden floor with a roof but no walls. Its purpose had been for drying vegetables. The property also had two small, unnamed streams that flowed through the village down to Mayberry Creek.

The many buildings and two streams made the property an ideal place for children to play. This likely was a consideration in Francis and Bookie's decision to take in foster girls for the Baltimore Catholic diocese of which Carroll County was a part. During the course of about 10 years, they raised at least six girls, who called them "Mom" and "Dad": Dolly, Terry, sisters June and Ann, Carol, and Jeannie. Jeannie's biological brother Frankie also briefly lived with them. Many of the girls stayed with them from their preteen years until after high school graduation. They even threw a wedding for Dolly, whom Fran-

Francis, Gladys, and their infant son Shown with several of their foster daughters

cis gave away. Unfortunately, Francis and Gladys had lost contact with all of them by the late 1970s.

Being rather rural, Mayberry also had very little light pollution, which made Francis very happy. True to his fascination with astronomy, he owned a small telescope on a tripod, and in the late 1960s and early 1970s, would set it up in the backyard. For some unknown reason, the habit among the children in the neighborhood was to use the archaic Southern convention of calling adults by Mr. or Miss plus first names. Thus, "Mr. Francis" and his telescope became a popular summer night attraction, and dozens of children got their first magnified glimpses of moon craters. Of course, this being the time of the moon landings, jokes about looking for astronauts were common.

The late 1960s and early 1970s also was when the family made several long road trips to the Midwest and into Canada. Francis, Bookie and numerous children would load into the family's VW bus and tow a pop-up camper. They would be gone for weeks, driving from campground to campground, with sleeping space split between the camper and the van and meals cooked at a camp fire. The couple thought these journeys might be the only chances for some of the foster girls to do any traveling in their lives so were eager to take them. Some memorable trips included Chicago, Niagara Falls, and St. John's Canada. Prior to this, Francis and Bookie also took many of the girls to the 1964 New York Worlds Fair, and Bookie sewed everyone shirts made out of the same flowered pattern to help keep track of everyone in the crowds.

The Mayberry property also was perfect for animals. Bookie was a lifelong animal lover, and Francis was (mostly) happily cooperative in her desire to have many. Over their roughly 16 years in Mayberry, they owned one pig, two steer, an old swayback horse (bought as present for Jeannie), about a dozen goats, at least nine dogs, and scores of cats. The last were divided into the few house cats and the many outside, semi-wild cats that Bookie allowed to be on the property and would feed. There were suspicions of people dropping off unwanted cats at night because previously unknown adults would occasionally appear, but in any event, Bookie gladly accepted people's strays as there was plenty of room in the many buildings.

One Easter – probably in about 1967 or 1968 – the family came home from Easter mass and Francis went out to the barns to feed the animals. The pig – named Piggly-Wiggly by the girls – somehow had pushed open the door of his building. Francis came back into the house and joked about the Easter pig's empty tomb. The family went in search of the pig, trudging for hours in the fields, woods and brambles around Mayberry. By Bookie's account, they were joined by 20 to 30 neighbors, adults and children, and sightings of Piggly-Wiggly were frequent with excited shouts as the half-grown animal invariably slipped out of the grasp or between the legs of one person or the other. Eventually, the large group surrounded him and slowly made the circle smaller and smaller. He made a dash for it, but a neighbor was able to tackle him and hold on, accompanied by the the shouts and laughter of everyone.

Francis and Bookie attended two Catholic churches during this time: first St. Joseph's in Taneytown and later St. John's in Westminster. Their only son, Sean, was born in 1965.

In 1967, Bookie began working as a home and hospital tutor for the Carroll County school system. In 1973, she took a position as a teacher at the adolescent section of Springfield State Hospital, a residential facility in Sykesville, Md. for people with mild emotional problems.

Meanwhile, in the early 1970s, Legg Mason went through some corporate restructuring that led to the layoff of many workers, including Francis. He had a difficult time getting work for about a year. To supplement his income, he worked various odd jobs, including briefly as a laborer on an egg farm where he collected and sorted eggs for later distribution to stores.

After about a year, because of his military experience, he secured permanent work with the Bay State Security Agency as a guard. His duty mostly was at the Random House book distribution facility in Westminster although he occasionally took extra, overnight work as a night watchman at other sites.

In 1976, Bookie received an MS in special education from Coppins State College in Baltimore. She had attended night classes during the few years before this.

In 1977, she had an opportunity to teach at an Alexandria, Va. school for emotionally disturbed teens, The Leary School. This job change led to the family's move to Virginia.

The Stafford Years

Stafford County, Va., is about 40 miles south of Washington, D.C., near the small city of Fredericksburg. The Stafford property was smaller than the Mayberry site – just an acre with only a three-bedroom house and a small barn. This led to a downsizing of the animals. Only four dogs, numerous cats, and a few goats made the move. Stafford was about 30 miles from the Leary School, meaning Bookie had to commute daily through heavy Northern Virginia traffic. In 1979, she took a position as the director of a group home for teenage girls in Fairfax, Va. It was named Oakton Arbor. The job still required a hard commute.

Following the move, Francis got a job with Pinkerton Security and worked for many years at the regional hospital, Mary Washington, in Fredericksburg. In the early 1980s, he had an opportunity to join the "Department of Defense" which, in this case, was a euphemism for the CIA. He worked at the agency's small facility at Fort Belvoir in Alexandria, where much of its analysis of satellite photography occurred. He found it quite humorous that he had to wear a sidearm and that he and a few other men his age – in their 60s – were the only protection for a building where important national security work occurred.

Bookie – who by then had begun going by her given name, Gladys – tired of the grind of the commute to Northern Virginia. Thus she quickly jumped on the 1983 chance to manage the opening of a coed group home for the Fredericksburg region named Rainbows Beginning. She led it until 1986 but lost the job when it was discovered that one of the overnight counselors let the boyfriend of one of the teenage residents spend the night. Although Gladys was unaware of this, she was the person in charge of the facility, and the board felt the need to fire someone higher up than the guilty counselor.

This led to her brief stint running the local SPCA, but she eventually started a business with a colleague, Joan. Their company, Employment Resources, offered job counseling and training to at-risk youth. They also started a small private school that they named The Star Center. It contracted with local school systems to serve middle and high school students who needed remedial or other special attention.

In 1992, Francis and Gladys' house was destroyed by a fire that likely started due to an old, worn wire leading to the back porch light. Fortunately, they had good insurance and were able to build a new house on the foundation of the old one. Unfortunately, they lost many heirlooms, including most of their photos. They rented a Fredericksburg apartment for about a year during the rebuild.

Francis retired in about 1994. This period saw the couple's best financial situation as Gladys' business was doing well, and they were able to erase debts including those related to their son's college education.

Deaths and After

In the summer of 1996, Gladys received a late diagnosis of breast cancer. It soon became clear that it had metastasized, and she succumbed to the disease within two months on 7 August 1996 at Potomac Hospital in Woodbridge, Va. She was 66. Francis lived in their home for another 15 months but suffered an unwitnessed heart attack and died there on 26 November 1997. He was 74. His death occurred on what would have been Gladys' 68th birthday, but that was a coincidence as far as is known.

Francis and Bookie's funerals were both held at St. William of York Roman Catholic Church in Stafford County, Va., and Rev. Gerald Weymes officiated both times.

They are buried together near Stafford at Quantico National Cemetery in Prince William County, Va. The single military-style stone bears his name and dates on the front and hers on the back.

Two-sided headstone of Francis and Gladys Oberle
Quantico National Veterans Cemetery, Section 12, Site 1487;
Triangle, Prince William County, Virginia

The Oberle School – Gladys is Remembered

In 2005, Gladys' business partner, Joan, lobbied the school's board of directors to rename it in Gladys' honor.

The Gladys H. Oberle School

The Gladys H. Oberle School – or simply The Oberle School as it is commonly known – is in Fredericksburg. It saw good growth, and in 2010 bought and moved into a larger building. It was still running very successfully as of this December 2013 writing, and the board was considering the purchase of adjacent land and another building to facilitate expansion.

Appendix IX – Family of Joseph and Katherine Oberle

Baltimore – Joseph Oberle, Sr. and his youngest son, Francis at Midhurst Road

Appendix X :: Suggestions for Further Research

Suggestions for Further Research

The following information is provided to assist anyone who wishes to do further research on elements of the family.

Oberle Research

Locating a birth record for my 3rd great grandfather François Joseph Oberlé id1154 would confirm that Balthassar (II) Oberlé id1675 is indeed his father, as I strongly suspect. See the appendix beginning on page 165 for details.

The idea that Seraphin (II) was sent to the Emden area (where he met his future wife Sarah) as part of his military service is based only on family stories. Locating Prussian military records or draft/recruiting records for the post-occupation (1871-1880) period in the Bas-Rhin area of Alsace could prove quite useful in filling in details of my great-grandfather Seraphin (II) id25 Oberle's life, particularly in clarifying how and exactly when he ended up in Emden. To date, however, I have been unable to locate any relevant records.

These same records might provide more information on Seraphin's brother Armand id1151 (15 May 1859-17 Jan 1943) and half-brother Augustin id2259 (1848-??). I have been unable to locate any information about Augustin after his birth.

Schreiber Research

My 3rd great grandmother Marie Anne Schreiber's death record, shown on page 34, says that she came from a town (or area) that looks to be "Bürckengal." The actual text is shown enlarged on page 25. So far, I have been unable to locate any town or area matching this, indicating that a) I am interpreting the text incorrectly or b) that it no longer exists. Resolving this might permit further research on her ancestry.

Kiwiet Research

What was the Kiwiets' connection to a shipping line? Was there a shipping line called "Kiwi"[185] or something similar operating out of Emden in the 1875-1885 time frame?

Although most records from Emden during the period when our Kiwiet ancestors lived there were apparently destroyed during World War II bombing raids, there might still be information about the family available from business records in Baltimore if the name and ownership of the company they owned (or were connected to) can be established, or if the name of the vessel could be determined.

Tom Jelks said that he recalls the Kiwiet Steamship Line (whatever its actual name was) had an office on the east side of Light Street in Baltimore, across

---

[185] The actual "Kiwi Line" today is, as might be expected, and Australian shipping company.

from the original First National Bank of Baltimore, and their ships docked at Fell's Point. According to Tom, there were three shipping companies side-by-side on Light Street at the time: The Bremen Steamship Line, whatever the Kiwiet Line was called, and a third company with a "Star" in its name (e.g. White Star, Blue Star, North Star, or similar). So far as I have been able to determine, Baltimore City Directories are not available through any of the on-line services, but can be viewed on microfilm at the Enoch Pratt Free Library in Baltimore. Unfortunately, I have not yet had the opportunity to do that.

I have so far been unable to locate the original birth record for Seraphin and Sarah's son Seraphin (III) in Emden, even though I have a citation[186] for it. The fact that a specific citation exists suggests that the records of St. Michael's Church in Emden may not have been destroyed during World War II, and locating the original, or at least a more comprehensive listing of transcriptions would likely provide more information on our Kiwiet ancestors. See page 60.

Other questions to consider, but which will likely remain unanswered, include:

Were the Kiwiets initially aware of Seraphin and Sarah's real relationship?

What was the reaction of the Kiwiets to Sarah becoming pregnant?

What, if any, impacts were there because of their differing religions? The Kiwiets were reformed Lutherans and Seraphin was a Roman Catholic.

Was there a specific motivation for Seraphin and Sarah to leave Europe and, if so, what was it?

Did they choose the United States and more particularly Baltimore as their destination specifically and, if so, why? The likely answer, of course, is that the family shipping line traveled back and forth to Baltimore, but this is speculation.

Boyle Research

My great-grandmother Catherine Boyle states that she was born in Ireland in January of 1848, and that she came to the United States in 1852.[187] To date I have uncovered no record of her arrival in this country. Since she would have been about four years old at that time, I also searched for her parents Edward Boyle and Margaret Kelly, with a similar lack of success.

It is possible, of course, that she was born in Ireland, emigrated to another country, and then proceeded to the United States, in which case she may have left Ireland at any time between January 1848 and 1852.

---

[186] Note that the citation refers to "Seraphin Kiwiet," not "Seraphin Oberle." See footnote 66 on page 62.
[187] See the discussion of her family beginning on page 89.

In County Donegal, only ten of the forty civil parishes were recording births, suggesting that locating civil birth records for her might present a problem. In the parishes of Conwal and Glenswilly (covering Letterkenny, Gartan, and Churchill, the areas where we believe she was born), birth records weren't kept until 1874, marriages records until 1877, and there are no death records extant.

As for Catholic Church records (since she was a practicing Catholic in the United States, and came from Ireland, it seems safe to assume that her family was Catholic), the parish church of Conwal and Leck in the diocese of Raphoe (which would have served Letterkenny and the surrounding areas) didn't begin recording baptisms until 1853, and marriages until 1857.

State registration of births, marriages and deaths didn't begin until 1864.

There is therefore, not surprisingly, no record of birth for a Catherine Boyle in any extant civil or church records of County Donegal.

I have confirmed the lack of any reference to Catherine or her parents with the following entity, considered to be the best source for genealogical research in County Donegal:

> Donegal Genealogical Committee
> Letterkenny
> County Donegal IRELAND

I was informed that the process of record discovery and transcription is ongoing, however, but that pursuing Catherine Boyle's birth would likely not be productive at this time.

In 1847, an Edward and Margaret Boyle of Glenswilly left Derry (Londonderry) with their son, age 13, on the ship Superior (of the J&J Cooke line) for Quebec, but there is no mention of a daughter Catherine. If this is indeed Edward Boyle and Margaret Kelly, then Catherine may not actually have been born in Ireland, although her tombstone indicates that she certainly believed she was.

There was an Edward Boyle who died at age 76 in Letterkenny during the period July-September 1899[188]. This would imply that he was born in 1823, which is in the range we would expect for Catherine's father. It is difficult to accept that his daughter Catherine came with someone else to the U.S. at the age of four without some other evidence, however.

There are a few couples named Edward and Margaret Boyle in the 1860 and 1870 U.S. Censuses, but none in the areas where we would expect to find our Boyle ancestors, and there is no child named Catherine with any of them in 1860.[189]

---

[188] Ireland, Civil Registration Indexes, 1845-1958: Film Number: 101600; Volume Number: 2; Page Number: 96; Digital Folder Number: 4201704; Image Number: 00389

[189] Recall that Catherine was working as a Nanny in Baltimore in 1870.

There is also a thirty-year-old Irish-born Edward Boyle listed in the indexes for Boston's Ward 9 in the 1855 Massachusetts State Census who was therefore born in about 1825. Because there are indications that someone in our Boyle or Goldrick ancestry spent some time in Boston, this Edward is certainly of the right age to possibly be Catherine Boyle's father. To date, however, I have been unable to locate a copy of the census to determine if this Edward had a wife named Margaret and a daughter named Catherine of the appropriate age (about six).

Goldrick Research

Martin Goldrick's tombstone clearly states that he was from County Sligo in Ireland, but I have been unable to locate any records to suggest when or where he arrived in this country.

Being able to determine his age might indicate whether he came as a child with his parents or as an adolescent or young adult. Based on the estimated date of his marriage to Catherine Boyle (about 1872), he would have to have arrived between his birth and that date. It seems likely therefore that Martin was in this country at the time of the 1870 census, but I have been unable to locate him.

A family of Goldricks was living in the Lauraville area of Baltimore in 1860, with a Martin Goldrick, aged 26. Based on the age on his tombstone, however, our Martin would have only been 16 years old in 1860, so this doesn't seem to be him. Given the unusual name, however, this bears remembering.

Martin's father, whose name my grandmother believed to be James, was likely born around 1822-1826, and only eight of the twenty-seven parishes in County Sligo had begun recording vital records by then. This suggests that Sligo research might not be very productive at all unless and until further information can be located about Martin in the United States.

The one exception to this might be the 1867[190] death record in Sligo of a James M. Goldrick, estimated to have been born in 1815. This would have meant that he was almost thirty years old at the time Martin was born, but certainly within a reasonable range.

Some Irish sources that might be useful include:

Sligo Heritage & Cultural Centre[191]
Stephen's St.
Sligo, County Sligo, Ireland

County Sligo Heritage Genealogy Centre
Aras Redden, Temple St.
Sligo, County Sligo, Ireland
Phone (071) 43728
e-mail heritagesligo@tinet.ie.

---

[190] Ireland, Civil Registration Indexes, 1845-1958: Film Number: 101583; Volume Number: 12; Page Number: 174; Digital Folder Number: 4200215; Image Number: 00452

[191] This organization is in the process of collecting and transcribing Church Records and Gravestone Inscriptions from the County Sligo area, and might be useful to check in the future.

Goldrick-Boyle Research

Martin Goldrick [id179] and Catherine Boyle [id171] were married with at least four children by the time of the 1880 census, but I have been unable to locate any record of the family in that census. Given the paucity of information on our Goldrick and Boyle ancestors, locating this could be quite useful.

APPENDIX XI :: INDEX OF SURNAMES

This is an index of surnames *other than Oberle* referenced in this book. If a particular surname appears more than once on a single page, however, it will only appear once in the index.

This index does not include names of those appearing as witnesses on historic documents (e.g. birth, marriage, and death reports) unless they are known to be related to our family.

Surname Index

A

Anstett...................i, v, 6, 7, 8, 12, 17, 51
Auer........................22

B

Bahr........................36
Bentz......................22
Berlier....................37
Borig......................xii, 119, 144, 260, 261, 262, 263, 264
Boyle......................i, viii, x, xi, xiii, 84, 85, 87, 89, 90, 91, 92, 93, 94, 95, 144, 173, 174, 175, 176, 178, 179, 181, 182, 183, 184, 190, 191, 196, 274, 290, 291, 292, 293
Brodnig..................8
Burger....................19, 45
Burke......................80

C

Christoph...............13, 49
Clodong..................37

D

Dachraus................36
Deumant................i, vi, 37, 39, 40, 41, 42, 167
Dieda......................x, 22, 41, 165, 167, 170, 171
Dillenschneider.....i, 13, 16
Dirkson..................i, vii, 60, 144
Dowd......................xi, 178, 179, 189
Drixel......................i, vi, 12, 38, 39, 40, 44, 45
Dunn......................viii, 94, 97, 196

F

Ford........................61, 63, 70, 77, 78, 80, 82

G

Gemmerle..............12
Gersinger...............22
Goldrick................i, iv, v, viii, ix, x, xi, xii, xiii, 77, 84, 85, 87, 88, 89, 90, 91, 92, 93, 94, 95, 96, 97, 98, 115, 116, 119, 120, 144, 174, 175, 176, 179, 194, 196, 219, 220, 230, 231, 232, 233, 234, 235, 236, 237, 238, 239, 256, 274, 292, 293
Gonce....................iii, ix, x, 115, 119, 120, 143, 144
Grandy..................70, 81
Greeley..................xii, 260, 261, 262, 263

H

Hartnett.................79, 80
Holland..................viii, xi, 60, 90, 178, 179, 181, 190
Hulshoff................iii, 120, 138

I

Iglehart...................209

J

Jacobi.....................xiii, 266, 268, 269, 270, 271, 272
Jelks......................vii, viii, 47, 58, 60, 61, 62, 65, 66, 70, 76, 77, 78, 81, 84, 98, 111, 289
Johnson..................82, 190

K

Kelly......................i, x, 89, 174, 178, 179, 183, 184, 185, 191, 290, 291
Kerber....................i
Kilhofer.................19
Kiwiet....................i, vii, xiii, 60, 61, 62, 63, 64, 80, 144, 150, 255, 289, 290
Kuemmert..............269

L

Langbour...............8
Laurent..................12, 34, 49, 52
Linkenheld.............11, 28, 37

M

Maroney..............xiii, 120, 144, 278, 279, 280
Mertz..................i, v, 9, 10, 11, 15, 17, 18, 22, 51, 245
Mettling..............37, 45
Miller..................xiii, 100, 119, 144, 220, 266, 270, 271, 272, 273
Müller.................i, iv, v, vi, 19, 21, 22, 24, 36, 39, 40, 41, 42, 43, 44, 45, 47, 49, 51, 53, 63, 165, 167, 171

N

Nickol.................70, 80

O

O'Connell............94

P

Perdue.................278, 280

R

Ramm.................8, 13, 15
Rinn....................91, 94, 97, 100, 175, 178, 179, 183
Rollin..................8
Rolling................36, 52, 167
Rubine................47
Ruffenach............i, iv, v, vi, vii, 12, 18, 36, 38, 39, 40, 43, 44, 45, 46, 47, 48, 49, 51, 52, 53, 58, 63, 167
Ruschmeyer.........36

S

Sali.....................11, 22, 171
Sands..................xi, 175, 176, 177, 179, 183, 185
Schaeffer.............47, 61
Schmidt...............11, 16
Schneider............36
Schott..................i, v, 6, 12, 13, 15, 16, 17, 18, 19, 20, 21, 22, 23, 24, 25, 51, 165, 166
Schreiber.............i, iv, vi, 13, 25, 27, 31, 32, 34, 35, 36, 46, 49, 50, 51, 165, 289

APPENDIX X – NON-OBERLE SURNAME INDEX

Schwaller..............23
Schwoerer.............8
Sennewick.............i, v, 12, 15, 16, 51
Smith.....................178, 179, 181, 185, 186
Spengler................11, 37
Stiltz.......................vi, 38, 44, 46, 49, 51, 58
Strasinger..............82

T
Trabert..................80

V
Vierling.................12

W
Weinmann............11

Z
Zabienski..............94

Appendix XII :: Family Group Sheets

Extending the Line…

As explained elsewhere, privacy considerations have dictated that, with few exceptions, names and personal information for the descendants of my parents' generation (listed in Appendix VII as generation 7 based on their removal from Balthasar Oberlé) are not included in this book.

For those who wish to add descendant names for use within their immediate family, the following pages provide a number of what are known in genealogical circles as Family Group Sheets, although I have modified them slightly to permit referencing back to one of the ancestors who is described in this book. Since the tradition of family bibles as family history archives has faded away, recording information on these may help future descendants to more easily connect the relatives they know to those discussed in this history.

Obviously, even for the 8th, 9th and 10th generations alone, many more sheets would be required but, since this is impractical, these sheets should be useful as examples, and many more examples can easily be located on the internet if desired.

Family Group Sheets: Generations ___ & ___   A

for _____ (from page ___)

Spouse's Name			
Spouse Born	Date	Place	
Spouse Baptized	Date	Place	
Married	Date	Place	
Spouse Died	Date	Place	
Spouse Buried	Date	Place	
Spouse's father's name			
Spouse's mother's name			

Child #: 1			Name	M or F
Born	Date	Place		
Baptized	Date	Place		
Died	Date	Place		
Buried	Date	Place		
Continued on page		(continuation sheet if this child has its own family)		

Child #: 2			Name	M or F
Born	Date	Place		
Baptized	Date	Place		
Died	Date	Place		
Buried	Date	Place		
Continued on page		(continuation sheet if this child has its own family)		

Child #: 3			Name	M or F
Born	Date	Place		
Baptized	Date	Place		
Died	Date	Place		
Buried	Date	Place		
Continued on page		(continuation sheet if this child has its own family)		

Family Group Sheets: Generations ___ & ___ (continued)

Child #:	4			Name	M or F
	Born	Date	Place		
	Baptized	Date	Place		
	Died	Date	Place		
	Buried	Date	Place		
		Continued on page		(continuation sheet if this child has its own family)	

Child #:	5			Name	M or F
	Born	Date	Place		
	Baptized	Date	Place		
	Died	Date	Place		
	Buried	Date	Place		
		Continued on page		(continuation sheet if this child has its own family)	

Child #:	6			Name	M or F
	Born	Date	Place		
	Baptized	Date	Place		
	Died	Date	Place		
	Buried	Date	Place		
		Continued on page		(continuation sheet if this child has its own family)	

Child #:	7			Name	M or F
	Born	Date	Place		
	Baptized	Date	Place		
	Died	Date	Place		
	Buried	Date	Place		
		Continued on page		(continuation sheet if this child has its own family)	

Family Group Sheets: Generations ___ & ___   B

for _____ (from page ___)

Spouse's Name		
Spouse Born	Date	Place
Spouse Baptized	Date	Place
Married	Date	Place
Spouse Died	Date	Place
Spouse Buried	Date	Place
Spouse's father's name		
Spouse's mother's name		

Child #:	1			Name	M or F
	Born	Date	Place		
	Baptized	Date	Place		
	Died	Date	Place		
	Buried	Date	Place		
		Continued on page	(continuation sheet if this child has its own family)		

Child #:	2			Name	M or F
	Born	Date	Place		
	Baptized	Date	Place		
	Died	Date	Place		
	Buried	Date	Place		
		Continued on page	(continuation sheet if this child has its own family)		

Child #:	3			Name	M or F
	Born	Date	Place		
	Baptized	Date	Place		
	Died	Date	Place		
	Buried	Date	Place		
		Continued on page	(continuation sheet if this child has its own family)		

Family Group Sheets: Generations ___ & ___ (continued)

Child #:	4			Name	M or F
	Born	Date	Place		
	Baptized	Date	Place		
	Died	Date	Place		
	Buried	Date	Place		
		Continued on page	(continuation sheet if this child has its own family)		

Child #:	5			Name	M or F
	Born	Date	Place		
	Baptized	Date	Place		
	Died	Date	Place		
	Buried	Date	Place		
		Continued on page	(continuation sheet if this child has its own family)		

Child #:	6			Name	M or F
	Born	Date	Place		
	Baptized	Date	Place		
	Died	Date	Place		
	Buried	Date	Place		
		Continued on page	(continuation sheet if this child has its own family)		

Child #:	7			Name	M or F
	Born	Date	Place		
	Baptized	Date	Place		
	Died	Date	Place		
	Buried	Date	Place		
		Continued on page	(continuation sheet if this child has its own family)		

Family Group Sheets: Generations ___ & ___   C

for _____ (from page ___)

	Spouse's Name		
	Spouse Born	Date	Place
	Spouse Baptized	Date	Place
	Married	Date	Place
	Spouse Died	Date	Place
	Spouse Buried	Date	Place
	Spouse's father's name		
	Spouse's mother's name		

Child #:	1			Name	M or F
	Born	Date	Place		
	Baptized	Date	Place		
	Died	Date	Place		
	Buried	Date	Place		
	Continued on page	(continuation sheet if this child has its own family)			

Child #:	2			Name	M or F
	Born	Date	Place		
	Baptized	Date	Place		
	Died	Date	Place		
	Buried	Date	Place		
	Continued on page	(continuation sheet if this child has its own family)			

Child #:	3			Name	M or F
	Born	Date	Place		
	Baptized	Date	Place		
	Died	Date	Place		
	Buried	Date	Place		
	Continued on page	(continuation sheet if this child has its own family)			

Family Group Sheets: Generations ___ & ___ (continued)

Child #:	4			Name	M or F
	Born	Date	Place		
	Baptized	Date	Place		
	Died	Date	Place		
	Buried	Date	Place		
		Continued on page	(continuation sheet if this child has its own family)		

Child #:	5			Name	M or F
	Born	Date	Place		
	Baptized	Date	Place		
	Died	Date	Place		
	Buried	Date	Place		
		Continued on page	(continuation sheet if this child has its own family)		

Child #:	6			Name	M or F
	Born	Date	Place		
	Baptized	Date	Place		
	Died	Date	Place		
	Buried	Date	Place		
		Continued on page	(continuation sheet if this child has its own family)		

Child #:	7			Name	M or F
	Born	Date	Place		
	Baptized	Date	Place		
	Died	Date	Place		
	Buried	Date	Place		
		Continued on page	(continuation sheet if this child has its own family)		

www.ingramcontent.com/pod-product-compliance
Lightning Source LLC
Chambersburg PA
CBHW071316150426
43191CB00007B/637